# Multinational Work Teams

## A New Perspective

## LEA's Organization and Management Series
*Arthur Brief and James P. Walsh, Series Editors*

# Multinational Work Teams

## A New Perspective

P. Christopher Earley
*Indiana University*

Cristina B. Gibson
*Center for Effective Organizations,*
*University of Southern California*

2002

LAWRENCE ERLBAUM ASSOCIATES, PUBLISHERS
Mahwah, New Jersey                    London

Lawrence Erlbaum Associates, Inc., Publishers
10 Industrial Avenue
Mahwah, NJ 07430

Cover design by Kathryn Houghtaling Lacey

**Library of Congress Cataloging-in-Publication Data**

Earley, P. Christopher.
Multinational work teams / a new perspective /
P. Christopher Earley, Cristina B. Gibson.
    p. cm. — (LEA's organization and management series)

Includes bibliographical references and index.
ISBN 0-8058-3464-8 (cloth : alk. paper
(ISBN 0-8058-3465-6 (pbk. : alk. paper)
1. International business enterprises—Management.
    2. Intercultural communication. 3. Teams in the workplace.
    I. Gibson, Cristina B.   II. Title.   III. Series.
HD62.4 .E23   2001
658.4´02—dc21

2001033503
CIP

Books published by Lawrence Erlbaum Associates are printed on acid-free paper, and their bindings are chosen for strength and durability.

Printed in the United States of America
10  9  8  7  6  5  4  3  2  1

To Elaine, for her seemingly endless
patience during my cross-cultural
adventures, and to Steve for providing
the most wonderful eternal cross-cultural
experiment a spouse could ever ask for!

### P. Christopher Earley

P. Christopher Earley is the Randall L. Tobias Chair of Global Leadership at the Kelley School of Business, Indiana University, and he holds the honorary chairs at Nanyang Business School (Singapore) and National University of Singapore. His interests include cross-cultural and international aspects of organizations such as the dynamics of multinational teams, the role of face in organizations, and motivation across cultures. He is the author of seven books and numerous articles and book chapters, and his recent publication include *Culture, Self-identity, and Work* and *The Transplanted Executive: Managing in Different Cultures* (both with Miriam Erez), *Face, Harmony, and Social Structure: An Analysis of Behavior in Organizations*, and "Creating Hybrid Team Cultures: an Empirical Test of International Team Functioning" (with E. Mosakowski, *Academy of Management Journal*). He is the Editor of Group and Organization Management as well as former associate editor of Academy of Management Review and a member of several other editorial boards. He received his Ph.D. in industrial and organizational psychology from the University of Illinois, Urbana-Champaign. He has taught on the faculties of London Business School, University of Arizona, University of Minnesota, University of California, Irvine, and he has taught executives and consulted for companies in England, Hong Kong, Israel, People's Republic of China, Singapore, South Korea, and Thailand, among others.

### Cristina B. Gibson

Cristina B. Gibson is currently holds a joint position as Associate Research Professor with the Center for Effective Organizations and with the Management and Organizations Department, Marshall School of Business, University of Southern California. Dr. Gibson received her Ph.D. in Organizational Behavior from the Graduate School of Management at the University of California, Irvine and her Bachelor Degree in Psychology from Scripps College in Claremont, California. Before joining the faculty at USC, she was Assistant Professor at the University of Wisconsin, Madison.

In her work with teams in multinational organizations, Dr. Gibson strives to increase performance, longevity and quality of work life for team members from various cultures. Dr. Gibson's research interests include communication, interaction and effectiveness in teams, the impact of culture and gender on work behavior, social cognition, and international knowledge management. She is co-editor with Susan Cohen of the forthcoming book *Emerging Perspectives on Creating the Conditions for Virtual Team Effectiveness* (Jossey-Bass) and her research has appeared in *Administrative Science Quarterly, Academy of Management Journal, Journal of Management, Journal of International Business Studies, Journal of Cross-cultural Psychology, International Executive, Advances in International Comparative Management, Journal of Managerial Issues, and Group and Organization Management.*

Dr. Gibson is the recipient of numerous awards recognizing her research, including grants from the Thomas J. Watson Foundation for International Research, the Carnegie Bosch Institute for Applied International Management, and the Center for Innovation and Management Studies. In 1996 she was awarded comprehensive funding from the National Science Foundation to investigate the implementation of teams in multinational corporations. Together with colleague Susan Cohen, she received a second four-year research grant from the National Science Foundation in 1999 to investigate creating conditions for virtual team effectiveness.

# Contents

## Figures and Tables

# Preface

The use of teams in educational, humanitarian, and business organizations has been increasing over the last several decades. For the most part, this increase reflects the belief that teams are an appropriate structure for implementing strategies formulated to deal with performance demands and opportunities presented by the changing business environment. Organizations are experiencing dramatically increased pressures for performance. They are being required to develop and deliver products and services at lower costs but with higher quality and increased speed. A great deal of the research and popular literature proffers teams of various sorts as an appropriate design response to these performance pressures for speed, cost, quality, and innovation. Much of the literature on quality management, for example, recommends teams to make improvements in organizational processes. This recommendation is based on the understanding that processes cut across organizational departments and that a process cannot be optimized without examining it in its entirety. What current research programs have failed to address, however, are the interests of multinational organizations with facilities in several countries. When adopting team-based systems across their global facilities, multinational organizations face special challenges. Intercultural theories of organizational behavior suggest that teams must be implemented in a manner that incorporates the cultural backgrounds of the members of a team; however, to date, a unifying theory explicating this process is nonexistent.

The purpose of our book is to extend and consolidate the evolving literature on multinational teams by developing a comprehensive theory that incorporates a dynamic, multilevel view of teams. Our model focuses on various features of a team's members, their interactions as a team, and the organizational context in which they operate. We use the concepts of integration and differentiation, and the notion of equilibrium, as a general force guiding the specific processes that link various levels of analysis in our model. Without question, multinational teams are not merely a management fad to be abandoned in the future. The globalization of business necessitates a cross-border approach to work with an increasing reliance on multinational teams.

The book consists of eight chapters. Chapter 1 introduces our basic assumptions and definitions and provides an overview of the remaining chapters. Chapter 2 is a comprehensive review of the literature related to multinational and multicultural teams, including a wide array of studies across an extensive time period for the interested reader. These various research studies provide the general, conceptual basis for our theory presented in the third chapter. Chapter 3 provides an overview of the specific model driving our thinking along with an extensive description of the component parts. The basic model is captured by a cubic representation with the internal elements housed within a general, societal context. There are six basic components to our model including individual and group elements, work and social structures, and two sets of catalysts, or processes, connecting individual to group elements as well as work to social structure.

Chapters 4 to 7 detail various aspects of the general model presented in chapter 3. In chapter 4, we revisit the individual and group-level elements of teams and their members. Chapter 5 focuses on the linking processes that connect various elements and structures. Chapter 6 focuses on the catalysts that give rise to changes in various elements and structures described in the theory section. By catalyst, we refer to facets of the team environment that move the team forward through various team dynamics. Chapter 7 provides a general integration of the model and an application of this framework for understanding multinational work teams (MNTs) in diverse cultural contexts. We apply the framework to several ongoing MNTs with whom we have worked extensively and discuss briefly the implications of our framework for management given the organizational and cultural contexts of these teams. Finally, in chapter 8, we conclude with a discussion of implications for research and practice, including a research agenda for the topic of MNTs in organizations.

## ACKNOWLEDGMENTS

Many individuals contributed to the creation of this book. Needless to say, our theory that we advance is the accumulation of our research and experiences that have been shaped by a number of key individuals. We have been exposed to many stimulating ideas from Michael Bond, Miriam Erez, Elaine Mosakowski, Nigel Nicholson, Harry Triandis, Lyman Porter, Jone Pearce, Susan Cohen, and Sue and Monty Mohrman to name just a few. Particular debt is owed to E. Mosakowski for the discussion of hybrid cultures and related phenomena. In addition, we are grateful to our home institutions and colleagues for their continued support as we worked on our book.

The first author wishes to thank the following for their support of this work: Randall L. Tobias Chair of Global Leadership and the Kelley School of Business, Indiana University; Nanyang Business School, Nanyang Technological University, Singapore for a Nanyang Professorship provided during the final stages of completing the book; and the Director and staff at the Sasin Graduate Institute of Business Administration, Chulalongkorn University in Bangkok, Thailand for providing a fertile environment from which to write and think about issues concerning international teams. Research assistance was provided to the first author by Clare Francis as well.

The second author wishes to acknowledge funding provided by the Carnegie Bosch Institute for Applied International Management Research, the University of Wisconsin Initiative for World Affairs and the Global Economy, and the National Science Foundation Grant #SBR 96-31748. In addition, she would like to acknowledge the time and effort extended by all of the respondents together with their associated staff that made the field research described in this book possible. Warmest regards and appreciation go out to Mary Zellmer-Bruhn at University of Minnesota, Rauol Zapata in Puerto Rico, Joylie Agustin and Ricardo Lim at the Asian Institute for Management in the Philippines, and Michael Segalla at the Hautes Etudes Commercials in France. The second author would also like to thank the following for administrative support, translations, and transcriptions: Paula Bassoff, Ryan Billingham, Peter Bruhn, Florence Brunell, Joan Donovan, Steve Gibson, Kerry Jung, Francisco Lloveras, Rachel Ritterbausch, David Robinson, Carol Troyer-Shank, and Richard Zapata at the University of Wisconsin. Both authors gratefully acknowledge the helpful comments provided on earlier drafts of segments of this work by Julian Birkinshaw, Brad Kirkman, Freek Vermeulen, and Mary Waller.

We would be remiss if we did not thank the editorial staff at Lawrence Erlbaum Associates as well for their patience and help in shaping our "diamond in the rough" into a rigorous presentation. Particular thanks go to LEA series editors Jim Walsh and Art Brief, whose invaluable comments and suggestions helped shaped this book. We also thank Anne Duffy and the staff at LEA who bore the burden of our coordination and writing of this book. Finally, we would like to thank our students and clients who have stimulated our thinking about international and intercultural issues.

# Series Foreword

"If we accept the idea that the globalization and international integration of companies is inevitable, then business and its study is at a crossroads of understanding. It is no longer acceptable to proceed with the study of teams as if its members are isolated from their cultural and national heritage." With these words, Chris Earley and Cristina Gibson embark upon the most comprehensive assessment of the multinational work team that we have ever seen. They begin by describing this emerging organizational phenomenon and then move to offer us a meticulous assessment of what we know and don't know about these international collaborations. Their original theory sprouts from this fertile ground. In the end, we are treated to scholarship at its very best. Grounded in our theoretical past and informed by a clear view of the current realities of business practice, Chris and Cristina present a theory of the multinational work team that will guide subsequent research for many years. We bring this new work to you with pleasure and pride.

*—Arthur P. Brief*
*—James P. Walsh*

# 1 Introduction and Overview

The internationalization of business, creation of a "global village" and similar influences remind us that a science of organizations and management is incomplete without the integration of concepts of culture, interdependence, and self-awareness. No longer is it appropriate to discuss organizational activities and employee actions without incorporating a more comprehensive view of where such activities take place. Not only must we include an immediate social context, but we must deal with the international and cultural aspects of the social world as well. More than ever, understanding of employee action requires knowledge of how action is related to the environment in which it is embedded. It is with this general focus, that we examine a number of significant issues derived from the way that people organize themselves in multinational work teams (MNT).

Given the increasing complexity of the workplace, much modern work requires a high degree of interdependence and interaction of employees. This interaction is often relegated to a work group, or team. People do not work within a social void, rather, they interact and are interdependent on others as they work and behave in an organization. People work together so as to perform various tasks and they work together for social needs as well. Given the prevalence of work groups in modern organizations, it is clear that they are an essential element in understanding cross-cultural aspects of work and organization. Our lives are organized around many groups such as families, work crews, religious groups, sports teams, and so forth. Much of what we do for business and pleasure revolves around the group. This is not to imply that all actions occur in a work group; many of our actions occur within aggregates rather than natural groups.

## WORK GROUPS AND TEAMS

Groups and teams are psychologically and sociologically distinct from casual aggregates of individuals (McGrath, 1984). Whereas a group has specific qualities involving roles, structure, and so forth, aggregates simply refer to a collection of individuals who gather for individual purposes and needs (e.g., audience at a movie). Of course, not all activities are group-based nor would we expect them to be. We perform actions for our individual needs in an individual context such as purchasing a favorite dessert, playing solitaire, or watching a movie on television alone. These behaviors do not constitute group behavior nor does their explanation fully apply to the dynamics of a group. Our focus is on the social context of work behavior in which people gather to perform some task or maintain group stability and relations.

McGrath (1984) who defines a group as a social aggregate that involves mutual awareness and potential mutual interaction. He uses families, work crews and task performance teams, and friendship (or social) groups as examples of groups, and he distinguishes groups from other social aggregates. Groups are distinguished based on three dimensions: size, interdependence, and temporal pattern. Social aggregates do not have the potential mutual interaction of a group. He argues that a group requires the following conditions:

> … it must include two or more people, but it must remain relatively small so that all members can be mutually aware of and potentially in interaction with one another. Such mutual awareness and potential interaction provide at least a minimum degree of interdependence; that is, members' choices and behaviors take one another into account. Interdependence, in turn, implies some degree of continuity over time: these relationships have, or quickly acquire, some history, and some anticipated future. *A time based, mutual interdependence can reasonably be termed "dynamic."* In other words a group is an aggregation of two or more people who are to some degree in dynamic interrelation with one another … this definition of group would normally include families (at least the residential unit core), work crews, and many social or friendship groups, but would normally not include units that fit all of the other kinds of aggregations in that list (cultures, communities, organizations, etc.). (p. 8)

Turner (1987) describes a group as one that is psychologically meaningful for the members to which they relate themselves subjectively for comparisons, and they adopt norms and values from this group. A member of a group accepts membership in this group and it influences the member's attitudes and behavior. He distinguishes the group from aggregate using an individual's attachment to the group as a reference group rather than mere membership.

A number of other definitions have emerged focusing on the cognitive aspects of group membership (Erez & Earley, 1993; Messick & Mackie, 1989). A focus on cognition emphasizes thought processes and information processing. Cognitive representations of groups consist of complex, hierarchical structures that contain elements such as category labels, attributes, and exemplars. A category representation refers to a category label (e.g., college professor), an abstracted prototype (e.g., list of features such as old and grey, beard, glasses, befuddled), and the projection of these characteristics to the group as a whole (stereotype). For example, a category label such as a "college professor" may have associated with it general prototypes of a professor such as being old and having a grey beard or wearing glasses. Stereotyping occurs if these prototypic characteristics are applied to the general population of college professors. Klimoski and Mohammed (1994) talk about a "team mental model" as a shared psychological representation of a team's environment constructed to permit sense-making and guide appropriate group action (Elron, Shamir, & Ben-Ari, 1998). When team members perceive shared understandings with other members, the positive affect and propensity to trust generated by such a discovery fuels performance improvement (Klimoski & Mohammed, 1994) and bolsters the group's belief in its capability to perform, often referred to as the level of group efficacy (Bandura, 1997; Gibson, 1999).

From a cultural viewpoint, Mann (1980) points out a number of interesting features of "natural groupings." A natural group refers to a group that exists of its own accord rather than the result of a laboratory manipulation. What is important about such a group is that it helps us understand the relevance of culture and society in a more direct fashion than through the use of laboratory, or ad hoc, groups. Ravlin, Thomas, and Ilsev (2000) take a perspective of understanding groups from a cultural perspective focusing on the conflict experienced within these groups (see Weldon & Jehn, 1998 for a similar approach).

Drawing from these perspectives, we adopt the major facets of McGrath's and Turner's views. A group or team refers to three or more individuals who interact directly or indirectly for the accomplishment of a common goal. A multinational team is a specific type of this more general form of team inasmuch as members must come from two or more different national or cultural backgrounds. For sake of simplicity, we use the idea of nationality as related to culture, although we freely admit that the connection between nation and culture is not a complete one. Within any given nation, there may exist multiple subcultures, and the national culture may not be completely shared (Rohner, 1984). Furthermore, nation–state is a relatively new concept in world history, and this is not to say that it will continue as a key feature denoting culture in the future. However, as we are operating (and writing this book) in a period for which nation and culture are highly coincident, we do not feel as if this is a major compromise to understanding team dynamics. Ultimately, we are referring to nationality as a grouping variable that captures differences among people in their cultural perspectives. In this sense, the term multinational and multicultural are used interchangeably as well in our book.

## CURRENT PERSPECTIVES ON MULTINATIONAL TEAMS

As we describe in chapter 2, there are a number of significant studies in the literature focusing on the importance of cultural influences and group functioning. In the management literature, there has been a call to understand the dynamics of group development with an emphasis on the compositional nature of a team from a cultural perspective (e.g., Jackson, May, & Whitney, 1995; Maznevski, 1994; Snow, Snell, Davison, & Hambrick, 1996; Tsui, Egan & O'Reilly, 1992). However, the study of group dynamics cross-culturally has been the focus of several cross-cultural and social psychologists. For example, the famous studies of Asch (1956) concerning conformity and social influence have been replicated in a number of cultures and societies. In his classic paradigm, Asch examined conformity effects by having individuals judge the length of one line relative to another. A subject initially made a judgment concerning the relative length of the line after which he or she was placed in a room with other "subjects" (confederates). The next phase involved the "subjects" reporting that one line (the shorter one in reality) was longer than another one, contrary to the real subject's earlier judgment. A conformity effect reflects a subject's consequent judgment and the extent to which it falls in line with the other subjects' judgments. This basic study has been replicated in a number of countries demonstrating conformity effects. Findings suggest that conformity effects are observed to a similar degree in many different cultures (e.g., United States, Germany, Japan, Brazil) and it is typically found that 30 to 35% of the subjects conform to the group standard.

Recent reviews of the teams and groups literature in management consistently show increasing interest in the area of cultural composition (Bettenhausen, 1991; Earley & Mosakowski, 2000; Erez & Earley, 1993; Goodman, Ravlin, & Argote, 1990; McGrath, 1984). However, few studies have appeared that more specifically address the issue of cultural composition (for recent exceptions see Argote & McGrath, 1993; Cox, Lobel, & McLeod, 1991; Earley & Mosakowski, 2000; Elron et al., 1998; Gibson, 1999; Jackson, May, & Whitney, 1995; Jackson, Stone, & Alvarez, 1992; Lau & Murnighan, 1998; Lawrence, 1997; Snow, Snell, Davison, & Hambrick, 1996; Thomas, Ravlin, & Wallace, 1996; Watson, Kumar, & Michaelson, 1993). Authors have noted the role of cultural influences in generating interpersonal conflict (e.g., Weisinger & Salipante, 1995; Yu, 1995) and differences in management styles (e.g., Earley, 1989, 1994; Kozan, 1989; Ohbuchi & Takahashi,

1994; Rossi & Todd-Mancillas, 1985; Westwood, Tang, & Kirkbride, 1992). This body of literature typically discusses cultural differences, such as individualism and collectivism, that collide in practice in the multicultural group, and does not specify the processes underlying the generation of intragroup conflict in multicultural groups. (for an exception, see Ting-Toomey, Gao, Trubisky, Yang, Kim, Lin, & Nishida, 1991 for their face-maintenance approach to differing conflict-handling styles).

What is lacking in the literature on cross-cultural teams is a comprehensive theoretical framework for understanding how these unique teams operate and function. Although a number of useful midrange theories of the multinational team have been proposed (e.g., see Earley & Erez's (1997), and Earley & Singh's (2000), Granrose & Oskamp's (1997) edited books for a number of very useful examples), the literature on international teams is lacking a comprehensive theoretical framework. It is our intention to provide such a framework for scholars working in this area.

## CONCEPTIONS OF CULTURE

Given our focus, it should go without comment that a thorough conceptualization of culture is needed. How then, can we define a culture and operationalize constructs appropriately? Central to this point is how one can place boundaries around a cultural grouping (Rohner, 1984). One possibility is that researchers should not simply identify the group using general characteristics but should examine according to a degree of identification, "Perhaps it is better to group people according to their degree of ethnocultural identification. Thus, you have an aggregate but it is operationally defined. You don't study Japanese-Americans, you study the extent to which there are clusters of Japanese-Americans who embrace and endorse patterns of behavior that are associated with a life style or world view." (Marsella, 1994).

There is a nontrivial debate concerning cultural groups and the concept of culture that wages in many fields including Anthropology and Organizational Behavior. How should the construct of culture be dealt with conceptually? A number of researchers have commented on this topic in recent years including Brett, Tinsley, Janssens, Barness, & Lytle (1997), Earley and Singh (1995), Geertz (1973), Leung and Bond (1989), Lytle, Brett, Barness, Tinsley, & Janssens (1995), and Martin (1992), among others. Although there are a number of points on which this discussion has focused, a major issue discussed by the various parties concerns the nature of culture as an entity. Although some view culture as a complex collage that is not properly understood from an elementalist perspective (Geertz, 1973), others argue that it can be understood using fundamental dimensions (Hofstede, 1991). Likewise, there is a debate whether or not culture is a real phenomena existing outside of the minds of various observers (Rohner, 1984). Although the definitions of a culture, society, group, or individual are critical in a complete analysis of behavior in organizations, they are only a starting point. Once the key issues concerning analysis and aggregation are dealt with, there is still the fundamental question remaining, namely, what are the reasons that general, cultural influences may impact individual behavior and action in an organization? In other words, the aggregation procedure does not help us better understand the conceptual framework that underlies such aggregation. Quite the contrary, our aggregation procedures must be informed by our conceptual linkages.

Culture is often defined as a shared meaning system or mental programming (Hofstede, 1991; Shweder & LeVine, 1984). It implies that members of the same culture share a common meaning and they are likely to interpret and evaluate situational events and management practices in a similar way. In contrast, members of different cultures who do not share a common way of interpreting and evaluating situational events are more likely to respond in a different way to the same managerial approach. Therefore, managerial practices found effective in one culture may be ineffective in another culture. For example, sociotechnical systems were implemented in North European countries (Trist & Bamforth, 1951) and individual based job-enrichment designs were implemented in the United States. (Hackman & Oldham, 1980). However, attempts to implement quality circles or sociotechnical systems in the United States were not highly successful (Lawler, 1986). Differential monetary reward systems are often rejected in Israeli Kibbutzim because they contradict prevailing norms of equality (Leviatan & Rosner, 1980). Differential rewards are well accepted in the private sector and in individualistic cultures which are guided by the values of equity rather than equality (Erez, 1986). Thus, the various types of management practices, and motivational techniques are evaluated in light of certain standards that vary across cultures. It seems that the successful implementation of motivational techniques and managerial practices depend on their congruence with the cultural context.

Few existing theories of organizational behavior provide a conceptual framework for understanding how culture, managerial practices, and work behavior are interrelated (see Erez & Earley, 1993 for one such example). Models of organizational behavior developed in the West do not take this aspect of cultural differences into consideration. Rather, situational effects are commonly interpreted as artifacts. The need to adjust to changes in a complex environment brings into focus the cognitive mechanisms of information processing that help explain how employees interpret and evaluate the situation and how these processes affect their behavior.

As we discuss in chapter 2, not all groups are integrated and fully functional. Thus, for a group to be integrated and effective, it must have several other important characteristics including an emergent and simplified set of rules and actions, work capability expectations, and member perceptions that individuals within a team develop, share, and enact after mutual interactions. To the extent these rules, expectations, and roles are shared (Earley & Mosakowski, 2000; Ravlin, Thomas, & Ilsev, 2000; Rohner, 1984; Shweder & LeVine, 1984), a strong culture exists. A strong culture is not meant to imply that everyone has the same understanding of all issues (a completely overlapping worldview for example), but there must be significant overlap among team members. Our thesis is that effective teams are those with a strong team culture because shared member expectations facilitate individual and team performance and communication. A strong team culture may derive from overlapping and pre-existing characteristics of team members or newly developed patterns of team member interaction. Additionally, selection into (or out of) a group is not necessarily a voluntary action on the part of a member. For example, an individualist may choose to leave a family group (e.g., sever ties with an overly critical parent or divorce a spouse) whereas such an option is not easily exercised by a collectivist (Erez & Earley, 1993; Triandis, 1995). Our definition does not require a particular size or age of an aggregate to constitute a group, although groups will vary qualitatively according to these dimensions. Finally, our definition requires that we consider the nature and structure of a group separate from the individual members. This final point seems necessary because much research on groups takes an individualistic perspective focusing on individual needs and motives (Turner, 1987).

(The reader should note some nomenclature as well that we adopt throughout our book. As stated, we use the terms "group" and "team" interchangeably and we use the terms "multinational" and "multicultural," interchangeably. We apply the group, or team, concept to a set of interacting parties coming from different national and cultural backgrounds. This is what we mean by a multinational team. In this sense, what we call the multinational team might as well be called a multicultural, transnational, transcultural, team. The critical parts of the definition were listed previously.)

So, how can we gain an increased understanding of team dynamics using a cultural lens? We live in a world of interaction and discourse from which our most fundamental self-perceptions are derived. We gain knowledge of ourselves and those with whom we interact based on many characteristics that become salient based on our cultural framework. To an American, the car one drives has symbolic significance whereas, to an Indian, schooling is an important sign of position and status. It is through various types of social interactions that all people define themselves within their social community, and this self-definition lies at the very heart of human endeavor. This is a particularly important issue as we approach our move into the global village. People struggle with a desire for self-understanding and self-awareness in the face of such variety and ambiguity as we are presented in a multicultural world. It is this struggle for self-definition in one's social system that is at the center of our approach.

Before we provide an overview of our book, it is important that the reader be aware of the general approach we adopt. In the next section, we examine the topic of levels of analysis because an international and cross-cultural theory inevitably crosses levels of analysis. We follow this discussion with an examination of the underlying philosophy in our approach to the study of groups and teams.

## LEVELS OF ANALYSIS

Much of the work done in the field of international and cross-cultural management reflects a basic disagreement among academics. What is the appropriate level of analysis for understanding cultural influences on work activities? Most research conforms to what Earley and Singh (1995) referred to as a "reduced" form of research design meaning that culture is treated as one of many exogenous factors that influence management processes. For example, one might examine the influence of a high uncertainty avoidance culture on strategic planning arguing that longer planning horizons will be adopted by high uncertainty avoidance cultures. At a microlevel of analysis, one might argue that people from a high power distance culture are more likely to respect highly autocratic leaders. These arguments reflect cultural factors isolated from one another and in relation to a very specific outcome.

Earley and Singh argued that a superior form of research design was reflected by a "hybrid" design, which includes several features. First, in developing research questions, intact systems are studied to identify important aspects of the systems. Second, hypothesized relationships are derived across systems and they are not necessarily unique to a given system. Third, constructs and relationships are assumed to be separable from the system in which they are embedded, but the mapping back onto an existing system may not be simple linear or additive. Fourth, specific relationships are interpreted using reduced parts of the system, but with reference to the general system. These interpretations can, in turn, lead to a further refinement of general principles. One example of this approach is reflected in Berry's Ecological Cultural Theory (1971, 1980). Briefly, Berry's theory looks at the influence of culture at various levels including general systems (e.g., political), midrange (e.g., social groupings), and micro (e.g., individual beliefs and values). His approach is wide-sweeping in scope while maintaining a focus on describing the linkages among elements of the framework.

However, cross-cultural and international management is still rife with the reductionist style of research, or worse, cultural variables are left implied but not stated. In this simplistic style of research, an author relies on a prior classification of a country's culture by other researchers (quite often,

Hofstede's classification scheme) and infers that his or her sample must match up because it was obtained from the same country (albeit, many years later). We would hope that this style of research has disappeared with the introduction of more modern methods, but the literature still reflects (and accepts) this type of work. Of course, there are exceptions to this in international and cross-cultural research such as Hofstede (1980a, 1991) and Schwartz (1992, 1993) who have bridged the gap between country and culture although they represent the exception rather than the rule. Additional efforts have been made including articles by Bond and his colleagues (e.g., Bond & Lee, 1981; Leung & Bond, 1989) as well as a special issue of Academy of Management Journal (edited by Earley & Singh, 1995) and work by House and his colleagues concerning an international assessment of charismatic leadership. However, this style of research is still the exception and not as commonplace as would be expected.

There are a number of reasons that the levels of analysis from micro- to macro-organizational research have not been spanned as frequently as one might desire. First, there is great comfort staying within one's disciplinary boundaries and not having to confront new assumptions derived from others' research ideology. Second, many researchers are trained to conduct research but on at a given level coincident with their discipline base. Third, we are creatures of our own social creation. The physicist sees the world through laws of strong and weak nuclear forces whereas an international management researcher sees it through businesses operating in diverse economies throughout the globe. Fourth, little formal cross-level theory exists useful to understand cross-level phenomena. Katz and Kahn's (1978) open systems theory, House and Rousseau's (1995) "meso theory" (also see Klein, Dansereau, & Hall, 1994; Rousseau, 1985), and Tosi's (1992) multilevel model are notable exceptions. Meso research:

> … concerns the simultaneous study of at least two levels of analysis wherein a) one or more levels concern individual or group behavioral processes or variables, b) one or more levels concern organizational processes or variables, and c) the processes by which the levels of analysis are related are articulated in the form of bridging, or linking, propositions. (House et al., 1995, p. 2).

House et al. argue that meso research is critical for the understanding of organizational phenomena because an organizational context is a unique influence that is the interactive product of person and context.

There are a number of reasons why it is important to conduct meso style research in organizations. Staw and Sutton (1992) suggest, "… organizations can magnify and blunt individual cognitive (and emotional and behavioral) processes, it is important to conduct research on the effects of aggregated beliefs (and emotions and behaviors) on organizational actions rather than to just assume that such effects will occur because they have been demonstrated in individuals or groups operating outside of the organizational context." They suggest that there are a number of influences from the micro to the macro levels in an organizational context such as powerful individuals who shape strategic thinking and decision making in an organization or the collective beliefs and values of individuals that make up the "climate" or "organizational culture." Likewise, macro-organizational variables influence the nature of individuals' perceptions and values within those organizations. This is at the heart of Granovetter's (1985) concept of embeddedness, namely, that the assumption of a simple, rational actor in the economic paradigm is inadequate to capture the sophistication of an individual who works within an organizational (social) context.

These concerns hold true (especially) for international and cross-cultural research in organizations as well. We focus on a particular problem confronting researchers who conduct cross-cultural research in organizations, namely, a poorly defined model. If we examine a phenomenon and leave out critical intervening constructs, we may easily misinterpret our findings. This dilemma is particularly relevant and salient to a cross-cultural researcher. Many have argued that one of the biggest dilemmas confronting cross-cultural psychology is that the inability to rule out alternative explanations of differences obtained in cross-cultural studies precludes firm conclusions concerning the importance of culture in an analysis of psychological phenomena. In conducting comparative or cross-cultural research, can a researcher adequately rule out competing hypotheses to those involving cultural differences? For instance, the first author recently reviewed a manuscript on the topic of group decision-making in a particular culture. The primary problem with the paper was that the authors failed to provide any substantial explanation concerning how cultural norms (their focus) might be related to the phenomenon of group decision-making. Although the study was posed as an exploration of group decisions in a "new" and infrequently studied cultural setting, no meaningful connections were made from the cultural context to the nature of group decisions. As a result, the model supported in the paper did not appear to provide unique ideas concerning group decision-making from a cultural perspective. Based on the research design, it was impossible for the authors to conclude that similarities or differences were driven by culture, or some other unspecified construct(s). This dilemma is an inherent problem with cross-cultural research because "culture" is typically confounded with other attributes of a society such as various institutions, economic systems, or it remains entirely unspecified or implicit in the model.

Crossing levels of analysis presents other problems as well such as Hofstede's (1980a) description of the ecological fallacy. Hofstede (1980a) described the difficulty of aggregating national data for use at other levels of analysis. Hofstede (1980a) collected survey information from respondents from over 40 countries throughout the world. In analyzing his data, he pointed out a difficulty using the individual as the appropriate level of analysis. His argument was that the phenomenon of interest, culture, was best dealt with at a national level, and so aggregation was the only solution. By not doing so, he argued, a researcher would commit the "ecological fallacy" created by inappropriate comparisons across levels.

Imagine we have a cultural value that is correlated with some individual characteristic such as need for achievement motive. Further, assume that for the three cultures examined in our study, the correlation within each culture of this value and need for achievement is +.5, but that the scatterplots for each relationship are structured such that Culture A is horizontally displaced from Culture B by one standard deviation and Culture C is horizontally displaced from Culture B by one standard deviation. If we examined the correlation of the cultural value to need for achievement in the entire sample (hence, at a "global" level), the resulting correlation is very close to 0.0 even though the relationship within each culture is quite strong. At a global level, we conclude that the value and achievement are unrelated. More recently, Schwartz (1992, 1993) has approached this problem in his international assessment of values at the individual and societal levels of analysis. His conclusions are that the two levels show different patterns of values, but that there exists significant overlap between the two. Other work along these lines includes Earley (1994), Earley and Mosakowski (2000), Gibson (1999), Klein et al. (1994), Leung and Bond (1989), Liska (1992), and Ostroff (1993) to name a few. Thus, although it is tempting to dismiss aggregation procedures as invalid and misleading, it is possible to yield useful comparisons across these levels.

## GENERAL APPROACH USED IN OUR BOOK

We can represent our general view of multinational teams using a set of cascading levels that overlap at particular exchange points. We illustrate and discuss this idea in chapter 3 and it is implicit in our discussion that MNTs operate within the context of active and influencing social environments (Weick, 1969). Further, these teams are collections of individuals who have personal agendas, possess unique values, and worldviews. Thus, we argue that it is inappropriate to describe and discuss a MNT as separate from either social context or individual member characteristics.

An additional caveat is in order at this point concerning the concept of culture that we use. There are a variety of schools concerning the concept of culture that can be crudely classified into the psychologist's two-by-two (Rohner, 1984), namely, behavior versus ideational crossed with realist versus nominalist. A behavior versus ideational dimension posits culture as represented as behavior and material embodiments (behavior) or in terms of ideas, beliefs, values, preferences, and other symbols (ideational). The dimension of realist versus nominalist refers to the existential nature of culture with the realists positing that culture exists outside of members of that culture and the nominalists arguing that culture has no form or existence separate from those who interpret and enact it. To the cultural nominalist, culture is a set of inferences made by an observer based on regularities or patterns of activity. In other words, it is a logical construct having no substance. The ideational realist, with some overlap with the nominalist position, best represents our use of culture. We focus our analysis on shared meanings represented by values and beliefs of individuals, and we argue that culture has significance separate from specific individuals within that culture.

## ORGANIZATION OF THE BOOK

We organize the book into eight chapters. Chapter 2 is a comprehensive review of the literature related to multinational and multicultural teams. In this chapter, we focus on a wide array of studies across an extensive time period for the interested reader. These various research studies provide the general, conceptual basis for our theory presented in the third chapter.

Chapter 3 provides an overview of the specific model driving our thinking along with an extensive description of the component parts. The basic model is captured by a representation with the internal elements housed within a general, societal context. There are several basic components to our model including individual and group elements, work and social structures, and the several sets of catalysts, or processes, connecting individual to group elements as well as work to social structure. In the third chapter, we discuss the overall framework along with how the various elements are interrelated.

Chapters 4 to 7 detail various aspects of the general model presented in chapter 3. In chapter 4 we revisit the individual and group-level elements of teams and their members. Our discussion focuses on the particular elements that are critical for MNTs such as roles and identity, affect, confidence, trust (individual level) as well as roles enacted, status hierarchy, and sense of shared history (team level).

Chapter 5 focuses on the linking processes that connect various elements, structures, and catalysts described earlier in the book. Our focus in this chapter is the description from a dynamic and time-based perspective of MNTs. We present a model of the general processes and sequences that a MNT undergoes during its development and functioning. Although an overly restrictive framework such as a traditional developmental approach (e.g., Tuckman & Jensen, 1977) espoused in the groups literature is out of place with our reasoning, we do provide a general pattern that MNTs follow including an initial stage of sense-making and exploration of self-identity and how this impetus influences subsequent group function-ing. That is, it is not the group development itself that is universal rather it is the member search for place and purpose within the team that gives rise to many common group-level developments. What is universal is a member's search for place and purpose within a MNT.

Chapter 6 focuses on the catalysts that give rise to various elements and structures described in the theory section. By catalyst, we are referring to facets of the team environment that move the team forward through vari-ous team dynamics. For example, a catalyst that influences the interplay of an individual-level characteristic such as a person's confidence (efficacy) as a team member with a group-level characteristic such as role enacted might be a change of group membership. That is, a team member's per-ceived confidence to enact a given role in the team may be changed as the group membership changes. As an example, an existing team member has high confidence in her capability to play the role of team leader. Team membership now changes because of an intracompany transfer of team personnel and a new member comes on board who is highly resistive of the existing team structure. The new member questions many aspects of the team including the leader's role as leader. The result of this is a power play and the new member builds a coalition and takes the team over. Membership changes acted as a trigger relating an individual-level feature (confidence) to a group feature (roles enacted).

Chapter 7 provides a general integration of the model and an applica-tion of this framework for understanding MNTs in diverse cultural con-texts. We apply the framework to several ongoing MNTs with whom we have worked extensively and discuss briefly the implications of our framework for management given the organizational and cultural con-texts of these teams.

Finally, in chapter 8 we present a brief overview of a research agenda for this work and the topic of MNTs in organizations. We focus our discus-sion on a number of organizational examples including new product de-velopment teams, sales and service teams, human resource teams, marketing strategy teams, and postmerger integration teams.

Our intention is to introduce a reader to these key concepts, propose a comprehensive theory of the multinational team and to invigorate the re-search streams concerning international team composition that were pre-sented by such scholars as Canney-Davison, Hambrick, Jackson, Maznevski, McGrath, and Ravlin, among others. The search for cross-cul-tural understanding and management effectiveness may be examined through the functioning of a MNT.

We conclude this introductory chapter with a few selected quotes from an article published in *The Times* from 1996 concerning the merger of Swedish pharmaceuticals firm, Pharmacia A.B. and American pharmaceuticals firm Upjohn, Inc. These were quotes made by senior executives from both firms after a number of meetings. One of the early sticking points of this joint venture was where to locate the merger headquarters with both companies wanting the other firm to travel to their own country. The resolution of this debate was a preliminary decision to have the joint headquarters on "neutral" ground (England) even though it meant a burden for both companies.

## Pharmacia Quotes:

"I think Europeans are much more international. We are used to working across borders, in different languages. We are used to treating people in a different way."

"While you can explain with brutal efficiency how high the costs are, you won't be able to find solutions in a collective-bargaining atmosphere if you don't understand the other side."

"It is important to respect the local culture."

## Upjohn, Inc. Quotes:

"We were astonished at European vacation habits."

"Americans have a can-do approach to things. We try to overcome problems as they arise. A Swede may be slower on the start-up. He sits down and thinks over all of the problems."

"In retrospect, we might have been a bit aggressive."

These quotes reflect a very practical, but fundamental, problem faced in the MNT. If we accept the idea that globalization and international integration of companies is inevitable, then business and its study is at a crossroads of understanding. It is no longer acceptable to proceed with the study of teams as if members are isolated from their cultural and national heritage. Teams composed of individuals from various national backgrounds do not come together and immediately differentiate themselves from one another based on engineering or accounting backgrounds, religious orientation, nor race. These are important characteristics admittedly, but they are incompletely shared as status markers across nations (Earley, 1999; Hughes, 1971). Rather, people most fundamentally notice their national and cultural backgrounds (Turner, 1985). It is this primary recognition that must be understood if researchers wish to move forward in their study of multinational teams.

# 2 Literature Review of Multinational Teams

Historically in the field of human resource management a strong emphasis on personnel selection and employees' performance appraisals has prevailed, and about 25% of all articles published in American I/O psychology journals in the 80s dealt with these two topics (Erez, 1994; Erez & Earley, 1993). Individual incentive plans were designed to reinforce individual performance, and differential incentive plans, including flexible, "cafeteria style" benefits were tailored to satisfy the needs of the individual employee (Cascio, 1989). From an historical perspective, this individualistic focus can be explained in light of the dominant stream in psychology, of the liberal individualist, which views the individual as self-contained, and as one whose identity is defined apart from the world (Cushman, 1990, Sampson, 1989). The emphasis on the individual per se detracts attention from environmental factors and their effect on organizational behavior.

However, the rapid environmental changes occurring in the last decade cannot be ignored. The two most significant changes in the work environment—the globalization of the market and the restructuring of companies—have a tremendous impact on employees' self-concept and self-identity, on work motivation and commitment to the workplace, and on organizational behavior and its consequent performance outcomes. The scope of the work environment and of work-related influences have increased dramatically. It involves confrontation with cultural differences in customers' needs, in partners' norms of behavior and work values, in human resource management practices, and in decision-making processes. As a result, there is a growing market for popular books on how to do business across cultures (e.g., Earley & Erez, 1997; Graham & Sano,

1984; Schneider & Barsoux, 1997; Trompenaars, 1997). The popularity of such books testifies that there are significant cultural differences in work behavior and that companies from Western societies having to do business across cultural borders are not well prepared.

Cross-cultural contacts have become pervasive at the national, regional, organizational, and individual level. All current societies contain multiple cultural groups (Berry, 1997; Goto, 1997), and most societies' workforces are also becoming more diverse (Moghaddam, 1997). This is evident in multinational companies (Dorfman & Howell, 1997; Granrose & Oskamp, 1997; Tung, 1997), but it is also true in other executive teams (Maznevski & Peterson, 1997) and in blue-collar work groups. In addition to internal organizational changes due to globalization and revolutionary developments in communication technology (Tung, 1997), interactions of various cultural groups take place in contacts with outside constituents, such as selling products to customers from many cultures (Ensher & Murphy, 1997).

Along with the increase in multicultural interaction and multinational teams, there has been a slow and steady increase in research addressing issues related to teaming across cultures. Bettenhausen's (1991) review of research conducted during the period from 1986 to 1989 identified only one study that included an examination of the effects of cultural, racial, or ethnic differences on group behavior. A review by Miliken and Martins (1996) indicates a dramatic increase in recent research with regard to diversity in organizational groups during the period of 1989 to 1994. However, the effects of cultural diversity in groups remain underrepresented in the literature, with only 3 of the 80 studies reviewed considering the effects of diversity with regard to national culture (Miliken & Martins, 1996).

In this chapter, we review this research, providing a summary of a wide array of studies that are relevant to multinational team functioning. Although our coverage of this research is not exhaustive, we were careful to select and include in this review the most pertinent and relevant theoretical frameworks and studies. This research provides the general, conceptual basis for our theory presented in the subsequent chapters.

At least three theoretical domains speak to the general topic of multinational teams. These domains can be informally characterized as: (1) multinational structures and technologies, (2) top management team composition and functioning, and (3) cognition, exchange and conflict. The first of these domains, multinational structures and technology, has foundations in organizational theory and information systems and thus approaches teaming from a more macro perspective with a focus on organizational context, technology, political systems, and economic systems. The second domain focusing on top management team composition, emanated from the strategic management tradition that emphasizes the decision-making power of the top managers constituting the dominant coalition of the firm. Finally, the third domain, cognition, exchange, and conflict, has origins in the organizational behavior literature and primarily addresses questions pertaining to the interpersonal and social aspects of multinational teams. Each of these three domains are addressed in turn next, along with implications for the theoretical framework we have developed in the remainder of this book.

## MULTINATIONAL STRUCTURES AND TECHNOLOGIES

A first body of research that informs our framework for multinational teams pertains to the context of the multinational organization and the technological tools that multinational teams utilize. Investigations of these issues have been conducted by strategy and organizational theory researchers, and help to ground our framework within the particular environment that multinational teams are often embedded.

**Technology.**    In today's organizations, more often than not, business success depends on expanding the global reach of an organization. The adoption of the transnational organizational model for a multinational enterprise is frequently acknowledged as a primary means of going global. The transnational organization meets challenges of global efficiency, while also being locally responsive, and encouraging ongoing learning processes. Using a transnational strategy, each organizational activity is performed in a location where it can be best accomplished (Bartlett & Ghoshal, 1987). Implementing this strategy often requires employees and business partners to be geographically and temporally distant from one another. Deploying information technologies is one means of overcoming spatial and temporal boundaries, thus designing an effective transnational organization depends on the effective deployment of advanced information technologies (Boudreau, Loch, Robey, & Straud, 1998).

The technology available to a team has a significant impact on how the team members interact with one another as well as others external to the group. Although the role of technology on group functioning is the topic of much research (e.g., DeSanctis & Jackson, 1994; DeSanctis & Poole, 1994; Lipnack & Stamps, 1997; Mankin, Cohen, & Bikson, 1996; McKenna & Bargh, 1998; Townsend, DeMarie, & Hendrickson, 1998; Warkentin, Sayeed, & Hightower, 1997), our emphasis is on the unique aspects of technology vis-à-vis the MNT. One of the most immediate effects of communication technology (e.g., Internet and e-mail) is that a MNT can keep in more direct contact among members even if geographic dispersion inhibits face-to-face encounters. We will address the advantages and disadvantages of these various forms of technology-mediated interactions in a subsequent chapter. For now, suffice it to say that technology such as e-mail, group-decision support systems, and other computer-mediated interventions are becoming more and more prevalent.

The numbers of people participating in virtual groups is increasing. Most North American households now own at least one computer, and over 40 million people are online, that is connected to the Internet, able to send and receive electronic mail (Dowe, 1997). Worldwide, the number of people online is doubling every year, and estimates are that 10% of the world's population will be online by the turn of the century (McKenna & Bargh, 1998). Whether virtual groups operate by the same principals as real-life or "face-to-face" groups has been a debating point for some years among researchers of computer-mediated communication (Lea & Spears, 1995; Walther, Anderson, & Park, 1994). Some authors have argued that the relative lack of social cues in e-mail interactions leads to a greater incidence of antisocial behaviors than would occur in face-to-face interactions, presumably because of deindividuation (Kiesler, Siegel, & McGuire, 1984). The buffering provided by an electronic system can have potentially devastating effects if the buffering is used to protect people from the normal social etiquette demanded in discourse.

However, electronic communications can provide useful opportunities if it creates a work environment that provides for enhanced interaction (Walther, 1997; Warkentin, Sayeed, & Hightower, 1997). Furthermore, other researchers have found that despite the greater anonymity of computer-mediated communication, group members form and adhere to norms just as they do in face-to-face groups (Spears et al., 1990).

Examining a particular type of virtual group, the newsgroup, McKenna & Bargh (1998) estimate that today, over 30,000 different newsgroups exist, covering general as well as quite specific interests. In series of three studies, these authors found that participation in a virtual group such as a newsgroup has significant effects on the transformation of an individual's social identity. Increased involvement led to increased importance of the group identity, which in turn increased self-acceptance of that identity even when it was a "marginalized identity" (i.e., concealable and culturally devalued identities such as people with epilepsy, former prison inmates, those with nonmainstream sexual interests or political views). These findings suggest that just as with nonelectronic group identities (Deaux, 1996), virtual groups are important to the daily lives of their members, and virtual group identities become an important part of the self. According to McKenna & Bargh (1998), as with face-to-face groups, the positive versus negative feedback of group members shapes one's subsequent behavior to the extent that belonging to that group matters to the individual.

The key appears to be the relational links developed among team members. For example, Warkentin et. al. studied a World Wide Web-based asynchronous computer conference system and found that teams using this computer-mediated communication system could not outperform traditional (face-to-face) teams under otherwise comparable circumstances. Relational links among team members were found to be a significant contributor to the effectiveness of information exchange. Though the virtual and face-to-face teams exhibited similar levels of communication effectiveness, face-to-face team members reported higher levels of satisfaction.

**Structures.** Many transnational organizations are meeting these challenges by developing three characteristics: alliances and partnerships, spatial independence, and flexibility (Boudreau et al., 1998). For example, companies such as Sun Microsystems, Nike, and Reebok, have been designed as a federation of alliances and partnerships with other organizations, allowing corporate functions to be easily integrated with functions provided by allied partners to enhance and extend corporate reach worldwide.

Using a contrasting strategy, Eastman Kodak is comprised of units with relative spatial and temporal independence. This increases the ease with which geographical boundaries are transcended, providing competitive presence in global markets and improving access to natural and human resources. Finally, companies such as Intel emphasize flexibility. Parts of the organization may be formed, disbanded, and reformed to respond rapidly to changing business needs. Comprising members from company locations in Ireland, Israel, England, France, and Asia, their new product development teams come together quickly, do their work and then regroup with a variety of other teams. This allows resources to be easily reassigned to respond to shifting opportunities in global markets (Solomon, 1995). Indeed, anecdotal evidence indicates that multinational teams have the potential to transform quickly according to changing task requirements and responsibilities (Armstrong & Cole, 1995). Experts agree that making all of these transnational strategies work requires an organization-wide commitment to cooperation among partners (Boudreau et al. 1998).

In an important study that bridges both the communication theory and multinational organizational theory, Ghoshal, Korine, and Szulanski (1994) found that interpersonal relationships developed through lateral communication mechanisms such as joint work in teams, task forces, and meetings, increased the communication effectiveness of multinational teams. The researchers examined subsidiary-headquarters communication and intersubsidiary communication based on data collected from 164 senior managers working in 14 different national subsidiaries within the consumer electronics division of Matsushita, a Japanese company, and 84 mangers working in nine different national subsidiaries of N.V. Philips, the Holland-based competitor of Matsushita. Findings demonstrated that lateral communication mechanisms had significant positive effects on the frequency of both subsidiary-headquarters and intersubsidiary communication. Given this link, the next step for future research is to investigate the relationship between across-border communication frequency and subsidiary performance.

Multinational organizational structure can indeed have an important influence on communication logistics. However, as argued by Huber and Daft (1987), the organizational task of information processing involves not only managing the logistics of its flow, but also facilitating the process of its interpretation. It is in creating shared meaning systems that create meaning out of ambiguous and equivocal information that networking mechanisms and organizational processes may play a vital role (Ghoshal, Korine, & Szulanski, 1994). We argue that the information logistics that formal structures attempt to induce can only function properly when the lateral processes needed for interpretation are also in place.

This point is echoed by Gomez-Casseres (1994) in his commentary on alliance networks that often involve multinational teaming. Call them networks, clusters, constellations, or virtual organizations, these groups often consistent of companies joined together in a larger, overarching relationships, and are often governed by teams. For example, Swissair's alliances with Delta Air Lines, Singapore Airlines, and SAS sought to increase bookings on transatlantic and European-Asian flights and to combine the procurement and maintenance of airplanes. In the multimedia industry, an array of alliance groups has sprung up in the past 2 years as the computer and communications industries have converged. Consumer companies have joined with consumer electronic companies, cable TV operators, telecommunication providers, and entertainment companies to develop new products and services. Gomez-Casseres argues that the collective governance structures that form to govern these alliances, such as IBM's Power Open Association and Sun's Sparc International, may help maintain network cohesion by binding together companies in a team-based representation system, but executives of the companies represented must always bear in mind that mismanagement can erode the group-based advantage that size and variety generate.

## TOP MANAGEMENT TEAM (TMT) COMPOSITION

A second body of research that informs our framework for multinational teams pertains primarily to demography and team composition, examining relative differences in observable characteristics such as age or functional background. This research highlights the strategic implications of multinational teaming and focuses on firm-level outcomes of interaction in such teams. The cultural diversity literature (e.g., Cox, 1993; Cox, Lobel, & McLeod, 1991; Jackson, Salas, & associates, 1992; Watson, Kumar, & Michaelson, 1993) studies team members' demographic backgrounds, and highlights demographic variables presupposed to relate directly to cultural attributes, values, and perceptions. The benefits of cultural diversity are often attributed to the variety of perspectives, values, skills, and attributes that diverse team members contribute (Maznevski, 1994). Finally, groups research addresses team composition effects (e.g., Hackman, 1976, 1990; McGrath, 1984; Tajfel, 1982; Tajfel & Turner, 1979; Turner, 1985). The groups literature suggests the relationship of heterogeneity to performance is mixed and subject to a number of constraints imposed by the work setting (McGrath, 1984; Nemeth, 1986).

**Interpersonal Processes.** Much of this research finds that team similarity is positively associated with team effectiveness and interpersonal attraction (Hambrick & Mason, 1984; Tsui et al., 1992). Homogeneous team members generally report stronger affinity for their team than heterogeneous team members (Ibarra, 1992). Attitude similarity and demographic homogeneity have generally been shown to be positively related to group cohesiveness (Jackson, 1992a). Demographically similar groups tend to exhibit higher satisfaction, and lower absenteeism and turnover.

These findings are consistent with the well-established principle that people are attracted to similar others (Byrne, 1971), and the proposition that heterogeneous groups experience more conflict (Jehn, Northcraft, & Neale, 1999). Indeed, research indicates that cultural diversity generates conflict, which in turn reduces the ability of a group to maintain itself over time and to provide satisfying experiences for its members (Earley & Mosakowski, 2000; Ravlin et al., 2000). Certainly, the degree of team heterogeneity has certain structural effects, such as increasing coordination costs (e.g., Steiner, 1972) and changing the number of opportunities that culturally different members have to interact with one another (Blau, 1977). Beginning with Steiner (1972), a stream of research has treated the composition of groups primarily in terms of the resulting process losses that prevent a group from reaching its performance potential. These process losses potentially result from the differing perceptions, attributions, and communication patterns that vary by national culture (Adler, 1991). This is particularly true for individuals who are different from the norm or majority in the group. The degree of distinctiveness of a particular cultural characteristics is important in that the more distinctive a person is, the more self-aware he or she becomes. This self-awareness leads a person to compare his or her behavior with the perceived behavioral standards of the group. It also makes it more likely that an individual's cultural norms for group behavior will vary from those of the group.

Many of these ideas were tested in a study conducted by Thomas (1999). Examining 24 multicultural teams performing five group tasks, he found that culturally homogenous groups had higher performance than culturally heterogeneous groups on all five tasks as rated by a panel of evaluators in terms of problem identification and quality of problem solutions. The degree of collectivist orientations of group members was directly related to their evaluation of group processes, including conflict, cooperation, cohesiveness, commitment, satisfaction, and trust. Finally, members' relative cultural distance from each other influenced their perceptions of group receptiveness. In terms of practice, Thomas (1999) suggests that these results highlight the importance of providing feedback concerning effective group processes for culturally diverse groups to reach their full potential. Effective interaction processes are important for all groups, but they may be especially critical for integrating the different viewpoints of culturally diverse groups.

***Relationships With Performance.***    At the same time, heterogeneity in top management teams has demonstrated some positive effects on performance. Organizational demography researchers often use external observable traits as surrogates for internalized mediating psychological states (e.g., Lawrence, 1997; Tsui, Egan, & O'Reilly, 1992). This view has historical roots in the strategic management literature examining firm competitive moves (e.g., Ginsberg, 1990; Hambrick, Cho, and Chen, 1996; Prahalad & Bettis, 1986; Pfeffer, 1983). Because so few members of top management teams are women and minorities, this research has investigated the impact of other demographic characteristics such as education and work function. For example, based on data from 199 banks, Bantel & Jackson (1989) concluded that both diversity of education and diversity of work function were positively related to measures of innovation when other factors such as organization size, team size, and location of operations were held constant. Hambrick et al. examined a large sample of actions and responses of 32 U.S. airlines over 8 years. The top management teams that were diverse, in terms of functional backgrounds, education, and company tenure, exhibited a relatively great propensity for action and both their actions and responses were of substantial magnitude. But they were also slower in their actions and responses and less likely than homogeneous teams to respond to competitors' initiatives. Thus, although heterogeneity is a double-edged sword, its overall net effect on airline performance in terms of market share and profits, was positive.

In related research, Duhaime and Schwenk (1985), for example, have shown how cognitive simplifications processes may influence acquisition and divestment decisions. Jemison and Sitkin (1986) discussed how obstacles to integration of divergent perspective may impede the acquisition process. Prahalad and Bettis (1986) demonstrated how the dominant logic for conceptualizing the business domain of a firm that is held by the top management team, links diversification to performance.

Finally, Ginsberg (1990) developed a sociocognitive model of diversification that grounds the role of top managers' belief systems in the cognitive and behavioral attributes of corporate strategy. He argued that the sociocognitive characteristics such as *complexity* and *consensus*, reflect the learning capacities of the top management team and are associated with the abilities of its members to collect and interpret information and to communicate among themselves. These sociocognitive capacities, in turn, influence decisions that pertain to diversification. These two capacities are particularly pertinent to our discussion of multinational teams, because in his framework, complexity is determined by two interdependent aspects: (a) differentiation, that is the number of constructs of the system, and (b) integration, that is the nature and extent of rules for integrating these constructs. Consensus, on the other hand, reflects the extent to which a diverse set of assumptions or beliefs has been synthesized into a commonly shared understanding. We return to the balance between these capacities in subsequent sections as we discuss process in multinational teams.

*Information Processing.* Recently, an approach suggesting that team information processing is the mechanism whereby TMT demographics are translated into firm performance has received increased attention. Information processing is defined as a team discussing and coming to a collective understanding of information (Corner & Kinicki, 1999). Although collective information processing is a complex phenomenon, it can be reasonably captured by team members' beliefs (Corner & Kinicki, 1999; Gibson, 2000b; Gibson, 2000c). Beliefs are defined as remembered cause and effect associations learned through experience (Axelrod, 1976; Thompson, 1967). Beliefs function as a storage mechanism for team members' knowledge and can be recalled and applied to strategic decisions. The effects of beliefs on outcomes can be captured by two variables: belief integration and belief variety (Ginsberg, 1990; Walsh et al. 1988). In one empirical study of these variables, Corner & Kinicki (1999) found that homogeneity with a team was positively related to belief integration, a positive relationship between experience and belief variety, a negative relationship between integration and firm performance, and a positive relationship between belief variety and firm performance. These findings illustrate that mediating mechanisms such as belief integration and belief variety may partially account for the previous pattern of inconsistent results regarding the relationship between TMT homogeneity, experience, and firm outcomes.

*Team Tasks.* A second approach suggests that the effect of cultural composition on acceptable output should be determined by the group's task. Nonroutine task performance may be facilitated by multiculturalism, whereas performance on routine tasks should either be unaffected or possibly even negatively impacted. Potential positive effects are only anticipated when the group has learned to manage its conflict, and the dimension of diversity is relevant to the task at hand (Thomas, et al., 1996).

Likewise, rather than having a uniformly positive impact, the effects of sociocognitive capacities of top management teams discussed previously, may depend on the nature of the decision-making task. For example, Sujan, Sujan, and Bettman (1988) argued that if the goal of effective sales-people is to discriminate among different types of customers, then sales-people who have highly differentiated cognitive construction systems compared to customers' should be more effective. If, on the other hand, the goal of effective salespeople is to uncover underlying similarities among different types of customers to best use the sales strategies available to them, then salespeople who have highly integrated cognitive construction systems in relation to customers should be more effective.

In a similar vein, Keck (1997) found that firms in continually disrupted contexts were more successful when they built teams that stayed together for longer periods but were functionally heterogeneous. This led Keck (1998) to argue that in turbulent contexts, cultural differences will be more disruptive than productive for heterogeneous teams. On a related note, Pelled (1996) developed a model of intervening processes linking demographic diversity to work group outcomes that recognizes both the types of diversity represented in the group (the demographic predictors) and the types of conflict experienced by the group (the intervening processes). She argues, for example, that as the visibility of demographic diversity increases, affective conflict within the group increase. In contrast, as the job-relatedness of demographic diversity increases, substantive conflict will increase.

***Team Tenure.*** Another potential moderator of the impact of TMT heterogeneity is length of time the team has existed together as a team. This is consistent with Pelled's (1996) model, as well as Elron's (1997) research on top management teams. Elron examined top management teams in international subsidiaries of multinational corporations. She found that cultural heterogeneity within the TMT was positively related to the level of issue-based conflict. Subsequently, issue-based conflict negatively affected TMT performance but had a positive relationship with subsidiary performance. No support was obtained for a negative relationship between cultural heterogeneity and cohesion. Elron argued that one possible explanation is that the negative effects of value dissimilarity on cohesion weaken over time, and in long terms groups like the TMT, become insignificant.

This notion was supported by Watson, Kumar, and Michaelsen (1993). These researchers investigated the impact of cultural diversity on group interaction and group problem solving over time. Their study involved 36 work groups of two types: (1) homogenous—consisting of all White Americans, and (2) heterogeneous—consisting of White Americans, Black Americans, Hispanic Americans, and foreign nationals. Over the course of

4 months, these work groups completed four projects. Various aspects of performance, including range of perspectives, number of potential problems identified, generation of multiple alternatives, quality of recommendations, overall performance and group interaction process were measured on a monthly basis. During the first 3 months, homogenous groups outperformed the diverse groups on several of the performance measures and reported significantly more effective process than the diverse groups. However, after 4 months, diverse groups scored significantly higher on range of perspectives and alternatives generated, and both types of groups reported equally effective group processes. Watson et al. (1993) conclude that diversity constrains process and performance among members of newly formed groups; however, limitations can be overcome, and eventually diverse groups will outperform homogeneous groups.

By the end of the study, the two kinds of groups became equivalent. Katz (1982) suggests that this reduction in process loss results from the tendency of a group to try to reduce uncertainty by relying on customary ways of doing things and to become more homogeneous through shared socialization and group experiences.

*Social Integration.* In an organizational setting, support for the link between demography and process was uncovered by Smith, Olian, Sims, O'Bannon, and Scully (1994) in their study of demographic heterogeneity in domestic TMTs. Smith et al. used data from 53 high-technology firms to test three alternative models of the effects of top management team demography and process on organizational performance: (1) a demography model, in which team demography accounts entirely for performance outcomes, and process has no impact; (2) a process model in which process contributes incrementally and directly to performance outcomes, over and above the team's demography; and (3) an intervening model, in which the effects of the top management team on performance outcomes are due entirely to the effects of its demography on process. Results demonstrated partial support for the intervening model, in which process is a mediator of the relationship between demography and performance, and the process model, in which demography and process variables each affect performance separately.

These results suggest a fourth, more complex model of top management team behavior, with greater emphasis on team social integration. In the Smith et al. study, social integration was related to both return on investment and one year growth in sales. Social integration is a multifaceted phenomenon that reflects the attraction to the team, satisfaction with other members of the group and social interaction among the group members (O'Reilly, Caldwell, and Barnett, 1989). Presumably, management teams that work well together react faster, are more flexible, use superior problems techniques, and are more productive than less integrative teams.

A similar model was proposed by Pelled, Eisenhardt, and Xin (1999), suggesting that work group diversity indirectly affects cognitive task performance through intragroup task conflict and intragroup emotional conflict. They argued that job-related types of diversity largely drive task conflict, while a "web of diversity types increase emotional conflict based on stereotyping and decrease emotional conflict based on social comparison" (p. 2). They further suggested that task routineness and group longevity moderate these diversity-conflict relationships. They tested these relationships in an examination of 45 improvement teams in the electronics industry, including team members' questionnaires as well as mangers' ratings of team performance. The findings suggested that task conflict is a relatively straightforward phenomenon driven by functional background differences. Emotional conflict was more complicated. The latter was increased by dissimilarity in race and tenure. The authors argue that this is because race and tenure attributes are relatively impermeable and so people find it difficult to identify with (and easy to stereotype) those of a different race or tenure. Surprisingly, emotional conflict was not related to performance. These findings coincide with those obtained by Jehn (1995), indicating that groups can manage the negative effects. Furthermore, task routineness reduced the positive associations between diversity and emotional conflict, suggesting that the management of task design can help to overcome the degree of conflict.

In a similar vein, Earley and Mosakowski found that a hybrid team culture may provide the basis for exchange and coordination within a diverse team to exploit member talents and resources. In contrast, a perceived sense of "teamness," or entitativity, appeared absent in the split teams. The moderately heterogeneous groups showed a great deal of communication problems, relational conflict, and low team identity. These intervening conditions have been found to have a dysfunctional impact on team effectiveness (Jehn, Chadwick, & Thatcher, 1997; Thatcher, Jehn, & Chadwick, 1998). With regard to Hughes's (1971) notion of trait hierarchies, Earley and Mosakowski showed that nationality is a primary status-determining characteristic within transnational teams. What remains unclear, however, is which auxiliary traits also matter and how these traits vary by cultural background. To some degree, Turner's Self-Categorization Theory (1985) sheds light on trait hierarchies. Self-categories may be ordered hierarchically by perceived importance, with people identifying with categories to varying degrees. People use trait categories to define themselves if sufficient overlap exists within a trait class. Inclusion at one level (e.g., apples and oranges are fruits), however, may not mean inclusion at a more proximate level (e.g., apples and oranges are not both citrus fruits). In this sense, societal membership may be an abstract category subordinate only to categories such as being human (Turner, 1985).

***Third Parties.*** Outside parties may influence the impact of heterogeneity in a top management team. Gibson and Saxton (2001) developed a framework relating type of third party input (direction, devil's advocacy, or expert advice), timing of input (either early or late), and team heterogeneity to team decision outcomes. They tested the framework using data collected from 106 five-person simulated top management teams participating in a complex, multiparty role play. Several characteristics of the simulation were experimentally manipulated. This design allowed for random assignment to conditions allowing them to rule out many potentially confounding characteristics of a natural organizational context. As a result, we can be relatively certain that differences in teams can be attributed to the experimental manipulations of type, timing, and heterogeneity.

Gibson and Saxton's (1999) findings demonstrate that type of third-party input, timing of the input, and heterogeneity of the team interact to affect decision outcomes, confirming the complexity of the decision-making process. Providing direction early in the process proved to be particularly productive for the team decision-making process. This relationship was also evident when direction was provided to heterogeneous teams, suggesting that the challenges diverse teams have in coming to a consensus and completing the decision-making process (Jackson, 1992b) might be offset by the presence of a third party helping guide the team and keep the members on task. Perceived team heterogeneity also interacted with third-party roles to affect decision outcomes. Specifically, devil's advocacy and expert information contribute more when teams were perceived by members to be homogeneous. This finding reinforces concerns that homogeneous teams can be limited in their diversity of perspectives and may be less creative (Jackson et. al., 1995). The presence of a third party in a devil's advocate role may challenge the team's assumptions and decrease the likelihood that groupthink will set in (Janis, 1972). Further, the advocate or expert role may help broaden the team's perspective and bring in information that is new or has been ignored. Both effects appear to lead to better decision outcomes for homogenous teams.

In short, in a controlled setting, Gibson and Saxton (2001) have established that third parties' involvement can interact with timing and team composition to enhance and sometimes mitigate the effects of team heterogeneity and homogeneity. Third parties may indeed facilitate the strategic decision-making process, but their findings suggest that it is not their direct involvement per se that matters; rather, it is the pluralism of perspectives third parties may provide that facilitates good decisions. Thus, to effectively use third parties, managers must understand how the third party role and timing may interact with the team's inherent characteristics in making effective strategic decisions.

***In-group Versus Out-group.***   In a multinational team, the role of outside parties is complicated by who is identified as "outside" versus "inside." In highly collective cultures, there is a strong sense of who is "in-group" and who is "out-group" (Earley & Gibson, 1998; Triandis, 1995). Individuals from a collectivistic society call for greater emotional dependence on one another than individuals from individualistic societies and their organizations are expected to play a stronger role in their lives. For example, in many Asian cultures, an individual's company is not only expected to provide a salary, medical coverage, and other benefits common to the West, but they provide housing, childcare, education, and even moral and personal counseling as well as political indoctrination.

Triandis and his colleagues (e.g., Bontempo, Lobel, & Triandis, 1989; Hui & Triandis, 1985; Triandis, Bontempo, Betancourt, Bond, Leung, Brenes, Georgas, Hui, Narin, Setiadi, Singha, Verma, Spanger, Tonzand, & de Montmollin, 1986; Triandis, 1989, 1990, 1995) argue that individualistic and collectivistic societies vary on a number of relevant dimensions germane to organizations. Collectivistic societies emphasize a number of characteristics including: priority is given to group goals and group goals are viewed as a means for attaining individual goals; concern for how one's actions will impact in-group members; tendency to share resources with in-group members; interdependence among in-group members is desirable; involvement in other in-group members' lives; perception that in-group values/norms are universally valid and a willingness to fight for these values; social behavior is strongly influenced by in-group rules; relationships are viewed as nurturing, respectful, and intimate; relationships are based on a principle of equality and altruism rather than exchange and equity; and, in-groups tend to be small and tight-knit as well as quite stable across time. Triandis argues that individualists belong to many groups and flow between them so as to attain personal interests and they will avoid a particular in-group should it place too many demands on the individual. The collectivist has a stable in-group membership whereas the individualist belongs to multiple in-groups and has to refresh membership and status in the group constantly. Triandis argues that the number of in-groups to which an individual belongs is a key aspect of individualism and collectivism (Triandis, 1995). Specifically, he argues that individualists form into a multitude of in-groups and stay with these groups until they impose on the individual. At this point, the individualist moves to another group for instrumental gains in order to avoid a restriction on his or her autonomy.

Thus, if the MNT consists of many people having strong collective orientations, then an outside party is likely to be truly viewed as "outside" and, therefore, viewed with suspicion. In an individualistic culture, the boundary between inside and outside is more fluid and so the outside party of today may be perceived as a group member tomorrow. The chief difficulty occurs if the MNT is highly mixed with regard to individualism and collectivism. In this instance, some group members will shun the outsider whereas others will bring the outsider into the group. This occurrence of new membership is described later in the next chapter, as we turn to a discussion of a theoretical framework that integrates the many conceptual and empirical works that have addressed multinational teams.

## COGNITION, EXCHANGE, AND CONFLICT

Finally, the largest body of research that informs our framework for multinational teams pertains to cognition, exchange and conflict across cultures. Here, we draw on the work of social psychologists who have examined Social Cognitive Theory, communication and linguistic theory, and industrial organizational psychologists who have studied processes of social exchange and conflict resolution. This research helps inform our model particularly with regard to the processes that occur inside the multinational team, as will be detailed next.

*Cognition.* Several streams of research demonstrate that group-level cognitive phenomenon differ from culture to culture. The basic thesis of a cognitive approach is that processing frameworks acquired in one culture persist and influence behavior even though circumstances might change (Walsh, 1995). In fact, the outcomes of culturally specific cognitions are the substance of much cross-cultural research. For example, the work of Nesbitt and colleagues (Choi & Nisbett, 1998; Choi, Nisbett, & Norenzayan, 1999; Choi, Nisbett, & Smith, 1997; Morris, Nisbett, & Peng, 1995) demonstrates how individuals and groups in different cultures interpret their immediate environment. They uncovered how distinct mental categories, differing links between categories, and negotiated understandings about cause-and-effect relationships form the perceptions that allow individuals and groups to act.

*Meaning of Teamwork.* Specifically examining these differing categories pertaining to teams, Gibson & Zellmer-Bruhn (2000), draw from linguistic theory to better understand how the meaning of teamwork varies across national and organizational cultures. These authors argued that it is not enough to observe that behaviors differ across cultures; we must be able to understand how those differences come into being. If one can determine the categories by which workers comprehend their environment, the available behaviors are clarified and the link between stimulus and behavior is elucidated. By understanding cognitive frameworks, it becomes clearer which values may be triggered and applied in a choice or decision context. In this manner, culture guides our choices, commitments, and standards of behavior (Erez & Earley, 1993; Schneider, 1989, 1993; Schneider & Angelmar, 1993; Schneider & DeMeyer, 1991).

Gibson and Zellmer-Bruhn (2000) also argued that it is important to realize that neither national culture nor organizational culture exist in isolation of the other. One of the few studies to address the relationship between culture at the national and organizational levels was conducted by Hofstede, Neuijen, Ohayv, and Sanders (1990). They argued that national culture consists of a more diffuse set of orientations that arise mainly from basic values developed early in life through the family and other socialization mechanisms. Although values play a role at the organizational level, organizational culture is based more on specific work practices that are acquired within the organization. Although the results of Hofstede's study point to a separation of national and organizational culture, it seems probable that some relationship between the two does exist. Many researchers have pointed to the complicated embeddedness of organizational cultures (Alvesson 1993; Beck & Moore, 1985; Myerson & Martin, 1987).

Organizational culture affects behavior directly by providing guidelines and expectations for organizational members. A similar statement can be made about the link between national culture and behavior (England, 1983). It is likely that national culture affects organizational culture (and perhaps in exceptional circumstances, vice versa) and that the two levels of culture may have contradictory effects on organizational behavior. Some evidence for this phenomenon was compiled by Gibson (1994). Gibson investigated how national culture influences characteristics of organizations such as specialization, standardization, formalization, centralization, and configuration. Based on exploratory interviews with managers in two cultural regions, she found evidence for three perspectives: (1) *structure as rational adoption of cultural rules*, (2) *structure as manifestation of cultural values*, and (3) *structure as reflection of cultural enactment*. Results suggested that an approach that allows for reciprocity among the three perspectives is most useful in understanding the impact of culture on organization structure. In a similar line of inquiry, Lincoln, Hanada, and Olson (1981) found that matching organizational culture with societal culture resulted in high job satisfaction. Based on this evidence, Gibson and Zellmer-Bruhn (2000) argued that that national culture must be considered along with organizational culture to fully understand the relation of an organization's culture to organizational functioning.

To investigate these ideas, Gibson and Zellmer-Bruhn (2000) selected four cultural contexts (the United States, France, Puerto Rico, and the Philippines) to obtain variation on the two cultural aspects identified earlier: power distance and collectivism. According to research conducted by Hofstede (1980a), employees in the United States tend to be relatively low in power distance and collectivism, employees in France tend to be high in power distance and low in collectivism, and employees in Puerto Rico and the Philippines tend to be relatively high in power distance and collectivism. The research was limited to the pharmaceutical and medical product industry to control for potential industry confounds; this industry was se-lected because production of pharmaceuticals is geographically dis-persed around the world. In each cultural context, the researchers studied the same six firms, selected due to the prevalence of teams across func-tional areas in each of the four cultural contexts.

Gibson and Zellmer-Bruhn (2000) traveled to each region of the world and conducted in-depth personal interviews with team members ranging in rank from hourly manufacturing employees to vice presidents, to gen-eral managers of country units. Interviewees represented a variety of func-tional team types, from manufacturing teams, to product management teams to sales teams and executive project teams. The sample also repre-sented a variety of levels in the organizations, and included both poor per-forming and high performing teams.

The researchers posed a series of questions to team members pertain-ing to concepts of teamwork, the function of the teams, team motivation, leadership in the teams, feedback and reward systems, sharing of knowl-edge and practices across teams, metaphors for teamwork, and the im-pact of culture on teams. Interviewees were also asked to discuss which factors they felt were the most important facilitators and inhibitors of team effectiveness. Finally, the researchers encouraged interviewees to discuss any additional issues pertinent to the use of teams in multinational compa-nies. Interviews were conducted in the native language of the interview-ees, with the assistance of a team of bilingual interviewers.

All interviews were tape recorded and transcribed by professional transcriptionists who were native speakers in the languages used in the study. As they transcribed, they translated the interviews into English. Any words that were not readily translated were left in the native language. This process resulted in a text database representing over 60 teams and consisting of over 1,000 pages of single-spaced text. The content analysis program TACT (Bradley, 1989; Hawthorne, 1994; Popping, 1997) was uti-lized to facilitate comprehensive text analysis.

Using these transcripts, Gibson and Zellmer-Bruhn (2000) examined con-cepts of teamwork, which they referred to as "teamwork metaphors" using an iterative process of both inductive and deductive analyses. Categories of teamwork metaphors were inductively derived, and then quantified. The four teamwork metaphors arrived at through this process were characterized as: (1) family; (2) sports; (3) community; (4) associates; and (5) military. The fre-quency of occurrence of these schema across cultures and organizations was then analyzed to deductively test research questions about variance in meaning. The significant main effects and interaction effects revealed by MANOVA indicated that these themes, or teamwork metaphors, vary across countries and organizations, even after controlling for gender and functional background. Specifically, the interaction of country by organization ac-counted for a significant portion of the variance in frequency of use of the *mili-*

*tary* category, the *community* category, and the *associates* category. This indicates that beyond the main country effects, organizations will tend to emphasize different teamwork metaphors in different countries.

Thus, the general expectations that country and organization would demonstrate significant main effects as well as interaction effects were thus confirmed. Furthermore, these differences appeared to coincide with cultural and organizational values. For example, as mentioned earlier one particularly pertinent aspect of culture is power distance, or perceptions regarding hierarchical relationships. Across the five teamwork metaphor categories, the family and military categories contained the most information about hierarchical relationships. Gibson & Zellmer-Bruhn's analyses suggested that respondents in the Philippines use both the family and military categories more than respondent in other countries. Filipinos are typically high in power distance. The authors argue that this provides evidence that cultural phenomena act as mechanisms through which the cultural context influences teams. Furthermore, understanding meaning assigned to the concept of teamwork can help provide guidance to organizations attempting to successfully adjust their team-based systems to multinational environments.

**Group Efficacy.**   A second stream of research pertains to collective cognitions known as group efficacy beliefs. group efficacy is analogous to self-efficacy at the individual level, defined as "a judgement of one's (or a group's) capability to accomplish a certain level of performance" (Bandura, 1986, p.391). People tend to avoid tasks and situations they believe exceed their capabilities. Efficacy judgments promote the choice of situations and tasks with high likelihood of success, and eliminate the choice of tasks that exceed one's capabilities. Self-efficacy has been mainly developed with respect to the individual (Bandura, 1986, 1997). However, a perceived collective efficacy is crucial for what people choose to do as a group, how much effort they put into it, and how persistent they are when facing failures (Earley, 1994; Gibson, 1999; Gibson, Randel & Earley, 2000; Guzzo & Shea, 1994; Guzzo & Waters, 1982; Guzzo, Yost, Campbell, & Shea, 1993; Parker, 1994; Prussia & Kinicki, 1996). For example, two groups of nurses who have equal training and supplies may hold very different beliefs about their group's ability to provide quality health care to the same group of patients. These beliefs may differ because the groups differ in the amount of information they have about their task, because they have different processes of sharing this information and communicating, or because they have different levels of commitment and identification among group members. Thus, groups that outwardly look similar in many respects, may form different beliefs about their groups' ability, due different group processes.

Bandura (1986, 1997) suggested that individuals hold performance beliefs about the groups to which they belong and that the strength of groups and organizations lies in people's sense of group efficacy that they can solve their problems and improve their lives through concerted effort (Bandura, 1986). Other researchers have verified the hypothesis that group beliefs about capability influence team performance (Campion, Medsker, & Higgs, 1993; Guzzo et al., 1993; Lindsley, Brass, & Thomas, 1995; Shamir, 1990; Zander & Medow, 1963).

For example, Campion, Medskar, and Higgs (1993) found that three group effectiveness measures for 80 work groups were correlated with 19 different work group characteristics drawn from the existing literature on group effectiveness. Of the 19 characteristics, the strongest predictor of effectiveness was the measure of group performance beliefs, or efficacy judgment. Furthermore, the extent to which the groups possessed confidence in their ability was the only characteristic that demonstrated a statistically significant relationship with all effectiveness measures. However, it is not clear how these judgments of group efficacy are influenced by social context. Bandura (1986) suggested that efficacy is, in part, socially constructed, and that such construction may differ as a function of national culture. Just as our culture teaches us what ideals to hold and what beliefs to endorse (Rokeach, 1973), it plays a role in how we construct our efficacy expectations (Bandura, 1986, 1997). Although research has focused on the nature of group decisions in organizations, relatively little is known about the nature of these decisions in varying cultural contexts (Mann, 1980).

Gibson (1999, 2000c) argued that group efficacy effects are complex and moderated by several contingency factors. Theoretically, it seems likely that group efficacy is distinct from the individual beliefs group members hold about themselves or the group, because group efficacy arises through group interaction and the process of collective cognition. That is, group efficacy forms as group members collectively acquire, store, manipulate, and exchange information about each other, their task, their context, process, and prior performance. Through processes of interaction, this information is combined, weighted, and integrated to form the group efficacy belief. These same collective processes do not occur during self-efficacy formation or when members form individual beliefs about the group.

Combining and integrating information in groups opens up the possibility that distortions will occur (Klimoski & Mohammed, 1994; Lindsley et al., 1995). When information is exchanged and integrated in a group, members negotiate interpretations of factors influencing past efforts and factors required to increase chances of success (Walsh, Henderson, & Deighton, 1988). Many factors may complicate this process by prohibiting or encouraging information exchange or by making salient certain categories of information (Goodman, Ravlin, & Schminke, 1990).

For example, when investigating teachers' group efficacy in their ability to teach mathematics, reading, and language arts, Parker (1994) found that group efficacy was associated with actual achievement in mathematics, but not with the other two domains. Parker (1994) suggests that this is due to the fact that "mathematics is a relatively concrete and 'culture free' domain as opposed to the more nebulous and culture-laden domains of reading and language arts." The nature of the task of teaching mathematics is different in content than the nature of teaching reading and language arts. Thus, characteristics of the teachers' task moderated the relationship between group efficacy and actual effectiveness. Findings such as these indicate that a contingency approach is needed to understand the impact of group efficacy beliefs.

Gibson's comprehensive research conducted between 1994 and 2000 supports the contingency approach to group efficacy (Gibson, 1995; Gibson, 1999, Gibson 2000a, Gibson, 2000b; Gibson, 2000c; Gibson, Randel & Earley, 2000). Gibson began with the premise that a focus on individual efficacy beliefs may have obscured the potential impact that efficacy beliefs at other levels of analysis (e.g. the group level) have on work performance, and that group performance beliefs may be especially important predictors in organizations that focus on team outcomes and in cultures that have a more collectivistic focus.

Gibson (1995) explored both factors that predict group efficacy and factors that impact the relationship between group efficacy and performance. Based on previous group research, she suggested that factors associated with group performance beliefs can be found within four domains—Characteristics of Group Members, Characteristics of the Group, Characteristics of the Task, and Characteristics of the Context; the last domain included cultural factors such as individualism–collectivism and field independence.

Gibson (1995, 1999, 2000a) investigated these factors in a series of two intercultural empirical studies using two distinct methods in each of two cultures. The first study involved a complex business simulation in two contrasting cultures (the United States and Hong Kong). Within each country, participants were randomly assigned to play a role in a simulated organization. Divisional groups within the organizations interacted for a 2-hour period during the simulation. Surveys designed to measure both self-efficacy and group efficacy were distributed at two points during the course of the simulation. Videotaped performance of the divisional groups was then observed by trained observers who were blind to the experimental conditions. In this manner, the relationships between variables in each category, efficacy beliefs, and performance were isolated and analyzed.

In the second study, Gibson (1995, 1999, 2000a) investigated several phenomena associated with group efficacy in a field setting. Efficacy correlates, efficacy beliefs, and performance among teams of nurses were monitored over an 8-week period. The nursing teams represented matched hospitals located in two contrasting cultures (the United States and Indonesia). This design allowed for an applied investigation of the relationship between group efficacy and variables such as identification (a Characteristic of Members), group reputation (a Characteristic of the Group), task interdependence (a Characteristic of the Task), individualism–collectivism and field independence (both Characteristics of the Context) and team performance. Additional insight into the application of the group efficacy construct was gained by conducting the study with actual work groups performing their normal daily tasks within a field context.

Across the two studies, Gibson's (2000a) findings demonstrated that member self-efficacy, group affect, and collectivism predicted between 27% and 49% of the variance in group efficacy. Interestingly, collectivism was negatively related to group efficacy. This finding is opposite to what was predicted, given that group members in collectivistic societies are often motivated to perceive their own group (or in-group) in positive terms. Instead, collectivists had lower levels of group efficacy.

One possible explanation for this finding may pertain to the concept of "face, reviewed earlier." Again, face refers to the evaluation of a person based on internal and external social judgments (Earley, 1999). A person's behavior in organizations reflects, in part, his or her attempt to establish and maintain face across a range of social settings (Earley & Randel 1997). Research suggests that people high and low in collectivism behave differently to maintain face (Erez & Earley, 1987). Collectivists (e.g., members of a kibbutz in the Erez & Earley study) often establish goals sufficiently low enough to ensure that all group members achieve them, thus ensuring that face would not be threatened. In contrast those low in collectivism (members of U.S. work teams in the Erez & Earley study), set quite high goals for themselves, in part due to a desire to appear competent in front of others. For the latter, face was maintained and strengthened by stretching and challenging the group, invoking competition.

Based on these findings, it is plausible that collectivists have modest performance beliefs in order to maintain face. For these groups, to have high efficacy and then perform less than expected would be a threat to face. On the other hand, for those low in collectivism, expecting the highest levels of performance, expressed as high group efficacy beliefs helps to maintain face.

With regard to the relationship between group efficacy and group effectiveness, Gibson's (1999) findings demonstrated that when task uncertainty was high, team members worked independently, and collectivism was low, group efficacy was not related to group effectiveness. In contrast, when groups knew what was required to perform a task, worked interdependently, and valued collectivism, the relationship between group efficacy and group effectiveness was positive.

This evidence for moderators may explain why relationships between group efficacy and group effectiveness have been modest in previous research. Arguably, it is under these circumstances of high task uncertainty, low interdependence, and low collectivism that groups have the most difficulty combining and integrating information about past performance, task constraints, or context. When groups know what is required to perform a task and can actively share information about their group and value it, their beliefs are better aligned with actual effectiveness. This research highlights the potential impact that the cultural context has on group processes. The impact of the cultural context is important for understanding the intercultural applicability of group efficacy, which becomes more critical as an increasing number of multinational organizations use teams in areas of the world with contrasting cultures. In addition to collectivism, there may be additional facets of culture associated with national borders that influence group efficacy and group effectiveness. Important research is currently being conducted investigating cultural characteristics, such as universalism–particularism, that were first identified by anthropologists Kluckhohn and Strodtbeck (1961). These cultural characteristics may have implications for group efficacy and should be incorporated into future investigations.

The nature of personal versus collective efficacy judgments continues to be questioned by researchers. Gibson et al. (2000) examined various conceptualizations of personal and collective efficacy including the view that collective efficacy may best be reflected by an average of individual team members' estimates of a group's capability. However, preliminary findings from their study suggest that there is a slight advantage for prediction in using a measure of collective efficacy based on a single judgment of estimated group capability derived from a group discussion process rather than the aggregation of individuals' personal estimates. To complicate matters, the weights attached to each group member's opinions may vary as a function of cultural background. Earley (1999) found that in high-power distance cultures, team members having high-status demographic characteristics had an inordinate amount of influence over a group's collective efficacy estimates in contrast with low-power distance cultures.

**Exchange.** In a third stream of research, the nature of social exchange across cultures has been examined. Foa and Foa's (1974) Resource Exchange Model is a useful tool for categorizing and structuring a wide array of resources as well as to describe their pattern of exchanges including functional relationships among interacting parties across cultures. According to their model, a resource is defined as anything that can be transmitted from one party to another. They define and categorize six major types of resources: love, or an expression of affectionate regard, warmth, or comfort; status, or an evaluative judgment conveying high or low prestige, regard, or esteem; information, or any advice, opinions, or instructions; money, or any coin or token that has some standard of exchange value; goods, or any products or objects; and, services, or any activities on the body or belonging to the individual (Donnenwerth & Foa, 1974).

To understand the relative contribution of these six resources to exchange, Foa and Foa hypothesized that two general, cultural dimensions underlie resource exchange. The first dimension, universalism versus particularism (Parsons & Shils, 1951), indicates the extent to which the value of a given resource is influenced by the persons involved in the transaction. For example, money is a universal resource, meaning that it does not really matter who provides this resource for it to have value to the recipient—or, in the case of a $20 bill found on the floor, if anyone provides it at all. In contrast, love is a highly particularistic resource whose source is extremely important in valuing it. If I am provided love by someone who I do not know, it has much less significance to me than if it is provided by my spouse. In this case, love represents a resource that is particular to the person providing it (and, arguably, the circumstances under which it is given). Second, Foa and Foa use the dimension of concreteness versus abstractness to describe the tangibility of the resource. Services and goods involve the exchange of some overtly tangible activities or products. In contrast, status and information represent abstract or symbolic resources because they are typically conveyed using verbal or paralinguistic behaviors.

An important aspect of the Foa and Foa model is that it is one of the few exchange models that has been tested in a cross-cultural and international context. Although the other models have received extensive attention in the western literature, it is unclear the extent to which they are culture-bound in their assumptions. For example, much of Homans's work (and work derived from his principles) has been based on an equity assumption of distributive justice. However, ample empirical evidence (see Leung, 2000 for a review) from the cross-cultural literature demonstrates that such an assumption is culture-bound, and that other allocation rules are used in various societies. Foa and Foa's model has been assessed in a number of different countries including Israel, Philippines, Sweden, and Spanish-speaking, Mexican Americans (Foa, Glaubman, Garner, Tornblom, & Salcedo, 1987). Their results provide empirical support for the etic (universal) nature of the resource exchange model including similar rank-ordering of resources and small differences in mean rank position of adjacent resources across their various samples.

Interestingly, Foa and Foa seem to discount the single consistent anomaly in their data, namely, that the information resource is "misbehaved" across their sampled countries. That is to say, the relative position (rank order) of information as a resource is inconsistent across samples and in the context of their framework. It is not at all clear why this anomaly occurs, however, it is conceivable that information plays a different role in relationships across cultures. In a high-power distance culture, information (represented by expertise) is emphasized as a symbol of power and status; this may not be the case in a low-power distance culture (Hofstede, 1980). Hofstede argues that, for example, teachers are respected as an important source of knowledge in high-power but not in low-power distance cultures. As a result, information seems to play a varying role in social exchange depending on the culture in question.

An important aspect of Foa and Foa's research is that resources are generally expected to be repaid in-kind. That is to say, if someone gives us love, we are expected to reciprocate with love and not another, more distant, resource (e.g., money). Studies by Turner, Foa, and Foa demonstrate that if unlike resources are used to reciprocate in an exchange (e.g., giving money in return for love), that repayment requires a disproportionate return, and the exchange may still be viewed as unsatisfactory for the parties. This suggests that the natural balance point, or harmony, will reflect norms of reciprocity and similarity. By reciprocity, we mean that in some cultures an exchange is expected to be two-way, but in others such an outcome violates expectations (i.e., insults the giver). By similarity, we mean that some resources may be interchangeable in certain cultures but not in others (e.g., Foa's difficulty in handling the resource of information). Thus, the nature of harmony within an interacting group depends on the type of relationship employed in a given culture.

**Distributive Justice.** A related stream of research has examined the concept of distributive justice across cultures. This research suggests that there are three general rules underlying concepts of distributive justice—equity, equality, and need. Tornblom, Jonsson, and Foa (1985) compared the use of three allocation rules (equity, equality, need) in the United States and Sweden. They hypothesized that the egalitarian emphasis characteristic of Sweden would result in a higher priority being placed on an equality exchange rule rather than need or equity whereas Americans would most emphasize equity over equality or need. The results of their study supported their hypotheses. Murphy-Berman, Berman, Singh, Pachuri, and Kumar (1984) examined the allocation rules of need, equity, and equality with respect to positive and negative reward allocations (bonus pay versus pay cuts) in the United States and India. As predicted, they found that Indian managers preferred a need rule over equality and equity whereas Americans preferred equity over the other two. They concluded that their results may reflect that in India people are less responsive to merit pay because societal status is determined largely by affiliation and caste rather than individual achievement.

Bond, Leung, and Wan (1982) and Leung and Bond (1984) examined reward allocation preferences in Chinese samples. They found that Chinese, who are considered to be collectivistic, use an equality rule in allocating rewards to in-group members more than do Americans (who are guided by individualistic values), but that there exists a general endorsement of an equity rule as well in both American and Chinese samples. More recently, however, Chen (1995) found a reversal of this typical pattern (Chinese preferring equality over equity and Americans preferring equity over equality) in his study of Chinese and American managers. He found that Chinese managers (People's Republic of China) were more inclined to use an allocation rule based on equity over equality with a heavy emphasis on material over social rewards.

Van Dyne, Graham, and Dienesh's (1994) research also speaks to these issues in their examination of organizational citizenship behavior, defined as the activities outside one's organizationally defined role that team members may engage in during work. Van Dyne et al. argue that a number of individual and contextual factors influence citizenship behavior through the mediating role of a covenantal relationship—a personal relationship resulting in action being performed without expectations of reciprocity. Over time, the vitality of the relationship itself becomes an important focus for those who have covenantal ties, and citizenship behavior is a way the relationship is maintained and strengthened. Fiske (1991), Foa and Foa (1976), and Van Dyne, Graham, and Dienesch (1994), among others, suggested that this form of relationship is characteristic of people who have a common family structure, shared history, closely linked outcomes, or closely shared cultural perspectives.

Farh, Earley, and Lin (1997) examined the relevance of cultural context, social contracts and justice for the display of organizational citizenship behavior in several groups of Taiwanese employees. They examined the relationship between citizenship behaviors and organizational justice in two studies in a Chinese context, using two cultural characteristics (traditionality and modernity) and one individual (gender) characteristic. Results showed a significant relationship for low traditionality (or male employees) and a weak or nonsignificant relationship for high traditionality (or female employees). Their results suggested that employees who perceive their interactions within an organization as recognized and legitimate are more likely to engage in citizenship behavior. This finding is consistent with Van Dyne, Graham, and Dienesch's (1994) argument that if a covenantal relationship exists, citizenship behavior is more likely to occur. For less traditional, or male, Chinese, justice perceptions stimulate citizenship behavior likely through the formation of a covenantal relationship of employee to organization. However, they argued that traditionalists, or women, are likely to have an expressive tie to their organization based on role expectations in society. These preexisting roles exist, in part, because of wu-lun, or the Confucian values people have come to endorse through socialization concerning their role in society. An expressive tie leading to citizenship behavior is not dependent on justice perceptions for traditionalists or women; rather, the tie flows from prior socialization and role expectations. If expressive ties do not already exist by virtue of cultural values, social structure, or gender-based socialization, justice perceptions will be related to citizenship behavior to the extent that they create an attachment between the employee and the organization (Lind & Tyler, 1988).

Farh et al.'s (1997) results were less powerful for the cultural value of modernity. Modernity moderated the relationship between citizenship behavior and the participative facet of procedural justice and distributive justice, as predicted, but few other consistencies were observed. Their results suggest there is an important limitation to the mediating role of a covenantal tie in the relationship between citizenship behavior and organizational and individual factors, namely, that the nature of social ties within a society influences the display of extra-role employee behavior. Some researchers have argued that organizational influences affect citizenship behavior by creating covenantal ties between employee and employer (Organ, 1990). Farh et al. concluded that traditionalists and Taiwanese women may already have formed a convenantal form of relationship with their organization, and so distributive and procedural justice would not predict engagement in citizenship behavior.

An additional finding on procedural justice that Farh et al. reported is that procedural justice in the form of supervisor behavior (interactional justice) was more important than the more formal aspects of justice, such as appeal mechanism and the opportunity to participate. Their findings are consistent with the Chinese tradition of personalism (also referred to as particularism) that describes the tendency to use personal criteria and relationships as a basis for decision making and action. Personalism is much stronger in Taiwan than it is in most Western countries. This personalism is reflected in such practices as differential advantage provided for some team members over others because of who they are (ascribed role) as opposed to what they accomplish (achieved role).

**Conflict and Communication.** Most previous research suggests that intercultural differences in communication occur due to differences in cognitive styles and cultural values (Glenn & Glenn, 1981; Gudykunst & Kim, 1984; Gudykunst, Ting-Toomey, & Chua, 1988; Triandis & Albert, 1987). Cognitive styles reflect methods of information processing.

In order to better understand intercultural communication difficulties, Gibson (1996) argued that it is useful to think about the communication process as comprised of five phases. During the first phase, often labeled the *encoding* phase, the sender constructs the message to be sent. During the second phase, sometimes referred to as the *sending* phase, the sender transmits the message. In the third phase, referred to as the *receiving* phase, the receiver acquires the message. During the fourth phase, often labeled the *decoding* phase, the receiver interprets the message. And finally, during the fifth phase, often called the *feedback* phase, the receiver responds to the interpreted message.

Gibson (1996) proposed that intercultural differences in communication are most evident during the first two phases of the communication process during which messages are *constructed* and *transmitted*. When such differences are prevalent, as is often the case when a work group is composed of members from diverse cultures or when work groups from different cultures must communicate, we might expect a disruption in the work flow and errors in work performance. Gibson proposed, for example, that during encoding, whether a communication sender will utilize an implicit versus an explicit style of language is dependent on the extent to which the sender's culture emphasizes a collectivistic versus individualistic value orientation. Implicit language carefully imbues messages within a more positive tone to decrease the chances of unpleasant encounters, direct confrontations and disagreements. Explicit language, on the other hand, communicates exactly what is meant in a much more direct manner, even if the message is negative or somewhat harsh (Rosch & Segler, 1987). Collectivism is likely related to the use of an implicit style of communication. Research suggests, for instance, that Chinese, Japanese, Koreans, and Indonesians make frequent use of qualifiers and ambiguous words such as "maybe," "perhaps," and "somewhat" to avoid confrontation, and members of these cultures tend to avoid negative responses while communicating with members of their own work group in order to preserve the sense of harmony within the group (Adler, Brahm, & Graham, 1992).

During transmission, Gibson (1996) proposed that utilization of formal versus informal channels of communication depends on the level of power distance that exists within the communicator's culture. Communicators in high power distance cultures are more likely to use formal communication channels that are authorized, planned, and regulated by the organization and are directly connected to its official structure. Those low in power distance are more likely to use informal communication channels, that is, routes that are not prespecified by the organization but which develop through the typical and customary interpersonal activities of people at work.

Such difficulties may indeed occur; however, Gibson (1996) argued that the intercultural differences evident in the first two phases of the process can be reconciled during the third, fourth, and fifth phases of the process, during which receivers acquire, interpret, and respond to messages. Furthermore, she suggested that the most successful multicultural work groups are those that are able to focus on these latter stages of the communication process and hone the skills necessary to overcome the difficulties associated with the intercultural differences apparent in the earlier phases of the process.

For example, during the third phase of the communication process, the receiver acquires the message being sent. Whether the message is sent in an oral, written, or visual format, the receiver must listen carefully to the message. Effective listening is one technique through which intercultural differences can be reconciled. Indeed, in one study of the patterns of success and failure in cross-cultural adjustment, listening skills were found to be closely related to interactional effectiveness (Nishida, 1985). Research suggests at least two keys for effective listening that apply regardless of the cultural background of the sender and receiver: *active listening* and *listening for ideas* (Morgan & Baker, 1985). In a similar vein, during the fourth phase of the communication process, the message sent by the communicator is decoded. Research suggests that when interpreting a message, a key method for avoiding intercultural miscommunication is *framing*. Framing has also been referred to as the ability to empathize with the communicator (Gudykunst & Kim, 1984). During the final phase of the communication process, the receiver responds to the sender's initial message. Here, a technique often referred to as *following-up* may be associated with intercultural communication competence (Hawes & Kealey, 1981). Following-up involves accurately repeating the communicator's message. Thus, Gibson's (1996) key points with regard to reconciling intercultural communication are that the first, and perhaps most important, step is developing an awareness of the features of communication that differ across cultures and an understanding of the characteristics of culture that drive these differences. Beyond this initial step, work groups must then work to develop skills as effective listeners, interpreters, and respondents to intercultural messages.

The framework developed by Larkey (1996) to explain communicative interactions in culturally diverse workgroups speaks to these issues. Larkey theoretically examined how individuals working within various types of work groups might be influenced in their perceptions of culturally diverse others. In particular, she contrasts the interpretation of differences using *categorization* versus *specification* in cognitive processing. Categorization operates by placing persons in to broad categories such as gender, race, or nationality. Once the cognitive category is evoked, additional information about the person is filtered through the schemata established for that category and either forced to fit or ignored. Categorization saves cognitive energy, but also blocks a person from noticing individuating characteristics of the perceived person. In contrast, specification is used as a person takes information about another person one piece at a time and composes a profile of the individual based on the unique set of observed characteristics.

Larkey (1996) argues that certain situations in work-group contexts emphasize categorization processes, whereas others encourage specification. Conflict or threat to individuals may strengthen cultural group identity and reinforce in-group/out-group perceptions, as do situations evoking competition among members. Providing individual rewards and punishments may serve to increase the already existing problem. Conversely, situations that threaten, challenge, or reward the workgroup in its entirety would create work-group identity and allow members to consider each others' individual characteristics. In cases of cohesive groups working together to reach common goals, ethnic or gender-group membership may take a back seat to work-group identity (Hofstede, Neuigen, Ohayv, and Sanders, 1990). Neuberg (1989) and Neuberg and Fiske (1987) showed that perceptions tend toward individuation when outcome dependency or goals for accuracy affect the person making the judgments about another. These factors are more likely to be present when group tasks and rewards create interdependence.

Larkey (1996) further argues that the type of cognitive processing (either categorization or specification) influences the degree to which behavior is exclusionary or inclusionary (the latter is more likely when specification occurs) and the extent of negative versus positive evaluation of others who are different (the latter is more likely when specification occurs). Cognitive processing may also be related to the degree of divergence, defined as adherence to cultural communication patterns in the face differences, as contrasted with divergence, defined as adjustment of communication style to match one's partner. Divergence or convergence in conversational patterns as described by communication accommodation theory is a well-known phenomenon of intergroup interactions based on categorization (Giles, Coupland & Coupland, 1991). The relationship between categorization patterns and accommodative behavior is affected by perceived differences in status. When such differences run along racioethinc lines, those in power are expected to diverge, maintaining their dominant style (Morrison & Von Glinow, 1990). Even in cases in which minority employees have achieved managerial status, such status may have been achieved through converging with the standard set by the majority (Ely, 1995).

**Conflict.** Convergence and divergence often lead to conflict. Previous research has established that workers in different cultures (e.g., the United States and China) experience conflict differently (Doucet & Jehn, 1997) and that when resolved, this successful resolution is linked to satisfaction with the cross-cultural interaction process, such as that which occurs in joint ventures (Lin & Germain, 1998). Walsh, Wang, and Xin's (1999) interviews with managers representing ten American–Chinese joint ventures uncovered numerous differences in perceptions regarding, for example, expertise and effectiveness, effort, allegiance, and time horizons that led to a sense of mistrust in many of the collaborations.

Successful resolution of such conflicts has also been the subject of much research. Kirchmeyer and Cohen (1992), for example, examined the effects of constructive conflict on decision-making groups that were culturally diverse. In a laboratory exercise, 45 four-person groups recorded their recommendations regarding a business problem, and afterward members individually completed a questionnaire on the experience. Ethnic minorities contributed considerably less to decisions than nonminorities did. However, with increasing use of constructive conflict, groups made more valid and important assumptions, and the performance and reactions of ethnic minorities improved at rates either the same as or greater than those of nonminorities. Thus, for managers facing growing ethnic diversity in the workplace, the practices of constructive conflict offer a promising approach to group decision making.

Finally, Larkey (1996) proposed that work-group members with different cultural backgrounds may differ in expression of opinions or points of view. There is evidence that varied ideation may be more likely in work groups with a few minority members. McLeod and Lobel (1992) determined that integrated groups produced more creative and more feasible solutions in a brainstorming task than homogenous groups. Jackson (1992a) reviewed the research on the effects of work-group members' differences in ability and personal attributes and concluded that those differences generally improve creativity and decision making. It is possible that similar processes operate for cultural differences, such as a range of differing worldviews or experiences bringing special cognitive abilities. For example, cognitive complexity associated with second-language acquisition at an early age (Lambert, 1977) may improve problem-solving abilities of members of bicultural backgrounds.

**Shared Understanding.** There is very little research describing factors that contribute to "understanding" in multicultural teams. It is often suggested that misunderstandings may be tempered by familiarity or experience with other cultures (Martin & Hammer, 1989). Ethnorelativism— or the tendency to accept, adapt to, and integrate cultural differences into one's worldview—may predict communication responses of understanding (Bennett, 1986). It seems likely that understanding would be the norm in work groups in which the opportunity to develop such attitudes and cultural knowledge exists and in which threats to personal resources are not present to trigger categorical-based processing (Larkey, 1996).

On a related note, research conducted by Gruenfeld, Thomas-Hunt, and Kim (1998) demonstrated that in freely interacting groups composed of majorities and minorities, statements made by those in the majority are higher in integrative complexity than those of minority-faction or unanimous group members. After participating in group discussion, subjects assigned to majority factions experienced an increase in integrative complexity, whereas subjects assigned to either minorities or unanimous groups experienced a decrease in integrative complexity. The authors argue that the increase on the part of majority factions is a consequence of minority influence. Minority members act as catalysts for divergent thinking among the majority. We return to this point in a subsequent chapter as we outline additional catalysts for processes in multinational teams.

Recent evidence also suggest that heterogeneity advantages, such as unique information and discussion of innovative ideas, dissipate over time. Kim (1997) found that laboratory groups with both task and team experience display a larger bias toward discussing common information and achieve lower task performance than groups with only task experience, only team experience, or neither task or team experience. This evidence supports the notion that experience may represent a necessary, but not sufficient condition for groups to reduce bias toward discussing common information. Kim argues that if progress is truly to be made in reducing discussion bias toward discussing common information, it may be that task and/or team experience must be based on feedback that is specific, credible, and diagnostic in order to form accurate and fully developed shared understandings.

These shared understandings emerging from team interaction have been called alternately a "hybrid culture" (Earley and Mosakowski, 2000), "third culture" (Casmir, 1992), team-based mental models (Klimoski & Mohammed, 1994), or synergy (Adler, 1991). A hybrid team culture refers to an emergent and simplified set of rules and actions, work capability expectations, and member perceptions that individuals within a team develop, share, and enact after mutual interactions. To the extent these rules, expectations, and roles are shared (Rohner, 1984; Shweder & LeVine, 1984), a strong culture exists. These characteristics need not be completely shared among team members just as cultural values are not uniformly shared among societal members (Rohner, 1984), but there may be significant overlap among team members.

Using a series of three studies, Earley and Mosakowski (2000) showed that effective teams are those with a strong team culture because shared member expectations facilitate individual and team performance and communication. A strong team culture may derive from overlapping and pre-existing characteristics of team members or newly developed patterns of team member interaction. Their paper showed that during the initial interaction phase, national heterogeneity had a detrimental impact on team functioning. This disadvantage was not a monotonically decreasing function; rather the impact was consistent (both split and heterogeneous teams were inferior) in contrast to a homogeneous team. Over time, however, the impact of heterogeneity on team performance and other team outcome variables was related in a curvilinear fashion. After forming ways to interact and communicate, highly heterogeneous teams appeared to create a common identity.

Several additional perspectives posit the importance of shared understanding for team functioning. For example, effective groups often display a shared conception of their expectations and rules (Bettenhausen, 1991; Hackman, 1990). A "team mental model" (Klimoski & Mohammed, 1994) is a shared psychological representation of a team's environment constructed to permit sense-making and guide appropriate group action (Elron et al., 1998). When team members perceive shared understandings with other members, the positive affect and propensity to trust generated by such a discovery fuels performance improvement (Klimoski & Mohammed, 1994) and bolsters group efficacy (Bandura, 1997). Carroll and Harrison (1998) found that length of service was positively related to a team's culture, and that the strength of this relationship varied somewhat by context.

According to Earley and Mosakowski (2000), team member characteristics influence the emergence of a shared culture in two general ways. First, team members' personal characteristics shape their expectations of appropriate interaction rules, group efficacy beliefs, and group identity. Second, these personal characteristics affect team members' expectations of how other members should act within the team. Thus, a person's demographic background influences self-construal as a team member and her view of others within the group (Lickel, Hamilton, Wieczorkowska, Lewis, Sherman, & Uhles, 1998; Markus & Kitayama, 1991). In a moderately heterogeneous team, subgroups or factions may exist if members perceive differences among themselves based on salient features (Lau & Murnighan, 1998; Mulder, 1976; Ravlin et al., 2000). Moderate heterogeneity is consistent with Lau and Murnighan's (1998) strong "faultlines." They suggested that demographic faultlines underlie how team diversity affects functioning. Faultlines are the "… hypothetical dividing lines that may split a group into subgroups based on one or more attributes." (p. 328). Analogous to the geological faultlines under tectonic plates, faultlines arise from a combination of team member attributes. Lau and Murnighan (1998) argued task characteristics moderate the display and functioning of faultlines to exaggerate or mitigate subgroup formations. Especially at early stages of group development, task type may exacerbate perceived differences among subgroups.

Thus, subgroup identities dominate a team with moderate heterogeneity (Jackson et al., 1995; Lau & Murnighan, 1998; Zenger & Lawrence, 1989). As challenges or threats confront the team, members retreat toward pre-existing subgroup identities for ego protection. Instead of forming a unitary identity, the team divides into pre-existing subgroups, creating a potential for relational conflict (Earley & Mosakowski, 2000; Jehn et al., 1997; Lau & Murnighan, 1998). For example, Fiedler (1966) conducted a study of heterogeneous groups with Dutch and Belgian members who reported a less pleasant atmosphere and experienced more communication problems than homogeneous groups. Subgroup identities provide for easy retreat that subgroup members hesitate to abandon. More likely is the persistence of multiple subcultures within a moderately heterogeneous team (Davison, 1994; Hambrick, Davison, Snell, & Snow, 1998).

Moghaddam (1997) points out the difficulty of changing organizational or cultural practices, because informal social norms often perpetuate stable interaction patterns despite strenuous official attempts to change them. Granrose and Oskamp (1997) focused specifically on how workers from differing cultural backgrounds can be socialized into effective organizational groups. In discussing the inevitable tension between differentiated treatment of employees and integrating them into a stable and consistent organizational culture, she emphasizes the importance of individual-organizational "fit" in producing organizational commitment and effective performance. Tung (1997) proposed several skills and competencies needed to deal effectively with diverse work groups and a variety of methods that can help to develop these skills. We return to her framework in subsequent chapters.

## SUMMARY

Three theoretical domains have provided a foundation for our framework for multinational teams: (1) multinational structures and technologies, (2) top management team composition and functioning, and (3) cognition, exchange and conflict. From the first domain, multinational structures and technologies, we have learned that the multinational structure can have an important influence on communication logistics and that the technology available to a team has a significant impact on how the team members interact with one another as well as others external to the team. Many organizations are finding that alliances, spatial independence, and flexibility assist in meeting the demands of globalization.

Within the second domain, top management team composition and functioning, we have learned that the relationship of heterogeneity to performance is mixed and subject to a number of constraints imposed by the work setting. Sociocognitive characteristics, the team task, context, third parties, and the length of time members have interacted all appear to moderate the strategic impact of heterogeneity.

Finally, within the last domain, researchers have demonstrated that collective cognition differs across cultures, in particular the concepts of teamwork that teams form differ. In addition, collective cognitive products such as group efficacy beliefs differ across cultures, as does the relationship of these beliefs to group performance. Furthermore, the nature of social exchange differs, depending on the extent to which the value of a given resource is influenced by the persons involved in the transaction and the tangibility of the resource, two factors which vary across cultures. The degree to which team members exhibit organizational citizenship behavior depends on the extent to which they perceive their interactions within an organization as recognized and legitimate based on cultural values. Finally, difficulties caused by intercultural contacts occur on many levels. They may involve threats to a person's social and self-identity, or "face," or problems in understanding and communicating with others. They may lead to workers' diminished commitment to the organization and poor organizational performance or intercultural contacts can also led to successful accommodation. When different cultural groups interact, there are several possible models that specify changes in the groups' cultural patterns. The implications of these three domains will be elaborated upon further as we discuss various aspects of our framework for MNTs in subsequent chapters.

# 3  Theory Overview

Most of the existing models of organizational behavior and work teams have been developed based on social psychological research generated in the last half of the 20th century. This research has been primarily laboratory-based using student samples performing on an ad hoc basis. More recently, the last 2 decades has seen a resurgence of interest in work teams from an organizational perspective based largely on field studies drawing heavily from psychological theory. Added to this emphasis are a number of popular-based texts on teams and groups with such titles as *The Wisdom of Teams* (Katzenback & Smith, 1993), *Business Without Bosses* (Manz & Sims, 1993), and *Inside Teams* (Wellins, Byham, & Dixon, 1994). In this chapter, we discuss a general conceptual framework useful for understanding the dynamics underlying multinational teams. We suggest nationality is a critical determinant of a person's self-identify derived through a shared meaning system with others (Earley & Mosakowski, 2000; Shweder & Levine, 1984). The next section reviews extant research on team diversity.

Campbell (1990) proposed that the improvement of conceptual models could be reached in three ways: It can be evaluated empirically; it can stem from evaluations of experts in the field of study, and it can be derived analytically. Empirical confrontation is essential for testing the meaning and validity of scientific hypotheses. What happens to a theory when it is not supported by empirical findings? The answer to this question is guided by two different approaches. One approach represents the school of logical empiricism that asserts that some theories are right and others are wrong, and that the empirical confrontation is a test of whether a given theory is valid. A push to empirically support a theoretical model may cause biases in interpretation. For example, data analysis consistent with a universalistic and individually oriented model of behavior may lead to a wrong interpretation of situational effects as artifacts, or as attributed to individual differences.

The second approach, contextualism, maintains that all theories are right, and that empirical confrontation is a continuing process of discovery of the contexts under which hypotheses are true and those under which hypotheses are false. According to the constructivist paradigm its role is to explore and discover the range of circumstances in which each of the opposite formulations hold. This approach enhances models of interaction that examine the boundary conditions of theoretical models. With respect to cultural effects, this approach allows for testing the moderating effect of culture on the relationship between various managerial techniques and employee behavior.

The second criterion for evaluating the quality of theoretical models is by expert evaluation. Researchers in the field of cross-cultural psychology and organizational behavior admit that their theoretical models are underdeveloped (Erez & Earley, 1993). Theories have been criticized for lacking validity generalization across cultures (Boyacigiller & Adler, 1991). Thus, on the basis of peer evaluation, present models of organizational behavior fail to account for cultural moderators.

The third criterion of theory evaluation is analytic. From an analytic perspective, cognitive and mediating processes provide the conceptual framework necessary for the development of a model of multinational teams. Such models help understand how employees process, evaluate, and interpret organizational cues of managerial practices in light of their cultural values and norms.

Our intention is to satisfy these three criteria provided by Campbell in his assessment of theory for our model of multinational teams. The importance of multinational teams (MNT) is evidenced not by well-developed research programs advocated by scholars but by the dominance of MNTs in the attention of global businesses. Somewhat surprisingly, MNTs have only begun to capture the research interests of scholars in the past few years (e.g., Canney-Davison & Ward, 1999; Earley & Mosakowski, 2000; Gibson, 1999, 2000a; Granrose & Oskamp, 1997; Hambrick, Cho, & Chen,1996; Larkey, 1996; Lau & Murnighan, 1998; Maznevski, 1994; Pelled, 1996). This despite an overwhelming call from practitioners concerning the need to develop procedures to integrate teams composed of people from many nations. A few examples from ongoing organizations will illustrate our point.

A joint venture consisting of two major partners might run into a number of potential problems because of strong subgroup identification—not an uncommon observation (Earley & Mosakowski, 2000). Many of these problems are evident in a takeover of Rover Motor Company by BMW. The mixture of a German emphasis on formal structure, hierarchy, and engineering precision with British traditionality, charm, and elegance has created a number of organizational difficulties (e.g., severe disagreements concerning marketing strategies for Rover automobiles) eventually resulting in the resignation of Rover CEO John Tower. Despite various assurances that the subsequent Rover CEO would be British, BMW chose to replace Tower with a German engineer from BMW's board. In commenting on his decision to withdraw from Rover, Tower suggested that the strong "guidance" from BMW was inconsistent with Rover's style of low-key leadership. Likewise, the recent trauma of GlaxoWellcome and SmithKline to complete their merger illustrates the difficulty of a "balanced" approach.

Perhaps the most recently celebrated example of multinational teams from a business perspective is described by Percy Barnevik, then CEO of Asea Burr Brown. Barnevik is an avid supporter of a team-based approach to management. In particular, he believes that the strength of a multinational company is derived, in large part, from its reliance on teams consisting of people from across its various countries in which it operates. After taking control of ABB, Barnevik reorganized the company in a matrix structure using overlapping teams consisting of multiple nationalities. Barnevik argued that the only way to really understand what is going on in a given region is through reliance on nationals, and the only way for these nationals to understand the global scope of the company is through active participation and representation.

A second example of multinational teams has occurred at the recently created Daimler-Chrysler. Coinciding with the merger of German auto manufacturer Daimler-Mercedes-Benz with the U.S. auto manufacturer Chrysler, the company created "postmerger integration teams" consisting of personnel from each company in each country. These teams were charged with the process of integrating the two companies, including creating a unified corporate culture that reflected both the national cultures involved in the merger. This task has proven to be a huge challenge, as will be discussed further in subsequent chapters.

Organizational researchers who recognize the heterogeneous nature of the work force have increasingly focused on the dynamics of teams with multicultural and multinational members (e.g., Argote & McGrath, 1993; Elron, Shamir, & Ben-Ari, 1998; Jackson, May, & Whitney, 1995; Jackson, Salas, & associates, 1992; Lawrence, 1997; Snow, Snell, Davison, & Hambrick, 1996). But what does team heterogeneity mean in a global context where nationalities, races, religions, and genders all matter? For example, gender role expectations may vary dramatically across cultures. Teams with both national and gender diversity may function differently than those with only gender diversity. We suggest current knowledge on team heterogeneity and performance does not adequately incorporate the complexity of nationally diverse teams.

## OVERVIEW OF CONCEPTUAL FRAMEWORK

Our model consists of both process and content features across several levels of analysis. A graphic presentation of our model is presented in Fig. 3.1. The model is intended to capture the key features of multinational teams in relation to environmental and personnel features.

Our model has a number of general features. At a structural level, the model contains both process and contextual features occurring at an individual, team, and organizational level of analysis. The overarching structure of the model links the individual and group elements through specific processes. For example, roles enacted by individuals within a team collectively may create fractionation within the team. Role-making and role-taking is a fundamental action of individuals when exposed to a social structure (Katz & Kahn, 1978; Markus & Kitayama, 1991). It is through the action of creating roles for oneself that fractionation and differentiation within a team may occur at a team level. Thus, in this example, individual-level influences give rise to team consequences through given processes. Our model provides a linkage among key individual and team characteristics.

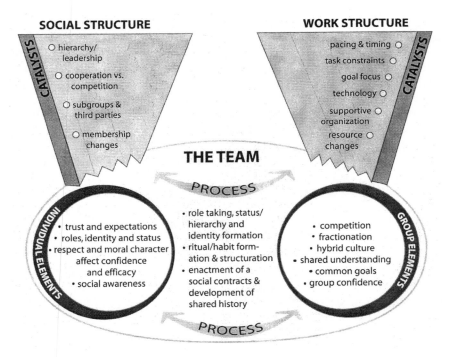

FIG. 3.1 Overview of Multinational Team Theory.

In addition to these elements and processes, we provide a mapping concerning the impetus for these processes. We refer to this feature of the model as catalysts. By catalyst, we mean that there are key features of the social and work structure that give rise to processes regulating the individual and group elements. For example, the presence of clearly defined subgroups within a multinational team (e.g., a six-person team having three French and three Indonesian members) acts as a catalyst for self-regulatory processes whereby an individual balances self and group-based identities (Brewer, 1993). These catalysts can be thought of as the motives giving rise to various processes that regulate self and collective identities of team members.

A final, and fundamental, feature of our model is an overarching principle of balance and equilibrium governing the various processes, elements, and catalysts contained within our framework. This feature is one of balance between desires of differentiation and integration. That is, we posit that all social regulatory processes in multinational teams balance a degree of integration and differentiation. We address this balance later in our discussion of the model.

We use a multilevel approach for a number of reasons, not the least of which is that multinational teams place demands on team members reflecting all levels of an organization. A new product development team, for example, that has members representing different functional areas located in different geographic regions, is responsible to the functional department head, the country managers, the research and development division, and the shareholders of the company. The team also has obligations to each member and to their customer base. The demands emanating from each constituent are often conflicting, and understanding the actions of the team requires knowledge of the various priorities they must juggle.

## EQUILIBRIUM: FORCES OF DIFFERENTIATION AND INTEGRATION

Equilibria or steady states are fundamental to physical laws of nature. A chemist defines a chemical reaction as in a steady state, or equilibrium, if the energy exchange is balanced with the transformation of atoms and molecules in a given system. It refers to chemical reactions that have come to completion, or complementary such that they cancel one another. To the physicist, a physical system is in equilibrium if the behavior of objects within the system is regular. Although the concept of equilibrium has long implied a steady state, or balance, more recent thinking and research (over the last three or four decades) has stimulated a large interest in dynamic equilibria and chaotic systems (Gersick, 1989; Gleick, 1987). In such systems, an equilibrium refers not to a static or predicted state, but of an observed, regular pattern that is not predicted from a determined relationship, rather, it is highly influenced by initial starting conditions. In such systems, initial starting conditions have a profound effect on the eventual behavior of the system. The concept of a dynamic equilibrium is simply illustrated in chemistry by considering a chemical reaction (e.g., the addition of acid to water) in which multiple chemical reactions continue in such a manner that they offset one another. Although there is the potential for further reactions, a tenuous balance is achieved unless further changes are introduced into the system (e.g., addition of more acid).

To an economist, the concept of an equilibrium is central to most theories. By equilibrium, it is meant, "Although the market price may be independent of any one agent's actions in a competitive market, it is the actions of all the agents together that determine the market price. The equilibrium price of a good is that price where the supply of the good equals the demand." (Varian, 1993). In a simple example of housing in London, the scarcity of available units makes certain that the demand for inexpensive housing is never fully satisfied. The result is that housing costs continue to increase until the point at which the market (renters) can no longer afford housing. Of course, this example understates the complexity of additional factors including demographic shifts, wage fluctuations, business cycles, government intervention, but the basic point remains, namely, that there exists some point above which renters will not pay for housing. In this simple example, the forces acting on the market are twofold, namely, the supply of housing and the demand by renters. If one plots the intersection of these two curves, supply versus demand, an equilibrium point is reached.

Of course, many economists have called into question assumptions of equilibrium and rationality in forming a new view of economic theory (Loasby, 1991). For example, Hahn (1984) describes a somewhat unorthodox view of equilibrium when he states, "An economy is in equilibrium when it generates messages which do not cause agents to change the theories which they hold or the policies which they pursue." Each agent uses relevant theory to interpret each message from the economy and thereby generates a given forecast. Based on each forecast, a given agent's policy generates particular actions (appropriate according to the policy), and these actions influence and change the system. What is important is not only that new information stimulates the development of new policies, but also that the system stays in equilibrium as long as the subsequent information from the economy does not require the agent to continue adapting or changing his policy. In other words, a change in the economy is a necessary, but not sufficient, condition for disequilibrium to occur. In his treatise on the basis for economic behavior, Von Mises (1949) makes a similar point in that he asserts that information exchange and psychological interpretations of market conditions underlie equilibria.

From a psychological perspective, the role of an individual actor within an economic system is significant and meaningful, because the identification of an agent concerning poor policies seems to imply an impact on the economic system given the lack of intermediate structures (Loasby, 1991). From a psychological perspective, Kahn's and Schumpeter's approaches are useful because they highlight the relative impact of knowledge and information as a source of change for a system. This suggests that shifts away from equilibria may be directly attributable to information that is gained or shared within a system, such as the signaling information conveyed in face. Many problems arise, however, from this information driven approach. For example, Mosakowski (1998) uses notions of primary and secondary causal ambiguity as a means of describing the difficulties firms have in adjusting to innovations within their industry. By primary ambiguity, she refers to changes that are not at all predictable but merely reflect random fluctuations. Secondary ambiguity refers to patterns that firms attempt to understand, but are largely influenced by complex factors not easily predicted. As a result, firms may attempt to model secondary ambiguity and use it on their behalf, even though such actions are futile.

Equilibrium and balance have been dealt with in other ways by organizational sociologists. For example, Giddens's (1984) notion of structuration points to a dynamic view of social systems. An equilibrium point is a constraining concept in his view because it creates an illusion of stability where none really exists. Giddens suggests that social systems be viewed in terms of several constructs including: structure, or the rules and resources organized as properties of a system; system, or reproduced relations between actors and collectivities that are organized as regular social practices; and, structuration, or the conditions governing the continuity or transformation of structures, and therefore, the reproduction of the systems themselves. Giddens (1984) uses the concept of structuration to capture the dynamic nature of social systems in stating,

> The concept of structuration involves that of the *duality of structure*, which relates to the *fundamentally recursive character of social life, and expresses the mutual dependence of structure and agency*. By the duality of structure I mean that the structural properties of social systems are both the medium and the outcome of the practices that constitute those systems ... The identification of structure with constraint is also rejected: structure is both enabling and constraining, and it is one of the specific tasks of social theory to study the conditions in the organisation of social systems that govern the interconnections between the two. (pp. 69–70)

Thus, for Giddens, the concept of an equilibrium is not viewed as static; rather he focuses on a given pattern of interaction that changes as a function of time. The impetus for this change over time comes from various influences with a social system including the actors, resources available, environmental shifts, and so forth.

The notion of equilibrium has a somewhat different role to play in conceptions used by the organizational ecologists and evolutionists (e.g., Hannan & Freeman, 1977; McKelvey, 1982). In this conceptualization, drawn from the field of biological evolution and ecology, equilibrium and balance are based on the relationship of actors within niches in their adaptation to the demands of the environment. Such a balance is never long-term because random fluctuations in the environment (e.g., changes or depletion of key resources) throw the system into a state of disequilibrium. In McKelvey's (1982) treatise on organizational evolution and dynamics, he suggests that a variety of forces including individual mutations and adaptations can influence the balance within a given ecosystem. Random or unpredictable events such as the discovery of oil reserves can have a profound impact on the nature of social structures and practices with a culture such as shifts attributable in Saudi Arabia, Kuwait, and their neighbors in the Middle East.

To the institutional theorist, equilibrium reflects a general process of imitation and transmittal. Institutional theory presumes that the practices engaged in by particular (usually powerful and influential) organizations are those that become the adopted standard for other, similar organizations (Scott & Meyer, 1994). In fact, institutional theory is sometimes criticized (e.g., Giddens, 1984) on the basis that the forces of institutionalization should grind innovation and change to a halt. In other words, the forces of mimetic, coercive, and normative isomorphism (DiMaggio & Powell, 1983) should lead to similar institutional structures and practices within a given industry, a finding that is with mixed empirical support (see Scott & Meyer, 1984; Zucker, 1987). Thus, equilibrium refers to a state of isomorphism such that the relevant actors within a system are copies of one another through process and structure.

To the social psychologist or organizational behaviorist, the concept of equilibrium may make reference to an individual's participation within a given social structure. For example, in group dynamics research, much attention has been devoted to the concept of the free rider (Olson, 1965) or social loafer (Latane, Williams, & Harkins, 1979). People are assumed to be maximizers or optimizers of their subjective expected utility by many psychological theories (e.g., expectancy theory such as that of Vroom (1964)). Such a constraint poses a problem for collective action as is suggested in Olson's (1965), *Logic of Collective Action*. Olson argued that participation in large groups, or collectives, is not likely because an individual may be better suited to gain for himself through defection and pursuit of individual gains. For instance, Olson (1965) argued, "A lobbying organization, or indeed a labor union or any other organization, working in the interest of a large group of firms or workers in some industry, would get no assistance from the rational, self-interested individuals in that industry" (p. 11). The dilemma, then, is that it is rational for an individual participating in a collectivity to pursue self-interests over those of the collectivity while assuming that the collectivity will ensure the attainment of a desire good. With both the collective action and social loafing paradigms, a sense of equilibrium is established by examining the concept of exchange. If individuals maintain their actions according to expectations for returns then an equilibrium exists. In other words, a balance is struck as a consequence of the expectations a person has in contrast to their efforts to pursue alternatives.

A somewhat different perspective is taken by Gersick in her work with temporal activities for task-performing work groups (e.g., Gersick, 1988; Gersick & Hackman, 1990). Gersick describes the role of time as an equilibrium notion, and points to a number of significant deficiencies in the existing groups literature that emphasizes a standardized process approach to group development (so-called stages of development including forming, storming, norming, etc.). She suggests that for task-performing groups, there is a critical "middle point" of temporal progression (not necessarily the chronological midpoint) that activates a group's progression. Additionally, she argues that group development is best thought of using a punctuated equilibrium notion that is often used in the physical sciences. A punctuated equilibrium suggests that certain groups will not continue to develop over their history; rather, they will reach a particular point and stabilize unless some critical event(s) takes place. For instance, a work team may form and develop norms for behavior but remain at this stage. Only with some dramatic event (e.g., a key member of the team leaves to take a job offer elsewhere) will the team continue its movement and development. Thus, Gersick points out that equilibria might be best thought of as temporary stable points subject to shifts due to significant environmental changes.

Another very important notion of equilibrium for our model illustrated at an individual-level of analysis is presented by Brewer in her Optimal Distinctiveness Theory (1993). According to her model, a person's self-concept is regulated as a balance between social integration with others in important reference groups and maintaining a differentiated self. In other words, any team member faces two simultaneous attractions (repulsion): a desire to be integrated with others who provide self-image and a desire to remain unique and a separated self. The relative balance of trait differentiation is also important according to work by Brewer and her colleagues (see Brewer, 1993 for a review).

Brewer's Optimal Distinctiveness Theory argues people psychologically trade off their individuality needs with team identity needs. What this implies for our theory is a highly heterogeneous group may initially experience a disproportionate emphasis on individuality with team members strongly aware of interpersonal differences. Counterbalancing forces may motivate the creation of commonalities among group members with a hybrid team culture as common identity. A "split" group may balance individual and team identities so members are not motivated to adjust this balance (Earley & Mosakowski, 2000; Ravlin et al., 2000). Although this result may satisfy individuals, it blocks team integration and entitativity. A recent study by Harstone and Augoustinos (1995) suggested a third subgroup may offset the difficulties of two subgroups. These authors demonstrated that the ingroup bias predicted by a minimal groups paradigm did not occur when individuals were divided into three, instead of two, subgroups. Fractionation of three or more subgroups may facilitate hybrid culture creation through greater information sharing about personal traits, backgrounds, and interests.

The importance of equilibria notions cannot be understated for our framework. We view the fundamental equilibrium underlying our model as the balance between integration and differentiation of self as individual, self as team member, and team as element in a larger social structure. That is, there are general forces that act as ultimate motivators for processes whereby these units described (self as individual, self as team member, and team as element in social structure) are regulated. As one of these units becomes too differentiated, then forces give rise to processes that lead to further integration. As an example, if a team is strongly integrated into a larger business unit (e.g., product design team), it may adopt artifacts to emphasize its unique identity such as a team name, symbols, reduced communication with other teams within the business unit, and so forth. These actions enable the team to maintain some semblance of uniqueness when strong pressures for integration exist.

## CONCEPTUAL FRAMEWORK—INDIVIDUAL LEVEL ELEMENTS

The individual level elements that are central to our model include: role identity, trust and expectations of others, respect for self/others and moral character, interpersonal affect, confidence and efficacy, and social awareness. We propose these elements based on the existing groups and teams literature, particularly for teams composed of individuals from various cultures and countries. Although the overlap for many of these elements exists for other types of teams (e.g., non-MNT teams), we emphasize these elements because they are critical for interpersonal relationships and team functioning in an international and intercultural context.

The first feature, role identity and formation, examines the nature of the various ways that people see themselves and others in a team context. People have a multifaceted and overlapping set of roles that they don just as they wear various types of clothing items. Just as with the clothing they wear, some of these roles are more evident than others and some take on special significance depending upon the circumstance.

With regard to specific actions or role-related behaviors, there are recurring actions engaged in by an employee that are coordinated with, and related to, actions of others in a predictable fashion (Katz & Kahn, 1978). It is this collection of interdependent actions and behaviors that constitute a social system in their framework. There are a number of potential difficulties with an individual's role because of these various interdependencies. The "role set," or collection of these interdependencies, suggests that understanding a social actor can only be fully accomplished through an assessment of the net or web of interdependencies entangling an actor's role(s). For example, a shop steward has a number of constituencies to which she answers. She must be cognizant of her workmates' interests balancing concerns of her superiors.

Trust and expectations of others are derived largely from the recent literature on trust in organizations (Curall & Judge, 1995; Golembiewski & McConkie, 1975; Gulati, 1995; Kramer & Tyler, 1996; Rousseau, Sitkin, Burt, & Camerer, 1998). Interpersonal trust can be characterized as, "… the willingness to be vulnerable to another party irrespective of the trustor's ability to monitor or control that party" (Mayer, Davis, & Schoorman, 1985). That is, it reflects a degree of predictability of another person's actions when given a chance for opportunism. Trust has also been thought of as confidence in the character, integrity, strength, and abilities of another person. In the social psychology literature, the construct of trust has been defined in a number of ways. Two general categorizations of trust are people's motivation versus credibility as well as generalized versus situational trust. Motivation-based trust reflects the expressed confidence that one party has in another's motives and intentions. This reflects the belief that other parties are motivated for cooperation and an unselfish orientation (Mellinger, 1956) and that the other person(s) will fulfill their obligations (Schurr & Ozanne, 1985).

Another feature critical to understanding the dynamics underlying MNTs is the respect and moral considerations of team members. Although the concept of morals and respect may be handled in a variety of ways, recent work by researchers interested in concepts of face (e.g., Earley, 1997; Ting-Toomey, 1994) has addressed the concept of interpersonal respect and morality. For example, Earley (1997) follows the Chinese tradition and discusses the moral aspects of face using the Chinese concept of "lian."

Fundamental moral character (as reflected by lian) is derived from two general groups of values in cultures, namely, social relatedness and moral imperatives. Social relatedness refers to the proper functioning in a social system. These values manifest themselves in the social system rather than within an individual. For example, affiliation and a sense of belongingness are values reflected in all cultures, and this is a type of social-relatedness value. Rebuffing such a value is viewed as sociopathology or neuroticism, and people who reject affiliation reject societal membership as well. Moral imperatives refer to universal dispositions of the person such as justice or goodness.

Self-control refers to an individual's restraint in the present on behalf of the future. For example, a student who pursues her doctoral studies may live as a pauper for a number of years in order to obtain the skills, knowledge, and credentials needed for a prestigious faculty position. Likewise, an organization that channels its extra profits into research and development rather than issuing extra dividends will ensure a more profitable future for itself (and its shareholders). Finally, Wilson's concept of duty refers to an individual's willingness to be faithful to obligations derived from society, family, and important referent others. For instance, Huston, Geis, and Wright (1976) looked at the actions of a number of "good samaritans" (people who intervened on behalf of others during a crisis). They found that many samaritans acted because it appeared to be the "right thing to do" rather than due to sympathy for the victims per se. It is through these four sentiments that Wilson argues people function and behave within a society.

The next feature of individuals within MNTs is the affect shared among team members. Interpersonal affect refers to an emotional reaction of one person toward another in a given circumstance. It reflects the views and orientation among team members. Affective relations among team members may be expressed through loyalty, trust, and commitment. Many scholars consider affective attachment of an individual to a team to be an implicit aspect of collective societies (Triandis, 1995).

Another characteristic of a MNT member critical to team functioning is the person's confidence for action, or what Bandura (1997) calls self-efficacy expectations. As reviewed earlier, perceived self-efficacy is a judgment of one's capability to accomplish a certain level of performance. Efficacy judgments promote the choice of situations and tasks with high likelihood of success and eliminate the choice of tasks that exceed one's capabilities.

A final individual-level characteristic of team members refers to a member's social awareness. We take this concept from Witkin and Berry's (1975) construct of field dependence as well as Hall's (1976) idea of low versus high context cultures. Field dependence/independence is associated with cultural variation. Witkin & Berry (1975) identified four antecedent factors of field dependence–independence—ecological adaptation, or the characteristic relationship between man and nature; social pressure pertaining to social conformity and sociocultural stratification; parent–child relationships; and biological factors.

## CONCEPTUAL FRAMEWORK—GROUP LEVEL ELEMENTS

Our framework focuses on five general elements of a group as we describe MNT functioning. These characteristics are not exhaustive, but they reflect the most fundamental elements of a team in an international context. These elements are competition within the group, factions and fractionation, hybrid culture and shared meaning and understanding, and common versus differentiated goals (priorities).

The first characteristic that we discuss reflects the nature of competition and cooperation within a team. Deutsch (1961, 1973) is one of the central figures who discussed the nature of competition within a group context. According to Deutsch, one can think of groups as focusing on a degree of competition when resources are perceived as scarce and nonrenewable and members' goals are nonoverlapping. Such a form of interdependence creates a sense of competition among team members and it interferes with normal team functioning. Competition is not inevitably harmful to a group but, if left unattended, frequently creates problems for the group that are difficult to resolve.

A second feature of a MNT at a group level is the sense of fractionation, or disunity experienced within the team. When organizational groups are composed of members of multiple cultures, a primary concern is that conflict between members of different cultural backgrounds will create disunity within the ranks. Ravlin et al. (2000) developed a framework for understanding the nature of conflict within a MNT based on the influences of belief systems regarding values and status, and the role that acceptance of these beliefs play in processes generating latent and manifest conflict within the group.

The third feature is the reverse side of fractionation, namely, the development of a hybrid, or team, culture (Casmir, 1992; Earley & Mosakowski, 2000). We adopt Earley and Mosakowski's term of "hybrid" culture, although alternative terms in the literature include "third culture" (Casmir, 1992), teamwork mental model (Klimoski & Mohammed, 1994), or synergistic culture (Adler, 1991). As we described earlier, a hybrid team culture refers to an emergent and simplified set of rules and actions, work capability expectations, and member perceptions that individuals within a team develop, share, and enact after mutual interactions.

A fourth group-level feature is the shared understanding and meaning that exists within a MNT. Several perspectives posit the importance of shared understanding for team functioning. For example, effective groups often display a shared conception of their expectations and rules (Bettenhausen, 1991; Hackman, 1990).

How might a unified team culture emerge? The answer depends on the basic motive for creating commonality within a group. We draw from several conceptual frameworks to describe this motive. Henri Tajfel and John Turner proposed complementary models of group process—Social Identity Theory (Tajfel, 1982) and Self-Categorization Theory (Turner, 1985, 1987). These theories assume individuals form group memberships based on relative similarity to others and individuals seek to distinguish their in-group from other groups by emphasizing differences from outsiders and derogating out-group members. Sociologist Everett Hughes (1971) argued individuals establish social roles relative to others based on "primary and auxiliary status-determining" traits. Hughes (1971) suggested people determine their relative status using hierarchically ordered primary trait categorizations.

A final aspect of MNTs concerns the nature of shared goals and priorities. This idea is related to our earlier discussion of Deutsch's notion of competition inasmuch as shared goals is often viewed as a central feature of cooperation (Deutsch, 1973). A great deal of research has focused on the impact of shared goals and common priorities on the success of teams (e.g., Coch & French, 1948; Steiner, 1972; Latham, Erez, & Locke, 1988; Goodman & Associates, 1986). Why do shared goals have such a pronounced effect on team functioning? This can be addressed in two different ways based on research from the field of goal setting (Locke & Latham, 1990).

The first impact of shared goals for a team is derived from the development of the goals themselves and the impact such development has on members' commitment to the goal. The second influence of the development of shared goals is through a cognitive influence on members within a team. In a series of studies, Erez and Earley (e.g., Earley, 1985; Earley, 1987; Erez & Arad, 1986; Erez, Earley, & Hulin, 1985) demonstrated that participation in the goal-setting process led to higher cognitive understanding of task and work requirements by those participating.

Latanè et al. (1979) documented the "social loafing" phenomenon. In brief, social loafing is the tendency of an individual participating in a group performance activity to withhold effort if her personal contribution is anonymous. With accountability, however, the incentive for an individual to loaf is removed. More recent work (see Harkins & Petty, 1983 for a review) suggests that the impetus to "defect" or loaf can be influenced by a variety of characteristics including cultural factors (Earley, 1989), anonymity (Harkins & Petty, 1983), "sucker" effects (Kerr, 1983), and cognitive demand (Weldon & Gargano, 1988). Studies demonstrate that a members sharing a common group goal are less prone to loafing (Harkins & Petty, 1983). This goal can be focused on specific work (Weldon & Gargano, 1988) or generalized social relationships derived from cultural commonality (Earley, 1993).

In the next section, we turn our attention to the process aspects underlying group dynamics that connect the individual and the group levels of the MNT. This section consists of six general topics including rules, roles, social contract, pattern of actions, status hierarchy, and sense of history.

## CONNECTING THE LEVELS: PROCESS DIMENSIONS

We pose three general classes of processes that link individual and group elements of teams (see Fig. 3.1). These three classes are role taking, status hierarchy and identity formation, rituals/habit formation and structuration, and enactment of social contracts and the development of a shared history.

A central team process that connects the individual to the group level of the team is role making and taking by members. Role taking and status differentiation are a central aspect of linking micro to macro aspects of team dynamics. On the structural level the self as a team member can be viewed as a collection of schemas, prototypes, goals or images that are arranged in a space (Sherman, Judd, & Park, 1989). Each schema is a generalization about what the self is, and it contains descriptive information about traits, roles, and behavior, as well as procedural knowledge of rules and procedures for making inferences and evaluation for its own functioning and development (Kihlstrom & Cantor, 1984).

Identity adoption and change are central to how people function with one another in a social context (Giddens, 1984; Turner, 1987). Role adoption is a key aspect of team functioning as well and it explains much of the cross-cultural variation observed in international teams (Ravlin et al., 2000). Roles are fundamental in shaping the expectations that members have for their own and others' actions. As we noted, there are other difficulties confronting a social actor with regard to roles. For example, roles may be ambiguous or in conflict resulting in problems. The consequence of role conflict, that is to say, an individual who has competing and conflicting roles received from powerful others, can be significant resulting in stress and health problems. Likewise, role ambiguity results in a number of dysfunctional consequences for an organization including increased turnover (Katz & Kahn, 1978) and reduced performance (Locke & Latham, 1990). To some extent, a highly useful aspect of a motivational technique such as goal setting is that it clarifies expectations concerning performance and employee behavior (Locke & Latham, 1990).

Second, rituals and habit formation as well as structuration are processes that link across levels. By rituals and habits, we refer to those patterns of actions that become scripted (Schank & Abelson, 1977) over time. On the structural level, the self as a team member can be viewed as a collection of schemas, prototypes, goals, or images that are arranged in a space (Sherman, Judd, & Park, 1989). Each schema is a generalization about what the self is, and it contains descriptive information about traits, roles, and behavior, as well as procedural knowledge of rules and procedures for making inferences and evaluation for its own functioning and development (Kihlstrom & Cantor, 1984).

The next process refers to the social contract that team members have with one another. This implicit or explicit team contract is critical for understanding the effectiveness of a team to operate as a unified force. Rules reflect the nature and style of exchange among team members. From a cross-cultural perspective, the nature of exchange becomes quite complex and ambiguous because the underlying principles governing concepts such as distributive, procedural, and interactional justice can vary a great deal (Bies, 1987; Brockner, Grover, O'Malley, Reed et al., 1993; Lind & Earley, 1992; Lind & Tyler, 1988).

The final process dimension connecting the individual and group levels of the MNT is the sense of shared history that the team acquires through mutual experience. This aspect of the team is the most elusive for a number of reasons not least because many teams do not remain intact sufficiently long to develop a history. A team's sense of history, however, is a central feature to the successful team for many of the same reasons that a sense of history is core to cultural transmission in a society.

In the next section, we turn to facets of the MNT context that we refer to as "catalysts." By a catalyst, we are referring to features of the team's environment that give rise to change within the team. These changes can be either productive or counterproductive for a team, but the point is that they are precipitated by some endogenous or exogenous influence on a team.

## CATALYSTS: SOCIAL AND WORK STRUCTURE

The catalysts underlying team dynamics from a social structure perspective are: membership changes, intervention by outside parties, subgroups, cooperation versus competition (conflict), hierarchy and leadership.

The first catalyst that we discuss, and likely the most powerful, is change in membership. A metaphor taken from the first author's hobby of saltwater aquariums is a good example of how membership change influences MNT dynamics. Introducing a new fish to a fish tank once the tank's inhabitants have acquired their own territories and status hierarchy is a great challenge (presuming that one wishes for the new fish to survive and prosper). Even fish two to three times smaller than the new inhabitant are often able to bully the newcomer to a point of danger for the new inhabitant. One trick used in aquariums for introducing new stock is to rearrange the seascape so as to disorient existing inhabitants and to break up existing territories.

In one sense, adding new members to a team is akin to adding new fish to the existing aquarium. Just as with the aquarium, some inhabitants may simply ignore the new addition while others will purposefully bully and harass the newcomer. This is true as well in teams with new members undergoing socialization and training concerning the team's social etiquette, hierarchy, etc. (Van Maanen & Schein, 1977).

In a MNT, changes of group membership are particularly difficult because a new member potentially brings in an entirely new "culture," or style of acting, that is not understood by a group. A cohesive MNT may provide additional socialization for such an individual or choose to shun and isolate the deviant. In a fractionated MNT, the new member may adhere to an existing subgroup, and in doing so, create a change in the balance of power. Members within a group may resist heavily taking on new members of the team if they believe that such additions will shift the existing power structure of individuals and subgroups. This is a common, and unfortunate, occurrence in academic departments as existing members resist change by blocking the addition of new faculty if they are threatened by such additions. If the new member brings new ideas (as is often the case in the MNT), then these existing members may be even more threatened and seek to block new members from joining the team even if it may hurt the existing team.

Outside parties play a role in the dynamics underlying a MNT as they do with other types of teams. Outside parties may influence a MNT in a number of ways such as providing new information and perspective concerning a MNT's environment and context. An outside party such as a third party is often brought in to settle a dispute between two groups. Although a discussion of this topic is beyond the scope of our book, we turn to a modest discussion of third-party interventions in a later chapter.

Another catalyst is the nature of subgroups within a team. This point is a particularly important one from the perspective of team culture as it relates to more general aspects of societal culture. Joanne Martin (1992) presents a characterization of three general forms of organization culture, namely, integration, differentiation, and fragmentation. Briefly, an integration view posits culture as shared meanings held in common. The differentiation view points out that there exist subgroups within any given organization that likely differ in their shared meanings from one another. Finally, a fragmentation perspective suggests that culture is a differential network of meanings that are interrelated and reciprocally related but poorly defined and inconsistent. One interpretation (Earley, 1997) of these perspectives is that they can be thought of using a factorial design have two factors. The integration view is a main effects perspective whereas the differentiation perspective is captured by an interaction term. Finally, the fragmentation view is best thought of as some form of within cell variance, or individual differences. Using this analogy, it becomes clearer that culture is not simply a monolithic construct capturing all of the minds within a given society, or a team. It is similar to Rohner's (1984) idea of complementary, but incompletely shared, meaning systems.

We find this conceptualization to be useful in that it provides a way of defining the boundaries for a team's culture (or an organization, community, or nation), and predicting the limits under which we might expect to see a culture truly "shared." Perhaps the most important clarification is to emphasize Rohner's, as well as Martin's (1992), point that any given group may consist of multiple subgroupings, or social subsystems. This means that any two individuals coming from the same team may, in fact, possess a number of differences in values and beliefs. The result of this in a team context is that as members aggregate into smaller subgroups, fractures within a team may occur leading to divisiveness and conflict (Lau & Murnighan, 1998).

Another catalyst for a team relates back to our earlier discussion concerning competition and cooperation. Our primary point here is that when a team is faced with external pressures for competition or cooperation that this may set in motion a number of team reactions. If the exogenous influence is competition, it may serve to bring the team members closer to one another. For example, traditional research on the prisoner's dilemma (Rappoport, 1961) shows that the rate of cooperation among game players increases if the experimenter monitoring the game is abusive to either of the participants. That is, an external threat heightens players' willingness to cooperate with one another. Exogenous competition such as a team's organization telling it that it needs to show some results for a project may bring team members together. Likewise, external encouragement by the host organization for team members to cooperate will likely cue cooperation among team members.

As described earlier, however, this cooperation and competition is subject to an important limitation derived from group structure and the presence of subgroups within the team. We argued earlier that if a pre-existing subgroup structure exists within the team, individuals will maintain their self-image and sense of worth from their various subgroups. The influence of an external threat such as an organization dictum for quick and decisive performance will act as a wedge to drive subgroups apart (Earley & Mosakowski, 2000). When people are faced with a threat to their self-image and status, their reaction is to regroup and attempt to rebuild that image. Goffman (1959) described this dynamic between two people as "facework" and he suggested that it was a powerful ritual for social interaction. Facework is a highly scripted procedure that individuals from a given culture engage in so as to help maintain one another's face, or projected self image (Goffman, 1959; Ting-Toomey, 1994). However, facework is most likely effective with individuals from the same cultural background because the scripted rituals of re-establishing face are unlikely to be understood from one culture to another. This is one of the reasons that if self-image is threatened externally by the dictates of one's company, the result may be a further development of subgroups because these are the people who "understand me."

Another reason that subgroups are likely to form if a team is faced with external pressures such as competition is that as a team experiences losses or setbacks, and member self-image suffers, the re-establishment of self-image is most easily accomplished by focusing on others within the team who are highly similar to you. That is, a person will turn to group members with whom they have much in common and will become some mutual admiration society. This provides a team member with some bolstering of self-image. Note that this is not the likely outcome of external dictates of cooperation.

One might argue that external pressure for a team to cooperate with other teams may further stimulate team members to bond with one another. In this instance, the external order to cooperate may lead team members to focus on their team uniqueness so as to differentiate the team from other teams.

The existing hierarchy and leadership inherent in a team will play a significant role as a catalyst for team dynamics. The influence of hierarchy is discussed to some degree in our prior section on status traits of team members. Within any given team there exists some hierarchy of power and responsibility. At the apex of this hierarchy is a team leader who may or may not be formally appointed by the team. Regardless, all teams have some form of hierarchy and leadership. Just how is this hierarchy responsible for triggering events within the team? If we look back at the impact of membership changes within a team we see the potential influence from one perspective. That is, when new members enter a team a new sorting out of "who is who" begins.

However, a leader presents a highly significant source of change for a team. Is this influence significantly different in a MNT as opposed to other non-MNT types of teams? This is an issue that we address later in our chapter on catalysts and context but a short answer is "yes." What is significant and different about leadership within a MNT is that no single leader is likely to provide a style and means of interacting with team members that is perceived as true leadership except in a few rare cases. The work on global aspects of leadership by Robert House and his colleagues in the GLOBE (House, 1998) project is instructive here. House and his colleagues have assessed various aspects of leadership in an international context sampling from over 50 countries worldwide. They have found that regardless of culture, there are some universal aspects of leadership including the existence of hierarchy and power, vision, personal integrity and commitment to action, and individualistic perspective. This type of leader in a MNT is likely to have a significant impact on the team's progress and path. More importantly, this charismatic leader is likely to stimulate cooperation and unity among MNT members.

In our next section, we turn to some additional catalysts that are derived from the nature of the work environment itself.

## CATALYSTS: WORK STRUCTURE

The structure of the work itself is based on a number of characteristics including the timing and scheduling of tasks, task constraints and requirements, resource changes, technology, supportive organization, and goal focus.

The first of these work characteristics refers to the timing and scheduling of tasks that are to be undertaken by the team. The influence of time and its impact on various organizational processes is the focus of much work by management researchers. We develop these arguments based on several ideas drawn from McGrath and colleagues' influential work on the psychology of time (see McGrath, 1988; McGrath & Kelly, 1986; McGrath & Rotchford, 1983 for excellent reviews). McGrath and Kelly (1986) propose a model of individual behavior and timing incorporating four central features: rhythm, mesh, tempo, and pace. Rhythm reflects endogenous temporal patterns of an individual such as biorhythms, life developmental cycles, sleep–wake cycles, and so forth. Mesh refers to both endogenous (to the person) timing mechanisms that coordinate and synchronize an individual's various rhythms as well as exogenous timing mechanisms (called "pace"). External demands and conditions can retime various rhythms such as the effect of an overseas assignment on an individual's biorhythms. Finally, the cadence and rhythm resulting from endogenous and exogenous influences result in the actual timing and sequencing of behaviors and actions reflected in the tempo construct. Graham (1981) proposed three cross-cultural time perceptions including procedural–traditional (emphasis on procedures and not time itself), circular–traditional (emphasis on time as holistic and epochal), and linear–separable (emphasis on time as a sequence of events with one following another). More recently, Bluedorn and his colleagues (e.g., Bluedorn & Denhardt, 1988), have discussed the importance of timing and scheduling for a variety of organizational phenomena including organizational behavior and strategy.

An assumption that time consists of unequal discrete units implies that a firm's strategist will perceive some moments will last longer than others will. We suggest this occurs when some moments are more important than others. Only an extreme view of path dependencies would suggest all moments in the past affect today's choices. More moderate views paint a picture of the past as pivotal moments interspersed with mundane ones (Arthur, 1988, 1989; Coombs & Hull, 1998; Scarbrough, 1998; Schilling, 1998). A similar texture to time also appears in Dierickx and Cool's (1989) time compression diseconomies and research on punctuated equilibrium (Anderson & Tushman, 1990; Beinhocker, 1999; Gersick, 1989; Romanelli & Tushman, 1986, 1994; Sastry, 1997; Tushman & Anderson, 1986; Tushman & Rosenkopf, 1992).

Anthropologist Edward Hall (1959, 1983) introduced the distinction between monochronic (m-time) and polychronic (p-time) time perceptions. He argued individuals differ in their cognitive styles related to time. An m-time perspective emphasizes schedules, segmentation, and promptness; a p-time perspective accepts several things happening at once. A p-time perspective stresses involvement of people and completion of transactions rather than strict adherence to structured schedules. Western culture is largely centered upon m-time (Hall, 1983) as reflected by schedules that guide nearly all facets of work and social life.

People view their work activities as sequential and distinct in Western culture's m-time. In Eastern and Middle Eastern cultures, p-time perspectives emphasize flexibility and multiple activities. For example, Trompenaars (1997) described a meeting of a South Korean manager with his Belgian boss. After entering the Belgian's office, the Korean manager noticed that his boss is on the phone. The Belgian motioned for his subordinate to "wait a minute" while the phone call is completed. The Korean manager interpreted this as an insult because the Belgian did not simultaneously carry on his phone conversation and greet his visitor. The m-time of the Belgian dictated a sequential approach to interaction, whereas the p-time of the Korean suggested taking on these activities simultaneously. Trompenaars (1997) observed that meetings in polychronic cultures can start anywhere from 15 minutes to a day late without parties being concerned because other circumstances may take precedent.

Most importantly from the MNT perspective is that concepts of time differ across cultures (Hall, 1983; Hofstede & Bond, 1988; Mosakowski & Earley, 2000; Trompenaars, 1997) and so members' views of the group's activities will as well. To a person having a strong focus on deadlines and schedules as is characteristic of German culture (Hofstede, 1991; Hofstede & Bond, 1988), the loose perspective that an Indian may have concerning when to begin a meeting becomes a strong potential source of conflict. This difference reflects more than simply observing a clock. It reflects an interest and willingness to pursue goals and focus on activities (Locke & Latham, 1990) and pursue growth and performance (Hofstede & Bond, 1988).

Task constraints and work requirements captures a number of aspects of the work being conducted by the team. One of the central features of task constraints relates to the composition of the MNT itself in relation to the work to be performed by the team (McGrath, Berdahl, & Arrow, 1995). Jackson provides an interesting, multilevel discussion of diversity of groups that is germane to our discussion of work and team dynamics. In general, as task interdependence increases, so does the potential for conflict within the team although some of this conflict may be productive and should not be automatically assumed to be a problem (Jehn, 1995). Thus, a task constraint such as the form of work interdependence experienced for task completion may act as a stimulus to bond team members together and improve performance as long as the conflict induced is task-, and not personally, relevant (Jehn, 1995). The problem, however, is that in the MNT we would argue that the likelihood of conflict being generated of a personal nature is much higher than in a team consisting of members having a common cultural background. Styles of interaction, face maintenance and facework, expectations concerning social etiquette, all are likely to be a source of unwanted personal conflict among MNT members that are less likely to occur in non-MNT groups. Work flow interdependence acts to make such conflicts more immediate and salient to all team members.

Changes in resources available are an obvious offshoot of the task constraints form of influence. As resources needed by the team become increasingly scarce, additional pressure experienced by team members will manifest itself as additional conflict. In some cases, well-integrated teams will use such scarcity as an impetus to come together further. However, in most cases, scarce resources will exacerbate existing conflicts and harm the team's sense of unity.

A team facing resource constraints is likely to experience additional conflict. In the formative stages of a MNT, this conflict will have a very damaging effect. Unlike a non-MNT, the natural tendency to form subgroups is high because national and cultural differences provide a very salient basis on which to group. A person's motive to seek and maintain status within a subgroup (Mulder, 1977; Ravlin et al., 2000; Sidanius, Pratto, & Rabinowitz, 1994) can be used to explain how resource scarcity may be related to the team members' cultural backgrounds. For example, in high-power distance cultures there is a natural tendency for members to seek and/or maintain personal status (Hofstede, 1980a; Smith & Bond, 1994). Two conditions in a high-power distance culture, acceptability of status differentials to exist and a desire to enhance one's position in a social hierarchy, lead group members to adopt the position taken by a high status member (Ravlin et al., 2000). Thus, scarce resources have an even larger impact in a team having high-power distance members because their position and status is most heavily threatened.

What seems to have received less attention is the proactive role that people take in shaping the technology around them to suit their needs for self-definition and face. A simple, but symbolic, example of this is the syntax that has developed on the Internet to convey personal information and affective state during email exchange. A smile or laugh, for example, is denoted with a ":)" as a means of conveying affect during "conversations." More importantly, syntax conveying relative status and physical characteristics has developed as well including gender, age, ethnicity, and so forth. These are important signals that are conveyed as a function of face demands. What remains relatively unexplored are the potential difficulties confronted with the use of electronic messaging in which parties desire face-related information but are unable to receive such information. Even the very use of technology may symbolize a loss of face for employees in certain cultures.

From a cultural perspective, technology represents a means of enacting general themes in a society. For example, in a tight culture there is a high demand for conformity to social practices and custom. Technology may be employed within an organization to monitor adherence to such social practices. An emphasis on social control and regulation is created through a reliance on technology as a means of enforcement. Just as important, in a tight culture, a willingness to accept such monitoring is likely to exist (even if it is not perceived as a desirable state of affairs). The obvious difficulty arises in a MNT representing wide ranges on cultural orientations related to privacy or social conformity. Thus, some members will gravitate towards technology as a means of monitoring one another whereas others will shun it.

The general context of the organization inside which a MNT operates is important as a catalyst for team action. Supportive organizational cultures will have a significant impact on the behaviors that team members enact. For example, Harris and Sutton (1986) examined the rituals and ceremonies used in the departure of individuals from their organizations such as a farewell party or testimonial. A striking example that conveys a culture of distrust and conflict is exemplified by the way a southwestern-based electronics company "fires" its employees. The practice is that after returning from lunch the former employee is surprised by a security guard standing by the employee's desk. The guard's function is to ensure that no company property is removed as the person clears out his or her desk. The guard escorts the employee out of the facility and the various security badges and passes are taken away—much like the symbolic breaking of the soldier's sword as he was dishonorably discharged from the cavalry. This symbolic ceremony instills a norm of distrust and reinforces the high price that is paid should an employee become disloyal to the organization (Erez & Earley, 1993).

The basic definition of organizational culture is captured nicely by Smircich and Calas's (1986) description of corporate culture as the sociocultural dynamics that develop *within* organizations; culture is viewed as an internal attribute of an organization rather than an external force that intrudes upon the organization. The idea of corporate culture has led to a number of different research streams. Some individuals view culture from an engineering perspective insisting that it refers to a coordination of systems within an organization such as culture and reward systems (Cummings, 1984) or an element essential for effective organizational change (Sathe, 1985; Tichy, 1982). Others view an organization as a living or dying system having an organization-level personality. For instance, Kets de Vries and Miller (1986) developed a typology of organizations based on manifestations of pathological personality types.

Smircich and Calas (1986) categorized the various frameworks used for studying organizational culture. These categories are: themes, paradigmatic perspective, and theory of knowledge perspective. The *themes* perspective refers to culture as a root metaphor. The five themes identified by Smircich and Calas are comparative and corporate culture, cognition, symbolism, and unconscious processes. The first two themes refer to culture as a variable denoting relationships between or within organizations. The other three themes refer to the use of an organization as a culture, that is to say, culture is what constitutes an organization from an expressive and symbolic process perspective.

The *paradigm* framework attempts to link culture and communication to organizational context and it consists of two major approaches. First, the functionalist paradigm is characterized by the objectivist, or positivist, approach used in most of the social sciences. The purpose of this approach is to develop useful law-like statements that enable the researcher to understand behavior within the context of specific corporate cultures. The second approach is the interpretive paradigm from an antipositivist view. In essence, interpretive research centers on understanding the dynamics of a corporate setting through the subjective perceptions of the viewer.

The third framework is the knowledge perspective, or the interests embedded in the organizational symbolism literature. Stablein and Nord (1989) use this approach to describe three cognitive interests derived from Habermas (1979). The *technical interest* focuses on the manipulation and control of the environment consistent with a functionalist approach. Second, a *practical interest* refers to a desire to understand meaning in a specific situation so that a decision can be made and action undertaken. The focus is on a consensually agreed upon decision rather than a more generalizable rule. Finally, an *emancipatory interest* refers to an interest in enhancing human liberties and responsibility in the world. The purpose of this approach is to determine the shared meanings of culture that have the potential to free individuals and give them liberty in individual action.

Empirical work suggests that "national," or societal-level, culture must be considered along with organizational culture in order to fully understand the relation of an organization's culture to organizational functioning (England, 1983). For example, Lincoln, Hanada, and Olson (1981) found that matching organizational culture with societal culture results in high job satisfaction. Ferris and Wagner (1985) found that a congruence of Japanese organization structure with Japanese values was positively related to the effectiveness of quality circles. A similar idea is forwarded by Ouchi and his Theory Z analysis (1980, Ouchi & Jaeger, 1978).

Schneider (1975) points out, "Where norms tell the actor how to behave in the presence of ghosts, gods, and human beings, culture tells the actor what ghosts, gods, and human beings are and what they are all about." (1975). Our argument is that "organizational culture" simply refers to the norms that regulate action within a particular organization and the heavy emphasis on the study of myths and rituals simply reflects the sense-making that individuals engage in according to the societal-level culture given these institutional norms. Perhaps the most important lesson to be learned is that organizational norms, rules, and functioning need to be consistent with a society's culture to avoid the individual from experiencing role ambiguity and alienation. Similar observations have been made in the work of Van Maanen and Barley (1984) in their work on occupational communities.

Thus, for the MNT, organizational supportiveness and culture may act to reinforce the cohesiveness of a team. Executive support for MNTs logically is quite crucial and such endorsement is likely to be linked to the team's effectiveness (Hambrick, Davison, Snell, & Snow, 1998; Maznevski, 1994). Supportive organizational cultures will help MNTs overcome obstacles and increase team members' attachments to one another. For example, Unilever operates with a strong "networked" form of structure (Goffee & Jones, 1995, 1998). Goffee and Jones refer to a networked organization as one having high sociability and low solidarity. Such a culture reflects strong friendships and communication within the company across its global operations with actions based on personal relationships rather than competitiveness. Unilever MNTs receive support from the corporate headquarters in terms of resources, acceptance for mistakes, and recognition for accomplishments.

The final element that we incorporate as a catalyst is a goal focus that might be introduced by the MNT's organization. We have already discussed to a certain degree the nature of schedules and timing as a facet of a team's actions. Likewise, the use of a team-based goal that is introduced externally or internally often will facilitate team interaction. Goals can, however, hurt a team if they act to place undue pressure on a team just as any other type of resource scarcity might do.

Goals generated by a MNT itself are likely beneficial because their development will act as a bonding ritual among group members. These goals reflect the common interests and attention of team members, and they make salient norms of cooperation and interdependence. Matsui and his colleagues (Matsui, Kakuyama, & Onglatco, 1987) found that group goals were effective for Japanese people. However, in individualistic cultures, group goals very often result in social loafing, and free riding, because group members in individualistic cultures do not share responsibility to the same extent as group members in collectivistic cultures (Earley, 1989). As a result, group performance tends to be less effective in individualistic than in collectivistic cultures unless employees are personally accountable for their performance. Perhaps one way to make group performance effective in individualistic cultures is to have the group members become personally accountable for their performance (Weldon & Gargano, 1988). Additionally, it is possible for a group goal to provide the accountability necessary for individualistic members to feel compelled not to socially loaf or free ride.

In the next section, we discuss several key process variables that connect our two categories of catalysts (social vs. work structure). These processes are rituals, structuration, and social enactment.

## CONNECTING THE CATALYSTS: PROCESS DIMENSIONS

There are three general processes that we draw on as processes that connect social and work structure catalysts to one another ritual/habit formation, role-taking and status, and enactment of social contracts. The first of these are rules and rituals that are enacted by an organization. Rules and rituals are employed by organizations to create predictability within an organization (Barley, 1990), and they help organizations connect the past to the present and future (Perrow, 1972). For instance, business meetings usually have their own protocols and procedures for conduct, including a ritualized placement of organizational members (seating charts), initiating event (calling to order), procedural pattern (who conducts the meeting), language (business-speak), and even closure (small talk signaling a completion of the meeting). These rituals are quickly acquired by new organizational members lest they be sanctioned by more "seasoned" members. Organizations are riddled with various rituals such as memos (and the modern counterpart, e-mail), accounting practices, and so on.

An area having received much research attention that has at its core roles and status is that of institution theory (Scott & Meyer, 1994). The study of institutions has long been a focus for sociologists, economists, and political scientists, and there has been an explosion of research on the topic during the last 20 years. Institutional theory applied to organizations can be thought of as the study of functioning through an analysis of persistent roles and procedures underlying action. Organizations are viewed as dependent on a wide environment that is the product of rational and nonrational impulses, and "… less as a coherent rational superactor (e.g., a tightly integrated state or a highly coordinated invisible hand) than as an evolving set of rationalized patterns, models, or cultural schemes … These may be built into the public polity, in the laws, or into modernized society through professional and scientific analyses or the models set by exemplary organizations." (Scott & Meyer, 1994).

An interesting example of an institutional arrangement is described by Steers, Shin, and Ungsom (1989) in his work on Korean Chaebols. Most chaebols are owned and controlled by a single family and are organized through a central holding company. Chaebols bear some resemblance to both of the Japanese intermarket and independent groups, yet they do not share most of the critical features of either form of Japanese organizational context. Chaebols generally reflect a narrow scope, and their resources are distributed unevenly across these differentiated functions, and they do not rely on the consistent relationships of subcontractors as do the keiretsu of Japan. Instead, they often buy or start new firms to care for their own production needs, and they utilize their ties to Japan for many of their supply needs. South Korean business groups reflect a centralized and integrated approach to economic activities whereas Japanese groups reflect "genuine associations of firms, some more tightly bound to the group than others." (Orru, Biggart, & Hamilton, 1991).

From a strict efficiency perspective (that is, structure and form follow an efficient process of production), it is not altogether clear why the Japanese, Korean, and Taiwanese institutional arrangements evolved in these various forms. However, within each country, organizations are formed along relatively similar lines. Homogeneity of structures within countries, but variance across countries, suggests that institutional forces are operating on organizations according to the unique cultural and economic circumstances reflected in each of the countries.

This synthesis view of the micro- and macrosociological influences within institutional theory is best represented in recent work by Scott and Meyer (1994), who pose a three-part model of institutions. In his layered model, institutions are the interactive product of three general components: meaning systems and social system patterns, symbolic elements including constitutive and normative rules, and regulatory practices that enforce these practices. Institutions, then, reflect these three general elements. Additionally, Scott poses that these institutional elements are influenced by, and influence, two other levels of the organization—governance structures and actors. The importance of an individual actor to the nature of institutions is one of cause as well as effect. That is, institutional influences on an organizational member occur through a number of mechanisms including socialization, identity formation, and sanctions according to Scott. Socialization reflects the most direct means through which organizational members are taught the "practices" and "rules" of an institution. In describing the reciprocal effects of individual actors on emergent institutions, Scott argues that through interpretation and innovation institutional rules and rituals are shaped.

The importance of an institutional perspective to an MNT is derived from the structures that members bring with them to the team and how these rules and practices evolve in the "new" team. In one sense, a highly diverse membership creates anarchy that provides members with an excuse to begin anew. A lack of consensus in a highly diversified team provides all members with an opportunity to reinvent what they believe are critical elements of a team regardless of their cultural backgrounds. In a highly homogeneous team, the existing rules and practices are simply reinforced.

As can be seen from this description, institutional theory (as it is presently depicted) characterizes social interaction and behavior as a product of institutional norms and rules evolving from various influences. Forces of various types create an impetus for demands and patterns of action in organizations that may or may not reflect true efficiencies in an economic sense. Further, these patterns (rules) influence the behavior of organizational members as they interact with one another. What is important from the ritual game of exchange in any given society is the sense of affirmation that partners derive from one another after successful encounters. These encounters reinforce our sense of self and they clarify our position in a social hierarchy.

Social enactment is the result of rituals, rules, and habits that people hold in a given institutional environment. What is important from our process perspective is that enactment reflects a person's position in a social hierarchy as well as a given work environment. Thus, the specific behaviors engaged in by a person varies as a function of the person's status at work, and not their status per se. That is, social enactment is quite specific to the work and social structure. For example, a well-accomplished athlete may command great respect from others in a sports setting but not in other settings. The degree of generalization for the athlete's status will reflect the social structure in which the athlete operates. For some social settings, the athlete maintains her stature regardless if it is work or nonwork (status generalizes beyond the confines of work). For other social settings, the athlete becomes less significant and high status. An American star soccer player commands little recognition and status in a nonwork setting such as a restaurant, whereas his British counterpart (in Britain) commands great respect and attention.

## SUMMARY

In this chapter, we have provided the foundation for our discussion of multinational teams through our general theoretical framework. Core to our perspective is the idea that a team is influenced by individual and team characteristics that lead to particular actions (and reactions) within a given social and work context.

We have defined individual elements of team members through roles and identity, trust and expectations, respect and moral character, affect, confidence and efficacy, and social awareness. Group, or team, elements include competition, fractionation (disunity), hybrid culture, shared meaning and understanding, common versus differentiated goals (priorities). Process dimensions connecting these levels include role identity formation, ritual development and structuration, and a shared sense of history.

The actions engaged in by team members are influenced by a variety of personal, interpersonal, and work factors. The unique aspect of a MNT not found in other types of work groups is that many of the underlying features of interpersonal interaction are not shared among group members. Rituals and rules for interaction differ across cultures and are incompletely shared by team members. Thus, even simple and preliminary forms of exchange require new thinking on the part of team members. As we described in the section focusing on hybrid team cultures, this lack of commonality among team members can pose a significant obstacle to overcome in the team as it develops. However, such a lack of commonality (shared culture) can, ironically, provide a strong basis for initial interactions of sense-making and social construction that will provide a team with a basis for moving forward. That is, the weakness of not understanding is a potential strength if such a lack provides an excuse for a MNT to develop its own new and unique team culture.

In the next few chapters, we will return to specific aspects of our model in more detail discussing these features more completely with additional examples from various MNTs with which we have worked. We now turn to a further discussion of the individual and group-level elements of MNTs.

# 4 Individual and Group-Level Elements

As discussed in chapter 3, our model consists of both process and content features across several levels of analysis. The overarching structure of the model links the individual and group elements through specific linking processes described in chapter 6. For example, roles enacted by individuals within a team collectively may create fractionation within the team. Role-making and role-taking is a fundamental action of individuals when exposed to a social structure (Katz & Kahn, 1978; Markus & Kitayama, 1991). It is through the action of creating roles for oneself that fractionation and differentiation within a team may occur at a team level. Thus, in this example, individual-level influences give rise to team consequences through given processes. Our model provides a linkage among key individual and team characteristics.

## CONCEPTUAL FRAMEWORK—INDIVIDUAL LEVEL ELEMENTS

As discussed in chapter 3, the individual level elements that are central to our model include roles, identity, and status issues, trust and expectations of others, respect for self/others and moral character, interpersonal affect, confidence and efficacy, and social awareness.

**Roles, Identity, and Status.**   The basis of rules/norms and the roles that people occupy is fundamental to any social structure. In this section, we draw upon conceptual work from symbolic interactionism (Blumer, 1969; Stryker, 1980; Turner, 1987) in discussing roles and rules. The roles that people enact are integrally tied with their self concept and identity (Erez &

Earley, 1993; Stryker, 1980; Tajfel & Turner, 1986). To understand how roles link personal and team identity with the social and organizational context, we draw from two general literatures. First, we discuss the nature of role taking and status using Status Characteristics Theory developed by Berger and colleagues (1974, 1977) as well as Stryker (1980). Second, we draw on Symbolic Interactionism theory (Stryker, 1980) as a means of understanding the dynamics of role enactment.

The social role is a critical and fundamental aspect of all relationships. It serves to integrate various actions and intentions of actors and it provides an important link of the individual to his or her social milieu (McAuley, Bond, & Kashima, 2001; Katz & Kahn, 1978; Smith & Bond, 1998). Role relationships are a central reference point in defining one's self-concept, which, in turn, regulates social behavior at least in some contexts (Stryker, 1980). It is not surprising therefore that cross-cultural researchers have used role relationships as a medium for investigating cultural-common frameworks of social situations. Triandis, Vassiliou, and Nassiakou (1968) reported a series of studies investigating normative behavior among members of various role relationships in the United States and Greece. Using data aggregated across subjects within two cultures, Triandis and his colleagues identified common behavioral dimensions and similar dimensional spaces for behaviors across the two cultures. Triandis (1977) labels the four dimensions defining normative behaviors within role relationships as association-dissociation (integration), superordination-subordination (power), intimacy (regulation), and hostility (activity). Additional studies of normative behaviors within role relationships have been conducted with Taiwanese subjects. Yang's (1970) study, also using aggregated data, revealed four main dimensions: association, hostility, superordination, and subordination. Chuang's (1998) individual differences study revealed two main dimensions: association-dissociation and superordination-subordination. Although these studies represent an important attempt to describe the social setting through relatively objective role relationships, a key point from our perspective is that the role itself has been the focus of attention in cross-cultural work for quite some time. In order to better understand the nature of role relationships, we must begin by reviewing the nature of role identities.

A framework useful in organizing the effects of multiple group memberships at the individual level is Identity Theory (Stryker, 1980, 1987). Identity theory holds that behavioral response patterns that are unique to situations involving group membership are organized as identities, so that a person has separate identities as a student, a family member, or as an employee. Identity theory differs from other models such as Social Identity Theory (Tajfel, 1982) or Self-Categorization Theory (Turner, 1987) in that its conception of identities is individual and involves role expectations and behaviors that are accepted and incorporated into the self (Earley & Laubach, 2000).

Stryker's Identity Theory explicitly brought social structural constraints into a symbolic interactionist conception of the self. In his theory, separate identities are ordered in a "salience hierarchy" in which highly salient identities are more likely to be evoked in response to a given situation. The salience of an identity is based on the individual's level of commitment to the social networks in which the identity is played out. Stryker (1987) defines commitment as "... the costs to the person in the form of relationships foregone were she/he no longer to have a given identity and play a role based on that identity in a social network ..." (p. 9). In a work group, respond to role-expectations using whichever identity is more salient in any given situation employees. Workers negotiate and decide among possible activities based on their identities created around role expectations surrounding their position in the formal structure, in a coalition, in an informal structure, or in an ethnic or other cultural group. Situations for which responses from multiple salient identities conflict become problematic, and the individual then responds with which ever identity holds a stronger commitment (Burke & Reitzes, 1991; Stryker, 1980).

There are a number of significant features of the Identity Framework. First, a central part of this framework affecting the relative salience of identities is control and coordination mechanisms used in organizational contexts (Earley & Laubach, 2000). Normative control evokes identities whose behavioral patterns are constructed around merged interests with the organization. In this sense, normative control merges identities based in informal organizational groups with identities based in the formal organization. People operating under normative control have high levels of organizational commitment, or in structural identity theoretical terms, have commitment to these merged identities (Burke & Reitzes, 1991). Bureaucratic control evokes identities whose subordinate behavioral responses are constructed around issues of legitimation, equity, and fairness embedded in organizational rules. This control form is susceptible to competition from identities whose behavioral patterns are based in the informal organization. Littler and Salaman (1984) argue that as organizations strike informal deals this lowers the salience of competing identities.

Second, the salience of identities in a cultural context as expressed in their culture-related values is important. If the ingroup is the organization, as is fostered by "clan-type" organizations (Ouchi, 1980), then the worker will respond to role expectations with the minimal efforts characteristic of normative control. A worker from a collectivist culture would tend to have a higher commitment to an identity that reflects the interests of his or her in-group, regardless of that in-group's relationship with the organizational structure. However, if a worker's in-group is not her organization, and especially if her in-group's interests are in potential conflict with the organization (e.g. class-based interests), then control methods must present role expectations in a way that favors evoking a subordinate identity over the competing ingroup identity. In addition, a cultural value that favors high power-distance relationships can support a worker's commitment to subordinate roles, facilitating the use of simple or bureaucratic control.

Third, Identity theory adds salient behavioral responses to those postulated by SIT and SCT, but also depth to the salience process beyond comparison of stereotyped characteristics among actors (Earley & Laubach, 2000). This extension can be seen in a hypothetical example of a work group in which two white Americans are training four Mexicans on technology transferred from a closed plant in the American's hometown. The Americans are an engineer and a machine operator who is a union member, and the Mexicans are a supervisor and three trainees. The union member as a central actor has a wide range of possible behaviors towards the Mexican trainees, from overt to covert aggression to mere compliance with the company to attempts to recruit them for the union. SIT and SCT would analyze his responses in terms of a set of demographic or organizational categories for himself and the Mexican trainees that would be possible for the situation. This analysis would examine the relevance for the potential categories, the extent to which the categories' definition fit the situation, and the differences between the potential sets of categories are contextually more relevant than the similarities. Of course, this interaction is only one set within the group context. The union member's behavior is potentially constrained by the presence of the American engineer, who may come from a minority category such as being female who, in turn, may have an ambiguous organizational relationship with him by being a professional and presumably aligned with management. Within the work group, the focal actor's behavior is presumably consistent, so whatever categories he selects to guide his own behaviors must somehow blend together to maintain some form of self-consistency.

Aside from the stereotypical behaviors based on whatever categories he assigns to himself and others, and Tajfel and Turner's key motives of self-esteem and uncertainty reduction (Thoits & Virshup, 1997), SIT and SCT offer few additional clues for which categories would become salient. The structural identity framework simplifies this analysis by focusing on the possible identities available to the actor and his commitment to each as determined by the consequences of inappropriate performances for each identity—for example, the loss of job for displays of hostility, the benefits of solidarity for unionizing the new plant, etc. This framework also assumes self-esteem and uncertainty reduction as motivators for identification but specifies uncertainty reduction in terms of consistency and self-preservation with respect to the maze of interests and power demands converging at each task.

Status characteristics can be diffuse or specific. Diffuse characteristics are those that carry general performance expectations that are not limited to the ability to perform one type of task and that are not necessarily rational.

Included in this category are such characteristics as gender, race, and age. Ridgeway and Walker (1995) define a status characteristic as an attribute on which individuals vary that is associated with widely held societal beliefs of esteem and worthiness. Because it is based in consensual beliefs, the status value of an attribute can change over time and vary among populations. The cultural beliefs that attach status value to a characteristic also associate it with implicit expectations for competence (Earley, 1997; Lau & Murnighan, 1998; Ting-Toomey & Cocroft, 1994). For example, in many societies including the United States, men are generally believed, rightly or wrongly, to contribute more to, that is, to be more competent on, a whole range of tasks than are women, hence gender is considered a diffuse status characteristic in those societies (Borgatta & Stimson, 1963; Elsass & Graves, 1997; Heiss, 1962; Kenkel, 1957; March, 1953; Shackelford, Wood, & Worchel, 1996; Stets, 1997; Walker, Ilardi, McMahon, & Fennell, 1996). In contrast, age is a highly relevant status marker in many Asian cultures including Thai society (Earley, 1999; Holmes, Tantongtavy, & Tomizawa, 1995). Specific status markers, however, may be only relevant only to one task, or category of tasks. Computer skills would be an example of a status characteristic of this type as would musical ability, engineering skills, athletic ability, nursing skills, and so on. It is important to emphasize that the assigning of value by individuals in a society to both diffuse and specific characteristics is often not a conscious process with the result that even very consciously "progressive" individuals can act otherwise at the micro-behavioral level. Research on the relationship between various status markers across cultures has tended to be sporadic and largely focused on characteristics relevant to western culture.

With regard to the status hierarchies employed within various countries, Earley (1999) explored the differential status attributable to particular demographic characteristics. More often than not, research conducted using various status markers relies on those characteristics that have historically accounted for a great deal of variance in the constructs that they are intended to predict. In the North American literature, these markers tend to be gender, race, age, and educational background (e.g., Jackson, Salas, & associates, 1992; Lawrence, 1997; Tsui, Egan, & O'Reilly, 1992). However, we do not have a fundamental understanding of why particular characteristics are relatively more salient than others in various cultures. Both Hughes and Turner assert the presence of a trait hierarchy within all societies. While this conception suggests that trait hierarchies are universal, Earley's results suggest (1) the effects of such a hierarchy on group decision-making as a function of cultural frame differ; and (2) the content of these hierarchies differs across countries. More importantly, we need to develop a more systematic way to predict the content of a trait hierarchy within a culture. However, Earley's work merely identified the characteristics nominated by key informants from each of the cultures he studied; he did not provide an ex ante framework predicting what characteristics might or might not be important in a given culture.

As we argued earlier in the book, trait hierarchies reflect the various social roles that a person may occupy in his or her society and it includes roles linked to traits including gender, race, religion, socioeconomic status as well as achieved roles including profession, education, etc. At the apex of our trait hierarchies is likely nationality. Indeed, research has shown that when individuals are confronted with members of other national or cultural groups, they regard the others, and themselves, primarily in terms of national or cultural orientations (Bochner & Ohsako, 1977; Bochner & Perks, 1971; Earley & Mosakowski, 2000; Meglino & Ravlin, 1998; Thomas, Ravlin, & Wallace, 1996). The presence of culturally different others makes culture salient. Demographic characteristics such as skin color and gender provide primary characteristics on which to differentiate group members (Fiske & Taylor, 1984). Differences among people also may be triggered by speech patterns, variations in dress, or normative behavior. Ravlin et al. (2000) suggest that an organizing principle for a society's trait hierarchy be based on the legitimacy associated with various traits consistent with Hughes's (1971) argument. Thus, those characteristics most highly associated with norms of legitimacy are at the top of the hierarchy.

An alternative view concerning the construction of a status hierarchy is offered in Status Theory (Berger et al., 1977). This perspective suggests that actors form expectations for self and other as a function of their expected advantage over those others (Berger et al., 1977). It applies primarily to short-term dyadic relationships with participants working on a task requiring collective effort to reach a goal [what Deutsch (1973) would refer to as promotive interdependence]. Both members of the dyad are assumed to be from the same culture and only salient characteristics, those with a direct or indirect effect, influence the dyad's interactions. Status characteristics with indirect influence on the successful performance of the task must distinguish between the two individuals to be salient. The result is that, unless both members of the dyad know for certain that an indirect characteristic is not relevant, they will treat that characteristic as if it were. Salient information, whether consistent or inconsistent, is used and the effect of each additional salient characteristic is attenuated. Further, for any individual, a status characteristic with more direct relevance to the task will carry more weight than one that does not.

Status Theory posits that the characteristics mix of individuals has important implications for power differences within a team. The more egalitarian the situation, the more the individual talents of the group members should be tapped. Where salient status characteristics are inconsistent or mixed in the expectations they create (e.g., a French manager having little formal education working with a team of highly educated French engineers), the group will be more egalitarian. Where salient status characteristics are consistent in this regard, the group will be more hierarchical. Drawing from this, we can infer that the higher the heterogeneity of a group, the more egalitarian it will be and the better it will achieve goals. Although lower status individuals might have increased the choice of actions available to the group, their ideas either remained unexpressed or were discounted by those of higher status.

For example, in the case of an American female doctor in a medical setting, her positive characteristic *doctor* will carry greater absolute value than her negative characteristic *female* (West, 1984). This relative ranking of characteristics is consistent with Hughes's (1971) notion of auxiliary status-determining traits as well. Hughes argued that certain characteristics are often associated with others (e.g., in the 1950s American culture, a physician was often associated with the auxiliary characteristic of being male). However, if these auxiliary status-markers are inconsistent with the primary characteristic, then the primary is somewhat denigrated or discounted. Thus, the male physician is seen as much higher status than the female physician is from the viewpoint of a "professional" despite their common professional background. Taken further, an auxiliary characteristic may even negate the status of a given marker if that characteristic has strong negative impact in a culture. For example, a Black engineer is discounted as a "token" at a computer firm, a female firefighter must have been "given" her job, etc. These inappropriate and unfair attributions illustrate the potential interactive effects of various primary and auxiliary status markers.

Empirical research is generally supportive of Status Theory (e.g., Berger & Zelditch, 1985; Webster & Foschi, 1988) and consistent with Bales's (1953) work. His research showed that groups homogeneous with respect to age, gender, and socioeconomic background and with no imposed structure formed stable participation inequities by the end of a one-hour session. The status hierarchies that developed reflected the participation inequities of the group members. People not only rank each other on the basis of physical, social and behavioral status characteristics, but carry with them a set of rules for doing so.

Status characteristics play a powerful role in short-lived groups; actors have little else on which to evaluate each other (Earley, 1999). In longer-term groups, one might expect that actors have more opportunity to evaluate objectively each other's skills, and so alter the ranking criteria used over time. However, a study by Cohen and Zhou (1991) showed that status-organizing processes in enduring research and development teams worked much like those in ad hoc groups. Although it is not appropriate to generalize from the results of any single study, the preliminary conclusion that we draw is that it is difficult for lower status individuals to overcome early impressions. Foschi (1996) suggests that it may be difficult for individuals to overturn initial performance expectations, because status characteristics not only influence performance expectations, but also create double standards for the evaluation of that performance.

If we examine status differentials within teams from a cross-cultural perspective, a number of cultural dimensions are directly relevant to understanding role processes (Butler & Earley, 2001; Earley, 1999; Smith et al., 1996). For example, a dimension typically used to describe on what basis status is accorded in different cultures is that of ascription versus achievement (McClelland, 1961; Parsons & Shils, 1951; Stovel, Savage, & Bearman, 1996; Weber, 1947) which Trompenaars (1994, p. 9; emphasis in original) describes thus: "Achievement means that you are judged on what you have recently accomplished and on your record. Ascription means that status is attributed to you, by birth, kinship, gender or age, but also by your connections (who you know) and your educational record (a graduate of Tokyo University or Haute Ecole Polytechnique). In an achievement culture, the first question is likely to be "What did you study?", while in a more ascriptive culture the question will more likely be "Where did you study?"

Smith, Dugan, and Trompenaars (1996) ranked North America very high on achievement whereas many Asian cultures are relatively high on ascription. Cultures are not simply more or less achievement- or ascription-oriented. Cross-cultural work also demonstrates that not only the actual characteristics on which status is accorded, but also the states of the characteristics themselves which vary by culture. For example, while many ascriptive countries value family background as a status characteristic, the Czech Republic, a highly ascriptive nation, is strongly opposed to using such a characteristic as a marker of status (Earley, Gibson, & Chen, 1999; Hampden-Turner & Trompenaars, 1994, p. 106). In some countries, having an upper class background (e.g., United Kingdom) is high status whereas in others a middle (e.g., Canada, Sweden) or working (e.g., Cuba, other former Communist states) class background is preferred. Complicating matters, within a culture, status characteristics themselves, as well as which state of a characteristic is positively valued, can change over time (Clarke, 1971; Prandy, 1998; Rallu, 1998; Stovel et al., 1996). Drawing on this distinction, Schneider and Barsoux (1997, p. 83) argue that, in French firms, senior managers provide "a high level of analytical and conceptual ability that need not be industry- or country-specific". In German firms, they have "specific technical competence, but also in-depth company knowledge," while in Chinese firms, they pursue "the Confucian tradition of patriarchal authority." The French preference for general analytical ability is satisfied through the elite system of grandes ecoles at the university level (Earley, 1999). Entrance to the grandes ecoles is based on achievement excellence in philosophy, mathematics and a range of other subjects in final secondary school exams. It is the graduates of these elite institutions who go on to assume top positions in industry and government. The German system tightly controls the provision of education through a series of achievement hurdles to the end of secondary education. With specific technical knowledge prized, students accepted to the dedicated engineering universities, especially those talented enough to attend the Technical University of Munich, get the top engineering jobs at the start of their careers and ultimately comprise the membership of the powerful company boards. In Chinese-run organizations, ascription is the predominant basis on which status is accorded. Family connections take precedence over academic qualifications with the result that many of the most respected and powerful firms are small in size relative to the top French and German firms as well as family-owned and managed. It is the elder family members who make important decisions.

Reports abound on the general challenge of working effectively across cultural boundaries (e.g., Earley & Erez, 1997; Schneider & Barsoux, 1997; Hampden-Turner & Trompenaars, 1994). It is also a specific challenge for the effective working of multinational management teams (Earley & Mosakowski, 2000; Gibson, 1999; Maznevski, 1994). Given that, in the achievement-oriented U.S., status hierarchies develop quickly and remain stable for the lifetime of the dyad or group concerned (Bales, 1953; Berger et al., 1977, 1985), it is likely also to be the case in ascriptive-oriented national cultures. Given that status is accorded on such different bases across cultures, can individual members of a multinational group read and accord status in a multinational group in order to develop an effective group culture with strong group goals overwhelming individual ones? And what are the implications for organizational level culture?

Despite these complexities, many multinational groups function effectively (Butler, 2000; Canney-Davison & Ward, 1999; Earley & Mosakowski, 2000; Maznevski & Chudoba, 2000). This suggests that according status across national cultures must be possible. Finding themselves in a situation where there is no "natural" social hierarchy around which initially to form, individual members of a multinational group, defined as one where none of its members share a nationality, reduce uncertainty by creating a social structure. In high heterogeneity, members of the group are likely to propose ideas regarding how to work together and what their goals should be. A broad range of these ideas is likely to be accepted by the group's members as all are seeking to preserve their positive self-identities through the positive reinforcement of the other group members. A solidaristic culture (Goffee & Jones, 1996) is likely to develop. If the organizational level culture is not supportive, then the group will modify their goals and culture, possibly putting their performance at risk.

Of course, roles that people adopt and are committed to are best understood in terms of some existing social patterns of rules. A role such as police officer is significant to the extent that it implies a set of rules and norms that are enacted as part of the role (e.g., giving traffic tickets to violators, arresting criminals using a particular procedure such as reading one's rights upon arrest). One example of such research on role structure was conducted by Bond and his colleagues who examined the nature of role dyads in Hong Kong Chinese and Australians (McAuley, Bond, & Kashima, 2001). In this study, they sought to separate a person's personality and individual differences characteristics from the actual social setting in which cultural interaction occurred. Drawing from work by Marwell and Hage (1970), they looked at a situational analysis relying on objective reports of dyadic relationships (e.g., mother-father, news reporter-politician, doctor-patient) and the results suggest broad structural similarity of culture-level relational space across these two cultures, with the four dimensions identified as complexity, equality, adversarialness, and containment of contact between members of dyads. Cultural differences were expressed in the location of specific roles within this common, four-dimensional space. Most importantly, the patterns for interaction were explained using four universal dimensions of role context.

A larger issue raised by the work of Marwell and Hage as well as McAuley et al. concerns the potential for separating social context from social roles. Marwell and Hage (1970) developed an empirically based taxonomy of role dyads defined in terms of physical context variables—occupants, activities, locations, and occurrences of role relationships. These variables were further expanded in terms of their scope (how many), intensity (how much), integration (overlap with other relationships), and independence (how much choice). This study produced a three-dimensional solution to describe the 100 role dyads. These factors roughly correspond to the regulation (visible, formal–private, intimate) and activity (intense–superficial) dimensions, respectively, found elsewhere (Haslam & Fiske, 1992; Triandis, 1977; Wish, Deutsch, & Kaplan, 1976). That is, these authors make the argument that culture influences roles and rules for interaction independently of the personalities of individuals involved in the social drama. Forgas and Bond (1985) and Pervin (1976) conducted studies aimed at exploring the subjective conceptual frameworks of social relationships for their subjects. The investigators first asked subjects to identify salient, representative social episodes from their lives, and then they accessed the conceptual structures in terms of subject-generated salient descriptors.

It seems to us that role identities are inherently subjective experiences and that the work by the "objectivists" (e.g., Marwell & Hage, 1970; McAuley et al., 2001) is an important complement to these subjective identities. That is, the role episodes themselves may have universal components of structure that act as a backdrop for the subjective experience of specific role identities. In a multinational team, the commonality of the structural elements can aid in the integration of subjective roles as long as the team members are aware of these role relationships. For example, if a team member knows that the nature of interpersonal relationships on a work team are highly intimate, intense, and prolonged from another member's perspective, this will help the team member understand the overtures of a member who seems overly concerned (from the original team member's perspective) with elaborate and detailed "getting to know one another" introductions.

**Respect for Self and Others.**     The second and third features are trust and the respect and moral considerations of team members. We present theses two features (trust and morality) together because they are closely intertwined. Trust presupposes moral actions and intentions. A useful approach to these concepts is presented in work on "face" (Earley, 1997; Ting-Toomey, 1994). Earley (1997) follows the Chinese tradition and discusses the moral aspects of face using the Chinese concept of "lian". According to Earley's (1997) Organizational Face Theory, lian refers to "… an evaluation by self and others concerning a person's adherence to *rules of conduct* within a social structure." (chapter 3). Furthermore, it reflects,

> Lian captures the basic moral character of a person that is acquired as a birthright (Hu, 1944), and it involves a person's respect derived from a society based on his or her adherence to the rules of moral conduct in a society. In this sense, everyone is born with lian and it is through moral acts that each person reaffirms it. However, lian is not some latent genetic characteristic. It refers to the social perceptions of self and others concerning a person's behavior and intentions. Through a variety of socialization experiences, children acquire the rules for appropriate (moral) behavior in their society just as adults learn the expectations concerning moral behavior in an organization. (p. 82)

Fundamental moral character (as reflected by lian) is derived from two general groups of values in cultures, namely, social relatedness and moral imperatives (Hu, 1944; Ting-Toomey & Cocroft, 1994). Social relatedness refers to the proper functioning in a social system. These values exist as a property of the social system and not simply as an individual differences characteristic. For example, affiliation and a sense of belongingness is a value reflected in all cultures, and this is a type of social relatedness value. Rebuffing social membership is the mark of a social outcast and misanthrope; people who reject affiliation reject societal membership. Moral imperatives refer to universal dispositions of the person such as justice or goodness.

The other aspect of face is referred to as mianzi, and it reflects the interactional aspect of face. That is to say, mianzi captures the aspect of face that reflects a person's interactions with others in her society. The metaphor of a tree and its bark is one that reoccurs in many Chinese sayings about face (e.g., "ren yao mian, shu yao pi," or people have face, tree has bark; Yan, 1995). This metaphor is a useful one not only because it depicts face as the outside which protects the inside (as bark protects the inside of the tree), but also because it demonstrates that there exists an important aspect of bark that aids in the definition of a given tree. Further, the bark provides the environment in which other creatures in the ecological system can live and flourish, just as face provides the setting needed for social systems to operate effectively.

Earley (1997; Earley & Randel, 1997) used the concept of face to understand how organizational members from various cultures might interact within and across cultures. He describes a conceptual framework for understanding face within an organizational context. The model consists of six basic parts: societal context, organizational context, organizational structure and content, social actor, harmony, and face. Societal context consists of six dimensions of culture: individualism and collectivism, tight versus loose (sometimes referred to as field dependence versus independence, respectively), harmony with nature, power distance, guilt versus shame, and masculinity and femininity. These dimensions constitute a collage in which face and interpersonal interaction is embedded. Organizational context in this model refers to the general situation in which organizations operate within a given society. The influences most salient and direct on a social actor, and most directly influencing harmony, are the aspects of an organization defined by its structure and content. Organization structure and content refer quite specifically to those influences inside of an organization that are thought to influence a social actor and social regulation of face such as technology, institutional roles and rules, intraorganizational dependencies, communication systems, and governance structures.

The psychological makeup of a person captures various immediate constraints acting on that individual that define how he interacts and behaves. A social actor provides an important link between culture and action and it is a dynamic structure interpreting the social patterns around it (Earley, 1997). However, viewing the social actor as independent from the social milieu from which he acts is an inadequate representation; there is no meaningful way to speak about people abstracted from their community (Sampson, 1989). Long term attachments and commitments to the social environment help define who people are (Sandel, 1982). Harmony reflects processes of social exchange, social regulation, and social discourse. It refers to the nature of interpersonal interaction and actions engaged in by social actors within a given organizational content and structure. In this context, harmony refers to the systems-level, dynamic processes through which face (and other behavior) is regulated. The impetus for face regulation is harmony, which becomes particularly relevant in a group context, as will be addressed later.

Earley & Randel (1997) present an example of how this view of morals and values can be applied to the multinational team. They use the example of the Japanese practice of group decision-making referred to as "ringi-sei" (Erez & Earley, 1993). In a cultural context where strong norms encouraging group conformity exist, the ringi-sei group decision-making system may derive strength from its ability to decrease the likelihood that participants' face will be threatened. The process in which groups engaged in a decision-making task move from an initial state where there is a lack of consensus to a final agreement includes numerous opportunities for group harmony to be put at risk. Without threats to group harmony during the decision-making process, the quality and innovativeness of the resulting decision may be jeopardized due to groupthink, a phenomenon in which group members do not voice their personal views due to norms for conformity (Janis, 1982). However, group harmony is critical in many cultural contexts. The ringi-sei system provides a structure that allows for the contribution of individual input to decisions while minimizing the threat posed to group harmony by the nature of decision-making tasks. Not only does the ringi-sei system offer a way of decreasing the threat posed to group harmony, but it also may enhance group harmony and the face of group members.

The participative nature of the ringi-sei system results in decisions that are formulated and approved by the entire organization. Approval for the decision is demonstrated by the written form of the ringi sho (distributed decision proposal) accompanied by the stamp of organization members at all levels of the firm's hierarchy (Lincoln, 1990; Jun & Muto, 1995). The collective effort put forth in forming a decision and the written endorsement of the decision by firm members offer confirmation of the interdependent self that is based on relationships with others (Markus & Kitayama, 1991). As the term implies, the interdependent self consists of a conception of the self as part of a relationship network among two or more people. Recall that a person's face makes reference to both self-identity and social identity. Through ringi-sei, the interdependent aspect of the self that relies on interpersonal relationships and social identity derived from group interaction are both emphasized and fortified.

Another example of how face can be used to understand team dynamics concerns job design. A great deal of attention has been focused on the use of individual-based versus group-based job design (Hackman & Oldham, 1980; Tannenbaum, 1980; Trist & Bamforth, 1951). The focus of much of this work has been on the sociotechnical approach to job design. Sociotechnical systems emphasize keeping work groups intact by integrating the methods of production with the needs of a group. The implication for group members is to allow them more discretion in their work, provide them control over their nonwork activities, etc. The advantage of this approach for group-oriented cultures is that these natural work groups are maintained so workers do not experience alienation. The basic features used in the famous Saab engine factory experiment (Tannenbaum, 1980) include: (1) assembly groups rather than assembly lines; (2) assembly of a whole engine by a group; (3) determination by group members of how work is to be allocated within the group; (4) a cycle time of 30 minutes rather than 1.8 minutes that is typical of the assembly line; and, (5) selection of work mates by team members. Rubenowitz (1974) provided a summary of several of the Scandinavian experiments in the sociotechnical system and he reported favorable reactions to the system by managers and employees. This approach is clearly consistent with the motives of growth and self-presentation reflecting collectivistic values of group togetherness and functioning.

From a MNT perspective, the Saab experience illustrates an interesting point about work structure versus group context. To some extent, the introduction of technology has the potential to remove direct, interpersonal contact and the type of interactions that are related to face. In the Saab experiment, the means of production were altered so as to provide an opportunity for continuing social relationships among work group members. By maintaining group structure, lian is supported through an in-group loyalty. Further, the opportunity to keep an intact group provides group members with the chance to further develop mianzi. An interesting aspect of mianzi is that it has greatest significance if given by a friend rather than a stranger. Thus, the motivational influence of mianzi is enhanced by the use of intact work groups in production.

Wilson (1993) reflects a concept of morality and their impact on a MNT in work. Wilson argued that there are four universal morals, namely, sympathy, fairness, self-control, and duty. He posited that these four sentiments constitute a moral sense in all peoples, and that there are discernible social and biological imperatives underlying these sentiments. Sympathy refers to a capacity for being affected by the experiences of others. For example, he discussed the case of a hospital benefactor who gives a generous gift, and receives public recognition in return. Although the benefactor may have provided the gift for public recognition, Wilson queries why observers would recognize the act if they suspected that the deed was not purely altruistic. He argues this is because people wish to encourage in one another the sentiment of sympathy. By fairness, he suggests that there are outcome and procedural standards by which actions are judged as fair or just, a finding well supported in an organizational context (e.g., Baron & Cook, 1992; Bazerman, Loewenstein, & White, 1992; Greenberg & Folger, 1983; Lind & Tyler, 1988; Rawls, 1971; Thibaut & Walker, 1975. For example, individuals provided with an opportunity to express their reactions to an evaluation system ("voice") experience stronger feelings of procedural and outcome fairness, and perform better, than individuals not afforded such an opportunity even if this opportunity occurs without concomitant decision control (Earley & Lind, 1987). Studies conducted in Hong Kong and elsewhere verify a cross-national similarity of procedural justice effects (Leung & Park, 1986; Lind & Earley, 1992).

Self-control refers to an individual's restraint in the present on behalf of the future. For example, a student who pursues her doctoral studies may live, as a pauper for a number of years in order to obtain the skills, knowledge, and credentials needed for a prestigious faculty position. An organization that channels its extra profits into research and development rather than issuing extra dividends will ensure a more profitable future for itself (and its shareholders). Finally, Wilson's concept of duty refers to an individual's willingness to be faithful to obligations derived from society, family, and important referent others. For instance, Huston, Geis, and Wright (1976) looked at the actions of a number of "good Samaritans" (people who intervened on behalf of others during a crisis). They found that many Samaritans acted because it appeared to be the "right thing to do" rather than due to sympathy for the victims per se. It is through these four sentiments that Wilson argues people function and behave within a society.

There are five types of moral imperatives that may be derived as values (Earley, 1997; Rokeach, 1973; Schwartz & Bilsky, 1987). First, there is the value of good versus evil. In all cultures, there are actions and views that certain behaviors are counterproductive for the culture and constitute "evil." For example, all social systems condemn the murder of societal members for personal gain. Likewise, most cultures condemn incest and patricide. These taboos have likely arisen because of biological needs although there are several notable exceptions typically attributable to a lack of appropriate social partners. Second, there is the value of justice that exists in all societies. This value has two important components, distribution and process. Although some people emphasize additional forms of justice, we broadly define distribution justice as related to all aspects of outcomes (reward or punishment) with process referring to all procedures through which outcomes are distributed or allocated. Thus, these two forms would encompass more specific forms that are discussed in the justice literature (e.g., Brockner, Grover, O'Malley, & Reed, 1993; Greenberg & Folger, 1983; Lind & Tyler, 1988). Third, there is the value of self-awareness that is to say that all individuals seek to determine their position and purpose in the world. It refers to the fundamental question of who we are in our social system. Self-definition is the single most critical value and it underlies many of our actions. Fourth, the value of spirituality exists in all cultures. That is not to say that all cultures have a sense of a singular god-like entity, but that there is a value that humans possess some characteristic that is unique. It is this point that relates to the idea of harmony or balance that is found in many cultures. Finally, duty refers to a person's relationship to her social system as well as collectives or in-groups. People invest their self-definition in their collective, and these results in a willingness of the individual to subordinate self-interests on behalf of the collective if required. It also captures the Parsonian characteristic of affectivity.

If we apply this notion of justice to an MNT we can see a number of interesting complications. Most obviously, people's concept of justice is universal but the specific form and definition of justice varies by culture. Distributive norms for allocating team resources will differ according to members' cultural backgrounds. For example, a dominant form of distribution found in India is based on need (to each according to their need) whereas in Germany it is based on equity (to each according to their accomplishment and contribution). If these members attempt to distribute resources within the same team, it is clear that problems may arise.

**Interpersonal Affect.**   Affect shared among team members is important for understanding the nature of MNTs. Affective relations among team members may be expressed through loyalty, trust, and commitment. Many scholars consider affective attachment of an individual to a team to be an implicit aspect of collective societies (Triandis, 1995). If we are discussing individualism and collectivism from a family perspective then it seems reasonable to assume that affect and loyalty are implicit. However, affect and friendship may mean very different things for the individualist and the collectivist who are dealing with a work group. For example, Japanese managers are reported to spend their dinners and evenings with their work colleagues as a natural extension of work. Americans interpret this action as work fanaticism and selflessness but an alternative explanation is that there exists a positive, affective bond between the managers and their subordinates that makes such after hours activities very desirable.

Affective sensitivity is particularly important for multinational teams even though this is a greatly understudied topic. The ability to sense fellow team members' moods and emotions can aid where cognitive recognition of differences in values or beliefs are unclear or in conflict. For instance, a member who empathizes with another team member may not be able to discern why the person is upset from an explanatory view, but if he realizes that there is some emotional distress then this is an important step in alleviating problems.

Affective sensitivity and empathy have received recent attention through a number of popular and scientific sources including Daniel Goleman's (1995) book, Emotional Intelligence. By emotional intelligence, Goleman describes a combination of factors that are emotionally based rather than cognitively based forms of intelligence. These include empathy, affective sensitivity to others, awareness of self, etc. His approach is a practical application and extension of traditional scholarship by researchers such as Gardner (1993), Salovey and Mayer (1990), and Sternberg (1985). An interesting example that Goleman (pp. 36–37) uses to describe emotional intelligence is that of a 4-year-old girl who is quite shy and a "wallflower." Although the child appears to be socially backward and withdrawn, her teacher discovers that she can correctly classify fellow students' preferences for play activities as well as playmates with re-markable accuracy. She is able to interpret the likes and dislikes of her classmates even though she is quite removed from the play activity.

The concept of an emotional intelligence, or awareness, is a compos-ite of several individual differences characteristics. Salovey and Mayer (1990) identified five sources of emotional intelligence in their frame-work. First, knowing one's own emotions is an extended form of self-awareness emphasizing the identification of emotion as it occurs. This reflects the ability to monitor one's feelings across time accurately in order to regulate behavior consistently with the social environment. Clearly, the self-awareness of personal emotion is critical to team func-tioning in several ways. Strong self-awareness enables a team member to understand how others will react to her personal actions as well as reg-ulate these actions accurately. Second, managing emotions refers to a person's ability to handle one's own emotions such as soothing oneself during tense periods, bringing oneself out of a depression, relaxing when distressed, etc. It is not merely enough to identify one's own emotions, effective team contributions require that these emotions are carefully regulated and managed.

Third, motivating oneself by using emotions to propel one toward de-sired goals is important. Emotional self-control such as delaying personal gratification and stifling impulses enables a person to regulate personal action toward team goals. Fourth, recognizing the emotional states of oth-ers is critical in a multinational team since the cognitive aspects of their statements and actions may be blurred due to cultural differences in be-havior. For example, a person from an affective neutral culture (Glenn & Glenn, 1981) does not display a great deal of emotive behavior and tends to be reserved. This means that someone who emphasizes the interpreta-tion of others' views and perspectives based on verbal and behavioral cues may have difficulties due to a lack of information. If a person is highly sensitive to the emotions of fellow team members, then a lack of overt be-havioral cues may not be such a problem. Finally, Salovey and Mayer argue that the ability to handle relationships is an important facet of emotional in-telligence. This reflects a social competence in dealing with others through managing their emotions. This is a key factor in such activities as leading others, negotiating, motivating, etc.

As described, emotional intelligence is very important in the multina-tional team—perhaps more so than a more homogeneous team. We have argued that a highly heterogeneous team presents team members with a unique challenge since many of the social and interpersonal cues needed to interact with one another are lacking or confused. This is the interesting aspect of emotional intelligence because it is not culturally bound. By this we do not mean that people from all cultures experience emotions in the same way from the same thing (e.g., humor is clearly interactive with personal and cultural experiences). However, evidence suggests that the experience of emotion itself does not differ across cultures. That is, happiness and love exist as emotions common to all cultures just as emotional expression (Ekman & Davidson, 1994) seems to be a universal phenomenon tied to biological mechanisms. This suggests that the cognitive interpretation of fellow team members' actions may be misleading and flawed given that behavior can be relatively scripted. However, the emotions that are experienced by team members and detected by the person having great affective sensitivity are in the unique position to step beyond these limitations. We are not arguing that such interpretation is devoid of cognitive and behavioral cues; people having high emotional intelligence and sensitivity receive their information about others through various sources. What this does imply is that the sensitive team member has a variety of sources through which to triangulate the intentions and actions of others.

Another important ability that emotional intelligence captures is the sense of one's own emotions and the capability to manage them. In the early phases of a multinational team's development, the confusion and sorting out that occurs gives rise to stress and the potential for conflict and anger. The effective team member is able to identify and manage her own emotions so that she does not send inappropriate signals to other team members. This capability also conveys a sense of confidence and efficacy that will lend itself to the team member's position and status within the team.

From a cultural viewpoint, there are at least two cultural values that bear relationship to affectivity in teams. First, Hofstede's (1991) concept of masculinity/femininity reflects a caring orientation among individuals. People from a feminine culture are concerned with proper social functioning and interaction among people. A nurturing and caring perspective focusing on people and their welfare is threatened if individuals place personal gain over interpersonal harmony and functioning. This suggests that the moral character of people be of central concern because such a focus helps to determine the potential of an individual to contribute to interpersonal welfare, and it reflects a person's likely "balance point." By a balance point, I mean that in a feminine culture it is important that people know one another's moral perspective to fully understand their true needs and wants. It reflects a desire to understand another person in a fundamental and personal way that is not attainable through a cursory examination of a person's wealth or position (i.e., to get to know the person and not just their role).

The second cultural characteristic is the traditional concept of shame versus guilt (Mead, 1967). In its most basic form, shame and guilt are related but not the same. Shame refers to a situation in which a person has failed to fulfill personal or community ideals for behavior and personal states whereas guilt reflects a situation in which a person transgresses moral imperatives of a society (Lazarus & Lazarus, 1994).

For example, we might say that a person who has a physical deformity (e.g., hunchback) experiences shame, but we would not necessarily conclude that this unfortunate person feels guilty about his handicap. However, if someone steals from her employer, but is not caught in doing so, she may well experience guilt but not shame. Thus, a critical dimension of these complex emotions is the degree of publicness implicit in the experience. Shame is a socially focused and oriented experience and guilt is a personal one. Using this general distinction, it becomes readily clear how this cultural dimension relates to the concepts of face and social action.

The origins of shame versus guilt from an anthropological perspective can be traced to a number of scholars including Benedict (1946), Levy (1973), Lynd (1958), Piers and Singer (1971), and Rosaldo (1989) to name a few. In fact, the distinction of shame versus guilt is one of the very few distinctions in anthropology that has stood the test of time for its universality. This may be attributable to the fundamental and bridging nature of the construct; shame is essentially a socially based experience whereas guilt is an individually based experience, and such a distinction maps on nicely to distinctions of societies based on self versus community. An early analysis of the contrast between shame and guilt was evidenced in Benedict's (1946) analysis of Japanese society and Pitt-Rivers's (1954) research with Spanish peasants. The mechanism through which feelings of guilt or shame are produced centers upon the family and community in most cultures. A society in which a child is trained by a large number of socializing agents, such as an extended family or tight community, a general shame-orientation is produced. A group member is afraid of a withdrawal of the love of others (Eberhard, 1967), of being suddenly out of synchronization with her environment, or of not meeting the trust that she has for herself. In many community-based cultures, the most important thing for a person is to avoid shame through the views of others. They have an internalized the norms of their group and important socializing agents, and much of their actions are based on avoidance principles (avoiding doing things that will bring on shame).

Guilt reflects "wrongdoing," an actual and real violation of moral standards for personal conduct, and it is typically coupled with experiences of remorse and guilt. The societal member avoids engaging in behavior that will put him in a position of violating his own code of ethics or standards for behavior. While the more "primitive" and developing types of cultures, with their emphasis on family and the social community, focus on shame, more industrially advanced and progressive communities focus on individual responsibility for action and a moral order driven by guilt. However, this contrast is not necessarily a simple and clean one as might be assumed based on discussion to this point. For instance, Rosaldo (1989) describes a number of his interpretations of the Ilongots

(a tribe of headhunters) concerning the concept of shame and its separation from a western concept of guilt. He stated,

> The difficulty with "guilt and shame" is that it sorts just "us" from "them," ask-
> ing how "they" achieve adherence to their norms and rules in lieu of mecha-
> nisms we use to an equivalent sort of end. What is not recognized is the
> possibility that the very problem—how society controls an inner self—may
> well be limited to those social forms in which a hierarchy of unequal power,
> privilege, and control in fact creates a world in which the individual *experi-
> ences* constraint.
>
> ... Thus, Ilongot "shame" is not a constant socializer of inherently asocial
> souls, but an emotion felt when "sameness" and sociality are undermined
> by confrontations that involve such things as inequality and strangeness....
> My point, in short, is that the error of the classic "guilt and shame" account is
> that it tends to universalize our culture's view of a desiring inner self without
> realizing that such selves—and so, the things they feel—are, in important
> ways, social creations. (pp. 148–149).

Eberhard (1967) describes some of the research conducted on the Burmese by Hitson (1959). He said that the Burmese, who are described as a
shame-based culture, also know the concept and experience of guilt. People describing the Japanese culture as a shame-based culture note that
the Japanese also are capable of feeling guilt as a result of personal actions
(Rosaldo, 1989). In Western culture, people certainly experience guilt
readily and for a multitude of reasons ranging from broken New Year's res-
olutions to having taken the last soda in the refrigerator to not having
walked the dogs on a given evening. Do westerners experience shame as
well? Certainly there seems to be evidence of this sort in many circumstances such as having a physical deformity or public embarrassment.
Thus, it appears that the distinction of shame versus guilt is much like that
of competition versus cooperation, namely, that both impulses exist in all
societies and it is the relative balance that determines the fingerprint for a
given culture (Mead, 1967).

Drawing on an organizational example, imagine an employee who has
set an ambitious work goal for his marketing team, but through several
personal mistakes that she ignored, but could have corrected, she has
caused the team to grossly underachieve their goal. The result of this failure is public teasing by other teams, and a formal warning from the company's hierarchy. In this case, the employee experiences both guilt and
shame. She experiences guilt about having let down his team members
through inaction or mistakes. She has violated her moral imperative for
making an adequate contribution to her team's progress by not trying to
correct several mistakes. However, she experiences a sense of shame as a
result of the ridicule and teasing from the other teams in the division. The
important question becomes one of understanding and predicting which

of these forces will contribute most directly (and heavily) to the manager's actions in the future. In a western context, it is likely that concern over having violated a moral imperative (not trying to overcome mistakes) will explain subsequent actions.

**Confidence and Efficacy.**    A fourth characteristic of a MNT member critical to team functioning is the person's confidence for action, self-efficacy expectations. In this section, we examine two aspects of confidence— individual and group-efficacy (also called collective) expectations (Bandura, 1997).

As reviewed earlier, perceived self-efficacy is a judgment of one's capability to accomplish a certain level of performance under a particular set of circumstances. Efficacy judgments promote the choice of situations and tasks with high likelihood of success, and eliminate the choice of tasks that exceed one's capabilities. Four sources modify the perceptions of self-efficacy (Bandura, 1997). First is enactive attainment based on authentic mastery experiences. Success raises perceptions of self-efficacy, and repeated failures lower them. It is not always quite this simple as demonstrated by early work (Campion & Lord, 1983). To be more precise, success and failure generally have consistent influence over successive efficacy expectations although high efficacy may lead an individual to reject or ignore failure feedback in the short term. Likewise, people who are chronically depressed and have low self-esteem may require numerous successes before they upwardly adjust their expectations (Bandura, 1997). Once a strong sense of self-efficacy is established the effect of failure is attenuated. To protect positive perceptions of self-efficacy people tend to attribute failure to situational factors. Second, vicarious experience is another factor that affects self-efficacy (Campion & Lord, 1982; Earley & Kanfer, 1985). Visualizing other similar people performing effectively positively affects one's level of self-efficacy. We rely on other models if we have no prior experience with the situation. People convinced vicariously of their inefficacy are unlikely to perform well whereas those who observe successful similar others are more likely to perform effectively. Verbal persuasion is the third factor that serves to enhance or inhibit efficacy expectations. Positive persuasion leads people to believe that they are capable of obtaining their goal, and consequently, they become more committed to the goal and allocate more resources to their mission. Commitment and effort result in a higher level of performance that further increases self-efficacy. Finally, Bandura (1986, 1997) argued that physiological state serves as basis for evaluating one's capability. Symptoms of fatigue, stress and anxiety indicate that a person is not at his/her best and, therefore, attenuate perceptions of self-efficacy. Two of these factors, vicarious experience and verbal persuasion, are expressions of social learning processes that take into consideration influences of the social environment.

A second feature of efficacy that we categorize as "individual level" is somewhat more problematic. This feature is group, or collective, efficacy. In one sense, this construct can be considered in both the individual and group-level elements of our model. We present it here in this category for sake of simplicity but we note that this concept is dual-listed in our framework. One of the reasons that group or collective efficacy is listed as both an individual and group level feature is because of its measurement (Bandura, 1997; Gibson, 1999, 2000a, 2000c; Gibson, Randel, & Earley, 2000; Guzzo, Yost, Campbell, & Shea, 1993; Shamir, 1990). A great deal of debate has occurred concerning the most appropriate way to define and measure this construct. Even the terms group versus collective efficacy reflect a split in some scholars' thinking on the topic (Shamir, 1990). We adopt Bandura's (1997) definition, "Perceived collective efficacy is defined as *a group's shared belief in its conjoint capabilities to organize and execute the courses of action required to produce given levels of attainments* (p. 477). The collective belief centers on the group's operative capabilities." (italics in original). The debate (see Gibson et al., 2000 for a review) around this construct seems to center on measurement issues whether it reflects: (a) an average of team members' personal estimates of efficacy concerning their own individual efficacy; (b) an aggregation of each team members' beliefs concerning team efficacy; or, (c) a collective judgment of a team concerning its capability (a single, collective judgment). Although the debate continues unabated, recent work by Gibson et al. (2000) demonstrated minimal differences among the various methods, and cross-cultural work by Earley (1999) suggests that collective judgments (method "c") may be problematic in high-power distance cultures as forewarned by Bandura (1997). Earley found that in high power distance cultures, team members having high status characteristics (e.g., age, education or gender) had a disproportionate influence on their team's collective judgment. Thus, as we consider the way that collective judgments of efficacy are formed we must be cognizant of the underlying implications for measurement.

Collective efficacy, however arrived at, reflects an important aspect of team functioning since it captures the motivational intensity of a team. A group's level of accomplishment is a function of coordinated individual contributions (Saavedra, Earley, & Van Dyne, 1993). Prussia and Kinicki (1996) illustrated this point in a study by concerning brainstorming in a laboratory context. They demonstrated that group performance was positively and directly related to collective efficacy, prior group performance, and vicarious team experience as well as negatively related to group affective evaluations. In addition, they found that collective efficacy mediated the relation of vicarious experience, negative feedback, positive feedback, and prior group performance on subsequent group performance.

There are a variety of influences that may serve to reduce, or undermine, collective efficacy. At a societal level, the functioning of governments and political parties can negatively impact collective efficacy by providing weak and diffuse goals for the public. In addition, a political system that is deaf to the needs and desires of the public reduces people's collective sense of control over events. Within an organization, collective efficacy is undermined if individuals do not feel as if their contributions are recognized or appreciated. Employees who view themselves as "another gear in a very large and complex machine" may not feel compelled to push themselves and their work. At an extreme, an employee may become withdrawn and lack commitment to organizational goals. Finally, at a team level, collective efficacy is reduced when team members feel disenchanted or detached from their team. Low personal identification with a team, low commitment to the team, and ill-defined sense of team purpose are antecedents of low collective efficacy within a team.

The point concerning threats to team efficacy is illustrated with a nice counter-example provided by some brief NASA (National Aerospace and Space Administration from the United States) history. Shortly after declaring the commitment of the United States to pursue space exploration and put a man on the moon within the decade, Kennedy was touring a NASA facility when he came upon a janitor. He asked the man his job at NASA to which the man replied that he was "putting a man on the moon". At all levels of the organization, the NASA staff was committed to a global vision set forth by President Kennedy. Thus, the conditions of ill-defined mission, low personal commitment and control, and anonymity/loss of personal identity did not exist for this janitor. Instead, he viewed himself and his actions as integral to NASA accomplishing its lofty goals.

Within a multinational team, individual and collective efficacy plays a significant role in team functioning. The interactive nature of the cultural context with individual and collective efficacy is illustrated by the study we described by Earley (1999). He formed three-person teams of managers coming from four countries—two high in power distance (France, Thailand) and two low in power distance (England, United States). Country of origin was fully crossed with status characteristic such that a single status characteristic (age, gender, or education type) existed with any given team resulting in twelve possible team types (country X status characteristic). Team members were exposed to a task after which they made individual judgments of their team's capability for a subsequent performance period. Next, they were asked to form a single, collective judgment to reflect their team perception of efficacy. Earley found that in the two high power distance cultures, team members possessing high status characteristics had an inordinate influence on the successive, collective efficacy judgment (either raising or lowering it) relative to an arithmetic mean of the aggregate team members' judgments. Further, the collective estimate of efficacy was more strongly tied to team performance on an interdependent task than the aggregated individual estimates. This "follow the leader" effect illustrates the potential influence of collective judgments of efficacy across varying cultural contexts. Of course, this raises an important issue concerning a multinational team – namely, what influence does cultural context play if the team is heterogeneous with regard to cultural membership. (Earley's study focused on teams within each country showing separate effects for homogenous teams).

As we reexamine the various factors influencing efficacy expectations we can see another complication for the multinational team. For example, enactive mastery reflects prior work experiences that are likely lacking for the multinational team member (or, at a minimum, limited to only a few team members). That is, the novelty of the MNT negates its contribution to efficacy bolstering. Vicarious learning and verbal persuasion are both factors that will influence team efficacy but it isn't clear if the MNT will have a sufficient "base" for understanding efficacy experiences conveyed in this fashion. For example, verbal persuasion styles differ greatly across cultural borders (Smith & Bond, 1994) and it remains unclear whether or not people coming from radically different cultures will rely upon others as their role models. As we argue in the next half of this chapter (group-level elements), if a hybrid culture is established within a team then we would predict that team members might rely upon one another as sources of efficacy. Styles of verbal persuasion as well as role modeling will be effective across the various members of the team in a hybrid culture. That is, a team member will trust and respect the verbal persuasions conveyed by fellow team members. Likewise, a team member will rely on the role modeling provided by others within the team.

Although we have not focused much on the other factor that changes efficacy, physiological arousal, it is likely to have a role in the MNT. Our argument is that physiological arousal will play a role in both inhibiting and increasing team efficacy. At the early stages of team functioning, the physiological arousal attributable to team interaction (social motivation due to the presence of others) will likely inhibit team effectiveness. Motivation and posturing as part of identity establishment will create additional tension to an already tense context. However, after the team has solidified a hybrid culture then physiological arousal will contribute to enhanced team effectiveness. This is not altogether different than what one would expect in a domestic team. However, the degree of interference is likely much more severe in a MNT because members operate in a stronger climate of confusion and ambiguity in the early phases of team functioning.

**Social Awareness.**    A final individual-level characteristic of team members refers to a member's social awareness. By social awareness, we are not referring to the same characteristic as we described before in the section on affective sensitivity, or emotional intelligence. Instead, we emphasize the cognitive aspects of a person's capability to determine cause and effect within a social environment. We take this concept from Witkin and Berry's (1975) construct of field dependence as well as Hall's (1976) idea of low versus high context cultures. Field dependence/independence is associated with cultural variation and Witkin and Berry (1975) identified four antecedent factors of it. First, ecological adaptation, or the characteristic relationship between man and nature. They classified societies into hunters and gatherers versus agriculturists and pastoralists (Berry, 1971). According to Berry, the ecological demands enforce members of a society to develop certain perceptual abilities. For example, hunters need to locate food and to return safely to their homes and they need to separate the stimuli from the environment and so they develop the field-independence style. Second is the social pressure pertaining to social conformity and sociocultural stratification. In tight societies intense pressure is put on the individual to conform. In loose societies there are few such pressures, allowing self-control to operate. Field independent societies can be differentiated from field dependent ones on the basis of family structure (nuclear versus extended respectively); social structure (egalitarian versus hierarchical-stratified); and social relation patterns (reserved-fragmented versus mutual dependence-integrate). It is suggested that agriculturalists, who cultivate the land and become permanent residents, develop tight social relationships compared to hunters. They live in extended families and experience a high level of interdependence.

Third, parent–child relationships affect the development of a certain cognitive style. This style reflects a demand for adherence to parental authority, encouragement of reliance on others, restriction of exploration, and lacks of emphasis on achievement constraint the development of psychological differentiation. This style of child rearing is known as "status oriented, or person-oriented. However, the "Growth nurturing style" enhances self-reliance, supportive interaction, positive reinforcement of curiosity, achievement striving, and more verbal articulation which corresponds with the development of field independence functioning. Finally, biological factors seem to affect the cognitive style. Research evidence demonstrates that androgen, which promotes the development of secondary male sex characteristics, is associated with field independent behavior, whereas estrogen, which promotes the development of secondary sex characteristics in the female, is associated with field-dependent functioning. Field-dependent and field-independent persons have different personality characteristics. First, they vary in the level of psychological differentiation that differentiates between inner and outer. Field-dependent persons are more likely to use the field as a referent for behavior, whereas field-independent persons perceive their identity as separate. A sense of separate identity entails the existence of stable internal frames of references for self-definition and for viewing, interpreting, and reacting to the world. Continuous use of external frames of references for the definition of one's feelings, attitudes and needs, suggests a less articulated sense of separate identity.

Another aspect of field-dependent–independent persons is the extent of reliance upon external social referent. Field-dependent persons rely more on external social referent than field- independent persons. This is particular true in ambiguous situations where they use information from others to resolve ambiguity. Field-independent people are less likely to be engaged in information seeking behavior than are field-dependent people. Again, this is in particular true in ambiguous situations, where field-dependent people use information from others to resolve ambiguity.

Finally, people who are field-dependent must behave in a socially facilitative fashion, and they have to be attentive to social cues in order to insure direct access to others. They are more likely to have an interpersonal orientation than field independent people are. Field-dependents enjoy being with others, are sociable, affiliative oriented, socially outgoing, interested in people, they seek relations with others, want to help others, have a concern for people, and show interest in social occupations. In contrast, field-independent people are somewhat cool and removed from others, concerned with ideas and principles rather than with people, task oriented and individualistic, and are interested in technical occupations (Witkin & Goodenough, 1976).

Field independence is a developmental variable capturing various patterns of thought and behavior. It varies along a dimension with the most global or diffused pattern at one end to the most articulated or differentiated at the other end. A person at the global end of the continuum is likely to be characterized as intellectually intuitive, perceptually holistic, emotionally expressive, socially dependent and other directed (Gruenfeld & MacEachron, 1975). A person at the articulated end is likely to be characterized as intellectually analytical and systematic, perceptually discriminating, emotionally self-controlled, socially independent, and self-reliant. Gruenfeld and MacEachron (1975) argued that positive relationships exist between certain growth nurturing style of child-rearing, socioeconomic class, and field articulation. They generalized from the individual to the society level, and hypothesized that the level of field articulation performance measures among managers from a particular country will correlate with indices of that country's economic development.

As discussed in chapter 2, one of the few studies to use concepts of field independence and dependence was conducted in recent work by Gibson (1995, 1999, 2000a). She investigated several phenomenon associated with group-efficacy in a field setting using nursing teams represented matched hospitals located in two contrasting cultures (the United States and Indonesia) over an eight-week period. This design allowed for an applied investigation of the relationship between group-efficacy and variables such as identification (a Characteristic of Members), group reputation (a Characteristic of the Group), task interdependence (a Characteristic of the Task), individualism–collectivism and field independence (both Characteristics of the Context) and team performance. She hypothesized that the level of field independence with a team would moderate the relationship of team efficacy to performance such that the efficacy-performance would be positive for field dependent teams and unrelated for field independent teams. However, she did not find a significant moderating influence of field independence in the relation of team efficacy to team performance as hypothesized.

Field dependence-independence seems to be associated with a cultural dimension of high versus low context dependence (Erez & Earley, 1993; Gibson, 1999, 2000a; Hall, 1976). Members of high-context cultures tend to use an affective-intuitive style, resembling the style used in poetry. They use associative communication that focuses on the experience of the communicator with the particular entity that is being communicated (Gudykunst & Kim, 1984; Ting-Toomey, 1985). This distinction is similar to the one between field dependent and field independent persons. Field dependent persons, compared to field independent persons, are more likely to pay attention to the source of messages than to the message itself, and they are more affected by the social appeal of the source of information (Larson, 1978). This dimension distinguishes between context-dependent communication and abstract communication. Cultures of the former group use context to ascribe meaning to messages, whereas noncontext cultures use abstract concepts to convey their messages. A high-context message is one in which "most of the information is either in the physical context or internalized in the person, while very little is in the coded explicit transmitted part of the message" (Hall, 1976). A low-context message is one in which "the mass of information is vested in the explicit code" (Hall, 1976).

High and low-context cultures influence the style of communication in conflict resolution. Individuals in low-context cultures are better able to separate the conflict issue from the person involved in the conflict than individuals in high conflict cultures (Ting-Toomey, 1985). In high context cultures to disagree openly or confront someone in public is a severe blow and an extreme insult, causing both sides to "lose face," in particular in the case of superior-subordinate communication. Individuals in high-context cultures perceive the conflict situation as expressive oriented. For them, the conflict issue and the conflict person are the same, hardly separable from each other. Therefore, in high-context cultures individuals are supposed to engage in a normative process of reciprocal awareness of one another. Within an MNT, differences in awareness of context will have an important impact on intra-team communication. Members from a high context background will tend to use fewer overt and obvious cues for signaling intent, status, etc. to fellow team members. Their low context colleagues may become frustrated with what they perceive to be a "wishy-washy" or ambivalent style of communicating.

The rules for handling a conflict differ across the dimension of high-low context. In high context cultures there are prescribed ways of handling the conflict, and once the cultural scripts are mastered, a relatively low degree of uncertainty and risk prevails. A potential for conflict is relatively higher between strangers in low-context cultures than in high-context cultures because in the latter case it is more likely that individual normative expectations of acceptable behavior are violated. On the other hand, interaction that deviates from cultural normative expectations is more easily identified in a normative homogenous system than in a normative heterogeneous system.

Individuals in high and low context cultures learn different attitudes toward conflict resolution. In low context cultures, characterized by action orientation, the conflict players are likely to assume a direct confrontation. In high-context cultures, they try to avoid direct confrontation, by employing a calculated degree of vagueness, typically when tension and anxiety mount. Low and high context cultures differ in their style of argument. For example, people in the United States (low context culture) for example, typically engage in the factual-inductive style of argument. People in Russia (moderate context culture) use the axiomatic-deductive style of logic; people in Arab cultures (high context culture) primarily engage in the affective–intuitive style of emotional appeal (Glenn, Witmeyer, & Stevenson, 1977). A factual-inductive style is based on facts and moves inductively toward conclusions whereas an axiomatic-deductive style proceeds from the general to the particular.

Differences between high and low context cultures affect communication between superiors and subordinates. This approach can be seen in superior-subordinate relationships. In low-context cultures, superiors directly criticize a subordinate for a poor quality of work. In a high-context culture superiors are very careful not to hurt the feelings of their subordinates when they have to criticize their work. For example, a North American supervisor (low context culture) is likely to say the following: "I cannot accept this proposal as submitted. You should come up with some better ideas" (Miyahara, 1984). A Japanese supervisor (high context culture) would say: "While I have the highest regard for your abilities, I would not be completely honest if I did not express my disappointment at this proposal. I must ask that you reflect further on the proposal you have submitted to me" (Miyahara, 1984). In conflict situations, members of low-context cultures handle conflicts by using the factual-inductive style or axiomatic-deductive style more than members of high-context culture use. Low context cultures tend to avoid direct confrontation. For example, an executive in China (high context culture) is advised to solve a conflict between two subordinates by meeting separately with the two of them, whereas in the United States the supervisor is advised to meet jointly with the two sides of the conflict (Bond, Wan, & Leung, 1985; Smith & Bond, 1994; Weldon & Jehn, 1995). Similar results were found in comparisons between conflict resolution of Mexicans (high context culture) and Anglo-Americans (low context culture) (Kagan, Knight, & Martinez-Romero, 1982). Mexican managers are most comfortable meeting with subordinates in private and avoiding direct contradiction and confrontation. Although common wisdom in managerial practice suggests for that Americans should avoid confronting subordinates in public, it is a frequent occurrence. It reflects a direct style that is preferred by Americans.

Thus, the concepts of high versus low context and field dependence reflects a MNT member's awareness of others with whom he works. It is this additional feature of a member that is critical for understanding the interpersonal dynamics that occur for an MNT as it comes together and develops. Individuals within a team who are high in field-dependence (high context) are constantly scanning the social setting for cues concerning what is going on in the team. Even rather subtle and indirect ones may be focused on as significant and important. For example, a team member (high field-dependence) may observe another team member consistently stop conversation as she encounters a third team member. From this, the field-dependent concludes that the status characteristics of the third member constitute seniority and the second member is falling quiet as a signal of respect. However, the field dependent may conclude that falling quiet is the second member's signal that he does not like the third person and does not wish to interact with her. Ironically, it may not be either of these inferences. The quiet may simply reflect a protocol of politeness to someone as they enter the room. If field- *independent* members are unaware of this subtle information-seeking, they may inadvertently miscommunicate with fellow members.

The next feature, trust and expectations of others reflect a degree of predictability of another person's actions when given a chance for opportunism. Trust has also been thought of as confidence in the character, integrity, strength and abilities of another person. In the social psychology literature, the construct of trust has been defined in a number of ways. Two general categorizations of trust are people's motivation versus credibility as well as generalized versus situational trust. Motivation-based trust reflects the expressed confidence that one party has in another's motives and intentions. This reflects the belief that other parties are motivated for cooperation and an unselfish orientation (Mellinger, 1956) and that the other person(s) will fulfill their obligations (Schurr & Ozanne, 1985). Deutsch (1973) focused a great deal on the motives and expectations of others in describing various forms of interdependence and cooperation. He suggested that these expectations lead an actor to interacting with others for whom these expectations are not met. Credibility-based trust reflects the informational uncertainty of situations and the sincerity of another's words and deeds. For example, Rotter (1971) defined interpersonal trust as an expectancy that the verbal and written commitments of one person could be relied upon. In Rotter's usage, trust does not require the actions or words of one person to be positive whereas others have this as part of their definition (e.g., Brewer & Kramer, 1985).

A key feature of trust concerns the expectations that one has concerning the actions of others. Trust reflects the expectation that another person will act on his or her behalf even if the opportunity for defection/opportunism presents itself. Thus, a critical component of a multinational team is that individuals within a team have a common set of expectations concerning the potential actions of fellow group members. Further, these expectations are such that team members "expect," or anticipate, that fellow group members will act on their and the group's behalf even if such actions violate self interest.

Expectations are essential to understand social interaction and structure. In a more formal sense, these expectations refer to the various roles that we play within an organization or other social system. As Katz and Kahn (1978) argue, "To the extent that choice of concepts can contribute to so complex a synthesis, the concept of role is singularly promising. It is the summation of the requirements with which the system confronts the individual member; it is the example most frequently given when one asks for a concept uniquely social-psychological and, for a concept in the vocabulary of a young science, it has a long history." The role episode as described by Katz and Kahn (1978) provides an interesting and useful starting point for discussing roles and a social actor. Role episode consists of two actors, in its simplest form, a role sender and a role receiver. A role sender conveys to the focal, or target, person a particular set of expectations concerning a role to be enacted upon which the recipient chooses to ignore or attend to various aspects of the role conveyed. It is through the focal person's role behavior that a role sender can interpret the nature of what was received, processed, and chosen to be acted on although the specific actions or events operating can be highly ambiguous. Additionally, there are exogenous (to this dyad) influences which may change the nature of roles sent, received, and acted on by the participants. Katz and Kahn pose three such additional influences, interpersonal factors, attributes of the person, and organizational factors.

A particular difficulty for a MNT member who is in an ambiguous role environment is that face-saving behaviors are often misdirected based on erroneous assumptions of who constitutes the role set, or set of expected behaviors. The team's leader tells a team member, new to a MNT, that it is important that everyone work together. What "important" means is often poorly defined, and the result are often an over- or underemphasis on working interdependently to the detriment of individual initiative.

Thus far, we have not made clear the contribution of roles and expectations to a member's actions in a team. Expectations are transmitted to a member concerning how she should act and behave based on general rules of culture, organization-specific demands, and individual-differences of other members in the role set. These expectations are particularly salient under several conditions. For instance, new members are highly susceptible to the demands imposed from the external role set because of the general ambiguity that they face and their inherent desire to reduce this ambiguity (Van Maanen & Schein, 1977). If there is a large status differential within a given role set and the culture is one which strongly emphasizes subordination to powerful others, a high power distance culture in Hofstede's (1980a) terms, then external role demands will have a strong influence (Mulder, 1977). External role demands will have a strong influence if the work environment is highly turbulent and unpredictable as well. An employee may adopt the reference point of other role incumbents to reduce uncertainty.

The influence of expectations on a team member comes from within the person himself as well. To complicate matters further, the line between external and internal demands can be quite fuzzy at times. Take an employee facing the demands of bribing foreign officials. What if the "external" demand is imposed by someone who has referent power (French & Raven, 1959) or charismatic authority (House et al., 1991; Weber, 1947) over the employee? It is conceivable that the external demand will be interpreted by the employee as an internal demand assuming that he internalizes the act as having legitimacy given its source.

There is an additional interactive relationship of a team member through the roles he enacts as we mentioned at the beginning of this chapter. To a certain extent, the members who interact with one another construct the role set that exists. A role set is an enacted and emergent property of a social system. It is only through the sense making of individuals within the social system do various roles emerge. Furthermore, these roles can be highly transient as a function of interactions among role incumbents as well as influences from outside of the role set. Role incumbents are shaped by the inconsistencies in a role set every bit as much as by the rational consistencies. Argyle, Henderson, Bond, Iizuka, and Contarello (1986) found that emotional restraint is highly valued in Chinese societies and there are numerous rules for emotional control that are strongly endorsed. Evidence shows that Chinese people report feeling emotions less intensely and for a shorter duration than other cultural groups (Wallbott & Scherer, 1986). Thus, a multinational team having Chinese and Americans, as an example, may have numerous difficulties with regard to standards for emotional display. The degree of impulsivity and affective display characteristic of the Americans will likely violate rules for display of the Chinese. Thus, social expectations play a significant role in the integration of a multinational team.

## CONCEPTUAL FRAMEWORK—GROUP LEVEL ELEMENTS

We use five general elements of a group as we describe MNT functioning. These elements are competition within the group, factions and fractionation, hybrid culture and shared meaning, and common versus differentiated goals (priorities).

*Intragroup Competition.* The first characteristic, competition and cooperation within a team reflect a number of facets. Deutsch (1961, 1973) is one of the central figures who discussed the nature of competition within a group context. According to Deutsch, one can think of groups as focusing on a degree of competition when resources are perceived as scarce and nonrenewable and members' goals are nonoverlapping. Such a form of interdependence creates a sense of competition among team members and it interferes with normal team functioning. Deutsch (1973) use the terms promotive versus contrient interdependence to capture the essence of cooperation and competition in his usage. By a promotive interdependence, he said, "... *promotive interdependence* has been used to characterize all goal linkages in which there is a positive correlation between the attainments of the linked participants. The degree of promotive interdependence refers to the amount of positive correlation; it can vary in value from 0 to +1." (pp. 20–21)

In contrast, Deutsch defined competition in terms of contrient interdependence, "Contrient interdependence is the condition in which participants are so linked together that there is a negative correlation between their goal attainments. The degree of contrient interdependence refers to the amount of negative correlation; it can vary in value from 0 to –1. In the limiting case of pure competition, a participant can attain his goal if, and only if, the others with whom he is linked cannot attain their goals." (pp. 20–21)

Competition is not inevitably harmful to a group but, if left unattended, it can create problems for the group that are difficult to resolve. Deutsch used three social psychological phenomena in order to understand the possible impact of competition on intra-team processes. First, the concept of substitutability suggests that one party will repeat and imitate the actions of another if they are perceived to heighten goal attainment for the imitating party. From a team viewpoint, this implies that a team will be less efficient under conditions of intrateam competition. Second, positive cathexis refers to the development of positive attitudes among team members. Under conditions of competition, negative attitudes are likely to arise as a competing party approaches goal attainment since this implies a lack of success for the other party(ies). Finally, Deutsch used the concept of inducibility, or the readiness to be influenced by another person. In a cooperative relationship, we would expect team members to be responsive to the needs of others and act accordingly. That is, if one person's actions interfere with another person's goal attainment, then he or she will change behavior. Under conditions of competition, we would expect the opposite pattern to occur. A cooperative orientation permits more substitutability and, therefore, a division of responsibilities within the team that would not occur under a competitive focus. This means a more productive and efficient use of human resources within the team. In addition, the positive cathexis induced through cooperation fosters more mutual trust and openness of communication as well as provides a stable basis for continuing cooperation even if the team is confronted with setbacks. More importantly, this cathexis stimulates a sense of commonality and similarity across team members, and this enhances empathy and social identity. Communication across members is enhanced and individuals are more likely to engage in extrarole behavior.

Tjosvold and his colleagues (e.g., Tjosvold, 1973, 1983; Tjosvold & Huston, 1978) conducted a series of studies using a framework of face and emphasized that people act in order to project a positive image in a variety of social settings (Deutsch, 1961, 1973; Goffman, 1998). Tjosvold suggests that people act on face in order to disconfirm views suggesting that the person is weak or incompetent through a variety of strategies including aggression towards the accuser, threats, control strategies, and claims of superiority among others. From this literature, individuals have been found to pursue strategies that reverse a disconfirmation (threat to face, or negotiator competency) even if such strategies result in reduced payoffs. In fact, the effect of such threats to face often result in intransigence such that the offended party will refuse further bargaining (Tjosvold, 1974).

Likelihood of cooperation is not merely a characteristic of the individual for that matter. Mead (1967) demonstrated in her classic study of primitive peoples that societal values maybe more or less oriented toward cooperation. This is one of the tenets of individualism–collectivism (Earley & Gibson, 1998; Triandis, 1995). The primary characteristics of individualism and collectivism include: relation of personal to collective interests and goals, family structure, individual discretion for action, locus of decision-making, emotional dependence on the collective, and social identity based in the social group. Additionally, Triandis (1989) suggests that other important dimensions of individualism and collectivism include: membership in a limited number of in-groups, sharing of resources, interdependency of relations among group members, and feelings of involvement of one another's lives (Hui & Triandis, 1985; Triandis, 1989, 1994). Collectivists are quite concerned by the implications of their actions on their in-groups and they feel interdependent on in-group members. They also emphasize the integrity and harmony of the in-groups (Hui & Triandis, 1985) over self-interests. The ingroup influences a wide range of the collectivist's social behaviors and he or she responds more fully to such guidance than do individualists. In addition, collectivists are thought to view out-group members with suspicion and distrust (Triandis, Bontempo, Vilareal, Masaaki, & Lucca, 1988). Collectivists will subordinate their personal interests to the goals of their collective, or in-group, and in-group membership is stable even when the in-group places high demands on the individual (Triandis, 1990). An individual belongs to only a few in-groups and behavior within the group emphasizes goal attainment, cooperation, group welfare, and in-group harmony.

Perhaps the most important aspect of individualists and collectivists concerns their goals and interests relative to the goals and interests of their collective. Individualists give priority to self-interests over those of their collective whereas collectivists do not distinguish between them (Earley & Gibson, 1998). To the collectivist, a collective goal *is* the individual's goal, and if self and collective interests do differ, he or she will subordinate personal interests for those of the collective. This, of course, is parallel to Deutsch's concept of promotive interdependence in a team context. However, strong collectivism can potentially produce dysfunctional results if an external threat exists. Triandis (1994) gives the example of an in-group that is so concerned with stopping an out-group from being successful that they allow themselves to come to harm. That is, the desire to make certain that outsiders are unsuccessful creates a myopia that leads to unfortunate and negative consequences for the in-group. This is, perhaps, one of the reasons that Earley and Mosakowski (2000) reported moderately heterogeneous international teams (having a few, but easily identified, subgroups) as being problematic relative to homogeneous or highly heterogeneous ones.

### Factions and Fractionation.

A second feature is the extent of fractionation experienced within the team. The contrient form of interdependence described by Deutsch (1973) provides fertile ground for which to observe fractionation. In MNTs a primary concern is that conflict between members of different cultural backgrounds will create disunity within the team. These subgroups often view one another as in competition and so the various dysfunctional effects described by Deutsch operate (low substitutability, negative cathexis, and low inducibility). The concept of cathexis and its impact on the development of a common identity within a team is particularly critical. This is indirectly supported by Jehn's (1995) research on task and interpersonal forms of conflict in teams. Jehn found that conflict that was task related was beneficial to team performance whereas interpersonal conflict was detrimental. Deutsch (1973) discusses such a "paradox" of competition by stating,

... competitive conflict, with its resulting losses to one or both of the parties involved, may be a necessary precondition to motivate the parties to en-

gage in a cooperative process. An affluent, complacent authority or majority may be unresponsive to a dissatisfied subordinate minority until the
threats and losses of a competitive conflict motivate it to seek a cooperative solution. (p. 31)

Ravlin et al. (2000) developed a framework for understanding the nature of conflict within a MNT based on the influences of belief systems regarding values and status, and the role that acceptance of these beliefs
play in processes generating latent and manifest conflict within the group.
They developed their conceptualization relying on a variety of theoretical
perspectives including theories of social information processing, social
identity, value congruence, status characteristics, and legitimacy.

An alternative to fractionation is the creation of a unified and cohesive
team (Casmir, 1992; Earley & Mosakowski, 2000). We adopted Earley and
Mosakowski's term of "hybrid" culture to reflect a tendency for a team to develop, share, and enact after mutual interactions. The shared nature of
these aspects of a team are not completely and perfectly overlapping, just as
cultural values and norms are not shared perfectly within any social system.

***Hybrid Culture and Shared Meaning.*** Effective groups often display a shared conception of their expectations and rules (Bettenhausen,
1991; Hackman, 1990). A "team mental model" (Klimoski & Mohammed,
1994) is a shared psychological representation of a team's environment
constructed to permit sense making and guide appropriate group action
(Elron et al., 1998). When team members perceive shared understandings
with other members, the positive affect and propensity to trust generated
by such a discovery fuels performance improvement (Klimoski & Mohammed, 1994) and bolsters group efficacy (Bandura, 1997).

How might a unified team culture emerge? The answer depends on the
basic motive for creating commonality within a group. We draw from several conceptual frameworks to describe this motive. Tajfel and Turner proposed complementary models of group process—Social Identity Theory
(Tajfel, 1982) and Self-Categorization Theory (Turner, 1985, 1987). These
theories assume individuals form group memberships based on relative
similarity to others and individuals seek to distinguish their ingroup from
other groups by emphasizing differences from outsiders and derogating
out-group members. Sociologist Everett Hughes (1971) argued individuals
establish social roles relative to others based on "primary and auxiliary status-determining" traits. Hughes (1971) suggested people determine their
relative status using hierarchically ordered primary trait categorizations.
People form early group attachments based on perceived similarities of
personal characteristics. Once formed, these similarities contrast with the
perceived dissimilarity of outsiders to enhance self-construal and worth
(Brewer, 1993; Markus & Kitayama, 1991) and strengthen group entitativity

(Campbell, 1958; Lickel et al., 1998). Which characteristic members as primary traits perceive depends upon their societal, cultural, and personal background. The likelihood of a unified team culture emerging varies as a function of group composition. In a highly heterogeneous team, few common bases for subgroup formation, self-categorization, and social identity exist. Members will attempt to create and establish a new shared understanding of team member status, team processes, role expectations, communication methods, and so on.

Hybrid culture depends upon group understanding emerging from team member interaction. Unlike a homogeneous or moderately heterogeneous team, a highly heterogeneous team cannot easily fall back on preexisting identity or subgroup identities because few commonalties exist. Perhaps more important, what constitutes primary traits is not shared. Thus, when external demands confront a highly heterogeneous team, it must form a hybrid team culture to move forward, although such formation may require significant time and effort (Lau & Murnighan, 1998).

**Shared Goals and Priorities.** A final aspect of MNTs concerns the nature of shared goals and priorities. This idea is related to our earlier discussion of Deutsch's notion of competition in as much as shared goals is often viewed as a central feature of cooperation (Deutsch, 1973). A great deal of research has focused on the impact of shared goals and common priorities on the success of teams (e.g., Coch & French, 1948; Goodman et al., 1986; Latham, Erez, & Locke, 1988; Steiner, 1972). Why do shared goals have such a pronounced effect on team functioning? This can be addressed in two different ways based on research from the field of goal setting (Locke & Latham, 1990) and group efficacy (Bandura, 1997).

The first impact of shared goals for a team is derived from the development of the goals themselves and the impact such development has on members' commitment to the goal. A common, but controversial, method of establishing a team goal is through participative decision-making (Erez, Earley, & Hulin, 1985; Latham, Erez, & Locke, 1988; Locke & Latham, 1990; Locke & Schweiger, 1979). Participation in goal-setting takes place at the beginning of the evaluation process, and as such, it is similar to the case of self-set goals, where goal-setting and commitment are highly related. Similar to self-set goals, participation allows a person to have more control over decisions concerning his/her own well being. A goal is more likely to be accepted when it is perceived to be under a person's control than when it is perceived as externally imposed.

Participation in goal setting enables the participants to have control over the decision, and therefore, it enhances the level of goal-commitment. The level of control could vary along four stages of the evaluation process: setting goals, monitoring, evaluating, and attaining outcomes. For example, goals could be set externally, the process of monitoring and evaluation is self-controlled, and the last stage of reinforcing goal attainment is, again, externally controlled. The highest level of control is experienced when a person has self-control over all four stages (Erez & Kanfer, 1983). The process of evaluating the significance of knowledge about what is happening with our personal well being generates emotions. "Only the recognition that we have something to gain or to loose, that is, that the outcome of a transaction is relevant to goals and well-being, generates an emotion (Lazarus, 1991). Thus, the process of goal appraisal is necessary not only for activating a response toward goal attainment but also for generating emotions.

The second influence of the development of shared goals is through a cognitive influence on members within a team. In a series of studies, Erez and Earley (e.g., Earley, 1985; Earley, 1987; Erez & Arad, 1986; Erez et al., 1985) demonstrated that participation in the goal-setting process led to higher cognitive understanding of task and work requirements by those participating. Thus, the creation of shared goals within a team will provide increased task knowledge and insights that will provide performance benefits. Improved performance will, in turn, enhance team member efficacy that will provide confidence for future mastery in a positive feedback loop.

However, collective efforts do not always facilitate team performance. In a series of studies of the "social loafing" phenomena Latanè et al. (1979) examined the tendency of an individual participating in a group performance activity to withhold effort if her personal contribution is anonymous. With accountability, however, the incentive for an individual to loaf is removed. Other work suggests that the impetus to withhold effort can be influenced by a variety of characteristics including cultural factors (Earley, 1989, 1993), anonymity (Harkins & Petty, 1983), and cognitive demand (Weldon & Gargano, 1988). Studies demonstrate that members sharing a common group goal are less prone to loafing (Harkins & Petty, 1983). This goal can be focused on specific work (Weldon & Gargano, 1988) or generalized social relationships derived from cultural commonality (Earley, 1993).

The importance of shared goals for a MNT comes through a number of mechanisms. First, shared goals provide a motivational basis for avoiding social loafing through the enhancement of a common identity. Having a shared goal implies that each team member is responsible for its accomplishment much in the same way that our NASA janitor felt personally responsible for putting a man on the moon. Second, shared goals can bolster team efficacy as we discussed. Goals provide a cognitive anchor for an individual's efficacy expectations (Earley & Erez, 1991). In the potential ambiguity facing a member from a MNT, these anchors can be important to keep team members focusing on team performance. Third, a team's focus and mission is clarified with a strongly held set of goals. Team goals provide direction as well as being motivational. Further, team goals can cue team members concerning strategy development (Locke & Latham,

1990). Fourth, the act of creating shared goals is itself motivating and it enhances individual team member attachment to the team and its objectives (Bandura, 1997). This occurs through a public and personal commitment process. Finally, shared goals can become a symbolic rallying cry for a MNT. For example, automobile manufacturer BMW instilled a rallying cry of "Beat Benz" throughout their company as a means of motivating their employees to take on the dominant position of Daimler-Benz (now Daimler-Chrysler). These symbols have tremendous importance and significance to the team member identification process.

## SUMMARY

The focus of this chapter was the identification and discussion of the individual- and group-level elements of our model. We discussed a number of individual elements: trust and expectations, respect and moral character, affective sensitivity, confidence and efficacy, and social awareness. The group level elements included: competition, fractionation (disunity), hybrid culture, shared meaning and understanding, and common versus differentiated goals (priorities).

The significance of the individual elements is observed in a multinational team in a variety of ways. Trust and role expectations of others provide an impetus for interacting with one another in good faith. This willingness to work in good faith is further strengthened by the moral character of team members. If we respect and trust one another, we are more likely to persevere in the face of adversity; such difficulties are likely to arise when people from many cultural backgrounds come together on a common team. Affective sensitivity or emotional intelligence operates in several different ways in the team. Given the potential for confusion that exists as people from different cultural backgrounds interact, affective awareness provides people with an alternative means for understanding how and why others react as they do. In the multinational team, this additional information is critical since the standard cues that a person relies on in a domestic context may be lacking. We discussed the importance of individual and team-level confidence or efficacy in understanding team dynamics. Personal efficacy provides a team member with sufficient motivation to persevere and to retry during initial difficulties of team performance. Further, confidence has an interactive effect with affective sensitivity and emotional intelligence because it has a spillover, or contamination, influence. That is, one person's confidence tends to influence other team members and bolster their confidence. Collective efficacy was presented as a feature capturing both individual and group-level elements. It provides a team with a sense of motivation and direction but it may be problematic from a MNT perspective. In the MNT, collective efficacy relies on the formation of a hybrid culture in order for the team to have sufficient shared knowledge to make it viable. Finally, we turned our discussion to a social awareness referred to as field-independence/dependence, or high versus low context cultures. Individuals who are field-dependent or from a high context culture are acutely aware of the various social cues displayed by others in their team. Further, these individuals are likely to provide relatively subtle cues of their own since they assume others are similarly able to pick up on these cues.

It is important to note that the individual elements do not exist in isolation of one another. A given individual could never be described by a single element (e.g., we would rarely refer to a person simply as "untrusting"). Rather, each individual team member can be characterized by a constellation or configuration of attributes, that together with their cultural background, status markers, and demographic characteristics make up a unified whole being. Furthermore, the specific attributes or characteristics that will be salient for a given member vary across members, situations, and over time (e.g., although I may not think of a team member as simply "untrustworthy," that may be the first attribute that comes to my mind about that person in a given situation). The constellation of individual elements that may exist in a hypothetical MNT is depicted in Fig. 4.1. The most

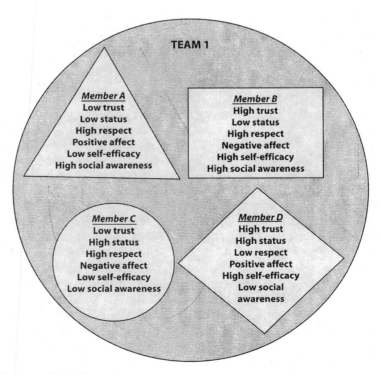

FIG. 4.1.   Individual Elements.

salient individual element for each member in this hypothetical context and point in time is highlighted. A key observation here is that even without considering the different cultural backgrounds and demographic characteristics of each team member in an MNT, the configuration of individual elements in the team is complex.

The group level elements began with a discussion of competition and cooperation. We described how promotive forms of interdependence are important for creating a cooperative environment for the team. Next, we discussed the importance of fractionation or disunity to a team's functioning. We used Deutsch's (1973) concept of contrient interdependence to discuss fractionation. We argued that if teams are composed of members of multiple cultures, a primary concern is that conflict between members of different cultural backgrounds will create disunity within the ranks. These subgroups may view one another as in competition and this has negative performance consequences. Third, we discussed the notion of a hybrid culture based on work of Earley and Mosakowski (2000). A hybrid culture refers to a newly developed set of expectations, norms, and rules for a team that provides a mechanism of commitment and attachment. Finally, we discussed how shared goals might positively impact team dynamics. Shared goals impact a team by increasing common knowledge and insights, reducing free-riding effects, and enhancing individual members' motivation.

Just as we argued for a configurational approach to understanding the interplay of the individual elements, we also advocate a configurational understanding of the group elements (see Fig. 4.2). Any given MNT can be characterized by all of the group elements at any given point in time. Although a particular group element may be more salient than another for describing that MNT at a given time, viewing the MNT based only on that group element is too simplistic. Figure 4.2 contrasts three MNTs with varying configurations of group level elements. The point here is that these elements may work in concert, or at cross purposes in comprising an MNT's identity. To fully understand any MNT, we must consider all the elements simultaneously.

In the next chapter, we turn our attention to the various linking processes that can be used to describe how individual and group-level elements relate to one another in a team context. We examine such processes as role adoption and adaptation, social construction, and structuration with the purpose of understanding the nature of team member sense-making in a multinational team.

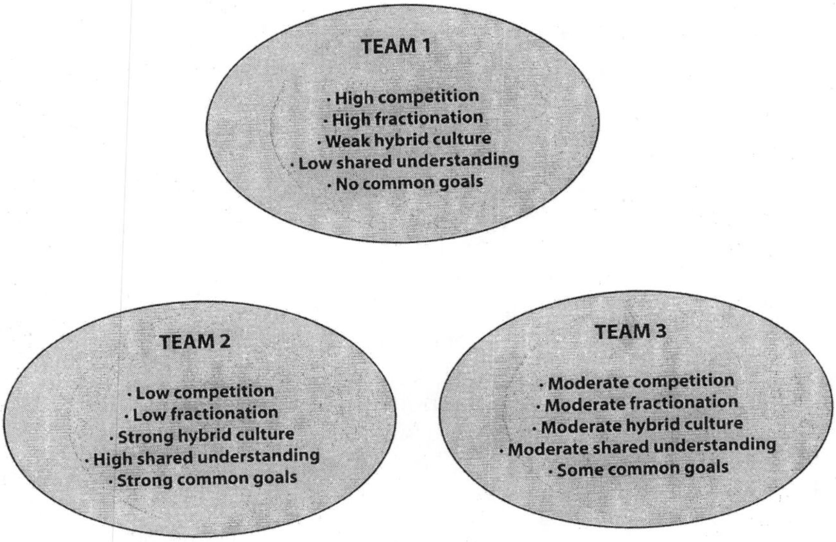


FIG. 4.2. Group Elements.

# 5 Linking Processes

The focus of this chapter is to describe the various processes that link the micro- and macrolevel features that we discussed in chapters 3 and 4. One of the most unique aspects of a multinational team, and what differentiates it fundamentally from other types of teams, is that many of the social cues and meanings are lacking, conflicting, or, at best, partially shared among team members. As we discussed early in our book, a multinational team differs from a domestic one in that the general meaning of action, even language used, is inconsistent. In a domestic team, there are still likely differences in the perceptions and values of team members, but a common cultural background provides at least some basis for interaction. In a multinational team, this common basis for action may be entirely lacking, or assumptions may be in direct conflict with one another. How then, do these micro- and macrofeatures of the social environment influence the nature of the team? To address this question, we examine a number of linking processes that are part of the multinational team environment.

By a linking process, we are referring to the change over time of team members' actions and a team's social functioning as a result of some influence. For example, an important microlevel feature of a multinational team is each member's personal identity in particular social roles. We have asserted that this identity is influenced by the macrolevel social environment of the work organization. It is the process of identity adoption and adaptation that we describe in this chapter that provides us with a way of predicting how macrolevel features of the work organization influence the emergent nature of a team member's personal identity adopted within the team. This identity is a complex amalgam of multiple role identities that are influenced by the nature of the cues available and social structure (macro-level features) through role-taking processes.

We break these processes into several categories of influence. First, we examine roles that people adopt, the rules that they comply with and internalize, and the formation of status, hierarchy and identity. Second, we discuss the importance of ritual and habit formation, and structuration as they determine team member interaction and reaction. Third, we describe the development of a social contract and shared history at various stages of a team's life cycle. Table 5.1 summarizes these process and the linkages they bring about in a multinational team.

## ROLE-TAKING, STATUS/HIERARCHY, AND IDENTITY FORMATION

There are general processes that we draw upon as processes that connect social and work roles with structure. Perhaps the most relevant theoretical framework concerning roles, status, and norms developed in an organization is that of institutional theory.

According to institutional theory, organizations are viewed as dependent on an environment that is the product of rational and nonrational impulses and an evolving set of rationalized patterns, models, or cultural schemes. Scott and Meyer (1994) present a useful overview of a prototypic, institutional model consisting of four parts. First, the specific nature of a given organization with its peculiar identity and activity patterns exists as a product of institutional forces. Second, the origins of environmental rationalization reflect macrosociological influences on the nature of organizing. Third, these origins give rise to particular dimensions of a rational-

**TABLE 5.1**
**Key Processes in MNTs and the Features Each Process Links Together**

| Processes | Features Linked by these Processes | | | |
| | Individual Elements | Group Elements | Social Structure | Work Structure |
| --- | --- | --- | --- | --- |
| Role-taking, status/hierarchy and identity formation | • Roles/ identity/ status <br> • Respect/ moral character | • Competition <br> • Fractionation | • Hierarchy <br> • Membership changes | • Task constraints |
| Ritual/habit formation and structuration | • Affect and affective sensitivity <br> • Confidence and efficacy | • Shared understanding <br> • Common goals | • Cooperation/ competition | • Pacing and timing <br> • Supportive organization |
| Enactment of a social contract and development of shared history | • Trust and expectations <br> • Social awareness | • Fractionation <br> • Hybrid culture | • Subgroups and third parties | • Technology <br> • Goal changes <br> • Resource changes |

ized environment such that rules or ideologies describing or prescribing given organizational practices create consistent changes in, and across organizations. Further, these general rules and ideologies give rise to the specific mechanisms that shape organizational functioning. That is, organizations develop and perpetuate policies and rules, ideas and beliefs, myths and rituals in the organizational identities taken on. The identity, structures, and activity patterns of an organization are the result of institutionalized patterns derived from a rationalized environment.

Institutional theory includes a number of additional key features. In traditional institutional theory, there is a high degree of emphasis placed on the importance of norms and values in shaping individuals' behavior and actions in an organization. Organizational actors are influenced by the basic nature of the norms and values endorsed and through socialization these norms and values are instilled in an employee. An updated view of institutional theory has evolved in the literature (Powell & DiMaggio, 1991). According to Powell and DiMaggio (1991), the new "institutionalism" differs from the traditional approach in a number of critical ways. First, in traditional institutional theory, the rational interests and purpose of an organization were viewed as perverted through political and conflict influences arising from individual actors' interests. That is, organizations created informal structures based on powerful cliques and coalitions that formed. These structures were thought to detract from the efficient functioning of the organization. In contrast, the new institutionalism views these emergent informal structures as the heart of formal structure.

Social roles and people's actions are a product of complex, symbolic processes encountered through daily, mundane experiences. Rules and norms for social interaction operate, and people are motivated to support and endorse these expectations as long as clear violations are avoided, or treated apologetically if they are created. People engage one another with an openness and willingness to overlook mistakes made by others, and much of their action becomes scripted, or ritualistic, as these interactions continue. For people to make sense of their social world, they employ tacit models of conversation and interaction through their everyday experiences. Garfinkel (1967) argued that most of the rules governing social actions are implicit and subtle, and so we only become aware of them if they are breached during the course of social interaction.

In his model, Scott and Meyer (1994) argued that institutions are the interactive product of three general components: meaning systems and social system patterns, symbolic elements including constitutive and normative rules, and regulatory practices that enforce these practices. In describing the reciprocal effects of individual actors on emergent institutions, Scott argued that through interpretation and innovation institutional rules and rituals are shaped. Institutions, then, reflect these three general elements. Scott suggests that institutional elements are influenced by, and influence, two other levels of the organization—governance structures and actors. The importance of an individual actor to the nature of institutions is one of cause as well as effect. That is, institutional influences on an organizational member occur through a number of mechanisms including socialization, identity formation, and sanctions. Socialization reflects the most direct means through which organizational members are taught the "practices" and "rules" of an institution.

The importance of an institutional perspective to an MNT is derived from the structures that members bring with them to the team and how these rules and practices evolve in the "new" team. In one sense, a highly diverse membership creates anarchy that provides members with an excuse to begin anew. A lack of consensus in a highly diversified team provides all members with an opportunity to reinvent what they believe are critical features of a team regardless of their cultural backgrounds. In a highly homogeneous team, the existing rules and practices are simply reinforced. The sense making that occurs in a highly diverse MNT provides a fertile ground for establishing new institutional rules for functioning.

Institutional influences may operate on a MNT through another means—legitimacy. Institutions legitimate themselves by imitating, or becoming isomorphic with other successful institutions. This imitation provides legitimacy from an insider's perspective as well as an outsider's viewpoint. In the case of a MNT, a newly formed team can legitimate itself in the eyes of its organization by imitating existing MNTs within the company or by taking on the personae of successful teams outside of the company. This is one of the simplest ways that a MNT can reduce the uncertainty and ambiguity experienced by a highly diverse MNT. Once formed and demonstrated successful, there exists a strong incentive to maintain status quo.

## RITUALS, HABITS, AND STRUCTURATION

As can be seen from the previous section, institutional theory characterizes social interaction and behavior as a product of institutional norms and rules evolving from various influences. Forces of various types create an impetus for demands and patterns of action in organizations that may or may not reflect true efficiencies in an economic sense. These rules and norms influence the behavior of organizational members as they interact with one another. What is important from the ritual game of exchange in any given society is the sense of affirmation that partners derive from one another after successful encounters. These encounters reinforce our sense of self and they clarify our position in a social hierarchy.

**Rituals and Habits.** By ritual and habit, we refer to patterned actions shared by a group of people reflecting systematic beliefs about some entity or process (Rosaldo, 1989). Rituals reflect cultural values and meaning but they do not always reflect great depth and significance. For example, many Spaniards begin their work day by stopping at a café for an espresso and morning chat with fellow workers. This interaction is relatively predicable and reliable but it does not necessarily reflect a high degree of collectivism as a cultural norm. Put more generally, Rosaldo (1989) notes:

> … rituals do not always encapsulate deep cultural wisdom. At times they instead contain the wisdom of Polonius. Although certain rituals both reflect and create ultimate values, others simply bring people together and deliver a set of platitudes that enable them to go on with their lives. Rituals serve as vehicles for processes that occur both before and after the period of their performance. Funeral rituals, for example, do not "contain" all the complex processes of bereavement. Ritual and bereavement should not be collapsed into one another because they neither fully encapsulate nor fully explain one another. Instead, rituals are often but points along a number of longer processual trajectories; hence, my image of ritual as a crossroads where distinct life processes intersect. (p. 20)

To understand rituals we must understand the nature of symbols (Stryker, 1980). The importance of symbols to meaningful relationships is determined by interpreting the interactions among societal members. Thus, a culture is viewed as a pattern of symbolic discourse that needs interpreting and deciphering in order to be fully understood. The researcher is also concerned with determining the dominant themes that specify the linkages among values, attitudes, and action as well as how the specific symbols within a subgroup or community reflect those of the society at large. For example, Harris and Sutton (1986) examined the rituals and ceremonies used in the departure of individuals from their organizations such as a farewell party or testimonial. A striking example that conveys a culture of distrust and conflict is exemplified by the way a southwestern-based electronics company "fires" its employees. The practice is that after returning from lunch the former employee is surprised by a security guard standing by the employee's desk. The guard's function is to ensure that no company property is removed as the person clears out his or her desk. The guard escorts the employee out of the facility and the various security badges and passes are taken away—much like the symbolic breaking of the soldier's sword as he was dishonorably discharged from the cavalry. This symbolic ceremony instills a norm of distrust and reinforces the high price that is paid should an employee become disloyal to the organization.

Looking back at our discussion of institutional theory, a critical aspect of Scott's view is that through enactment, an institution's rituals and habits are shaped and reshaped. Rituals are established but they are not unchangeable. As the social environment changes and evolves, and new members enter the institutional environment, rituals and habits change. To describe these changes, Scott and others draw on Giddens' (1984) view of structuration and work by anthropologists on cultural meaning systems. Through daily actions and activities, the context in which behavior is embedded and interpreted is changed. In this sense, people's desire to regulate their position in a social structure (according to organization-specific, and culture-general, rules and practices) reinforces and changes the organization.

One example of how these changes may manifest themselves is illustrated by the way people seek status in an organization, or what reaffirms "face" (Earley, 1997; Goffman, 1959; Hu, 1944; Ting-Toomey & Cocroft, 1994). In one major European food and personal products company, managers pride themselves on a very open and "friendly" environment. Over the last decade, the increasingly international nature of the business and the number of markets that the company has engaged in throughout South America, Africa, and Asia has led to a schism in views of the company. The Europeans generally emphasize the traditional norm of networking and friendly environment whereas the emerging markets have managers who are much more competitive and confrontational. The cultural norm de-emphasizes direct confrontation and disagreement. However, during the past 5 years, the company has been trying to move its culture to a more competitive and confrontational form with the belief that this will create a more energized and productive environment. However, direct confrontation creates tension that is unaccustomed by many of the Europeans. To deal with the perceived loss of face due to direct confrontation, a ritual approach has evolved with the Europeans such that they address their colleagues from the developing markets as "the debaters" when they see them. If a disagreement arises, a European will quickly say "Of course, this is the way you do things in [country X] but we Europeans do it in this way." Often, they will seek out fellow Europeans to reinforce their position with their confronter. After this, they remind the aggressive party that the company is, after all, one extended family and so disagreements are to be expected. More importantly, these actions have positive consequences that become institutionalized such that managers from other emerging markets have come to expect this diffuse style of verbal fencing so that their European colleagues may maintain status. In this manner, individual actions give rise to collective practices and rituals.

**Structuration.** The second process connecting social and work structure is reflected in Giddens's (1984) notion of structuration. Giddens points out the importance of routine in maintaining social structure and he reflects this in his concept of structuration. Structuration refers to the continual reproduction of social structure by social members as they interact in daily activities. He suggests that people act to control diffuse anxiety such that they develop and maintain routines as they interact socially with a reliance on scripted behavior to reduce anxiety. This general view is consistent with Goffman's work in as much as social order is based on the enactment of these subtle, ritualized forms of interaction. Collins (1988) furthers this idea as he describes the nature of social structure. He suggests that social structure is best thought of as a series of interaction sequences that are based on a scripted style. People invest cultural resources and emotional energies in interactions that support a given hierarchy as a function of cultural and emotional resources. The rules for social interaction, expectations for behavior, and social regulation in a work context are best thought as rules, rituals, and ceremonies emergent from institutional practices.

Implicit in this discussion has been the idea of social enactment. By this, we are referring to the actions of individuals as they engage their work. As people work, they engage in a multitude of work and nonwork behaviors. Many of these actions are enacted as a way of maintaining and enhancing personal position in the social hierarchy. Such actions are referred by various terms including impression management, face saving, posturing, and so on. It is often thought that people socially enact according to their core values, we must be cautious not to assume a direct connection between values and social enactment. Whereas cultural values are shared prescriptions of beliefs within a given social system, it is possible to think of values as somewhat independent of social enactment.

Another aspect of process is pattern of actions. This is probably the least understood aspect of team interaction from an international perspective although its basis in social cognitive psychology is well known. By pattern of actions, we are referring to scripted and schema-based behavior in a given social context (see our discussion in chap. 6 on collective cognition as well as Schank & Abelson, 1977; Wyer & Srull, 1980). Models of social cognition have mainly conceptualized the mechanism through which relevant information is processed, stored and organized into a certain structure. Following this approach the self in a group context can be viewed as a person's mental representation of his own personality formed through both experience and thought (Erez & Earley, 1993). This representation is encoded in memory alongside mental representations of other objects, reflected and imagined, in the physical and social world (Kihlstrom, Cantor, Albright, Chew, Klein, & Niedenthal, 1988). It is a system of self-schemas or generalizations about the self derived from past social experiences. [A schema is hypothesized to have a dual nature of structure and process. As such, the self is both the knower and what is known (Markus & Warf, 1987). The content of self conceptions and identities form the structure, and anchors the self in the social system, whereas self-evaluation deals with the dynamic dimension of the self (Gecas, 1982).]

On the structural level the self as a team member can be viewed as a collection of schemas, prototypes, goals or images that are arranged in a space (Gibson, 1999, 2000b; Sherman, Judd, & Park, 1989). Each schema is a generalization about what the self is, and it contains descriptive information about traits, roles, and behavior, as well as procedural knowledge of rules and procedures for making inferences and evaluation for its own functioning and development (Kihlstrom & Cantor, 1984). Thus, a team member's self-concept is multidimensional consisting of many role identities (Gecas, 1982), and relevant traits and characteristics (Markus & Wurf, 1987).

People differ in the components of their selves and in the relative importance of these components. The various attributes of the self seem to be organized in a hierarchical order. The general self is at the top of the hierarchy, followed by more specific self-attributes (Kihlstrom & Cantor, 1984). The hierarchical structure is also conceived in terms of central and peripheral traits, with the central traits as more substantial for the self (Lau & Murnighan, 1998; Turner, 1987). Individuals are known to be more committed to their central roles because they are more consequential to their conduct of behavior (Stryker, 1980). The amount of information included in the self must be enormous, including information concerning our past, present, and future. However, not all the information is accessible all the time. In information-processing terms, the self represents declarative knowledge (consisting of abstract and concrete factual knowledge) of those attributes and features of which it is aware, at least in principle. The aspects of personality brought to our attention at any particular time are determined by contextual factors (Kihlstrom et al., 1988).

It is in this sense that a pattern of action takes shape within a MNT. Team members carry with them the pattern of action (and interaction) that they have acquired through experience and time in their own cultural frame. These actions cover a wide variety of behaviors and they are those that arise when ambiguity is faced in a new team. For example, some of the frustration faced by team members when they first enter into a new group of diverse national background is that no one quite knows what is appropriate behavior. If one wishes to make a point, does one simply interject? Should a group member make a point after finding out what everyone else's position might be in order to avoid causing others to lose face (Earley, 1997)? How should the group's goals be established (as well as what might those goals be)? Even such basic features as taking turns for presenting one's ideas become problematic in this type of context. In the absence of other information, a team member in an internationally diverse group may well realize that her style may be inconsistent with the styles of other team members.

Thus, our schema for action within a group context may well be relied upon in an ambiguous situation but with potentially disastrous results. In an internationally diverse MBA group that Earley dealt with some time ago, the first meeting of the team was fraught with many problems. At the onset, the lone American member took up the group's pen and began writing on the whiteboard a listing of everyone's responsibilities. Before getting too far with his task, a fellow group member (Austrian) asked him why he thought that he should have this responsibility. The American replied that he thought, "someone needs to get us moving on our group assignment." To this, the Austrian asked why the American thought that he was "that someone." The Austrian suggested that the preferred person to take this role was the member having the most work experience and graduate training. Clearly, this was a clash of patterned action concerning the establishment of group locomotion.

To understand the relationship of the social actor to his social system, sociologists often focus on the relationship between the individual and the system. The relative contribution of each to social consequences is a central debate that has taken place between social system sociologists and social action sociologists. For social system sociologists, social actors are pictured as being very much at the receiving end of the social system. Their existence and nature as social beings, their social behavior and relationships, and their very sense of personal identity as human beings, they are determined by it. Social action is thus entirely the product and derivative of social system (Dawe, 1978, p. 367).

The division of social system versus social action theorists was addressed by Giddens with structuration theory (Butler & Earley, 2001; Giddens, 1991). Giddens was concerned with how social classes perpetuate themselves across time and space despite shifting memberships within social classes across time and qualitative changes in terms of what is meant by upper, middle or lower class. Despite many threats to stability and consistency, Giddens observed that social classes remained recognizable to members and nonmembers alike. How did a new class emerge as existing ones were retained? Giddens argued for a duality of structure whereby individual actors both influence and are influenced by social structures. Social classes exist because human beings create them; if social classes continue to exist and exert influence, then they do so because human beings act to allow them to continue to exist and exert influence. If they change or indeed cease to exist, then they also do so because human beings acted to change them or cause their demise.

Most studies adopting a structuration theory perspective have focused exclusively on this duality of structure. Giddens's discussion of perpetuation (i.e., the replication *and* revision) of social classes illustrates how these two theoretical views might be reconciled. An individual from the lower class behaves differently from one from the upper class because he or she is forced to by the preexisting strictures of the class to which each belongs. He or she could simply not do otherwise. This argument, however, fails to account either for the creation of social structures in the first place, or for changes in classes over time. In contrast, social action sociologists propose that the social system is derivative of social action and interaction, a social world produced by its members, who are thus pictured as active, purposeful, self- and socially creative beings. The language of social action is thus the language of subjective meaning, in terms of which social actors define their lives, purposes, and situations; of the goals and projects they generate on the basis of their subjective meanings (Dawe, 1978, p. 367).

Both informal and formal observation shows that most of the time people do not change their actions. If only a few individuals in a social system change their actions, then changes overall are likely to be very small or slow. Giddens argued that the reason that change usually happens rarely or only very slowly is that change involves the reduction of personal security, a basic human need. The greater the degree of change, the greater the loss of personal security. Thus, most of the time social structures are replicated, rather than revised, over time. Structuration theory, however, is fundamentally about *order*, not *stability* (Butler & Earley, 2001). There are times when significant individual action, simultaneous action by a larger number of individuals, or cumulative action over time results in social structure revision. These actors are more likely to consider incorporating that social structure into their own social system.

Structuration theory examines the nature of the self and the role of reflexivity in developing and maintaining the self-identity of actors. This individual-level process is key to the replication and revision of social structures. Giddens characterized the reflexive monitoring of activity, a cognitive process, as a chronic feature of everyday action involving the conduct of self and others. Actors not only monitor continuously the flow of their activities, they also routinely monitor aspects, social and physical, of the contexts in which they move.

Thus, structuration constitutes a sociological theory of action but not necessarily one of behavior (Butler, 2000). To use Marx's well-known example, bees and humans both build things; bees build hives and humans build, among other things, buildings. The bee builds hives by instinct, and it does not reflect what shape of hive is the most attractive, unique, cheapest, or most likely to receive an award, as humans do. For sociologists behavior is instinctual and action is reflexive (as discussed in Giddens, 1971). Actors know what they are doing and why, and can usually explain their actions at what Giddens terms the discursive level of consciousness. What knowledgeable actors cannot always do, however, is explain their motives for acting at the discursive level (1984). Motives tend to remain at an unconscious level. In between these two levels lies a third: practical consciousness, a vague area of consciousness. This middle level of consciousness is fundamental to structuration. It is the level of consciousness that links the discursive rationalization of unconscious motives to the replication and revision of social structures. Most cognitive activity leading to routine behavior is itself routine processing (e.g., Wyer & Srull, 1989), hence the central role of the practical level of consciousness to the replication of structures. Actors introducing change do so more often than not by activating their discursive level of consciousness, and, in turn, those who experience the change also activate their discursive level of consciousness to make sense of and respond to the change they are experiencing (Barley & Tolbert, 1997). When the members of a social system (i.e., group) become aware of a potential change in social structure (e.g., a new technology or cross-cultural contacts), it becomes less likely that cognitive activity will remain routine, and the revision, rather than the replication, of social structures is more likely to occur.

A number of organization and management scholars have used structuration theory as the lens through which to explore their change-based research questions. Generally, these questions have revolved around the large-scale social phenomena of the type in which Giddens was originally interested (e.g., Hinings, Brown, & Greenwood, 1991; Pettigrew, 1985; Ranson, Hinings, & Greenwood, 1980; Riley, 1983; Sahay & Walsham, 1997; Walgenbach, 1993; Wilmot, 1987). However, a number of interesting examples of group-level phenomena have been addressed.

An example of a change more relevant to us is the introduction of new technology as this stream of research often focuses on the team level. Indeed the largest body of empirical research (e.g., Barley, 1986; DeSanctis & Poole, 1994; Orlikowski, 1992) taking a structuration theory perspective focuses around technological appropriation or change as such changes are comparatively easy to observe and measure. DeSanctis and Poole (1992) studied "the degree to which technology can channel structurational processes" in small groups using Group Decision Support Systems (GDSS) for the first time to agree on budget allocations. As there were no right answers to the group task, change of consensus was used as a proxy for quality. They found three different patterns of appropriation, or adoption of practice. Half the groups used faithful appropriation, the one with the least process loss and the highest quality. In spite of the technology, however, the other half were less efficient in terms of appropriation. These groups acted contrary to the premise of GDSS designers by reinterpreting the role of the support system in their work. Although this study was focused on technological adoption, it is rich with theoretical and methodological insights into the application of structuration theory to micro level processes.

Weisinger and Salipante (1995) compared homogeneous and multicultural subunits in not-for-profit organizations. They use structuration theory to explain how domestic voluntary organizations in the United States create a pluralistic membership by initiating cross-unit interactions where the focus is on the organization's superordinate identity. Both homogeneous and multicultural subunits in their study were comprised of Americans. Membership was differentiated primarily in terms of race in multicultural subgroups. Their work demonstrates how actions in homogeneous groups are revised successfully once individuals are placed in multicultural groups, but it does not address how the move from mono- to multicultural membership takes place.

Maznevski & Chudoba (in press) argue that both culture and technology are important social structure characteristics and use DeSanctis & Poole's (1994) Adaptive Structuration Theory to show how effective outcomes in multinational virtual teams are,

> Within the structure of the technology available, effective interaction incidents match form to function and complexity, which are in turn affected by task and group characteristics. The temporal rhythm is structured by a defining beat of regular, intense face-to-face meetings, followed by less intensive, shorter interaction incidents using various media. [The authors] speculated that the length of time required between the face-to-face meetings depends on the level of interdependence required by the task and the degree of shared view and strength of relationships among members. (p. 42).

Maznevski and Chudoba do not distinguish between degrees or types of "multinational-ness" nor do they directly compare multinational with nationally homogeneous teams. From their study, it is difficult to tease apart culture and technology effects. Further they studied teams at various stages of their lives whereas the most critical incident from our perspective occurs when the teams are formed, when culture first comes to the attention of the group members and so is at its most salient.

Butler (2000) focused on how heterogeneous and homogeneous national groups of executive MBA students react differently to critical events that lead to differences in the setting and achieving of goals. She found that during the initial periods of newly formed multinational groups, individuals are more likely to act consciously around critical incidents such as initial group formation and deadlines and agree on a broader range of action and outcome goals to be replicated across time. An implication of these results is that the two types of teams may be best suited for different types of tasks with varying longevity (Butler & Earley, 2001). For example, multinational groups may be better suited to longer-term, highly interdependent projects where new learning is required, whereas nationally homogeneous teams may be better suited to shorter-term projects where the task requires less interdependent working and new learning.

An elaboration and extension of his structuration notions is represented by Giddens work on modernity (1991). In his presentation, Giddens makes explicit how reflexivity of action differs in the late modern age from that of traditional societies. Individuals now colonize the future to secure a sense of self-identify. Giddens defines colonization of the future as "the creation of territories of future possibilities, reclaimed by counterfactual inference" (1991). He suggests further that, "In a post-traditional social universe, an indefinite range of potential courses of action (with their attendant risks) is at any given moment open to individuals and collectivities. Choosing among such alternatives is always an 'as if' matter, a question of selecting between 'possible worlds.' Living in circumstances of modernity is best understood as a matter of the routine contemplation of counterfactuals, rather than simply implying a switch from an 'orientation to the past,' characteristic of traditional societies, towards an 'orientation to the future'" (1991). For example, individuals living in the late modern age have a choice of what, if any, religion to follow. They are aware of these choices primarily through interaction with people of differing faiths and beliefs. Such interaction comes about, because, in contrast to the members of traditional societies, individuals of the late modern age are members of social systems that imperfectly coincide. Being a member in a social system that does not strongly coincide with existing values means individuals need to make choices about which social practices to adopt. Individuals seek to colonize the future as an intrinsic part of their planning and this helps minimize threats and risk to the person. As Giddens points out, "Thinking in terms of risk becomes more or less inevitable and most people will be conscious also of the risks of refusing to think in this way, even if they may choose to ignore those risks." (Giddens, 1991).

In assessing the future risks to self-concept, individuals make decisions about what to do (i.e., set future goals). These future goals link back to each individual's self-identity and the motives (Erez & Earley, 1993) underlying the sense of self. To colonize the future, an individual must visualize himself acting prior to doing so, that is he must see himself acting in the future (i.e., working toward and achieving future goals). In this way, he can do things for the first time, and, equally, do things differently from the way he previously did them. Indeed, he has probably seen others act differently through membership in imperfectly coinciding social systems. Thus, a middle-class actor may work to promote or demote himself by acting in a way that leads others to perceive him or her as upper or lower class.

Choice of profession, for example, could lead to a promotion or demotion. The child of middle-class professionals may choose in adulthood to become a manual worker or marry into an upper-class family and, thereby, change his or her position in society (i.e., an individual actor acting to influence existing social structures. At the same time, he may or may not be accepted by the members of the world he wishes to enter (i.e., existing social structures acting on the individual actor). Despite his efforts, society may still view the middle-class person as still middle-class despite the "new wealth and circumstance." This may be especially true for societies having a more rigid and delineated social structure, and illustrates well the "duality of structure" between individual action and social structures. Equally, the middle-class child who remains a middle-class adult chooses to remain so by adopting an occupation and lifestyle commensurate with the middle class. At the time of action, not all risks are known. Although not all consequences of an action are intended or foreseen, "in modern social conditions, the more the individual seeks reflexively to forge a self-identity, the more he or she will be aware that current practices shape future outcomes" (Giddens, 1991, p. 129). It is through such reflexive future thought and the setting, working toward, and possible achieving of goals that the social structures are maintained or changes are brought about.

If individuals colonize the future through the setting, working toward, and achieving of goals, then for groups, these individual future goals should also result in the establishment of future goals of some sort. Zander and Medow's (1963) synthesis of prior work addressing the issue of personal versus group goals is key. They summarized much of the existing work using three points. First, strong group-oriented motives of members are associated with effective team performance. Second, a desire for group goal attainment often overwhelms a desire for the attainment of personal goals. Third, a desire for group success increases as a group experiences prior success. Weisinger and Salipante's (1995) work suggested that newly formed multicultural groups need an organizational culture high on shared interests and goals to develop a team culture needed for task success. If there are differences between multinational and nationally homogeneous teams in terms of the setting and achieving of goals, as appears to be the case, then thought and action at the discursive level of consciousness among the members of each type of team is a unifying explanation.

## SOCIAL CONTRACT AND SHARED HISTORY

Another important process linking various aspects of team dynamics is determined by the social contract and shared history that a team experiences. A social contract refers to the assumptions underlying exchange and reciprocity within the team, and we draw from Fiske's (1991) work, *Structures of Social Life*, as well as work by Foa and Foa on social exchange among others.

Early work on exchange relationships can be traced to Homans (e.g., Homans, 1958; 1961) and his initial conceptualization of exchange and distributive justice. He suggested that social behavior can be viewed as an exchange of goods such as the symbols of approval or prestige,

> Social behavior is an exchange of goods, material goods but also non-material ones, such as the symbols of approval or prestige. Persons that give much to others try to get much from them, and persons that get much from others are under pressure to give much to them. This process of influence tends to work out at equilibrium to a balance in the exchanges. For a person engaged in exchange, what he gives may be a cost to him, just as what he gets may be a reward, and his behavior changes less as profit, that is, reward less cost, tends to a maximum. Not only does he seek a maximum for himself, but he

tries to see to it that no one in his group makes more profit than he does. The cost and the value of what he gives and of what he gets vary with the quantity of what he gives and gets. It is surprising how familiar these propositions are; it is surprising, too, how propositions about the dynamics of exchange can begin to generate the static thing we call "group structure" and, in so doing, generate also some of the propositions about group structure that students of real-life groups have stated (Homans, 1958, p. 606).

Thus, social exchange refers to interactions in which some form of resource is given to, or taken from, others. It is important to note that his formulation does not simply capture an economic exchange in which expectations of repayment are explicit, and in-kind, but involve intangibles such as vague types of resources to be exchanged having indeterminate repayment schedules (Blau, 1989). It is also quite significant that Homans viewed the structure of an exchange as an important determinant as to the content and nature of the exchange.

Emerson (1962) viewed social exchange in terms of power differentials and dependencies among various people in social groups. He argued that social relations typically entail mutual dependencies. Unequal power relationships do not always lead to an equalization of power. For example, an employee who depends on her supervisor for job-relevant information is in a weaker power position since the supervisor is capable of withholding such information. However, this relationship is typically bi-directional such that a supervisor is ultimately judged by her ability to get an employee to perform her work effectively. Emerson's approach has much in common with the social exchange work of Thibaut and Kelley (1959; Kelley & Thibaut, 1978) who discussed dyadic exchange from the perspective of relative power and dependence. They developed an extensive and elaborate framework for understanding social exchange and dependencies in their research. An interesting and important point that they raise in their model concerns the paradox of integration in a group context. For example, a person who establishes links with a group shows that she has interests in common with them and shares the values that they endorse. To establish and strengthen her participation in the group, she demonstrates that she values what the group has to offer and endorse. However, in doing so, she has demonstrated a dependence on the group as a source of reward and legitimization. The characteristics that attracted her to become a member of the group repels her because a group having reward power over her implies that at some future point the group may demand repayment of rewards. The potential obligation for reward repayment keeps her somewhat at a distance.

In his work on social structure, Blau (1989) was concerned with social exchange as well. He argued that social exchange is best thought of as a product of structured social relationships in which dependencies are based on these structures. He suggested that two basic principles underlie social exchange: first, an individual who receives a reward from another person is obligated to that person; and, second, to discharge this obligation, a person must furnish benefits to the person who provided him with benefits. Blau further distinguished social exchange from other forms including economic, altruistic, and involuntary exchange. It is the altruistic form of exchange that Von Mises (1949) referred to as an "autistic exchange," meaning a one-sided exchange without the aim of being rewarded by the recipient or other parties.

In discussing social exchange, Blau uses the interesting example of a person who is magnificent in his giving as someone who uses exchange as an opportunity to gain great power. He suggested that an ability to distribute valuable possessions becomes a socially defined mark of superiority (Blau, 1989). He said,

> The ability to distribute valuable possessions becomes a socially defined mark of superiority. The extreme illustration of this process is found in the institution of the potlatch among the Kwakiutl and other Indian tribes. These ceremonies are, to quote Mauss, "above all a struggle among nobles to determine their position in the hierarchy to the ultimate benefit, if they are successful, of their own clans." For this purpose, feasts are given in which the host not only distributes but actually destroys huge quantities of valuable possessions in order to shame others who cannot match his extravagance into submission. (Blau, 1989, p. 109).

In this sense, high status is acquired through the great expenditure of wealth, or as Mauss (1954, as cited by Blau, 1989) points out, "The rich man who shows his wealth by spending recklessly is the man who wins prestige."

Another important perspective on social exchange was described by Foa and Foa (1974) in their Resource Exchange Model. Their model can be used to categorize and to structure a wide array of resources as well as to describe their pattern of exchanges including functional relationships among interacting parties. According to their model, a resource is defined as anything that can be transmitted from one party to another. They define and categorize six major types of resources—love, or an expression of affectionate regard, warmth, or comfort; status, or an evaluative judgment conveying high or low prestige, regard, or esteem; information, or any advice, opinions, or instructions; money, or any coin or token that has some standard of exchange value; goods, or any products or objects; and services, or any activities on the body or belonging to the individual (Donnenwerth & Foa, 1974).

Foa and Foa hypothesized that two general, cultural dimensions underlie resource exchange to understand the relative contribution of these six resources to exchange. The first dimension, universalism versus particularism (Parsons & Shils, 1951) indicates the extent to which the persons involved in the transaction influence the value of a given resource. For example, money is a universal resource meaning that it does not really matter who provides this resource for it to have value to the recipient—or, in the case of a $20 bill found on the floor, if anyone provides it at all. In contrast, as mentioned earlier, love is a highly particularistic resource whose source is extremely important in valuing it. If someone who I don't know provides me love, it has much less significance to me than if my spouse provides it. In this case, love represents a resource that is particular to the person providing it (and, arguably, the circumstances under which it is given). Second, Foa and Foa use the dimension of concreteness versus abstractness to describe the tangibility of the resource. Services and goods involve the exchange of some overtly tangible activities or products. In contrast, status and information represent abstract or symbolic resources because they are typically conveyed using verbal or paralinguistic behaviors.

The resource exchange model is depicted graphically using these two independent dimensions of culture in which the six resources are represented with a circle. The resources appear at 12:00 (love), 2:00 (services), 4:00 (goods), 6:00 (money), 8:00 (information) and 10:00 (status) positions. Each of the classes of resource are represented as points, but are best thought of as ranges such that each has elements more or less related to adjacent resources. For example, an expression of love such as the verbal statement, "I love you" has much in common with the adjacent element of status and information (i.e., more symbolic) whereas an expression of love such as a hug or kiss is more concrete (ironically, related to goods and services?). Finally, the ordering of the resources indicates their relative similarity. For example, love is closest to status and services whereas it is furthest from money. Information is proximate to status and money but distant from services.

The Foa and Foa model is one of the few exchange models tested in a cross-cultural and international context. While other frameworks (e.g., Blau or Homans) have received extensive attention in the western literature, it is unclear the extent to which they are culture bound in their assumptions. For example, much of Homans's work (and work derived from his principles) has been based on an equity assumption of distributive justice. However, ample empirical evidence (see Leung, 1997 for a nice review) from the cross-cultural literature demonstrates that such an assumption is culture bound, and that other allocation rules are used in various societies. Foa and Foa's model has been assessed in a number of different countries including Israel, Philippines, Sweden, and Spanish-speaking, Mexican Americans (Foa, Glaubman, Garner, Tornbolm, & Salcedo, 1987). Their results provide empirical support for the generality their model including similar rank ordering of resources and small differences in mean rank position of adjacent resources across their various samples.

Fiske (1991) examines an interesting perspective on exchange in social interaction in his book, *Structures of Social Life*. He identified four basic forms of social behavior, and he argues that these are universal aspects of social exchange. The first form is *communal sharing* and it refers to the behavior observed in a family context. Resources in such a circumstance are shared according to need, and people monitor their consumption of community resources themselves. The second form is *authority ranking* and it refers to resource allocations based on status differentials. For example, in traditional Chinese society, the eldest son receives command over the family's resources after the death of a father. The third form is *equality matching* which refers to a distribution of resources based on an equality principle. In other words, each person (by virtue of their humanity) equally deserves of a comparable share of resources as each other person in a community. In this form of exchange, there is an emphasis on reciprocity and fairness, and it is characteristic of western systems of justice. Finally, the fourth form is *market pricing* which refers to an equity-based distribution of resources using general market principles. In this case, if someone spends twice as long working in a company, she should receive twice as much in terms of reward.

According to Fiske, social behavior is based on these four universal resource exchange principles, but that the specific form generally endorsed varies within and across societies. As a result, a common institution such as marriage occurs as an etic, but its underlying impetus may differ. For example, in certain cultures people may marry for love (e.g., communal sharing), but in other cultures they may marry for position and status (e.g., authority ranking). An important aspect of Fiske's argument is that all four principles exist within each society, but that they vary in relative magnitude of importance, as well as specific manifestation. So, market pricing may be very important in the United States, but less so in Indonesia. Further, in the United States it may manifest itself as individual achievement over others in a business context, but as family ties in Indonesia. However, it is present in both countries. Thus, a useful aspect of Fiske's analysis and model is that these four exchange principles are acting in a quasi-independent fashion within any given culture. This suggests that social relationships may be governed by principles that are, at times, complementary, independent, or even conflicting. In terms of an equilibrium perspective, Fiske suggests that social equilibria are tenuous and fluid because of the complexity of interaction among the four resource principles.

The importance of social exchange in understanding team processes is relatively straightforward yet quite unpredictable. People who are from various cultural backgrounds will bring with them into a multinational team expectations of exchange and reciprocity based on their personal experiences and cultural backgrounds. For example, team members from a country such as China with its dominant focus on an authority ranking arrangement will focus on exchanges that reinforce and legitimate the symbols and positions of authority in their view (e.g., expectation that aged members deserve more rewards than younger members). In contrast, members from a country such as Sweden are likely to invoke practices of communal sharing with an expectation that all members are of comparable and equal status. Obviously, if these two groups come together in a common team, then the relative position and status of a team leader may be problematic with one group revering and the other group neutralizing the authority of the leader. This general logic can be applied to other forms of exchange.

As Fiske (1991) notes in his description of communal sharing, "… is a relationship of equivalence in which people are merged (for the purposes at hand) so that the boundaries of individual selves are indistinct. It is characterized by the fact that people attend to group membership and have a sense of common identity, whereas the individuality of separate persons is not marked. Members of the group are undifferentiated with respect to the dimensions to which people are attending" (p. 13).

In a Market Pricing relationship, people place value in a single universal metric through which they can compare any two persons or associated goods. In a market relationship, individuals seek to influence others through various means, and although some trust and mutual support exists, individuals do not view the relationship itself as an end. People share common characteristics (e.g., come from the same town or region) and some common goals, but each person views himself as the central point of an interaction. Although an authority ranking exchange is relatively stable and long-lived, a market pricing exchange can be quite short-lived such as the single exchange between a shopkeeper and an out-of-town visitor in need of supplies. However, market arrangements need not be terribly short-lived; as long as interacting parties find their exchanges to be mutually satisfactory, market pricing relationships can be quite long term. However, this need not be the case because a single defection by one party ("unjust" action) will disrupt the relationship. In a multinational team, market pricing arrangements suggest a norm of exchange based on expectations of gain from others. That is, people will cooperate and interact with one another to the extent that they anticipate receiving desired goods from others. The standard for judging satisfaction with team membership is based on the receipt of positive outcomes; if positive outcomes are not forthcoming, or better alternatives exist elsewhere, a team member is likely to leave the team physically and/or psychologically.

Another important facet of social process is the shared history of the parties within the multinational team. In one sense, this idea is captured by the national cultures from which the members come. However, the organizational context itself imposes its own unique character as well (Martin,

1992). Regardless, culture (national and organizational) is often defined as the shared meaning that people attach to various facets of their lives (Rohner, 1984). Schein defines culture as,

> The pattern of basic assumptions that a given group has invented, discovered, or developed in learning to cope with its problems of external adaptation and internal integration, and that have worked well enough to be considered valued, and, therefore, to be taught to new members as the correct way to perceive, think, and feel in relation to these problems (Schein, 1985, p. 6).

As we have argued earlier, the unique nature of the multinational team with its ambiguities and dynamism lends itself to a recreation of the team's immediate culture. This reconstruction of team member values and norms is influenced by the "cultures" that they bring with them including their national as well as organizational cultures. Although it is likely that their national cultures may differ from one another in a number of ways, their organizational culture may pervade since it provides a basis of commonality across members.

As we stated earlier, culture is not simply a monolithic construct capturing all of the minds within a given society. Meaning systems can be complementary, but incompletely shared (Rohner, 1984). We again go back to the work of Martin (1992) and the notion that there are at least three general forms of organization culture: integration, differentiation, and fragmentation. An integration view posits culture as shared meanings held in common, the differentiation view points out that there exist subgroups within any given organization that likely differ in their shared meanings from one another, and a fragmentation perspective suggests that culture is a differential network of meanings that are interrelated and reciprocally related but ill-defined and inconsistent. We argue that these forms may all co-exist in the same organization.

The importance of a shared history for a team comes in various forms. First, a shared history is a basis for common understanding of identity (Stryker, 1980) and roles. What should a leader do within the team? How should dissenters be dealt with and how should team members regulate one another's actions? These are critical questions for team functioning that are often a matter of social history for the team. If members come from the same general background, many of these questions are already defined and answered. Second, shared history reinforces each member's commitment to the team and their role (Maznevski, 1994; Stryker, 1980; Turner, 1987). Having a shared history provides the basis for myths and rituals that reinforce membership within a given community of individuals (Rosaldo, 1989). Finally, the development of the history is itself a commitment device for the team. That is, through various shared experiences a team develops for itself a sense of temporal continuity that helps members identify and commit themselves to one another.

Roles and rules, rituals, and shared history are processes central to understanding how MNT members may resolve the ambiguity of being part of a multinational team. All of these facets are individual processes that collectively shape the general social structure of the team.

## SUMMARY

In this chapter, we have examined a number of processes that link various micro- and macrolevel features of multinational teams and help us better understand team functioning. Our emphasis has been on showing the generally interpretative nature of multinational team membership and how such subjective interpretations give rise to particular team dynamics.

The interpretive perspective is useful in demonstrating how individual and group elements are linked to one another. One example that we discussed was the nature of roles and role taking in multinational teams. When first encountering a new team, a process of social identification and personal alignment occurs in a team. People seek to answer the question as to who they are relative to others within the team as well as the purpose and goals of the team. Although some people argue that the developmental phases through which teams progress are not structured or lock step (Gersick, 1988), we argue that the initial stage of a multinational team is necessarily one of personal identification of self and team. This occurs because team members nearly always face sufficient ambiguity concerning one another that a social comparative process must take place. This is one of the ways that multinational teams differ from other types of teams. Whereas the design teams observed by Gersick in her research did not require such initial identification (necessarily) because members had already in common a sense of one another vis-à-vis their own cultural norms and expectations (both nationally as well as organizationally). In a multinational team, this identification process necessarily takes place because the various social cues are absent or confused.

A second aspect of linking processes that we explored were the habits and rituals that occur. Self schema and cultural schema provide individuals with a way of predicting one another's actions in many cases. If these schema are absent or inconsistent with incoming experiences, then team members must sort through and reintegrate various new types of information. An example of this is a person the first author worked with in Thailand who was from the United States. His job was to head up the administration of the international airport in Thailand just outside of Bangkok. He commented that one of the most taxing trials of his new position was to "relearn" what Thai people were like and how his subordinates might perceive him. For example, he observed that within the Thai business culture, there was a distinction made by Thais who were of Thai descent versus those Thais having a Chinese ancestry. In much of modern Thai business, the Chinese-Thais have a significant influence in business activities. However, in the government and the military most senior positions are occupied by "Thai–Thais." Other Thai managers have told the first author that in private businesses, senior positions are nearly always dominated by Chinese–Thais—in part, because many of these businesses are based on Chinese extended families with strong connections to Hong Kong, China, and Taiwan. The American commented that since the airport authority was run by the government but many of the related commercial firms were run by Chinese–Thais he had to be cognizant of who he had deal with whom in running the airport authority.

Next, we turned our attention to the importance of a shared history to a team's functioning. The shared history and experiences influence team functioning in a number of ways. Group elements such as cultural concepts of competition interact with individual elements through such mechanisms as face and face-saving. Within all cultures, people have a positive sense of self that we call face and there exist scripted patterns for interacting with one another in order to maintain face. Goffman referred to this as facework in his dramaturgical theory of action. From the perspective of the multinational team, what is important is to realize is that people do not share the same perspective on what constitutes face, facework, and face-saving (Earley, 1997). A threat to face in a high context society such as Japan may well be seen as innocent and "constructive" conflict in a culture such as the United States. Indeed, many difficulties in intra-team dynamics are attributable to differences in what constitutes appropriate social behavior in various cultures. Contradicting one's boss in a meeting is often acceptable in the United States in many cases whereas such conflict is rarely tolerated in Japanese business culture. Instead, the Japanese have a variety of social settings outside of the workplace that allow and encourage such confrontation (Erez & Earley, 1993).

A shared history is important as well for another reason. A shared history is a needed building block for a multinational team and this gives rise to the creation of a history if one is absent (Earley & Mosakowski, 2000). By creating a shared sense of history, team members create for themselves an emergent and simplified set of rules, norms, expectations, and roles which team members share and enact. This emergent culture offers a common sense of identity that is group specific, provides a basis for team member self-valuation, and facilitates team interaction and performance (Casmir, 1992; Klimoski & Mohammed, 1994). Thus, the absence of an initial shared history gives rise to the motivation to create one, and this process of creation gives rise to unity through the development and delineation of roles and expectations for one another.

Finally, another process that we discussed was that of social structure and enactment. A key point from Giddens's work on this topic is that social structure is not static; rather, social structure is an ongoing and evolving process whereby team members create and recreate the structure that they are in. It is somewhat of a paradox in the sense that the team forms a sense of structure and this team construct tends to perpetuate itself across new team members and new tasks. However, new members and new tasks give rise to an evolving structure as well. In this sense, structure is both cause and effect of itself and team members' sense of the team is likewise cause and effect of itself. The ongoing evolution of a team thus reflects the existing concepts of team members enacted imperfectly across time. It is for this reason that the early phases of team development are particularly critical since the structure will tend to be recreated over time even if membership changes.

In the next chapter, we turn our attention to the various catalysts that we presented in our model. These exogenous variables influence team dynamics by altering the likelihood that a given team process might occur. Generally, these catalysts often act to speed things up in team dynamics but this is not always the case, as we will describe. However, we argue that these features are important in understanding the functioning of a MNT from a dynamic perspective. The catalysts consist of those characteristics influencing the social structure and the work structure. The social structure is influenced by third parties, subgroups, cooperation versus competition, hierarchy/leadership and the work structure is influenced by timing, task constraints, technology, organization support, resource changes, and goal focus.

# 6 Catalysts for Change and Development in Multinational Teams

By way of review, a key component of our model is equilibrium between the dual forces of differentiation and integration. We incorporate a dynamic view of equilibrium, similar to that proposed by Giddens (1984), in that equilibrium is not static; it is a pattern that changes as a function of time. Also drawing upon the work of Brewer (1993), the fundamental equilibrium underlying our model is the balance between differentiation and integration of self as individual, self as team member, and team as element in a larger social structure. As one of these units becomes too differentiated, then forces give rise to processes that lead to further integration.

The impetus for this change over time comes from various influences within the social system, including the actors, resources, and environment. The purpose of this chapter is to elaborate upon these impetuses, which we refer to as catalysts. By a catalyst we are referring to features of the team or its environment that might guide reactions, acting as stimuli to bring about or hasten change in the team's development. In chemistry, this is referred to as the process of catalysis and like chemical catalysts, these factors in MNTs change the rate of the reactions that occur, with out themselves being used up, processed or changed. For example, hydrogen peroxide slowly changes to water and oxygen, but in the presence of platinum metal, the reaction proceeds rapidly. The platinum metal increases the rate at which the reaction takes place, but it does not increase the amount of the product formed (Hill & Kolb, 1998). In short, the catalysts serve as agents or reagents, substances that bring about changes and cause reactions between one element and another.

The changes that occur can be either productive or counterproductive for a team, but the point is that they are precipitated by some endogenous or exogenous influence on the team. These influences, or catalysts, can also be used as techniques for guiding an MNT that finds itself "stuck" on a given process phase, unable to move forward and complete the collaborative thinking process that often must proceed effective collective action. As the catalyst works to bring about change, it helps to establish a new equilibrium among opposing forces in the MNT. For example, changes in timing or pacing (e.g., the introduction of a new deadline) can establish a new equilibrium among past, present and future focus in an MNT. Addition of new technologies helps to bring about equilibrium between standardization and flexibility. Changes in leadership establish a new equilibrium between role ambiguity and hierarchy. Introduction of third parties in MNTs brings about a new equilibrium between fractionation and integration. We discuss these dynamic processes and others below. The catalysts and the equilibria they help establish are summarized in Table 6.1.

## WORK STRUCTURE CATALYSTS

The first general domain of catalysts to change in MNTs pertain to the structure of work, including the timing and pacing, task structure, the nature of goals, technology needed to accomplish task work, the organizational context that supports task work, and the availability of resources. These factors can be viewed as distinct from those pertaining more to the social and interactional structure of the MNT. However, as will be elaborated on in chapter 5, work structure and social structure catalysts do act in concert to catalyze change and are interconnected through critical team processes.

### Pacing: Equilibrium Among Past, Present, and Future Focus.
Businesses today operate in competitive environments that are increasingly global, turbulent, and unpredictable (Bartlett & Ghoshal, 1991). In response, organizations often rely upon autonomous teams in the race against time to respond and adapt to such environments (Galbraith, 1974; Mohrman, Cohen, & Mohrman, 1995; Waller, 1999; Waller et al., 1999; Weick & Roberts, 1993). This race has developed into a push for the "better–faster–cheaper" proliferation of marketable knowledge by teams, and central to this push is the notion of time (Gleick, 1999).

However, such a focus is complicated in MNTs because team members from different cultures are likely to have very different time perspectives— also referred to as time orientation (Hofstede, 1993; Kluckhohn & Strodtbeck, 1961). The key distinction in the cross-cultural literature has been between *present* as opposed to *future* time perspective (Hall, 1983;

**TABLE 6.1**
**Catalysts to Change in MNTs and the Equilibria They Help to Establish**

| Category | Catalyst | Establishes Equilibrium Among ... |
|---|---|---|
| Work Structure | Pacing and timing | Past, present, and future focus |
| | Task constraints | Task uncertainty and configuration |
| | Goal changes | Growth and stability |
| | Technology | Standardization and flexibility |
| | Supportive Organization<br> - Standard processes<br> - Organizational culture<br> - Training and development<br>  - Reward, recognition, and promotion | Alignment and adaptability |
| | Resource Changes | Control and commitment |
| Social Structure | Leadership<br> - Performance management and coaching<br> - Appropriate use of technology<br> - Cross-cultural facilitation<br> - Career development<br> - Building trust<br> - Networking | Role ambiguity and hierarchy |
| | Cooperation vs. competition | Conflict and consensus |
| | Third parties and subgroups | Fractionation and integration |
| | Membership changes | Isolation and incorporation |

Jones, 1988; Levine, West, & Reis, 1980; Mosakowski & Earley, 2000; Zellmer-Bruhn, Gibson & Aldag, 2000). Future time perspective (FTP) is an overall attitude toward time that focuses on the future (Nuttin, 1985). FTP involves a belief that behaviors performed in the present increase the probability that a desired future goal will be attained, and FTP societies tend to value goals whose attainment can only occurs in the future (Jones, 1988). FTP has United States and Western European roots, particularly in the Puritan/Protestant concept of eschewing hedonism in this life in order to attain future rewards. Most Anglo cultures, including the North American culture, tend to be FTP cultures (Erez & Earley, 1993; Jones, 1988; Levine, 1997; Levine, West, & Reis, 1980; Spadone, 1992).

Conversely, present time perspective (PTP) supports the idea that behaviors taken today have no more effect on the probability of attaining a future goal than do future behaviors that could be taken as the goal nears. According to Jones (1988), "If putting off today does not materially alter the probability of successful goal attainment, there is little reinforcement for anticipatory goal behavior." Similarly, although FTP-oriented societies tend to value future goals more than other goals, PTP-oriented societies often have a generally-held value that enjoying today is more important than worrying about enjoying tomorrow. As such, these societies tend to focus on the immediate social environment, and emphasize expressive behaviors rather than instrumental ones (Jones, 1988). Examples of PTP cultures include African-Americans (Jones, 1988); Brazilians (Levine, West, & Reis, 1980); Latin Americans (Epstein, 1977); and the Thai (Spadone, 1992).

Despite this large body of cross-cultural literature providing evidence of the subjectivity of time, much of the empirical management research relies almost exclusively on objective time measures based on past events or historical dates (Mosakowski & Earley, 2000). Longitudinal studies of population dynamics incorporate clocks tied to precipitating external events or intraorganizational transitions. These clock-setting events are defined objectively, based on the date industry sales began (e.g. Barnett, 1997; Mitchell, 1989), regulatory changes occurred (e.g. Carroll & Swaminathan, 1991), or top managers were replaced (e.g. Amburgey, Kelly, & Barnett, 1993; Carroll, 1984).

Although the subjective view of time is not clearly represented in strategy research, there is an increasing interest in subjective views operationalized as either shared views of strategy (Peteraf & Shanley, 1997; Reger & Huff, 1993) or idiosyncratic perspectives that might alert individuals to entrepreneurial opportunities (Kirzner, 1973, 1979; Mosakowski, 1998). Few, if any, strategy studies focus on the subjective perceptions of time, pacing, rhythms, or dynamics. In the organizational behavior literature, notable examples include Gersick's (1988) study of how group members' perceptions of time and deadlines trigger group progress and Zaheer, Albert, and Zaheer's (1999) call to incorporate subjective views of time scales.

Furthermore, much of the groups research involving time assumes a future-oriented approach to time in that deadlines are assumed to be equal motivators for all study participants (cf. Gersick, 1988, 1989; Lim & Murnighan, 1994; Parks & Cowlin, 1995; Waller, Zellmer-Bruhn, & Giambatista, 1999). Similarly, some organization theories assume a future-oriented time perspective. For example, goal setting theory (Locke & Latham, 1990) and prospect theory (Tversky & Kahneman, 1986) assume high value placed on future time belief, even though such belief is not shared by many of the world's peoples (Jones, 1988; Levine, 1997). What we believe we know about the impact of time and timing in organizations and teams may not apply in a multicultural context that mixes people holding different time perspectives. As discussed earlier, concepts of time differ across cultures (Hall, 1983; Hofstede & Bond, 1988; Mosakowski & Earley, 2000). Time perspective, both focuses individual attention on the present or the future and potentially influences individuals' attitudes and behaviors. Based on this existing research, it seems reasonable to believe that differences in time perspective may lead to team members perceiving time resources and team efforts to coordinate activities under time-constrained conditions very differently (Waller, Gibson & Carpenter, 2001).

Perhaps the strategy research closest to a subjective view of time is work that identifies how multiple views of time influence strategic actions (Mosakowski & Earley, 2000). For example, Mitchell's (1991) study of dual clocks suggests that entrants and incumbents are affected by different clocks: a clock associated with all entrants' actions versus a clock associated only with incumbents' actions. Although Mitchell (1991) constructs his dual clocks with objective measures similar to those described previously, acknowledgment of dual clocks allows that, to some extent, time is in the eye of the beholder. Brown and Eisenhardt (1998) emphasize diversity in the rhythms experienced by firms. Without clearly deciding whether interfirm differences in rhythms are attributable primarily to differences in internal social rhythms or external environmental rhythms, they allow for different perceptions of rhythms.

The effect of placing individuals who may hold very different perspectives of time into MNTs, and asking those teams to collaboratively create and share knowledge, is vastly under explored (see Ancona & Chong, 1996; McGrath, 1988). For example, knowledge creation in MNTs typically involves an intense, collaborative integration of knowledge from different systems of meaning and different "thought worlds" (Dougherty, 1992; Fleck, 1979; Mohrman, Gibson, & Mohrman, 2000; Waller, Gibson & Carpenter, 2001). This collaboration typically involves the generation of ideas and plans (McGrath, 1984).

Within MNTs, present time perspective (PTP) and future time perspective (FTP) differences among team members can negatively impact collaborative knowledge creation processes (Waller et al., 2001). Interpersonal interactions could easily become conflictual due to the PTP-oriented individuals' need to develop social relations and the FTP-oriented individuals' emphasis on instrumental interactions. Similarly, FTP-oriented individuals may tend to focus most knowledge creation activities on knowledge that leads to the attainment of future goals, while PTP-oriented individuals may focus on activities for knowledge creation that lead to more proximal goals. The adherence to and valuing of deadlines, milestones, and time-oriented devices such as Gantt charts, which plot project progress against projected time frames and milestones, could differ drastically between PTP- and FTP-oriented individuals, making collaborative knowledge creation quite difficult and slow. This overall mismatch of time focus within teams may result in inefficient, conflicting, laborious interactions during knowledge creation activities, and ultimately slow efforts to collaboratively create knowledge.

The sum total effect of these differences could result in what Steiner (1972) refers to as process losses within groups, in that the differences bring about complexities in the coordination of work in MNTs that put a marked strain on processes. In many respects, this is the essence of team-work, as expressed by McGrath (1984) "… performance is related to the coordination of group members' efforts, rather than simply to the ability of the best member, worst member, or average member." This leads some researchers to theoretically argue that key tasks in teams, such as knowl-edge transfer, is likely to be negatively impacted by time heterogeneity (Waller et al. 1999).

Assume, for example, a transferring team that is more future–time-ori-ented attempting to transfer knowledge to a more present time oriented receiving team. The transferring team may attempt to transfer knowledge in the most expedient manner possible, omitting time for the development of interpersonal relationships between the teams' members. The format of the knowledge may be presented by the transferring team in terms of acronyms or mathematical shorthand, with little opportunity for the re-ceiving team to interact. Finally, the transferring team may present knowl-edge in terms of its usefulness for future goals. Conversely, the receiving team, having a more present time orientation, may constantly attempt to develop interpersonal relationships with their counterparts, interrupt the transfer process with questions, and stop to couch the knowledge being transferred in terms of present issues.

In MNTs that have developed rhythms or pacing, external changes in tim-ing, deadlines, or pace and or the introduction of new members with differ-ent time perspectives may act as a catalyst for these dysfunctional consequences, setting in to motion a series of ineffectual processes. Waller et al. (2001) argue that whether or not this occurs is dependent upon several important factors pertaining to the content and process of task completion. If knowledge creation is the task, for example, they suggest that these fac-tors might include: (1) knowledge characteristics (i.e., whether autono-mous and systemic), (2) process characteristics (i.e., supplementary or complementary, and (3) location of team members (i.e., degree of geo-graphic dispersion). If knowledge transfer is the task, Waller et al. argue that whether or not time perspective heterogeneity is a problem depends on: (1) goal congruence between teams, (2) the timing of the knowledge transfer activities, and (3) the procedural expectations of the teams.

Pressing deadlines are also likely to increase group cohesiveness and draw members' attention away from their subgroups and to the group as a whole (Heilman & Hornstein, 1992; Sherif, 1966). Individual or subgroup differences may be put aside to complete a project on time or to compete with a major competitor. In the short run this can minimize the impact of subgroups (Lau & Murnighan, 1998), but whether the effects of such expe-riences can continue after a crisis has yet to be investigated.

Successful change and innovation in MNTs may require thinking simul-taneously about multiple time horizons. Brown and Eisenhardt (1998) conceptualize the treatment of time in organizations as "balancing on the edge of time"—rooted in the present, yet aware of past and future. Their research indicates a tendency to slip off the edge toward the past or future, driving managers to focus too much on either. If there is too much attention paid to the past, strategies and organizations become locked into dated competitive models. Air France and Renault are organizations potentially suffering from this. The "Gallic inertia" has consistently caused these organizations to lag in adopting innovations such as hub-and-spoke connections and baggage automation in the airline industry, and just-in-time production in the auto industry. However, if managers forget the past, then they fail to take advantage of experience and thus are slow to change. In contrast, if too much attention is directed toward the future, organizations get too far ahead. A potential example here is Sony's fierce marketing for firewire card technology for digital imaging editing at a time when many computer hardwire configurations and camcorders cannot yet support this technology.

Brown and Eisenhardt (1998) warn against the establishment of rhythms around events, and instead advocate "time pacing" in which change is triggered by passage of time, rather than the occurrence of events. Launching a new product or service every 6 months rather than in reaction to a change in the market as a competitive response is an example of time pacing. Their research suggests that managers who use time pacing—as distinct from speed—as a strategic weapon are more successful, particularly in high-velocity industries. We discuss this point further in chapter 7.

On a final note, we must emphasize that individuals operate within boundaries defined by their social collectives to maintain their status within a group (Earley, 1997; Stryker, 1980; Tajfel & Turner, 1986). Concepts of time may be held for social purposes such as maintaining or enhancing one's "face" or status (Mosakowski & Earley, 2000). A team member with a punctuated view of time may focus on long-term planning around hypothesized past critical events in an effort to predict and plan for the punctuated change. More importantly, this member will create institutional practices, select key personnel, and implement decisions that further reinforce a "wait for the event" approach.

In summary, our key point here is that time can be viewed as subjective and that MNTs will often consist of members with different views of time. These differing perspectives may have distinct links to organizational successes and failures, particularly in knowledge intensive environments (Giddens, 1989; Scott & Meyer, 1994). As we reviewed earlier, Giddens's (1989) concept of colonizing the future illustrates how the actions of individuals within groups can guide more macrolevel organizational outcomes based on individuals' social constructions. Zaheer et al. (1999) provide a parallel discussion of aggregation effects attributable to time in their presentation of time scales. They suggest that a subjective perspective of events may differ radically depending upon the scale (time-frame width and frequency of sampling) of time used. Thus, it is insufficient to view a person's concept of time as passively acquired from one's culture or social structure. Individuals will adopt and adapt to views of time that are personally reinforcing and, in turn, create social institutions to perpetuate such views.

### Task Constraints: Equilibrium Between Task Uncertainty and Configuration.

Task uncertainty has also been referred to as manageability (Mohr, 1971) task predictability (Comstock & Scott, 1977), task complexity (Wood, 1986) and task routineness (Pelled, Eisenhardt, & Xin, 1999), but the underlying logic is the same. Processes will be different in groups faced with unstable, complex, unpredictable tasks as compared to groups in which the task is known, certain, and stable (Goodman & Associates, 1986). The task uncertainty framework developed by Gist and Mitchell (1992) focuses on the degree to which it is known that if "x" is performed then a given outcome will result. In a group context, "x" might represent task strategies for effective performance. Task strategies are clear under conditions of low task uncertainty and the group can be confident that certain strategies lead to effectiveness. Under conditions of high task uncertainty, strategies are not known, and thus must be established through a lengthy process of interaction and examination in the group in which assumptions are checked, educated guesses are made and tested, and additional information is gathered and exchanged (Wood, 1986).

Task complexity describes the required acts and information cues and sets the upper limits on knowledge, skills, and resources individuals need for successful task performance (Wood, 1986). Component complexity is the number of distinct acts that need to be executed in the performance of the task and the number of distinct information cues that must be processed in the performance of those acts (Wood, 1986). As the number of acts increases, the knowledge and skill requirements for a task also increase, simply because there are more activities and events that an individual needs to be aware of and able to perform. For example, building a house is more complex (i.e., involves more distinct acts) than sawing a log.

Coordinative complexity refers to the nature of relationships between task inputs and task products. The form and strength of the relationship between information cues, acts, and products, as well as the sequencing of inputs, are all aspects of coordinative complexity. Thus, coordinative complexity includes timing, frequency, intensity, and location requirements for performance of required acts. As an example of coordinative complexity, compare the simple linear combination of behavioral acts that are needed to paint a wall with the more complex programming of acts needed for an individual to assemble a radio. In the case of the radio assembly, the acts performed in one part of the task are contingent upon acts performed at other stages and several acts may need to be performed simultaneously.

Finally, dynamic complexity captures the changes in the states of the world that effect the relationship between task inputs and products. In dynamically complex tasks, changes in either the set of required acts and information cues or the relationship between inputs and products can create shifts in the knowledge or skill required for a task. Performance requires knowledge about changes in the component and coordinative complexities of a task over time. Tasks performed over longer time horizons will generally be more dynamically complex, as will tasks that are relatively unique (Wood, 1986). Variations in task environment factors such as resource availability or social support have been shown to lead to temporal changes in the nature of tasks performed (Galbraith, 1973; Thompson, 1967).

Task routineness focuses on the extent to which a task has low information processing requirements, set procedures, and stability (Jehn, 1995). Routineness determines the richness of information required for a group's task, that is, whether a group needs to draw on different knowledge bases. Task routineness can have a significant impact on the dynamics of heterogeneous teams such as MNTs, particularly with regard to task conflict. According to Pelled et al. (1999), there are two possible effects that task routineness can have on the relationship between heterogeneity and task conflict. One possibility is that task routineness diminishes the association between diversity and task conflict. When tasks are well defined and straightforward, team members have little need to exchange opinions or challenge each other. Hence, in teams with routine tasks, even if members have diverse backgrounds, there is only minimal room for task conflict based on those backgrounds. In teams with nonroutine tasks, there is more room for task conflict so group members with diverse backgrounds are more likely to exchange opposing opinions and preferences derived from their backgrounds. The tendency for diversity to trigger task conflict may therefore be heightened by task nonroutineness, or diminished by task routineness.

An alternative possibility is that task routineness will have the opposite effect. Early theories of optimal arousal (Berlyne, 1967; Fiske & Maddi, 1961; Hebb, 1955) suggested that people have a preferred level of arousal, a preference for stimulation that is neither too low nor too high. Drawing on these theories, Zuckerman (1979) postulated that people engage in behaviors that decrease stimulus input when they are under aroused. Empirical evidence is consistent with this notion (Zuckerman, 1979, 1984). An implication of Zuckerman's theory, referred to as sensation-seeking theory, is that people who are under stimulated will seek experiences and interactions that offer them greater arousal. Since group members performing routine tasks may experience suboptimal levels of stimulation, they may seek opportunities to debate about their tasks to make work more exciting. They may elicit opposing task perspectives from people with different backgrounds seeking to engage in challenging discourse. In contrast, team members performing nonroutine tasks may be sufficiently aroused by a group's task and may be less motivated to draw out additional conflict for the sake of excitement.

Pelled et al. tested these two competing reactions to task routineness in a study of 45 teams from the electronics divisions of three major corporations involved in monitoring and modifying work processes. Team composition varied according to function, tenure, and race. Team outcomes were measured by team managers and team characteristics were measured by surveying team members. They found that the interaction of task routineness and functional background diversity had a significant positive association with task conflict suggesting that functional background differences were more likely to trigger task conflict when tasks were routine then when tasks were non-routine, coinciding with the second effect described above.

In addition, they found that the interaction of task routineness and race diversity had a significant negative association with emotional conflict. Thus, task routineness reduced the positive association between diversity and emotional conflict in teams. The authors suggest that this reduction of association is due to a process similar to that described in conjunction with the first effect described above. When tasks are routine, team members are unlikely to seek emotional conflicts with people of different backgrounds. This is consistent with the research demonstrating that people do not typically seek unpleasurable arousal when under stimulated (Gallagher, Diener, & Larsen, 1989; Zuckerman, 1979). People performing complex tasks may be more anxious and, consequently, rely more heavily on cognitive mechanisms for simplifying information processing (Staw, Sandelands, and Dutton, 1981). In contrast, when tasks are routine, people have less need for such cognitive mechanisms such as categorization of in-group versus out-group based on diversity. Thus, the tendency for diversity to trigger categorization and emotional conflict will be weaker when tasks are routine. Also consistent with this finding is the research on displaced aggression that suggests that the association between diversity and emotional conflict will be weaker when tasks are routine. Studies have shown that frustrating work conditions lead to more interpersonal aggression among employees (Chen & Spector, 1992; Storms & Spector, 1987). Because routine tasks tend to be less frustrating than complex tasks, members of groups with routine tasks may have less frustration to vent and, consequently, less inclination to blame or "pick on" people of different backgrounds, compared to members of groups with complex tasks (Pelled et al., 1999).

For tasks that begin as uncertain, like many projects that MNTs face, structure can be imposed, and this is the process of structuring or configuring.

Certainty is not necessarily the result, but perhaps an underlying order, configuration, or disposition can be discovered. As predictability increases, teams are able to develop decision scripts. Several organizational theorists (e.g., Gioia & Manz, 1985; Gioia & Poole, 1984; Lord & Kernan, 1987) have developed theories of the role of "scripts" in organizations. According to Gioia and Poole (1984), for instance, through the use of recalled decision scripts, teams have structured expectations not only about the appropriate processes to be used to accomplish work, but also about the likely subsequent events that will result from their actions. Based on Eckblad's (1981) scheme theory, Lord and Kernan (1987) suggest that scripts can help explain how organizational behaviors come to be predictable.

Taken as a whole, this research would suggest that task uncertainty results in increased cognitive strain, decreased predictability, and a decrease in the team's comfort level with the task. Thus, based on the recall of scripts, groups have structured expectations about the appropriate processes to be used to accomplish work and about the likely subsequent events that will result from their actions (Gioia & Poole, 1984; Gioia & Manz, 1985). Gradually, the scripts evolve into routines. Routines occur regularly and are often taken for granted by members of the work group, although they might appear odd to outsiders (Gersick, 1988; Waller, Zellmer-Bruhn, & Giambatista, 1999; Zellmer-Bruhn & Gibson, 2001). When carried out under the guidance of a recalled script, behavior is enacted with minimal cognitive strain, prior knowledge and feedback substitute for an explicit and detailed analysis of each part of a complex task, and the task is performed more efficiently (Lord & Foti, 1985). Indeed, the response to the new incoming information is itself a routine, with the team responding in a similar fashion regardless of the input or stimuli being perceived (Bandura, 1986; Hackman, 1990; Lindsley et al., 1995).

The degree to which this occurs likely varies across teams. It has been argued that teams can be order along a continuum ranging from dense integrated cognitions to few integrated cognitions (Corner et al., 1994). Likewise, some teams may be characterized by integrated knowledge structures and others may be characterized by emergent knowledge structures (Ginsberg, 1990; Weick & Bougon, 1986). Construction of emergent versus integrated knowledge structures is analogous to the distinction between automatic versus controlled processing at the individual level. An emergent knowledge structure is constructed in an ad hoc way to deal with a novel problem or issue through a lengthy process that requires extensive cognitive energy. Once a structure has been constructed there is substantial inertial and process efficiency value in retaining it to interpret future issues (Weick, 1979). Emergent structures may then become so integrated and entrenched over time that the construction portion of the process occurs more quickly as team members apply a repeatedly used structure to new data. Eventually, the team may begin to suffer from knowledge structures that are too highly integrated. When integration is moderate, group members are likely to attend to a variety of information, and this will facilitate their performance. Thomas and McDaniel's (1990) results offer preliminary support for this conclusion. Top management teams with many highly integrated cognitive structures used less variety of information for environmental analysis than did top management teams with less integration. Similarly, Wellens' (1993) case study observations suggest that optimal group situation awareness is achieved when enough overlap occurs to maintain group coordination while allowing enough division to maximize coverage of the environment.

In some industries, it may be most advantageous to manage uncertainty such that a midrange level is the steady state. Brown and Eisenhardt (1998) argue that organizations can experience the continuous innovations necessary to compete in some markets if they stay at the "edge of chaos." This same principal applies to MNTs. The edge of chaos has been described as a "natural state between order and chaos, a grand compromise between structure and surprise" (Kauffman, 1995). The notion behind the edge of chaos is that change occurs when teams are sufficiently rigid so that change can be organized to happen but not so rigid that it cannot occur. On the one hand, too much chaos makes it difficult to coordinate change. There is no coherence and confusion sets in. On the other hand, too much structure makes it hard for a team to move. Strategies become brittle and prone to unexpected collapse. The edge of chaos lies in an intermediate zone where teams never quite settle into a stable equilibrium but never quite fall apart either. As Brown and Eisenhardt correctly point out, the intermediate zone is where systems of all types—biological, physical, economic, and social—are their most vibrant. The edge of chaos captures the complicated, uncontrolled, unpredictable but yet organized behavior that occurs when there is some structure but not much. This has been referred to as "adaptation" or "self-organization" (DeSanctis & Poole, 1994; Giddens, 1884; Maznevski & Chuboda, 2000; Thompson, 1967), and captures our notion of maintaining rhythms and balance among opposing forces in MNTs, in particular the tension between task uncertainty and configuration.

In a recent empirical investigation, Mohrman, Gibson and Mohrman (2001) examined a theoretical model that included self-organizing activities as one key component of knowledge sharing among groups consisting of researchers and practitioners. The other elements included joint interpretive forums and perspective-taking. The general research question that guided their investigation was, "What are the roles of joint interpretive forums, perspective-taking, and self-organizing in determining collaborative use of knowledge?"

By self-organization, Mohrman et al. were referring to action-oriented (behavioral) and cognitive processes that members use to redesign and reorganize their organizations (Thompson, 1967). The behavioral component is manifest during periods of transition, at which time an organization's form and processes are continually changing as a result of managerial decisions (Huber & Glick, 1993) and ongoing improvisation and learning throughout the organization (Tenkasi, Mohrman, & Mohrman, 1998; Weick, 1990, 1993; Weick & Westley, 1996). Organizations in transition generally undergo a vast number of change initiatives that involve collectives of organizational members trying to determine how to do things differently. MNTs might be set up to house formal self-design activities, such as design, planning, and implementation teams. Many informal interactions will also be oriented to making sense of and deciding how to operate within the changing organizational context.

The cognitive component of self-organizing involves collective cognition. As described in earlier chapters, collective cognition is the process involved in the acquisition, storage, transmission, manipulation, and use of information among collectives (Gibson, 1999, 2000b; Hutchins, 1991; Wegner, 1987). In an organization, knowledge is distributed across individuals and across external storage systems, such as electronic files or intranet sites. Collective cognition occurs as a series of transactions when information is exchanged among individuals. Interactions that take place during self-design help bring problem-relevant information to light (Sniezek & Henry, 1990) and influence the individual-level cognitive processes of each group member (Larson & Christensen, 1993). Social interaction also serves as the vehicle by which individuals' perceptions, judgments and opinions are combined to generate organizing solutions.

Less important here, but addressed further below, the second component of the Mohrman et al. (2000) framework is joint interpretive forums. This concept builds on Argyris and Schon's notion that learning is facilitated by creating occasions for reflection (e.g., Argyris & Schon, 1978). Joint interpretive forums bring together members of different communities to *jointly* reflect and interpret information. They enable the surfacing of different knowledge structures for collective examination. The final component of the Mohrman, et al. framework, perspective-taking, refers to the recognition of knowledge, values, meanings, assumptions, and beliefs from a different community (Boland & Tenkasi, 1995; Duncan & Weiss, 1979; Shrivastava, 1983). This is a critical process to manage subgroups and fractionation in groups, as will be discussed later.

To test the usefulness of the three components of their model, Mohrman et al. (2001) examined the extent to which each occurred and the interrelationships among them in the context of a previously conducted research project that followed ten companies during fundamental transitions in their organizational forms. Extensive interviews with members of the organizations who participated in the research project, followed by quantitative statistical analysis to model the relationships, indicated that knowledge sharing was related to the extent of self-organizing activities and joint interpretive forums.

In summary, it is important to understand the various ways in which uncertainty impacts MNTs. When tasks are nonroutine, diversity is likely to result in greater task conflict. In contrast, task routineness can reduce the positive association between diversity and emotional conflict in MNTs. Realistically, some degree of uncertainty is unavoidable in the turbulent context in which MNTs often operate. Thus, all teams face a trade-off between emergence and integration processes. When integration is moderate, team members are likely to attend to a variety of information, and this will facilitate their performance. This highlights the role of self-organizing, or configuration, as a catalyst to knowledge sharing and subsequent behavior change in MNTs. In the face of uncertainty, configuration structures information, but the group can bypass a lengthy exploration of potential task characteristics. Like some chemical catalysts, configuration lowers the energy required to start a reaction, while still bringing about the desired change process.

***Goal Changes: Equilibrium Between Growth and Stability.*** A third category of catalysts to change in MNTs are changes in goals. In chapter 4, we discuss the importance of common goals, and the consequences of differentiated goals. Realistically, however, goals often evolve over the course of the life of an MNT. New goals may be added, original goals may evaporate and become less relevant, and priorities may mutate. This evolution can have substantial impact on the MNT. We argue that such changes have particular implications for the rate of growth as opposed to stability in the team.

In the early phases of a team's life cycle, it is critical that the team leader and sponsor(s) painstakingly clarify the mission, purpose, agenda, accountability, and time frame for the MNT (Canney-Davison & Ward, 1999). For example, in the first few meetings, the entire team must become well versed in the organizational strategy and policies, putting the purpose of the team in context, jointly identifying priorities, mission, purpose, objectives, and key success criteria. Research conducted by Snow, Snell, Canney-Davison & Hambrick (1996) on over 50 transnational teams showed that explaining how the purpose of the team fits in with the overall organizational strategy helps team members to understand why they should put the energy into working across organizational, geographical, and cultural barriers.

However, even when these steps have been taken, it is in the very nature of MNTs that the goals of the team will change. As mergers and acquisitions occur and organizations downsize and grow, objectives evolve. A problem that is becoming increasing common, particularly for part-time team members in overly downsized organizations, is participation on multiple MNTs (Canney-Davison & Ward, 1999). Loyalties can be spread so thin that the individual does not feel "at home" anywhere in the organization. This may lead to increased turnover on the MNT, and role conflict for the individual team member. Difficulties can also arise if MNT members perceive there are parts of the organization that are not supporting their work. A team member may feel obliged to defend their part of the business that is only minimally represented on the team and that may make it difficult for that member to support the team fully. Similar difficulties can arise if the decisions taken by a team impact the livelihoods of some of the local colleagues of team members.

Furthermore, as the team itself grows and evolves, hidden agendas may emerge and create what Mitchell (an accomplished trainer at GlaxoWellcome) calls "strategic moments" in which the team needs to renew, review, and undergo training and development (Canney-Davison & Ward, 1999). In many teams, strategic moments are emotional and traumatic processes in which opinions are shared, frustrations are vented, and conflict is brought to the surface. If the ground rules have been set tightly and clearly the team may actually have much greater freedom for creative interaction and the task and norms are less likely to dominate. If multiple options and rich pictures have been generated, the team leader should expect the energy to rise as these options are forged into one path of action. If this happens, strategic moments can be very healthy.

Drexler and Sibbtet's (1988) team model stresses that teams move from freedom at the beginning of their teamwork, to constraint at the half-time point, back to freedom as they have accomplished their task. This can be represented in Figs. 6.1 and 6.2 (diagrams of funneling that is functional versus dysfunctional, cf. Canney-Davison & Ward, 1999). If after a short early argument dominant norms force people to fall in line or leave, the dominant pattern will force the team onto a narrow path early on and the material gathered will be limited and only a narrow outcome will emerge. If, however, participants initially argue through many divergent points of view, with intense discussion focused toward a point of maximum constraint where they have to agree, the richness of the initial debate and subsequent focus and decision making allows a broad, rich, inclusive end product. We discuss this further in the section on conflict as a catalyst next.

Beyond these initial interactions, changes in goals may evolve as a result of feedback. When the team acts and feedback is available about performance, this information is likely to generate a feedback loop. Feedback is first perceived, then filtered and stored. Group members share subjective impressions of what has occurred or what may occur and these impressions are utilized to form future cognitions (Gibson, 2000b). This is a critical issue because these collective interpretations are eventually stored in the team's memory and can form the basis for future performance throughout the life of the team. When the information is positive, this may encourage accumulation of more knowledge, and

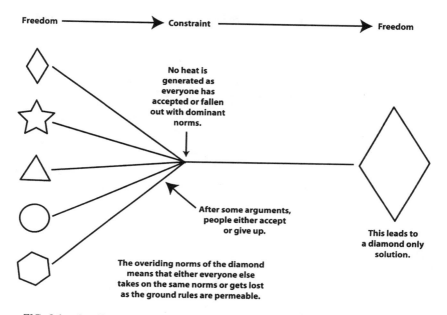

FIG. 6.1.   Ineffective use of freedom and constraint in teamworking.

repetition of the cycle. When the feedback is negative, it will likely encourage reexamination.

Preliminary evidence offers support for the relationship between feedback and accumulation of knowledge in teams. In a laboratory study of 81 four-person groups that performed a series of brainstorming tasks, Prussia and Kinicki (1996) found that performance feedback was related to both group affective evaluations and performance expectations. In fact, feedback may be so critical to collective information processing, that it might serves as a "limiting reagent." Limiting reagents are reactants that are used up first in a reaction, after which reactions cease no matter how much remains of the other reactants (Hill & Kolb, 1998). Examples from biochemistry are the essential amino acids (lysine, tryptophan, valine, etc.) that must be included in our diets. When the body is deficient in one of them, it cannot make proper proteins.

However, cognitive integration, decisions and actions in a team might react with another catalyst—social comparison—in which behavior is compared to some other team (Gibson, 2000b). That comparison may then form the basis for a re-examination of the teams' knowledge stores (Bandura, 1997; Lindsley et al., 1995). In other words, teams may look out-

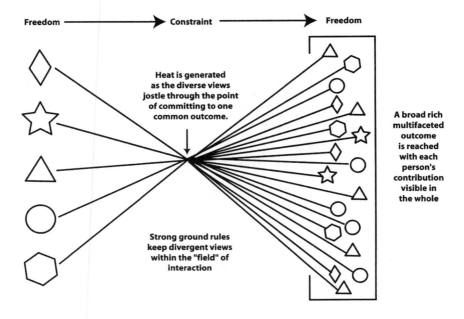

FIG. 6.2. Effective use of freedom and constraint in teamworking.

ward to "referent others" following action. These referent others serve as models or standards that guide re-examination. If the comparison is positive, this is likely to encourage repetition in action and decisions, resulting in the reinforcement and perpetuation of routines. If the comparison is negative, this encourages re-examination of the team's actions, and subsequent growth periods to counteract periods of stability in action.

In summary, all of these forces are likely to be complicated, and even exacerbated in MNTs. The evolution of goals is complicated by the frequent existence of multiple competing goals for each member of the MNT who represents a different geographic area or organizational subunit. Strategic moments may be heightened and less easy to manage and resolve given that the face-to-face interaction may be limited in the MNT, and thus socioemotional cues are less pronounced. The amplification of divergent views in the early stages of the MNT's life cycle may generate strong entropy leading the team toward early integration as the team struggles to establish order. This may curtail the healthy discussion of different opinions, options and perceptions, reducing creativity. Feedback about the team's goal accomplishment may be particularly sparse in the multinational context, given the potential disconnect among varied tracking systems and performance evaluation systems. Finally, the often unique configuration of cultures, organizations, and interests represented on each MNT may make it difficult for a team to locate "referent other" teams that can serve as examples for social comparison processes. This makes it nearly impossible for a team to identify an ideal prototype that can be used to pattern their behavior. Thus, the context of the MNT presents a particular challenge for balancing growth and stability in the team. Managing this process requires additional attention to technology, organizational structure, and resources as outlined in the next few sections.

***Technology: Equilibrium Between Standardization and Flexibility.***
Early research on alternative forms of communication (e.g. face-to-face, telephone, e-mail) assumed that different media inherently possess characteristics that make them more or less effective for certain tasks (Cohen & Gibson, 2001). This perspective was based on information richness theory (e.g. Daft, Lengel, & Trevino, 1987). For example, Sproull and Kiesler (1991) noted that face-to-face communication conveyed social context cues strongly and presented research to suggest that meeting together was useful early in a decision process to determine team goals, to secure commitment to them, and to break down work tasks.

This makes sense, given that people rely primarily on nonverbal signals to help them navigate social interactions. According to some estimates, about 93% of the meaning of a message is contained in the nonverbal part of the communication such as voice intonation (cf. Thompson, 2000). Some researchers have asserted that nonverbal (body orientation, gesture, eye contact, head nodding) and paraverbal behavior (speech fluency, use of uh-huhs, etc.) is the key to building "rapport"—that feeling of being "in sync" or "on the same wavelength" (cf. Thompson, 2000). When the person we are interacting with sits at a greater distance, with an indirect body orientation, backward lean, crossed arms, and low eye contact, we feel a much lesser degree of rapport than the same person sitting with a forward lean, open body posture, nodding, and steady eye contact. These non-verbal and paraverbal cues affect the way people work and the quality of their work in a team.

Interesting, asynchronous, distributed communication is growing at a faster rate of popularity than are other forms of communication such as the telephone and videoconference. The telephone has been around for 120 years, but less than half of the people in the world have ever made a phone call; in contrast, the Internet is only about 30 years old, and current estimates are between 200 million to 1 billion Internet users. E-mail conveys much less rapport, but can be very effective. Comparing two groups of students, one taught in a traditional classroom and the other taught on the Internet, it has been found that even though text, lecture, and exams were standardized for both classes, the virtual class scored an average of 20% higher than the traditional class on examinations. Further, the virtual class had significantly higher peer contact, time spent on class work, a perception of more flexibility, and greater understanding of the material. It is worth noting that virtual students reported greater frustration, but not from the technology, rather from their inability to ask questions of the professor in a face-to-face environment. However, this same frustration lead to greater involvement among classmates, who formed study groups. Thus, performance differences were most likely attributable to collaboration among students instigated by the technology.

In part due to findings such as these, recent research extends information richness theory by considering the effects of the social context in which communication is embedded, and argues that group norms and organizational culture influence the appropriate use of specific technologies (Markus, 1994). For example, Nemiro (1998) found that some of the MNTs in her dissertation sample used e-mail—a relatively lean medium—to work effectively on creative and unstructured tasks. Extending this idea even further, research on communication technologies has taken a "structuration" perspective (DeSanctis & Poole, 1994; Giddens, 1984; Maznevski & Chudoba, 2000). As we have discussed earlier, this approach acknowledges the reciprocal relationship between aspects of technology and social context—each influences the development of the other (Maznevski & Chudoba, 2000; Orlikowski, 1992). The structuring of technologies in use refers to the process through which users manipulate their technologies to accomplish work, and the ways in which such action draws on the particular social contexts in which they work (Majchrzak, Rice, Malhotra, King, & Ba, 2000).

For example, Johnson & Rice (1987) showed that an interplay of individual, group, managerial, and organizational actions and policies influenced the level of adaptation, which they referred to as reinvention, of word processing units. Leonard-Barton (1995) discussed the role of managers in mutually adapting technology, users, and organizations. Finally, Rice (1994) reviewed the empirical research on the interplay of computer-mediated communication and information systems with pre-existing social and organizational structures. They concluded that technology adaptation evolves over time—sometimes gradually, sometimes interrupted (Tyre & Orlikowski, 1994), and sometimes as intentional policy management (Johnson & Rice, 1987; Orlikowski, Yates, Okamura, & Fujimoto, 1995). It is constrained by pre-existing structures (Barley, 1986) of the organization and its associated tasks, technology, and the group (DeSanctis & Poole, 1994). People make small adaptations to their work, technology and organization, there is a role played by pre-existing conditions in affecting what adaptations are feasible and helpful, and adaptations often unfold in response to a series of misalignments with these pre-existing conditions.

Using this adaptive structuration approach more recently, Majchrzak and her colleagues (2000) conducted an in-depth case analysis of a virtual team working on a highly innovative project over a 10-month period. This team was engaged in the process of adaptively structuring their technology to meet their work needs. These researchers found that technology adaptation processes can be understood as a series of appropriations in which technology, the group's work and task structure, and the organizational structure all evolved. The evolution of these structures occurred when the group found the structures to be misaligned. It was only when these changes finally yielded a set of structures that were in alignment that the team was able to achieve successful outcomes.

In contrast to adaptive structuration theory (DeSanctis & Poole, 1994) they concluded that a technology's spirit—the general intent of the technology with regard to values and goals—is not fixed, even though it may be so in the mind of the technology developer. Instead, groups may actively change the technology spirit, if allowed to do so. Perhaps most importantly, fit with initial spirit is not essential for successful group outcomes. Instead, success is achieved when the spirit is sufficiently flexible to be molded to the needs of the workgroup and organizational structure; so it is the fit of the spirit with the structures that is more important than the initial nature of the spirit (Majchrzak et al., 2000). Finally, adaptive structuration theory proposes that appropriations of technology affect a group's decision-making process, which in turn affect outcomes. Majchrzak and her colleagues found instead that the process is much more iterative and synchronous, whereby appropriations of technology, the work group's decision-making process, and organizational structures are all happening at once. They summarize by stating:

> We found that the team initially experienced significant misalignments among the pre-existing organizational environment, group, and technology structures. To resolve these misalignments, the team modified the organizational environment and group structures, leaving the technology structure intact. However, as the team proceeded, a series of events unfolded that caused the team to reevaluate and further modify its structures. This final set of modifications involved reverting back to the pre-existing organizational environment, while new technology and group structures emerged as different from both the pre-existing and initial ones. (pp. 569–570).

Of particular importance in MNTs, the effective adaptation of information technologies allows for the interactions and the creation of shared repertoires will. At a minimum level, members of MNTs need to be able to use electronic communication. To achieve high levels of effectiveness, however, it will be necessary to also create repositories of team knowledge and information. Such repositories may contain email archives, electronic versions of reports, drawings, meeting notes, reference material, or

prototypes, among other data. Stein and Zwass (1995) refer to such repositories as organizational memory information systems. In a team that seldom meets face-to-face, the existence of repositories are particularly
critical to archive raw data, analyses, and decisions and ultimately, to create a sense of shared history of the team (Cohen & Gibson, 2000).

Anecdotal evidence suggests that when MNTs use a variety of communication technologies effectively, overall effectiveness of the team increases (Maznevski & Chuboda, 2001). Factors to consider in selecting
technologies include: permanence, symbolic meaning, experience and
familiarity, time constraints, organizational and functional cultures, and
access to technology training and support (Duarte & Synder, 1999). Perhaps the two most interesting of these are permanence and symbolic
meaning. Permanence is the degree to which the technology is capable of
creating a historical record of team interactions or decisions (Poole &
Jackson, 1993). Although the concept is fairly straightforward, many teams
overlook the importance of a permanent record, a factor that is exacerbated when language differences play a role in the degree of comprehen-
sion across team members. Having a record to refer back to helps to
ameliorate these differences and aids in interpretation. Symbolic meaning
refers to the context over and above the message that is implied by the
technology (Innis, 1991). With symbolic meaning, the act of selecting one
technology rather than another such as a handwritten thank-you letter
rather than one typed adds meaning to the message.

Research into the impact of technologies on MNTs is hardly existent. Increases in productivity are anecdotal and company specific. As reported
earlier, most academic research has focused on group decision support
systems. Feature of these systems such as anonymity, automated record
keeping, parallel communication, automatic translation, and time to think
in a second language with out being interrupted, suggest they may be extremely helpful for MNTs. Although many North Americans emphasize the
exchange of words and specific explanation of ideas, other cultures—such as the Japanese—depend very strongly on the context of the
discussion, facial expressions, postures, and tacit understanding, all of
which are lost in group decision support systems or groupware (Ishii,
1990). The limited case studies on MNTs have also demonstrated that
team members often develop preferences for certain modes of communication and have different levels of technological proficiency.

Thus, there is some speculation, but no systematic exploration, as to
technology considerations based on cultural factors (Duarte & Synder,
1999). For example, members from high power distance cultures may participate more freely with technologies that are asynchronous and allow
anonymous input. However, the danger of anonymity in high power distance cultures is that members with high status might have less opportunity for establishing face and thus become dissatisfied or inactive

communicators (Earley, 1997). Members from highly collectivistic cultures may prefer face-to-face interactions. Members with high uncertainty avoidance may be slower adopters of technology. They may also prefer technology that is able to produce more permanent records of discussions and decisions. Finally, members from cultures with more "feminine" orientations may be more prone to use technology in a nurturing way, especially during team formation.

Information systems managers supporting MNTs must help the team to focus on helping the team to use technology to undertake activities such as encouraging members to share common experiences verbally or electronically, creating shared artifacts even if they are thrown away later, and creating the opportunity for creative dialogue (Majchrzak et al., 2000). These functions are of far greater benefit than making sure everyone uses all the new features of every tool. A second key function, elaborated upon below in the next section, is making sure that technology adaptations conform with the larger organizational goals and tasks structure. Adaptations may be necessitated by prior misalignments, appropriations, and reinventions, or may reflect misunderstandings about or inadequate access to existing technology structures. This may then lead to even greater problems and defeat of wider, more long-term goals (Gasser, 1986; Johnson & Rice, 1987). A third key function of information systems support is to find ways to incorporate informal forms of interaction (private message spaces) into the technologies whenever possible, allowing for changes in initial coordination protocols as the team's relationships and understandings evolve. Thus, according to Majchrzak and her colleagues, "an ideal technology implementation should not be defined as one in which misalignments do not occur, because adaptations large and small will be needed; instead, an ideal technology implementation should be defined based on the ability of the team to resolve its own misalignments and the range of structures available to appropriate."

In summary, in terms of catalysts to change, differences in information technology platforms and tools, and insufficient support for the implementation and use of technologies, can be major barriers to integration. Basically, there is no ideal set of technologies for all teams (Duarte & Synder, 1999). There are basic computer-mediated capabilities that most teams will benefit from, including e-mail, calendaring and scheduling systems, whiteboards, and document sharing. Clearly, the increased use of company intranets, the World Wide Web, and groupware tools such as Lotus Notes are moves toward integration of information technology systems. MNTs need to have a clear strategy for matching technology for the task at hand, and for managing transitions to new technologies that can potentially bring about major change in the team. Because MNTs are more likely to use new, leading edge technologies, they will be more dependent on technological support staff than traditional teams. Minimally, MNT members should be able to integrate their own data and tools with each other as well as those of the people with whom they work in their own co-located organizations. MNTs will be able to develop effectively only if systems are compatible and enable connection and collaboration. With the importance of technology-enabled integration in mind, we argue that MNTs need to develop policies for using and adapting a variety of technological options, and that the more they do so, the more integrated the team will be.

### Supportive Organization: Equilibrium Between Alignment and Adaptability.

Supportive organizational contexts can help MNTs overcome obstacles and increase cohesiveness. At least four important components of the organizational context are critical: (1) standard organizational processes, (2) organizational culture, (3) training and development, (4) reward, recognition, and promotion systems (Canney-Davison & Ward, 1999; Crandall & Wallace, 1998; Duarte & Synder, 1999).

### Standard Organizational Practices.

The first aspect of the organizational context that is critical for MNTs is the standard organizational processes that comprise the day to day work of the team. This might include the means by which teams develop charters, estimate costs, plan projects, and techniques for documenting and reporting progress (Duarte & Synder, 1999). In successful MNTs the three foundations of work design—people, decisions, and information locus—are dramatically different than in unicultural, colocated, or traditional teams (Crandall & Wallace, 1998). For example in traditional teams, people focus on narrow tasks as individual contributors to the work being done. In MNTs, work design may include combined sales and service roles or broad roles that combine many steps in a customer-focused work process, whether customers be internal or external to the organizations represented in the MNT (Crandall & Wallace, 1998). Furthermore, in MNTs speed is often critical and this runs contrary to the typical controlled and hierarchical decision making processes in traditional organizations. In MNTs, decision making is often more dispersed, and decisions are made close to the customer. Finally, information in MNTs is more widely distributed and available as opposed to the "knowledge is power" approach in traditional teams.

To establish this work design, MNTs often find it useful to restructure around processes rather than functions, adopting a customer-focused approach to operations that cuts through functional departments and silos. Similarly, a work design matrix that does away with "jobs" and moves toward an array of skills associated with processes is more effective. These steps might be facilitated through the use of project-management software packages, or the "balance score card" approach. This approach involves defining why the team exists, what value-add the team has for the corporation, and what the team's customers expect of it. The team then defines primary measures of effectiveness, such as cost, cycle time, quality, or human resource efficiency. The final critical step in the balance scorecard approach is activity based, defining what processes and activities can be used to accomplish goals and objectives. A given team's score card is then often "rolled up" into an overall balance score card for a unit or organization and therefore serves as a means of aligning the team with the rest of the organizational strategy.

*Organizational Culture.* The second dimension of organizational support is organizational culture. Using the typology developed by Smiricich and Calas (1986), for MNTs we would advocate thinking about organizational culture using the "paradigm" framework, and more specifically, the functionalist approach in which useful law-like statements enable the researcher to understand behavior within the context of specific corporate cultures. For example, research suggests that an adaptive, technologically advanced, and nonhierarchical organization is more likely to succeed with MNTs than is a highly structured, control-oriented organization (Apgar, 1998). Thus, for MNTs it is important to develop organizational norms and values that focus on collaboration, respecting and working with people from all cultures, keeping criticism constructive, and sharing information (Duarte & Synder, 1999). Norms must honor different ways of doing business in different cultures, including the legalities such as copyrights and data sharing (Grimshaw & Kwok, 1998).

*Training and Development.* Members must be trained in the skills that represent the depth and breadth of the processes. This is a frequently overlooked area (Duarte & Synder, 1999). For example, team leaders at the World Bank believed that underfunded technological training for team leaders and members was one reason that their efforts to implement groupware did not fully succeed; money was spent on the technology, but not on teaching people how to use it (O'Dwyer, Giser, & Lovett, 1997). Training in technology usage is not enough; team members also need training in meeting facilitation and in knowledge management techniques such as knowledge repositories and chat rooms. Johnson & Johnson's Learning Services offers support to MNTs in enhancing collaboration skills in cross-cultural and functional interactions using what it calls "The Series." NASA's Web site for project managers contains a place where "lessons learned" are stored. It also has a bulletin board where project managers can ask questions and receive suggestions from other project managers.

*Reward, Recognition, and Promotion Systems.* Finally, with regard to supportive reward, recognition and promotion systems, the design of reward systems that recognize the skills needed to operate in a cross-national (and often cross-functional or cross-organizational) environment are critical. Typical reward and recognition systems favor individual and functional work. One of the most common changes accompanying the transition to work teams is the implementation of team-based rewards (Kirkman & Shapiro, 2000b; Johnson, 1993). Specifically, such rewards are made contingent upon the performance of an employees' team as a whole and are shared among team members. Compensation specialists have argued that individualistic reward systems compensate employees for individual effort and performance at the expense of team goals and performance (Kanin-Lovers & Cameron, 1993; Schuster & Zingheim, 1993). Although some research has demonstrated the positive impact of team-based rewards, efforts to design and implement reward systems to promote team effectiveness have largely been unsuccessful in organizations (DeMatteo, 1997). One of the possible reasons for failure is the reward-recipient's perspective regarding the extent to which team-based rewards are beneficial (Dulebohn & Martocchio, 1998).

In a sample of 618 line-level employees representing 57 work teams in a Fortune 50 insurance company, Kirkman & Shapiro (2000b) examined the impact of various individual-level factors such as employees' collectivistic orientation, team-related attitudes, and justice perceptions, on employee receptivity to team-based rewards. They found that employees were generally more receptive to team-based rewards when they were: collectivistic, preferred teams, were committed to their teams, perceived a fit between team-based rewards and other organizational changes, rated their teams as highly task interdependent, and perceived procedural and interactional justice. The authors suggest that from an organizational change perspective, managers ought to do what they can to create an organizational culture that is supportive of collectivistic and team-based values. Positive team-related experiences in the workplace, accompanied by team-based rewards, may increase employee values of collectivistic versus individualistic approaches to work.

Finally, with regard to promotion, some team members in MNTs may fear that since they tend to be globally dispersed from head quarters, they may be looked over for promotional opportunities if they are not seen every day. Evidence suggests that managers who lose visual and verbal proximity to their employees often put up the strongest resistance to alternative work and team arrangements (Apgar, 1998). Given the fundamental nature of this issue, we address it further in subsequent sections.

In general, it is important for these four basic domains of the organizational context to be in place and well aligned. However, inevitably, changes will occur as organizations merge, acquire other organizations, downsize, or grow. Thus, a critical balance must be maintained between alignment and adaptability. At a practical level, most senior executives are trying to find ways of making their large firms act more like small firms. For example, in the words of WPP chairman Martin Sorrell, "Every CEO wants the power of a global company with the heart and soul of an entrepreneurial company" (Gibson & Birkinshaw, 2000).

Thus the challenge is to obtain balance between exploitation and exploration (March, 1991), or between alignment and adaptability (Tushman & O'Reilly, 1996). According to March (1991), organizations must work to achieve an appropriate balance between exploration and exploitation as they move forward. By exploration, he refers to search, experimentation, discovery and innovation as reflected in activities such as creating new technologies and developing new markets. Exploitation refers to refinement, choice and effective implementation of existing processes such as selling existing products to existing markets. In their start-up years organizations focus on exploration, and at this stage, they demonstrate a high capacity for adaptation. Gradually, as organizations grow larger they develop systems and procedures that shift the emphasis towards exploitation. Alignment tends to be high, however, as bureaucracy and inertia take hold, exploration-oriented activities are "driven out" and the organization begins to stagnate. Framed in this way, organizational renewal can be seen as a shifting of the balance back towards exploration-oriented activities such as search, creativity, agility and entrepreneurship that maximize adaptation, while still maintaining alignment. [Of course, March suggests that the picture is somewhat more complex than this in that the rate of learning attributable to exploration may be differentially effective depending upon the type of work undertaken by an organization as well as changes in environmental circumstance. For example, the introduction of information technology may provide for rapid scanning of the market and increase variability of market focus for some companies (exploration) while acting to codify production methods and expertise for other companies (exploitation)].

In the research literature, the path to achieving this balance has been described by various terms (Gibson & Birkinshaw, 2000). At one end of the spectrum we have the decisive leadership approach, in which organizational renewal is seen as being driven by the chief executive and his/her bold decisions to enter important new markets or invest in certain risky technologies (Gibson & Birkinshaw, 2000). At the other end of the spectrum we have the culture change approach in which the creation of an invigorating culture or behavioral context fosters a spirit of entrepreneurship and enthusiasm among employees, which in turn leads to a greater focus on exploration-oriented activities (Gibson & Birkinshaw, 2000). Top management's role in this model is to nurture the supportive behavioral context (e.g., Bartlett & Ghoshal, 1987; Hurst, 1995; Markides, 1999).

Finally, as a midrange approach, is the realignment of the organization's structures and systems, which covers everything from reporting relationships to HR policies. According to this perspective, the main obstacle to renewal is the bureaucratic organization structure that prevents managers from responding to new opportunities. The solution is to break up the existing structure—by spinning off activities, desegregating large units, and delayering the management hierarchy (e.g. Peters, 1994; Tushman & O'Reilly, 1996).

Using this latter approach, Gibson and Birkinshaw (2000) propose that balance of exploration to exploitation is the result of implementation of sets of enabling management systems, established as strategic complementarities (Milgrom & Roberts, 1993), that create adaptability necessary for long-term success. In organizations focusing on exploitation, objectives are clear, roles and responsibilities are well-defined and understood, decision-making authority is clear, the right things are accurately measured, and there is accountability for results. In organizations focusing on exploration, initiative is valued, inconsistencies and discontinuities are objectively evaluated, experimentation and some failure are tolerated, and there are processes for modifying institutional systems (World Economic Forum/Booz-Allen & Hamilton Report, 2000).

Gibson and Birkinshaw (2000) report on a five-step process examining which sets of systems result in the greatest degree of adaptability in specific contexts: (1) interviews with top executives of seven multinational firms, (2) interviews throughout two business units of each firm, (3) surveying a stratified random sample of 200 employees at four hierarchical levels of the two business units (senior management, middle management, line management, and non-management), (4) identifying and understanding the key enabling systems through qualitative analysis of interview notes and quantitative analysis of survey data, and (5) feedback sessions in each firm. Consistent with March's (1991) simulation, Gibson and Birkinshaw found evidence that exploration and exploitation influences are not mutually exclusive; there is a modest positive correlation between the two capacities. Companies that score above the overall mean on both outperform industry peers on key financial indicators. Across companies, the key systems predicting alignment are: vision/strategy, decision making, and capital allocation. The key systems predicting adaptability are: incentive compensation, knowledge transfer, and risk management. In general, more senior management attention is focused on achieving alignment than on adaptability.

In summary, it is generally important for these four basic domains of the organizational context—standard organizational processes, organizational culture, training and development, and reward, recognition, and promotion systems—to be in place and well aligned. The context of the MNT presents unique challenges in developing these systems. Furthermore, inevitably, changes will occur as organizations merge, acquire other organizations, downsize, or grow. The formidable task for the MNT is to identify which set of systems is critical in their own context, and how those can be managed to promote optimal levels of exploration and exploitation.

### Resource Changes: Equilibrium Between Control and Commitment.

Organizational infrastructures can either facilitate effect teamworking or cause MNTs to expend valuable energy and brain power trying to over come organizational obstacles. Some form of matrix structure is the typical structural arrangement of many multinational firms. In a matrix structure, employees (or teams) report both to a functional supervisor and to a project supervisor. Imagine functions as the rows in a chart, and projects as the columns, with teams or individuals in each cell created by the crossing of these two reporting structures. Matrix structures became fashionable in the late 1970s and early 1980s. The parallel reporting relationships acknowledge the diverse, conflicting needs of functional, product, and geographic management groups and provide a formal mechanism for resolving them (Bartlett & Ghoshal, 1990). The multiple information channels allow organizations to capture and analyze external complexity. And its overlapping responsibilities are designed to combat parochialism and build flexibility into an organization's response to change.

The authority and power in these structures is very diffuse and the dominant power base (e.g., line managers, functional heads, country managers, team leaders) often reflects the organizational culture (Canney-Davison & Ward, 1999). Furthermore, in many instances, the matrix proved all but unmanageable—especially in international context. Dual reporting leads to conflict and confusion, the proliferation of channels created informational logjams , and overlapping responsibilities often produced turf battles and a loss of accountability. Separated by barriers of distance, language, time, and culture, managers often found it virtually impossible to clarify the confusion and resolve conflict (Bartlett & Ghoshal, 1990).

Thus, in a matrix structure, it is critical that the locus of decision-making authority be clarified: either with the MNT leader or the line manager. Even if an MNT is clear where it fits in the organization and who it reports to, it can still suffer from conflicting demands and divided loyalties. Sometimes a line manager is under pressure to deliver a set of objectives that contradict the needs of an MNT.

Furthermore, most international projects cross-functional boundaries. This means that the MNT leader needs to work with many different line managers. It the team is composed of part-time members who are also members of other teams, the team leader has to negotiate with line managers over the resources that are dedicated to the team (Canney-Davison & Ward, 1999). The required level of commitment to the team, skills, and time frames may all be up for grabs. Involving line managers in the design of the team is one way to address this issue, but even still there may be ongoing conflicts around staffing resources.

MNT leaders may not have clearly designated power in the organization, yet they are often held accountable for success or failure of the team. One of the key questions for MNT leaders is "who carries the weight of successful implementation and performance?" (Canney-Davison & Ward, 1999). In general, the more control a team has over its own success or failure, the higher the motivation to perform well, but also the greater the need for shared responsibility for managing resources.

According to Devanna, Fombrun, & Tichy (1984) the critical "management task is to align the formal structure and human resource systems so that they drive the strategic objectives of the organization." The currents which shape policy choices within HRM can also be understood as the interplay of stakeholders' concerns (which may be contradictory) with situational factors such as labor market conditions and legal constraints (Beer et al., 1985). These policy choices affect longer-term consequences such as individual well-being, organizational effectiveness, and societal benefits. Thus, cultural concerns may impact on the HRM policies implemented by a firm. For example, the policies of a firm based in France might be influenced by the high value put on social welfare issues. If the firm operated a subsidiary in the United States, where issues such as job security have a lower profile, its overall HRM policy would still be constrained by the general policies of the head office (Cray & Mallory, 1998).

While HRM policies do vary dramatically from firm to firm and country to country, two basic approaches that have been contrasted in the literature are the American model and the European model (Brewster, 1995; Gratton, Hailey, Stiles, & Truss, 1999; Huselid, Jackson, & Schuler, 1997). Common themes in the American model are: (1) an integrated HR strategy is critical to the achievement of organizational effectiveness, (2) responsibility for HRM decisions should be devolved to line managers, (3) there should be an emphasis on the development of a strong organizational culture to ensure that behaviors are consistent with the values and philosophy of management, and (4) the HRM system should focus on the individual in terms of appraisal, training, and reward systems (Beaumont, 1992; Brewster, 1995; Clark & Mallory, 1996; Cray & Mallory, 1998; Gratton et al., 1999).

Empirical research supports this characterization. Using a large sample of 293 U.S. firms, Huselid, Jackson, and Schuler (1997) contrasted a technical versus strategic approach. Technical effectiveness encompasses those activities associated with a high level of knowledge and expertise, occupational specializations, and professional criteria for judging effectiveness, including recruiting, selection, performance measurement, training, and compensation. Strategic effectiveness involves designing and implementing a set of internally consistent policies and practices that ensure a firm's human capital contributes to the achievement of its business objectives (Huselid et al, 1997; Jackson & Schuler, 1995). Huselid et al. (1997) found that among U.S. firms, levels of technical human resource management effectiveness were higher than their levels of strategic human resource management effectiveness. These results suggest the extent to which technical human resource activities have become institutionalized. Institutionalized activities, they argued, are inadequate means of differentiating from competitor and thus are not powerful tools for gaining competitive advantage. Thus, the potential gains to be made by large U.S. firms through increased human resource effectiveness may be greater to the extent firms focus on making improvements within the domain of strategic human resource activities (p. 184).

HRM in this standard American version is likely to transfer most readily into the management repertoire of nations characterized by lower power distance (Clark & Mallory, 1996, cf. Cray & Mallory, 1998). In these cultures, there is likely to be a greater a willingness to delegate responsibility for HR and a willingness of individual employees to take responsibility for their own development. Equally critical, the model would transfer to nation's characterized by low uncertainty avoidance, contributing to the recognition that there are risks attached to this delegation. Finally, the model may transfer to nations characterized by high masculinity, including the belief that the way employees are managed makes a critical difference to their effectiveness. This implies that the "American model" would transfer most readily to Anglo countries (United Kingdom, Australia, Canada, and New Zealand).

In contrast, Brewster (1995) has proposed a European model of HRM which recognizes the differences in employee relations between Europe and the United States. There are three common elements within the European nations that transcend national boundaries: (1) a recognition of the importance of human resources as a source of competitive advantage, (2) the delegation of responsibility for HR to firm and/or line managers, and (3) the integration and mutual reinforcement of HR strategies and overall strategy. Brewster argues that this model has developed because: "European organizations operate with restricted autonomy: constrained at the international (European Union) level and at the national level by culture and legislation, at the organizational level by patterns of ownership, and at the HRM level by trade union involvement and consultative arrangements" (p. 3).

Of course, with that said, there are national differences. For example, Sweden's strong collectivist culture inhibits the development of a more individualistic orientation toward compensation and employer-management relationships, while the Dutch "feminine" culture discourages Dutch employees from accepting hard HRM practices (Clark & Pugh, 1997). In France, the presence of powerful owner-employers restricts the decentralization of HRM functions. The German HR manager operates within a very highly defined set of legal constraints over specific work practices and under the structure of federally mandated works councils. This means that German practitioners will take a much more formal and static approach to most HRM functions than the British or American counterparts and will be much less proactive in attempting to launch new policies or revise old ones (Cray & Mallory, 1998; Lawrence, 1991). For the British HR manager, the HR function is dominated by the relationships between employee groups, the production units, and specific work practices.

There are a number of other factors that influence the international HRM policies a firm will adopt. The firm's international experience, including the degree of international involvement and its international strategy, has been shown to have an important impact (Adler & Ghadar, 1990; Cray & Mallory, 1998; Rosenzweig & Nohria, 1994). External factors such as industrial sector and the cultural profile of the host country will also shape the formulation of HRM policy for a particular country (Schuler, Dowling, & De Cieri, 1993).

One of the important determinants of a firm's policy is the orientation of upper-level management (Cray & Mallory, 1998). There are three general attitudes that a parent firm may adopt regarding international HRM (Taylor, Beechler, & Napier, 1996): adaptive, exportive and integrative. Firms with an adaptive approach are less concerned with fitting in with local practices. Organizations with an exportive attitude toward HRM stress rules and practices that can be applied to all settings. The integrative approach implies a consistent overall framework within which local standards are applied. These contrasts in HRM functions across nations result in real challenges for developing a consistent approach to managing human resources within a global corporation. All three of these approaches have met with various criticisms both from American and European researchers (see Brewster, 1995 for a review).

In summary, we agree with the new trend toward creating a wider perspective on human resource management that interweaves government, market, and labor-management relations. This approach, argued convincingly by Brewster (1995), suggests that business strategy, human resource strategy, and human resource practices interact with national culture, power systems, legislation, education, and employee representation. The recent research findings demonstrating significant differences between nations in their human resource management practices provide support for this model. The approach also highlights the importance of the multinational firm, and more specifically the multinational team, adapting their human resource management to local practice.

## SOCIAL STRUCTURE CATALYSTS

A second general domain of catalysts to change in MNTs pertains less to the task of the MNT and more to the social context, including the interaction, roles, status and relationships within the team. We have identified four general categories of social structure catalysts: leadership, cooperation vs. competition, third parties and subgroups, and membership changes. Like the task structure catalysts, these catalysts serve as means of resolving key tensions in MNTs. We provide a detailed discussion of each below.

### The Leadership Factor: Equilibrium Between Role Ambiguity and Hierarchy.

In teams, leadership roles: (1) direct the flow of incoming information between various other components in order to attain processing objectives, (2) help to identify, from the group's repertoire of activities, previously "experienced" task information that matches incoming stimuli, and (3) provide a means of utilizing this information. Those in leadership roles, or members engaging in leadership behavior (if leadership is shared), may perform the function of "encoding" or "organizing" information, acting as catalysts that guide the group from accumulation of group knowledge to active consideration of that knowledge. These individuals are often engaged in assigning information gathering activities among team members, interpreting information, and resolving disagreements and/or directing individual team members into action, thus facilitating examination of information. Again invoking the language of chemistry, a leadership catalyst helps bring about activation energy—the minimum energy needed to get a reaction started.

Many organizations implement MNTs as a form of self-managed work team (Kirkman & Shapiro, 1997; Kirkman, Gibson, & Shapiro, 2001; Kirkman & Shapiro, 2000a; Kirkman & Shapiro, 2000b). Self-managing work teams (SMWTs) are a special category of teams that perform many of their own managerial tasks, such as goal setting, monitoring, and reward allocation. Over the past 15 years, many organizations have exported self-managing work teams to global affiliates, and this trend has extended to include MNTs. However, research indicates the team members respond differently to the implementation of self-managing work teams, depending on the values derived from the countries they represent (Kirkman, Gibson, & Shapiro, 2000; Kirkman & Shapiro, 2000a).

Specifically, Kirkman and his colleagues investigated over 378 work teams working in eleven organizations located in nine countries using observations, interviews, and survey data. Employees were generally more receptive to self-management when: (1) they valued equality in organizations more than status and power differences (i.e., low versus high power distance); (2) valued work activities more than non-work activities (i.e., when they were doing oriented rather than being oriented); and (3) believed they (rather than external forces) control their personal and organizational outcomes (i.e., were free will oriented rather than deterministic).

Given the potential variance in receptivity to self-management across cultures, these authors warn against a blanket approach in which all facilities of a multinational implement teams in the same manner. To adapt the form of a SMWT in countries such as Argentina, Mexico, and the Philippines, where employees are typically uncomfortable taking initiative without the permission of their managers (i.e., high power distance countries), Kirkman et al. suggest that the level of self-management characterizing the teams should be reduced, at least initially. In these countries, managers might retain their responsibilities to a large degree at least until team members get comfortable with the idea of taking on more responsibility and autonomy.

In addition to adopting the form of the SMWT to mesh with a country's particular cultural values, Kirkman et al. also argue that managers should also adapt their SMWT implementation strategies to be consistent with employee cultural values. In countries that are, on average, low in power distance like the United States, employees will most likely want to have a say in how the teams are formed, the specific nature of the reward and evaluation system to be used, and the type of tasks to be performed. Conversely, in countries that are characterized by higher levels of power distance such as Argentina, China, Mexico, or the Philippines, employees may not eagerly respond to chances to participate in SMWT implementation decisions. For example, researchers studying the implementation of SMWTs in Mexico have recommended that top organizational leaders must be more intimately involved in the implementation of teams than would ordinarily be the case in the United States. Due to the high level of power distance in Mexico, top management may need to take a strong, positive stance toward SMWTs and set clear expectations to legitimize their implementation.

As a final implementation strategy for self-managing teams, employees most likely to readily accept teams and self-management can serve "translator" and "bridge" roles for teams in contexts where many employees are likely to resist either teams or self-management (Kirkman et al., 2000). They may also be excellent candidates for the role of facilitator and can help in designing training programs to improve the general level of acceptance among team members in challenging contexts. Thus, as part of an integrated selection system (i.e., application, interviews, personality and ability instruments, and reference checks), managers could assess potential new hires on their level of individualism–collectivism, power distance, doing versus being orientation, and determinism versus free will.

In those situations in which stronger external leadership is needed, there are at least four key competency areas leaders can contribute to MNTs: (1) performance management and coaching, (2) appropriate use of technology, (3) cross-cultural facilitation, (4) career development and transition of team members, (5) building trust, and (6) networking (Duarte & Synder, 1998).

With regard to performance management, the key is to develop awareness of a number of different compensation and reward systems across national contexts. With regard to technology, experience using a variety of different electronic communication and collaboration technologies and the ability to support and lead virtual meetings (e.g., using video-conference or groupware) is key. With regard to cross-cultural facilitation, leaders must be able to constructively discuss dimensions of cultural differences, create ways of working that accommodate and optimize cultural differences, and plan team activities while taking into account the cultures of team members (Earley & Erez, 1997). This includes the development of what O'Hara-Devereaux and Johansen (1994) call "third ways" of working—techniques for working or interacting that do not elevate one culture bias over another. For example, one team leader from North America made the mistake of taking a typically North American management custom—publicly recognizing an individual team member for his work—and applying it to a multicultural setting. To make matters worse, he singled out, complimented, and gave a generous individual performance reward to a team member from Japan in front of the entire team (most were from Japan and China). For a North American this may have been slightly embarrassing, but for the Japanese team member, to be singled out for high performance in front of other team members who had also contributed to the team's performance was not only embarrassing, it was more of a punishment than a reward.

In the area of career development and transition, the key is to assist members in joining the MNT and facing potential subgroups and conflicts (see discussion later). Building trust involves stating personal values, keeping commitments, accurately portraying the team's work to management, and building personal relationships in a short period of time. Finally, networking refers to the ability to identify important stakeholders and plan collaborative activities.

With regard to building trust, there has been more and more attention in the literature on MNTs and virtual teams on the role of trust (e.g., Handy, 1995). Handy suggests, for example, that if we do not find ways to build trust and understand how technology affects it, people will feel as if they are always in a very precarious state. Because geographically dispersed MNT members may be outside a normal physical distance conducive to establishing trust (opportunities for regular interactions face to face with the immediate work group or in-group), this makes the task of developing and maintaining trust even more critical for performance (Duarte & Synder, 1999). In a geographically dispersed MNT, team members may never have the opportunity for face-to-face contact or to use other traditional sources of information that provide the basis for developing trust. In an MNT, creating trust requires a more conscious and planned effort on the part of a team leader. Trust requires leadership to set and maintain values, boundaries and consistency (Duarte & Synder, 1999).

Finally, with regard to networking, the key is to create links across boundaries. Networks might include team members, mangers from local and remote functional areas, customers, vendors, suppliers, and partners. In this regard, the leader's role is to analyze relationships with important people across these different boundaries, noting patterns of good and poor relationships and what may cause them, and noting what can be done to address the poor patterns (Duarte & Sydner, 1999). A large portion of the leader's time needs to be spent finding ways to create shared perceptions among outsiders about the team and its goals. The network has to be broad and strong enough to withstand competing priorities and changing requirements, to obtain needed resources, and to instill a sense of trust in the team and its work.

In summary, without leadership and facilitation, roles in an MNT are often ambiguous. Role ambiguity is a condition in which members lack a basic understanding of either the function they play in the group, the activities they are responsible for, or potentially how the group fits into the larger organizational context. We would argue that member roles serve an essential guiding function that enables MNT members to make more efficient use of each other's personal store of problem-relevant information. Preliminary evidence suggests that when members know which other members of the group have expertise in which specific knowledge domains, the amount of unshared information they actually discuss increases significantly (Stasser, 1991). Clearly defined roles enable this sharing. We discuss this further in chapter 5.

However, as we noted previously, many MNTs exist in "adaptive environments" (Duarte & Synder, 1999). These environments do not follow rational, structured rules. Teams have not yet developed satisfactory responses to the problems they face, and may not even know what questions to ask. There is no specific plan of action or tool of logic that can solve a particular problem. Many workers are uncomfortable in this environment since it is riskier, requires more effort, and generates uncertainty and discomfort. As a leader, helping MNTs to face adaptive situations is a process of mobilizing and enabling rather than planning and controlling. Traditional styles of leadership do not serve well in adaptive situations and therefore require leading and working "from a different place" (Heifetz & Laurie, 1997). This process is discussed further in chapter 7.

**Cooperation and Competition: Equilibrium Between Conflict and Consensus.** Conflict is an important part of group process (e.g., Argote & McGrath, 1993). Conflict can be defined as "… a process in which one party perceives that its interests are being opposed or negatively affected by another party" (Wall & Callister, 1995, p. 517). Key in the MNT is the process-based and perceptual nature of the phenomenon, the involvement of more than one entity, and the element of opposition. Interests include values and other value-related phenomena, such as goals, behavior, attitudes, or possessions (Deutch, 1980; Putnam & Poole, 1987). Given the central role of values in the self-schema, challenges to values are powerful bases for the development of conflict particularly in multicultural groups, in which cultural values are likely to be salient (Ravlin et al., 2000).

There are several layers or levels of conflict (Pondy et al., 1982). Latent conflict occurs because differing values specify different goals, modes of behavior, attitudes, and preferences for culturally different group members; it is not recognized, but may create group process problems anyway, as described later (Ravlin et al., 2000). Perceived conflict is that for which individuals recognize a difference in goals or other value-related phenomena. Many conflicts are suppressed but this is unlikely to happen if conflicts relate to values central to the individual's personality (Pondy, 1967; cf. Ravlin et al., 2000). Personalization and/or characteristics of the parties involved, such as their relative status or their similarity to one another, are factors that may cause escalation to the perceived conflict stage. Finally, manifest conflict is actual conflict-oriented behavior occurs between the two entities.

Conflict is a multifaceted, unavoidable process, and a positive influence on effectiveness under some conditions (e.g., Amason, 1996; Jehn, 1995). Functional conflict is often task oriented and viewed as a way of surfacing more ideas, criticisms, and opinions of group members regarding task performance, and can make a positive contribution to group performance. Dysfunctional conflict is often relational, focusing on interpersonal relationships and personalities, and is detrimental to the group. Functional conflict could potentially have positive developmental influences on individual group members (e.g., Jehn, 1995; Ravlin et al., 2000; Williams & O'Reilly, 1998).

Ravlin et al. (2000) developed a model for conflict in multicultural teams. They argue that members initially make distinctions between others' belief systems resulting in judgments of similarity or difference. These assessments result in a perceived status hierarchy of members based on comparative evaluations (e.g., Sidanius, Pratto, & Rabinowitz, 1994). Because values are a core part of the self-schema (Markus & Wurf, 1987), and have implications for many aspects of perception and behavior (e.g., Meglino & Ravlin, 1987), perceived differences on value and value-related dimensions can challenge an individual's feelings of legitimacy. Furthermore, Ravlin et al. argue that when there is a lack of agreement on the group's status ordering, these challenges to legitimacy tend to lead to overt functional and relational conflict. The process is moderated by several factors, including an individual's interpretation of legitimacy (ethnocentrism), his or her perceived place in the status hierarchy, level of cognitive moral development, and whether he or she is in the minority or majority on the dimension of interest.

Teams that have consensus have reached common expectations of the task and team, allowing them to predict the behavior and resource needs of team members more accurately, thus facilitating performance (Cannon-Bowers & Salas, 1990). Walsh et al. (1988) refer to this component as "realized consensus," Corner et al., (1994) refer to it as "consensus frame" and Klimoski and Mohammed (1994) refer to it as "sharedness." However, when all group members agree on nearly all pieces of knowledge and information, the group may gradually suffer from biases associated with groupthink (Janis, 1982).

There is some preliminary empirical support for this effect. Walsh et al. (1988) investigated the schema employed by strategic decision-making groups participating in a simulated business environment and found that groups marked by low consensus actually performed better than decision-making groups marked by high consensus. Likewise, based on their case study observations, Cannon-Bowers, Salas and Converse (1993) argue that knowledge of team members may overlap to the point where shared cognitions become a liability, and the potential for individual contribution is lost. Finally, based on her case study of a fire brigade, Langfield-Smith (1992) argues that it is not necessary for members of a group to have complete consensus. She suggests that the repeated cycles of interaction in response to changing circumstance leads to the best performance.

Particularly under conditions of task uncertainty, there is a tendency for cultural norms to become salient and conflict to be viewed from the lens of the particular culture. Evidence for this effect was obtained by Thomas, Ravlin, and Wallace (1996). These researchers examined the influence of cultural differences on process and outcomes of five culturally homogeneous groups (all Japanese) and eight culturally heterogeneous groups over the course of 10 weeks. The Japanese participants reported significantly less positive assessments of group outcomes and processes then did their non-Japanese counterparts. The least positive assessments were those of Japanese participants in heterogeneous groups. These may have resulted from an inconsistency between the functioning of the groups and the expectations that Japanese participants had for behavior. Furthermore, because they were not familiar with ad hoc task groups, the Japanese participants were faced with a substantial amount of uncertainty regarding the appropriate behavior in task groups. In these cases, we would expect a reliance on cultural norms for behavior in the group, such as the maintenance of harmony for the Japanese. The Japanese group members in the Thomas et al. (1996) study indeed had a higher expectations of group harmony (wa) than their counterparts from other cultures, and therefore perceived even low levels of conflict as very salient.

In summary, for our purposes, it is important to note that conflict and debate are major catalysts in MNTs, and that the likely cultural differences in the way in which status and hierarchy are perceived, mean that MNTs are particularly susceptible to conflict. As mentioned earlier, when it occurs, the group may on the one hand, be spurred toward additional interaction and the associated sub-processes of retrieving, exchanging, and structuring information, before it is able to integrate knowledge, makes decisions or take action. In contrast, building a consensus in a group is likely to move it onward toward complacency. Neither path is necessarily good or bad. In fact, iterative movement between the phases of interaction and examination is probably healthy in most groups. Taken together, the preliminary evidence indicates that agreement and integration are important factors in the collective cognition that occurs in MNTs; however, conflict and debate may also serve a necessary role in prompting the team to act outside routines and controlled processing of information. In fact, any given conflict might serve to establish what is referred to in chemistry as an "active site"—that spot on a molecule in which a reaction takes place—thus focused attention to conflicts as sources of change is warranted.

### Subgroups and Third Parties: Equilibrium Between Fractionation and Integration.
A third category of social structure catalysts pertains to group membership, whether it be membership in groups external to the MNTs or subgroup membership with in the MNT. Most MNTs have somewhat fluid membership, with the "team" being defined loosely as a core set of members, together with a set of peripheral members that may or may not be considered official members of the team at any given point in time, depending on the life cycle stage of the team, the particular task at hand, and/or competing priorities that keep such peripheral members busy outside the scope of work of the team. Thus, MNTs are fertile ground for the challenges posed by subgroups, and for the influence of third parties, discussed next.

How people define their membership, as part of the larger group or as part of the subgroup can have serious impacts on group processes. Information perceived from in-group members tends to be more influential than similar information from out-group members (Abrams, Wetherell, Cochrane, Hogg, & Turner, 1990). Thus, if subgroup members define each other as in-group members, this can seriously isolate the subgroup.

If subgroups form explicitly and each subgroup meets individually and independently from the larger group (as they often do in MNTs), additional forces can contribute to solidify the subgroup structure and strengthen rifts in the larger group (Lau & Murnighan, 1998). In particular, cohesive subgroups may find themselves polarizing and taking positions that become increasingly extreme. Persuasive arguments theorists (e.g., Vinokur & Burnstein, 1978) suggest that group members who support similar attitudinal positions will find that, as other members support that position using arguments different form their own, they each have more reason to become even more extreme than they were before.

MNTs with salient subgroups are likely to have a shorter sense making process. Sense making is necessary because knowledge is subjectively generated and consumed by different communities in relationship to that community's unique thought-world (Dougherty, 1992; Fleck, 1979), interpretive conventions (Brown & Duguid, 1991), and specific social processes (Barnes, 1983). Structuration theory (Giddens, 1974; Poole & DeSanctis, 1994) argues that human behavior and understanding is contextual, guided by contextually determined interpretive schemes, norms, and power relationships that shape sense-making. Knowledge from another community will be rejected if it is discrepant from the receiving community's conventions (Mohrman, Gibson, & Mohrman, 2001).

Kanter and Eccles (1992), for example, noted that managers and academics at a conference regarding network research used very different kinds of data to draw conclusions. Managers tended to use egocentric and asymmetric data that viewed the network from their personal position in it and in terms of its implications for accomplishing their purposes. Academics depicted very complete networks and dealt with gross characteristics that, in the eyes of the practitioners, sacrificed the very subtlety and nuance that were paramount. Thus both theory and experience argue for a broadening of perspectives so they can interpret, communicate, and make sense of each others' thoughts. This is difficult, because meaning systems are often tacit and taken for granted by a community; people often assume that the rest of the world's perspectives are more similar to their own than they actually are (Compton, 1980). Furthermore, one party may assume that its knowledge is superior to that of another party (e.g., Howes, 1980).

When subgroup members are similar on many dimensions (e.g., gender, nationality, age), sense making can be relatively straightforward because group members will expect that the members share similar scripts. With weak subgroups, group members are less likely to expect that others will have similar scripts, and a longer sense making process may be more typical (Lau & Murnighan, 1998). An open exchange of information within the larger group can limit the kinds of subgroup polarization that entrench subgroup conflict.

When subgroups do form and persist early in an MNTs development, they become an important part of members' memories and provide the foundation for group norms (Bettenhausen & Murnighan, 1985; Feldman, 1984). Subgroups also tend to emerge when subsequent conflict arises and they tend to reinforce themselves through time if they become active early in a group's development (Lau & Murnighan, 1998). Network theorists suggest that people with similar demographic attributes tend to socialize together (Ibarra, 1993). This relationship building can emphasize subgroup divisions, and the off-work activities can enhance understanding and relationship among the subgroup members so that they become more internally cohesive (Lau & Murnighan, 1998).

Recruiting group members with different and/or unique combinations of attributes may reduce the probability of subgroup formation and the kinds of intragroup conflicts they can cause. Outsiders and inactive peripheral members, often known as "third parties" can also assist in this regard. From a theoretical perspective, third parties can be broadly defined to include any individual or set of individuals formally employed or contracted by an organization to provide input for strategic decisions (Gibson & Saxton, 2001). Excluded from this definition are informal contractors such as family, friends, and other acquaintances. Third parties have a profound impact on organizations today. Attorneys are involved in decisions with direct, indirect, or potential legal implications related to acquisitions and alliances, human resource policies, and a range of other strategic decisions. Accountants play a major role in assessing tax and other implications for major and minor corporate investments and for measuring performance. Management consultancy at firms such as Andersen, McKinsey, Booz-Allen and Hamilton, and Price Waterhouse Coopers have been expanding at a prodigious rate. Since 1990, revenues in the business as a whole have been growing by 10% or more a year, and in the leading companies by as much as 20 to 30% (Wooldridge, 1997). Andersen Consulting, one of the largest, has quadrupled its revenues in the first 6 years of its existence to more than $4.2 billion a year, with predicted earnings of $8 billion by 2000 (Wooldridge, 1997a).

Despite the extent of involvement of third parties in organizational decisions, existing research has done little to measure the impact of third parties on decision processes or outcomes. Third parties such as consultants are occasionally mentioned (e.g., Fischhoff & Goitein, 1984; Hambrick & Mason, 1984; Miles & Snow, 1978; Robinson, 1982), but as incidental players as opposed to central figures in strategic decision making. Third parties are rarely, if ever, the focus of theoretical or empirical research.

Third parties and specifically consultants do make appearances in strategy literature and related books. Robinson (1982) recognizes that third parties, including consultants, lawyers, accountants, and bankers, play an important role in organizational decisions. Greiner and Metzger (1983) have written a book devoted to the topic, and flesh out why and when companies might use consultants. Others document the explosive growth of the consulting industry in domestic as well as international engagements (Ashton, 1991; Suryanarayanan, 1989; Wooldridge, 1997b). Ginsberg and Abrahamson (1991) note the value of external advocates as change agents. There is also a body of literature that investigates third-party intervention in dispute resolution (e.g., Karambayya & Brett, 1989). However, despite this literature, there is limited empirical evidence that demonstrates that teams with third parties will be more effective than those without.

A noted earlier in chapter 2, Gibson and Saxton (2000) argue that it is the *differential* effect of consultant involvement that is of strategic interest. Companies vary in whether, how, and when they involve consultants in strategic decisions (Saxton, 1995; Greiner & Metzger, 1983). Gibson and

Saxton's (2000) empirical investigation demonstrated that type of third-party input, timing of the input, and heterogeneity of the team interacted to affect decision outcomes. In particular, for heterogeneous teams, third parties were particularly helpful when they provided input that can be characterized as "direction" early in the decision-making process. This type of input helped in clarification of the goals, objectives and mission of the team, assisted the team in establishing direction and momentum toward effective accomplishment of desired outcomes, and aided the formulation of second-order goals and actions steps that serve as means to accomplishing the relevant ends (Saxton, 1995).

Thus in summary, if subgroups form explicitly in an MNT and become cohesive, the subgroups often polarize and take positions that become increasingly extreme. MNTs with salient subgroups are likely to have a shorter sense making processes within the subgroups, and more conflicts between subgroups. The challenges MNTs have in coming to a consensus and completing the decision-making process might be offset by the presence of a third party helping guide the team and keep subgroups on task. Third parties may indeed facilitate the strategic decision-making process in MNTs, but it is not their direct involvement per se that matters; rather, it is the type and timing of third-party input, and the role they play in bridging subgroups that facilitates effectiveness.

***Membership Changes: Equilibrium Between Isolation and Incorporation.*** Changes in membership in MNTs is the final social structure catalyst to change we have identified in our research. When important members leave and/or influential members join an existing group, the changes in a group's dynamics can be truly significant. For example, the addition of new members into established groups introduces the possibility of creating new subgroups or resurfacing old ones. Existing members share some understandings of group norms, past group history, and group tasks; newcomers rarely have this kind of knowledge. Jackson, Stone, and Alvarez (1992) propose that a single newcomer tends to experience strong pressures to conform unless he or she shares some demographic similarities with at least one existing group member. Thus, the first member of noticeable societal minority who enters an established homogeneous group of societal majority members may not be in a strong position to alter existing group norms (Lau & Murnighan, 1998).

Hollander (1964) suggests in his analysis of group entry, new members typically keep quiet until they have established themselves enough to have their ideas heard. However, when new group members share similarities with established group members, the new versus old member distinction becomes less important, and if subgroups exist or form, new members may join old members with whom they share similarities. Single group members may latch onto any possible similarity and any available subgroup to provide themselves with some interpersonal security (Lau & Murnighan, 1998). In contrast, minority subgroups may seek support from new members to allow them to reintroduce controversial issues that had been rejected by the group, especially when they have not internalized the stronger subgroup's positions. New members then hold the promise of possible support for minority subgroup members' suppressed desires.

A person who does not fit into established subcategories will lead perceivers to form a new subcategory in order to allow the perceiver to categorize that person (Fiske & Neuberg, 1990). This reevaluation process means that the initial importance of subgroups early in an MNT's life cycle will diminish over time. Knowledge of others' values, personalities, hobbies, or political preferences, will fragment a group's initial subgroup structure (Lau & Murnighan, 1998). Similarities among otherwise diverse group members are likely to surface over time.

Perhaps the most important dynamic to consider regarding membership changes is the potential impact these changes have on the collective cognition, shared understanding, and mental models within the MNT. Research in this domain is very limited and emerging, but preliminary evidence suggests that cognitive convergence—the development of similar cognitive structures among team members over time—is critical to shared understanding (Monier, 1999). Specifically, Monier (1999) examined convergence among 17 teams and found that cognitive convergence predicted performance on a team problem-solving task. Teams performed better when members began with diverse mental models and became similar over time. This research implies the importance of some stability of membership overtime, with the caveat that if properly managed, socialized and integrated, new incoming members might also demonstrate similar cognitive structures to those already developed in the team.

Using a social network approach, Joshi and Caligiuri (2000) came to similar conclusions. These researchers examined socials interactions among team members from six national subsidiaries to determine the relationships among participation in social networks and effectiveness. Centrality in the communication network was positively related to subsidiary effectiveness and cohesion. These results highlight the difficulty that entrance of new members, or frequent turnover of existing members, often poses in developing an effective social network within the team.

In summary, membership changes in MNTs pose significant challenges to developing inclusive team culture that encourages incorporation as opposed to isolation. New members impact subgroup formation and operation, cognitive convergence, and development of social networks. Stability of membership is not always feasible, nor entirely recommended, but relative consistency in a core set of MNT members, together with explicit policies for incorporation is advised.

## SUMMARY

In this chapter we have reviewed general domains of catalysts bringing about change in MNTs. With the task structure domain, we emphasized that pacing is a key catalyst. Time can be viewed as subjective and MNTs will often consist of members with different views of time. These differing perspectives may have distinct links to organizational successes and failures, since the actions of individuals within groups can guide more macrolevel organizational outcomes based on individuals' social constructions. Thus, it is insufficient to view a person's concept of time as passively acquired from one's culture or social structure. Individuals will adopt and adapt to views of time that are personally reinforcing and, in turn, create social institutions to perpetuate such views.

Task constraints are equally important catalysts. When tasks are nonroutine, diversity is likely to result in greater task conflict. In contrast, task routineness can reduce the positive association between diversity and emotional conflict in MNTs. Realistically, some degree of uncertainty is unavoidable in the turbulent context in which MNTs often operate. Thus, all teams face a trade-off between emergence and integration processes. When integration is moderate, team members are likely to attend to a variety of information, and this will facilitate their performance. This highlights the role of self-organizing, or configuration, as a catalyst to knowledge sharing and subsequent behavior change in MNTs.

Evolution of goals also acts to bring about change in MNTs. Multiple competing goals for each member of the MNT who represents a different geographic area or organizational subunit is a fact of life. The amplification of divergent views in the early stages of the MNT's life cycle may generate strong entropy leading the team toward early integration as the team struggles to establish order. This may curtail the healthy discussion of different opinions, options and perceptions, reducing creativity. Thus, the context of the MNT presents a particular challenge for balancing growth and stability in the team.

Managing this process requires additional attention to technology, a fifth category of task structure catalysts. Differences in information technology platforms and tools, and insufficient support for the implementation and use of technologies, can be major barriers to integration. MNTs need to have a clear strategy for matching technology for the task at hand, and for managing transitions to new technologies that can potentially bring about major change in the team. Minimally, MNT members should be able to integrate their own data and tools with each other as well as those of the people with whom they work in their own co-located organizations.

A supportive organizational context can assistance in this process, and acts as a sixth category of catalysts to change. It is important for four basic domains of the organizational context—standard organizational processes, organizational culture, training and development, and reward, recognition, and promotion systems—to be in place and well aligned, but also adaptable. Research suggests that alignment and adaptability are both important predictors of firm performance in multinational organizations and that alignment and adaptability result from different combinations of internal systems across geographic and industry contexts. The challenge for the MNT is to identify which set of systems is critical in their own context, and how those can be managed to promote optimal levels of alignment and adaptability.

A final category of task structure catalyst we reviewed encompasses human resource changes in teams. An approach that simultaneously considers business strategy, human resource strategy, and human resource practices and how they interact with national culture, power systems, legislation, education, and employee representation is particularly well suited to MNTs. The approach also highlights the importance of adapting human resource management to local practice in the multinational firm, and more specifically the multinational team.

Beyond task structure catalysts, we discussed four categories of social structure catalysts. The first of these is leadership. Without leadership and facilitation, roles in an MNT are often ambiguous. We argued that member roles serve an essential guiding function that enables MNT members to make more efficient use of each other's personal store of problem-relevant information. Preliminary evidence suggests that when members know which other members of the group have expertise in which specific knowledge domains, the amount of unshared information they actually discuss increases significantly. Clearly defined roles enable this sharing. As a leader, helping MNTs to face adaptive situations is a process of mobilizing and enabling rather than planning and controlling. Traditional styles of leadership do not serve well in adaptive situations and therefore require leading and working using self-management techniques.

This more flexible style of leadership facilitates cooperation and competition, the second social structure catalyst we discussed. Conflict and debate are major catalysts in MNTs. Because there are likely to be cultural differences in the way in which status and hierarchy are perceived, MNTs are particularly susceptible to conflict. When conflict occurs, the group may on the one hand, be spurred toward additional interaction and the associated sub-processes of retrieving, exchanging, and structuring information, before it is able to integrate knowledge, makes decisions or take action. In contrast, building a consensus in a group is likely to move it onward toward complacency. Neither path is necessarily good or bad. In fact, iterative movement between the phases of interaction and examination is probably healthy in most groups.

Subgroup formation and third party consultation constitute a third category of social structure catalysts. If subgroups form explicitly in an MNT and become cohesive, the subgroups often polarize and take positions that become increasingly extreme. The challenges MNTs have in coming to a consensus and completing the decision-making process might be off-set by the presence of a third party helping guide the team and keep sub-groups on task. Third parties may indeed facilitate the strategic decision-making process in MNTs, but it is not their direct involvement per se that matters; rather, it is the type and timing of third-party input, and the role they play in bridging subgroups that facilitates effectiveness.

Finally, membership changes acts as a catalyst, in that such changes in MNTs pose significant challenges to developing an inclusive team culture that encourages incorporation as opposed to isolation. New members im-pact subgroup formation and operation, cognitive convergence, and de-velopment of social networks. Stability of membership is not always feasible, nor entirely recommended, but we argued for relative consis-tency in a core set of MNT members, together with explicit policies for in-corporation. In the next chapter, we provide the integration and application of our framework to multinational teams. We do this through the use of an extended case analysis conducted by Gibson through her work on a major research grant of international business teams.

# 7 Profiles of Elements, Catalysts, and Dynamic Processes in Operative MNTs

As we discussed in chapter 3, our basic model is captured by a cubic representation with the internal elements housed within an organizational and societal context. There are six basic components to our model, including: (1) individual elements, (2) group elements (3) context, (4) work structure catalysts, (5) social structure catalysts, and (6) a set of basic processes, connecting individual to group elements and the context in which these elements are embedded. In this chapter, we provide a general integration of our model of MNTs, including elements, catalysts, and dynamic processes. We apply the model to five ongoing MNTs with whom we have worked extensively. Our intent is to "tell the story" of these five teams, and in doing so to illustrate how the model can be utilized for understanding MNTs in diverse cultural contexts.

Our involvement with these five teams included observations, extensive interviews, 360-degree team assessments, and surveys exploring the elements and processes. The second author, Cristina Gibson, conducted these investigations together with her colleague Mary Zellmer-Bruhn and a team of translators in conjunction with the Multinational Implementation of Teams Project, a four-year program of research with funding from the National Science Foundation (SBR # 96-31748), the University of Wisconsin Initiative for World Affairs and the Global Economy, and the Carnegie Bosch Institute for Applied International Management.

The research comprises a comprehensive multi-method investigation of team effectiveness in multinational organizations. "Team" was defined as a group of individuals who work together interdependently to produce products or deliver services for which they are mutually accountable. Key factors explored in the project include team effectiveness, degree of direction provided by external leaders, group-efficacy motivational beliefs, cultural phenomenon, processes, practices, and various facets of the organizational context.

Phase I of the project consisted of exploratory interviews. A total of 111 individuals were interviewed representing 59 teams across six organizations and four cultures (U.S. France, Puerto Rico, and in the Philippines). The organizational contexts for the research were selected based upon two general guiding principles: (1) all were within the same general industry to control for possible industry-related effects; and (2) only organizations that had facilities in each of the four countries were included. We selected the pharmaceutical and medical products industry because production of pharmaceuticals is geographically dispersed around the world.

Gibson and Zellmer-Bruhn traveled to each region of the world and conducted in-depth personal interviews with a wide variety of members from each organization (See the Appendix for a copy of the interview protocol). All interviews were tape recorded and transcribed by professional linguists and transcriptionists. A Phase I report based on interview analyses was compiled, translated, and sent to all 111 respondents in three languages. Country comparisons and organizational comparisons were included. Managerial implications and suggestions for future research were proposed.

In Phase II of the study, Gibson and her colleagues (Gibson, Zellmer-Bruhn, & Schwab, 2000) developed a survey assessment based on the cross-cultural interviews. Potential items were derived using content analysis, items were refined , and initial instrumentation created. Extensive translation and back translation procedure were utilized to ensure equivalence of meaning across three foreign language versions (English, French, and Spanish) of the measures. A comprehensive bilingual analysis of the instrumentation was conducted and then a multiple constituency approach was used to pilot test the measures in the field to ensure that team leader, team member, and team customer versions of the instruments were equivalent and produced high interrater reliability (see Appendix A for survey instruments utilized).

In the third phase of the study, the survey assessment was administered to over 3,000 participants (including members, leaders, and customers) in five of the organizations across the same four countries that participated in the interviews. A total of 1,041 completed surveys were returned, representing 166 teams. Based on survey results, customized team-level feedback reports were distributed to all teams to disseminate major findings of the third phase of the project and facilitate team development among industry participants. For the MNTs that we describe here, names of the team members, team configurations, and organizations have been disguised to protect the confidentiality of the participants.

The MNTs we include represent a variety of team types, structures and industries. They vary in the number of cultures, geographic regions, and functions represented on each team. The nature of the collaborative work they perform together varies dramatically across teams. We begin each team story by discussing this general background information. Next, given that our objective here is illustration as opposed to diagnosis, we do not attempt to describe every feature of our model in each team. Rather, we highlight what we believe to be the subset of most critical individual and group elements in each team, the catalysts that were most potent, and the processes that appeared to have the greatest impact on the dynamic equilibrium in each team.

## THE ASIA PACIFIC STRATEGY TEAM (APST)

I'm very heavy on my belief in teams, the use of teams. And when I came here, I started coming up with teams that would be involved with certain activities. One of the most active ones would be the strategy team, composed of heads of all the regions.
—*Mike, Director of Strategic Initiatives, Asia Pacific Strategy Team, Pharmco*

**Context.** The Asia Pacific Strategy Teams consists of 12 members, each of whom represents a different pharmaceutical product within a variety of countries in the Asia Pacific Region. The team had been in existence for approximately four years when we first began our work with them. Using the categorization scheme developed by Cohen and Bailey (1997), the team considers itself a "parallel" team, meaning that it pulls people from different work units or jobs to perform functions that the regular organization is not well equipped to perform. Parallel teams typically have limited authority, and often make recommendations to people higher up in the organization. Parallel teams are often used for problem-solving and improvement activities. The objective of the APST is to develop a consistent marketing strategy across products and nations within the region.

The APST members are all employed by one organization ("Pharmco"), that develops, manufactures, sells, and distributes pharmaceutical products. This organization is a leading research-driven company whose mission is to provide society with superior products and services, innovations and solutions that improve the quality of life and satisfy customer needs. According to annual reports, the organization also strives to provide employees with meaningful work and advancement opportunities and to provide investors with a superior rate of return. In the popular press reports, company representatives have stated that they view their ability to excel at competitively meeting customer's needs as dependent upon the integrity, knowledge, imagination, diversity and teamwork of employees.

Figure 7.1 depicts the APST, indicating the demographic characteristics of each team member. Eight nations and three ethnicities are represented on the team. There are three women and nine men on the team. Members range in age from 28 to 53 years, educations range from a bachelor's degree (4 members), to a master's degree (6 members), and two PhDs. Tenure in the organization ranges from less than 1 year to 20 years, and team tenure ranges from 1 year to 3 years. Most team members consider themselves in marketing, with one indicating sales and one indicating finance as a functional home. For the most part, the members of the APST are each directors or senior directors of regional marketing for their respective products. The exception are the leader (Mike), who holds a director's position in strategic initiatives and one member (Nate) who does not have specific product representation, but instead serves as economic advisor for the region.

The APST is a high performing team. Table 7.1 provides a comparison of the scores received by the APST and the other teams described in this chapter on both team outcomes and processes. Internal team customers rated the team as highly effective in terms of outcomes (customer satisfaction, goals, productivity, quality, and timeliness). The customer ratings received by the team on process effectiveness were uneven across the four processes we assessed (attitudes, cohesion, communication, conflict resolution), as discussed below cohesion is low but the team is very effective at conflict resolution. Based on our model, we would argue that the APST's success can be explained primarily by the combination of several key catalysts and elements, including third parties, hybrid culture, effective approaches to subgroups, processes associated with adaptation, and several factors in the organizational context that have encouraged this adaptation. Each of these is discussed in turn below.

**Catalysts.** In comparison with most of the MNTs in our sample, the APST can be considered moderate in terms of demographic heterogeneity. Although national heterogeneity is high (8 nations represented), all members share the same functional background, and have similar levels of education and tenure, thus overall heterogeneity is moderate. In a moderately heterogeneous team, subgroups or factions may exist if members perceive differences among themselves based on salient features. As reviewed in chapter 2, moderate heterogeneity is consistent with Lau and Murnighan's (1998) strong "faultlines"—hypothetical dividing lines that may split a group into subgroups based on one or more attributes. They suggested that demographic faultlines underlie how team diversity affects functioning.

Pharmco: Asia Pacific Strategy Team

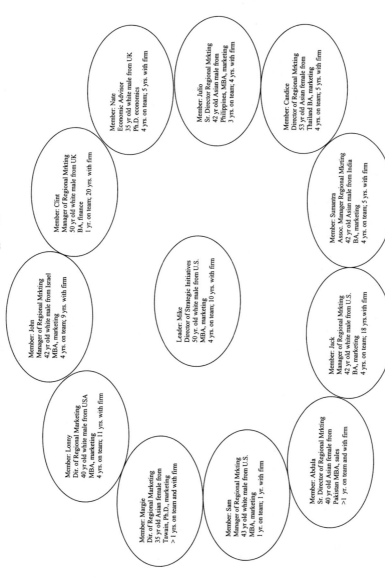

FIG. 7.1. Asia Pacific Strategy Team.

**TABLE 7.1**
Customer Ratings of MNT Outcomes and Processes

| | Overall Avg. of All Teams in Sample (N = 166) | APST | BPT | SST | LLT | HRPT |
|---|---|---|---|---|---|---|
| **CUSTOMER RATINGS OF TEAM OUTCOMES** | | | | | | |
| Customer Satisfaction | 5.2 | 5.7 | 5.7 | 5.6 | 4.2 | 4.7 |
| Goals | 5.4 | 5.5 | 5.9 | 4.6 | 5.6 | 5.0 |
| Productivity | 5.1 | 5.8 | 5.7 | 4.9 | 5.0 | 4.8 |
| Quality | 4.8 | 5.1 | 5.8 | 4.8 | 5.2 | 4.3 |
| Timeliness | 5.1 | 5.3 | 5.0 | 4.7 | 4.7 | 5.5 |
| **CUSTOMER RATINGS OF TEAM PROCESSES** | | | | | | |
| Attitudes | 5.2 | 5.9 | 5.3 | 4.9 | 5.4 | 4.9 |
| Cohesion | 5.1 | 4.9 | 5.6 | 5.2 | 5.0 | 4.4 |
| Communication | 4.8 | 4.9 | 4.8 | 4.8 | 5.3 | 4.3 |
| Conflict | 5.0 | 6.2 | 5.3 | 5.2 | 5.2 | 4.1 |

Following Gibson & Vermeulen (2000), we computed scores for each team in our sample that capture the potential for faultlines to occur based on various combinations of member attributes, including age, gender, ethnic background, functional background, and team tenure. These faultlines suggest where potential subgroups might form. The more alignment there is of different individual member characteristics, relative to other members, the more distinct the subgroup. For subgroups to emerge, there must be overlap between certain members which is not shared by others. As a result, faultlines are most likely to occur in teams of moderate heterogeneity (Earley and Mosakowski, 2000; Lau and Murnighan, 1998). On the other hand, teams of moderate heterogeneity *can* be free of faultlines; when the demographic differences are dispersed across different members.

Among the five teams profiled here, the ASPT received the highest score on the measure of potential faultlines. For example, in the ASPT, a likely subgroup might consist of the five Asians, three of whom are also the only women on the team, and most of whom have relatively little organizational tenure. A second subgroup might consist of the other seven members of the team (from the United States or United Kingdom). A strong faultline might then separate these two subgroups.[1] Some evidence for such faultlines in the APST is revealed in the team's low cohesion score of 4.9 on a 7-point scale, compared to the overall average of 5.1. Evidence of the subgroup was also expressed in interviews, such as this statement by Abdula, the Senior Director of Regional Marketing in Pakistan:

> Women in the workforce I think fosters teams. And that's just a, in my opinion, female trait. I think teams have a better chance of becoming more like a family based on the fact that women do a better job of keeping families together. I just think that's the way we're made. So it's a pretty biased opinion that I have on that subject, that others in the team don't share. But I think that's one of the positives that would come from having women in the team. So, yeah, I guess anything else I was going to say is along those lines—it's so apparent with the physicians that we call on that it is difficult for those certain customers, if they come from India, or if they're Asian, to respect us as reputable sources. Then there are certain physicians that would much rather deal with men. So I usually just allow them to do that and turn those over.

Candice, Director of Regional Marketing for Thailand, concurs. She stated:

> I think that there is a gender, I don't want to call it a problem, but, sometimes you're very aware of, of your gender when you're speaking with certain people. I think that is a cultural issue, and it definitely can affect how people have

---

[1] By way of comparison, the faultline potential in the APST is similar to Group Number 3 depicted in Lau & Murninghan's (1998) Table 1. Group Number 3 had moderate diversity, but consisted of two White males in their 50s on the one hand, and two Black females in the 30s on the other; thus, the potential for a faultline between these two subgroups is very strong.

related when they have to work collectively. My perception of one of our team members is that he was very threatened by, I don't want to say strong women, but women who were good at what they did. And he felt very threatened by that and you could tell.

Representing Regional Marketing in India, Sumantra had this to say about the subgroups in the team:

I think that other cultures are more supportive of teams than Americans. The Asian cultures are very family oriented, group-oriented, you know, everyone works together and helps each other out. And I don't see that so much in the Western culture. The Western culture supports more independence, whereas the Asian culture supports interdependence.

As reported in chapter 2, research suggests that if subgroups form explicitly and each subgroup meets individually and independently from the larger group the subgroup structure might strengthen rifts in the larger group (Earley & Mosakowski, 2000; Lau & Murnighan, 1998). MNTs with salient subgroups are likely to have a shorter sense making process. When subgroup members are similar on many dimensions (e.g., gender, nationality, age), sense making can be relatively straightforward because group members will expect that the members share similar scripts. With weak subgroups, group members are less likely to expect that others will have similar scripts, and a longer sense making process may be more typical (Lau & Murnighan, 1998).

Subgroups tend to emerge when subsequent conflict arises and they tend to reinforce themselves through time if they become active early in a group's development (Earley & Mosakowski, 2000; Lau & Murnighan, 1998). Abdula, the one team member with a sales background on the team, described this situation as follows:

I never really considered myself to be a salesperson. When I originally came to Pharmco, I wanted to be in marketing, and they said, well you have to start out in sales. Pharmco hires a lot of really good people, I mean really sharp people, and you work your territory, and you are compensated, and you are judged, and you are promoted on the basis of what you did. People that are very successful, feel a good deal of internal satisfaction from that. And now at the team level, I'm always kind of struggling with that. You've got strong personalities all working together as a team. And sometimes that's not always the best, so there can be a lot of power struggles between certain groups.

An open exchange of information within the larger group can eliminate the kinds of subgroup polarization that entrenches subgroup conflict. As mentioned above, the APST is very effective at conflict resolution, scoring 6.2 on the seven point scale in which 5.0 was average across the entire sample (see Table 7.1). Julio, the Director of Regional Marketing from the

Philippines had this to say as he reflected on some of the forces in the team that served to strengthen the conflict resolution skills:

> You know, there is this funny thing about our values. Because there is always two sides of a value. You know. For me as a Filipino, one of the things would be the "pakikisama" system, which is trying to be together in certain endeavors. To reach the objective of, you know, harnessing everybody's effort towards something good, then that's a very potent word to capitalize it. Then there is this peer pressure approach that is a part of helping in that. In Filipino we call it "bayanihan." Yeah, bayanihan. Bayanihan is like, in the provinces we would have such houses, like huts. During the rainy season, the village would carry it on their shoulders, one whole group. If one person fell, then the house would fall, you know. So in the same sense, if you have a weak link in the team, then it won't work out. Bayanihan is a very good example. But I guess it's a model of how you now, how to utilize this. But by and large, I think, we all share the Filipino desires to be accessible, to be part of a team, to have fun, to always want to do positively in every team.

Effective conflict resolution was also likely encouraged due to the to the presence of a second catalyst to change highlighted in our MNT model: third parties. As we reviewed in chapter 2, third parties can be broadly defined to include any individual or set of individuals formally employed or contracted by an organization to provide input for strategic decisions. Gibson and Saxton (2001) demonstrated that type of third party input, timing of the input, and heterogeneity of the team interacted to affect decision outcomes. In particular, for heterogeneous teams, third parties were particularly helpful when they clarified goals, objectives and mission of the team, assisted the team in establishing direction and momentum toward effective accomplishment of desired outcomes, and aided the formulation of second order goals and actions steps that serve as means to accomplishing the relevant ends (Saxton, 1995).

In the APST, Nate, the Economic Advisor, can be considered an active third party. Being from the United Kingdom and holding a PhD, Nate also increased the level of heterogeneity in the team, potentially reducing the tendency for subgroups to form. Nate had this to say about his role:

> I would not consider myself an advisor to the representatives, but again, a resource I guess, a consultant for, to keep them abreast of current updates, new drugs that are coming out, new treatment patterns, new issues with respect to total quality management and outcomes. All of those things, as well as managed care, updates there. So I guess I would, yeah, I think a resource is the best way to look at my role.

Reflecting on the team composition, an APST internal team customer said this about Nate:

The agenda for each meeting will probably cover the concerns of this month. But also a lot of different materials. For example, each rep would come up with a presentation about their region, what's the problem, what's going on, what are the successes, so that they can share among themselves, and the advisor, he's one notch higher in terms of knowledge from the headquarters. And they draw out these people within their teams. So, these people are the ones providing insight.

A second set of catalysts that may have worked to counteract faultlines in the APST is membership changes. Most MNTs have somewhat fluid membership, with the "team" being defined loosely as a core set of members, together with a set of peripheral members that may or may not be considered official members of the team at any given point in time, depending on the life cycle stage of the team, the particular task at hand, and/or competing priorities that keep such peripheral members busy outside the scope of work of the team. Members with differing priorities and commitment levels bring a certain amount of stress, as expressed by Sam, the team member from the United States:

> This is the most upheaval that Pharmco has been through since they did their first huge expansion in 1988, so there's a lot of I wouldn't want to say, unrest, but unsettledness, just because of the new people that are coming on. And the people that have the experience and the tenure are being promoted, and many times staying out in the field, but also many time going to manage. So there are a lot of people that will be new.

However, recruiting group members with different and/or unique combinations of attributes may reduce the probability of subgroup formation and the kinds of intragroup conflicts they can cause. Particularly if they lead to the development of a key element in the team: hybrid culture.

**Individual and Group Elements.** As reviewed in chapter 2, a hybrid culture refers to an emergent and simplified set of rules and actions, work capability expectations, and member perceptions that individuals within a team develop, share, and enact after mutual interactions (Earley & Mosakowski, 2000). To the extent these rules, expectations, and roles are shared (Rohner, 1987; Schweder & LeVine, 1984), a strong culture exists. Earley and Mosakowski found that a hybrid team culture may provide the basis for exchange and coordination within a diverse team to exploit member talents and resources. Lonny, the Director of Regional marketing from the United States, had this to say about the hybrid culture that has developed in the APST:

> My counterpart [Margie in Taiwan] and I work together phenomenally. We are just, like—we're complete opposites, and it, we use it to the maximum.

You know? We just complement each other really well. But, she is the more meticulous, you know, number crunching kind of, pay attention to detail, and I am more the big picture, and, you know, here's the big project. She is very happy doing that side; I am very happy doing mine. And we're very, very successful. I think that when they hire for the clusters [such as the APST], they should really take a look at the personality of the team they're putting them in. And I don't … I know they do to a certain degree, but it would be nice if we could also take a look at this person, have 'em work with us, see what they're like and see in our minds how they would fit into our cluster. I don't think they want to give us that power. But I think it would actually be really be worthwhile and prevent a lot of headaches down the road.

**Processes.**     A key process highlighted in our MNT model is adaptive structuration. A key point we borrow from Giddens's work on this topic is that social structure is not static; rather it is an ongoing and evolving processes whereby team members create and recreate the structure. The empirical work of Majchrzak and her colleagues, reviewed in chapter 5, suggested that the evolution of these structures occurs when the teams find the structures to be misaligned with their tasks. Team success is achieved when the initial structure is sufficiently flexible to be molded to the needs of the workgroup and organizational structure; so it is the fit of the team structure with the strategy that is more important than the initial nature of the structure.

As a rule, the organizational context at Pharmco focuses more on adaptability than on alignment. As shown in Table 7.3, the APST received the lowest score of all teams on the scale measuring global integration, indicating little pressure in the team to adopt standardized practices across cultural contexts. In contrast, the team's score on local responsiveness was extremely high, indicating that the challenges the team faces are unique, and that practices developed outside the team may not readily meet its needs. This approach may underlie the success of this team.

As discussed in chapter 5, all organizations face a potential trade-off between alignment and adaptability, and a supportive organizational context helps to establish the equilibrium given the unique environment that a team faces. Gibson and Birkinshaw's (2000) company-by-company analysis revealed that different systems are better predictors of alignment and adaptability in some organizations than others. They proposed that balance is the result of implementation of sets of enabling management systems, established as strategic complementarities, based on the industry, market, stage of growth and institutional context in which an organization is embedded. In organizations that have achieved an optimal level of adaptation, initiative is valued, inconsistencies and discontinuities are objectively evaluated, experimentation and some failure are tolerated, and there are processes for modifying institutional systems (WEF/BAH Report, 2000).

This appears to be the case as Pharmco. As expressed by Julio, the director from Guatemala:

> Managers within Pharmco have a lot of autonomy. And when you have a company this size—and I know it will be similar for the other pharmaceutical companies—from what I can understand, I think it's even to a greater extent with Pharmco—it's like having a million little companies—there's a lot of diversity between the regions. And within the regions, between the managers. So there's always some standard Pharmco laws that are for the whole. But those types of things, as far as best practices, there's a lot of diversity between managers. The product groups. Because they develop the strategies for the entire nation, but then the good thing that has been allowed to change within Pharmco in the last three or four years is that then the regions can take that and make it work for their area. In the past, there was a lot less flexibility. And a lot of that has to do with a complete change of upper management within Pharmco.

At an individual level, openness and respect for others helps to establish the flexibility necessary to develop adaptation and a hybrid culture. Clint, the Manager of Regional Marketing from the United Kingdom, had this to say:

> The key things are open-mindedness and flexibility. They have to be able to be tolerant. I mean even if you've been in the territories for 25 years, you have to be willing to say, okay that's something I didn't know. Whereas a lot of people—if you've been with the company a long time—you're kind of reluctant to say, "Oh, okay, this youngster just taught me something." So I think you definitely have to have an open mind, you have to be able to be taught, and you have to have flexibility when you are working with many different individuals.

Encouraging this style of relating is an important intervention in MNTs that we will discuss further in our last chapter. Here, we now move on to our second case study.

## BIOMEDICAL PRODUCTION TEAM (BPT)

> I think we have, you know, we've done a lot in terms of empowering. [chuckles] An abused word, "empowering." But in the sense that, you know, we feel that we can manage the work. We can recommend certain ways of doing things during meetings. It's really open, as a matter of fact. Leadership in the team as far as facilitating, as far as that kind of leadership, is very much expressed in the team membership.
> —*Juan, Production Specialist, Biomedical Production Team Puerto Rico, Biomedco*

**Context.** The Biomedical Production Team consists of 9 members responsible for the manufacturing and packaging of a granulated biomedical product. The team works in a cellular manufacturing environment inside a large modern production facility located in Puerto Rico. When we first began our work with the BPT, the team had been in existence for approximately 5 years. Using the categorization scheme developed by Cohen and Bailey (1997), the BPT is a work team. This type of team is responsible for producing goods or providing services. Their membership is typically stable, usually full-time, and well-defined.

Figure 7.2 depicts the BPT, indicating the demographic characteristics of each team member. The United States and Puerto Rico are the two geographic regions represented on the team, participants from the United States are White, those from Puerto Rico are Latino. There are two women and seven men on the team. Members range in age from 25 to 51 years, education ranges from an associates degree (three members), to a bachelor's degree (four members), to a master's degree (two members). Tenure in the organization ranges from 1 year to 20 years, and team tenure ranges from 1 year to 5 years. All members are Production Specialists. Given these demographic attributes, the BPT scored low on heterogeneity and low on faultlines.

The members of BMT are employed by one organization ("Biomedco"). In corporate communications, Biomedco describes itself as "people with a purpose, working together to make the lives of people everywhere healthier, striving in everything we do to become simply better as judged by all those we serve: customers, shareholders, employees and the global community." Biomedco's source of competitive advantage is the energy and ideas of their people. Their strength lies in what they value: customers, innovation, integrity, people, and performance. Their focus is personal commitment and team spirit, and the creation of a common culture around the world that enables them to make people's lives healthier through their product line.

It is within this context that the BMT has become arguably the most effective team we describe in this chapter. As demonstrated in Table 7.1, the team received very high ratings of both outcome and process effectiveness from internal team customers. Our MNT model suggests that this is primarily due to positive affect, confidence, and high expectations at the individual level, and shared meaning and common goals at the group level. Impetus for development of these elements has been several key catalysts including leadership and a supportive organizational context. Rules, roles, and structuration serve as the mechanisms by which these catalysts have brought about a transition to high performance. Each of these factors are discussed in the sections that follow.

**Catalysts.** We begin our exploration of the MNT model in the Biomedical Production Team with a discussion of the key catalysts in this con-

Biomedco Puerto Rico: Production Team

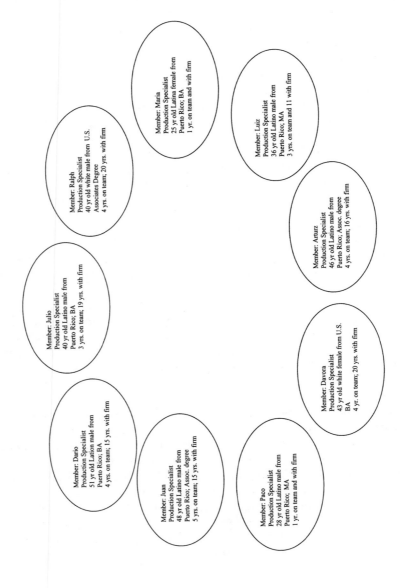

Member: Dario
Production Specialist
51 yr old Lation male from
Puerto Rico; BA
4 yrs. on team; 15 yrs. with firm

Member: Julio
Production Specialist
40 yr old Latino male from
Puerto Rico; BA
3 yrs. on team; 19 yrs. with firm

Member: Ralph
Production Specialist
40 yr old white male from U.S.
Associates Degree
4 yrs. on team; 20 yrs. with firm

Member: Maria
Production Specialist
25 yr old Latina female from
Puerto Rico; BA
1 yr. on team and with firm

Member: Juan
Production Specialist
48 yr old Latino male from
Puerto Rico; Assoc. degree
5 yrs. on team; 15 yrs. with firm

Member: Luiz
Production Specialist
36 yr old Latino male from
Puerto Rico; MA
3 yrs. on team and 11 yrs. with firm

Member: Paco
Production Specialist
28 yr old Latino male from
Puerto Rico; MA
1 yr. on team and with firm

Member: Arturz
Production Specialist
46 yr old Latino male from
Puerto Rico; Assoc. degree
4 yrs. on team; 16 yrs. with firm

Member: Davora
Production Specialist
43 yr old white female from U.S.
BA
4 yr. on team; 20 yrs. with firm

FIG. 7.2.    Biomedco Production Team.

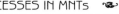

text. Perhaps the single most important key to the success of the BPT is the delicate equilibrium they have achieved between ambiguity and hierarchy through their unique approach to self-management. As depicted in Table 7.2, using our survey scales as a basis of comparison among teams, the BPT team has only moderate decision making authority, but high self-management scores. Based on the work of Manz and his colleagues (Manz & Sims, 1993), these latter scale scores indicate that the team is strongly encouraged to:

1. rehearse and plan activities before performing them;
2. set their own goals for performance standards;
3. look for performance problems and critically evaluate them when they occur;
4. feel good about itself when it performs well;
5. expect high performance of itself, and
6. track its own performance.

However, critical in this context is that the team also has a great deal of support in terms of direction outside the team.

This approach coincides well with the recommendations of intercultural researchers reviewed in chapter 5. According to Hofstede (1980), Erez and Earley (1993), Earley and Erez (1997), and Kirkman, Gibson, and Shapiro (2001), among others, the cultural value of power distance has important implications for whether an employee is receptive to self-management or not. Power distance is defined as the extent to which people in a society accept status and power inequalities as a normal and functional aspect of business. Countries that are "high in power distance" are thus those whose citizens generally accept status and power inequalities; and those "low in power distance" are those whose citizens generally do *not*. Puerto Rico is high in power distance. It is in these contexts that Kirkman et al. suggest that top managers should adapt their self-managed work team implementation strategies to be consistent with employee cultural values, specifically, the exact form of the self-management used will have to be permanently or gradually adapted to more closely mesh with the deeply held cultural values of country members. Failure to do so will likely result in the same counterproductive effects. Our interviews suggest that the BPT has followed this strategy, as illustrated in the following excerpt:

> Interviewer: In your opinion, is this team self-managed? Or do they still receive quite a bit of direction and leadership from outside of the team?

> BPT team internal team customer: I guess they are self-managed in the sense of they know how much is supposed to be delivered in a certain month. They come up with their daily itinerary. So in terms of managing the task, they are self-managed. But of course they also receive certain direction

# TABLE 7.2
## MNT Member Ratings of Self-Management and Decision Making

| | Overall Avg. of All Teams in Sample (N = 166) | APST | BPT | SST | LLT | HRPT |
|---|---|---|---|---|---|---|
| ***SELF-MANAGEMENT*** *DEGREE TO WHICH TEAMS ARE ENCOURAGED TO:* | | | | | | |
| Planning | 5.0 | 5.3 | 5.4 | 5.1 | 4.8 | 7.0 |
| Set Goals | 5.4 | 5.9 | 5.9 | 4.9 | 6.0 | 7.0 |
| Team Critique | 5.0 | 5.2 | 5.8 | 5.3 | 5.4 | 7.0 |
| Accomplishments | 5.4 | 6.1 | 5.5 | 4.5 | 6.0 | 7.0 |
| High Expectations | 5.7 | 6.2 | 6.5 | 5.5 | 6.0 | 7.0 |
| Track Performance | 5.5 | 6.0 | 6.1 | 5.4 | 5.6 | 7.0 |
| ***DECISION MAKING*** *AUTONOMY DEGREE TO WHICH TEAMS ARE INVOLVED IN:* | | | | | | |
| Develop Member Skills | 5.0 | 5.3 | 5.2 | 3.3 | 5.2 | 6.5 |
| Plan & Schedule Work | 5.4 | 5.7 | 6.0 | 4.1 | 5.4 | 7.0 |
| Plan & Determine Goals | 5.3 | 5.7 | 6.1 | 3.9 | 6.2 | 6.5 |
| Team Membership | 4.2 | 4.4 | 5.1 | 3.4 | 4.6 | 6.5 |
| Internal Leadership | 4.3 | 4.4 | 4.9 | 3.4 | 5.4 | 6.0 |
| Evaluate Team Performance | 4.6 | 5.0 | 5.1 | 3.9 | 5.4 | 6.5 |
| Assign Tasks | 5.0 | 5.4 | 5.5 | 4.6 | 6.0 | 7.0 |
| Peer Evaluations | 4.3 | 4.8 | 4.4 | 3.4 | 5.4 | 6.5 |

and guidance in the sense of, you know, coaching, training, activity, and in terms of costs or reports that, that would have to be requested outside of the group level. So, looking at it as solely self-managed—probably not yet. But, the majority of the task would be self-generated from the team.

Members of the BPT concur. When asked about the implementation of self-management in the teams, Dario had this to say, indicating that leadership at Biomedco is a careful balance between self-management and external direction:

> Through our training, we find here certain new ideas, new concepts. So that is a growing factor. And Biomedco recognizes invention, by just putting the names on the bulletin board, or the newsletter, and congratulatory memos from the district manager or from the president himself. And you know, not costly, but very effective ways of encouraging the individuals to participate. But there will always be resistance, definitely. So it takes a lot of leadership. The leaders have to do a lot of convincing.
>
> Interviewer: Do you feel especially that early on an outside manager needs to play that role?
>
> Dario: Yes!
>
> Interviewer: Do you feel that the manager could, could back out a little bit as the teams become accepted?
>
> Dario: Uh, back off? No, he, he would have to be always there. I would always believe a leader should be active. But what is, what is the goal he is going to be active at is a different thing. He should be active in facilitating and coaching. But he should not be active in dictating. Those are two different ways of being active. But you know, he can be active in developing someone to take his place instead of be running the show.

The external leader that provides most of the support to the BPT had this to say about the process of self-management:

> I would say that teams do not always reach a good decision. There are teams that take a lot to administer. I mean, you cannot have the self-managed team concept, and use it like, that is the solution. That's part of the solution. In other situations, when you have a team sometimes, let's say, I have a vision and I want to get to a point, which I do, and right now we are at a stage here where I am being in some areas in a way, directive in some areas. That way is not negotiable because otherwise we will get to a place that I already have gone through a certain experience and I have a certain background that is difficult to translate this background to them and all this experience that I have just because, not because I am more intelligent or whatever, it is because I go to meetings and I participate in other things that they don't. Therefore, I must go ahead and decide certain things.

In addition to maintaining the delicate balance between ambiguity and hierarchy, the BPT is also embedded within a very supportive context and has developed strong internal team norms. As evidenced in Table 7.3, the team perceived effective feedback and recognition systems within Biomedco and rated the training and resources as relatively effective. Juan had this to say about the training available to the team:

Our team is continuously developed, both in terms of, you know, training—whether it will have to be on the behavioral aspect, like, you know, communication skills and interpersonal skills. And something also like technical, like problem-solving activities. Tools and techniques. The team is always upgraded in terms of knowledge, skills, habits, so they are more effective. Because if you are able to do that, then you know, you will function better.

This quote highlights the importance of developing skills in order for team members to be effective at self-management.

**Individual and Group Elements.**    Perhaps due primarily to the balance between self-management and external direction and ample training, there is strong positive affect on the team, an extremely high confidence level, and high expectations for performance. These all feed into the development of shared meaning and common goals on the team. Top management in Biomedco has worked very hard to enable teams such as the BPT to develop common goals and high performance expectations. The President of the company described this effort as follows:

We have a team, the BPT that is making [name of product] that is working excellent. We have one in the utilities that is working excellent. The thing that is important for a team is that the, it has to be very clear what is the charter, also what are the boundaries of their empowerment, okay? It's that it has to be under a certain framework, let me put it that way and that, it does work because, see, what teams bring is collaboration and it forces you to collaborate.

**Processes.**    As we discussed in chapter 6, the key linking processes that enable catalysts to produce change in the individual and group elements include rules, roles, rituals and habits. Documentation and tracking are key processes that have become habitual in the BPT, as evidenced in the high score on the "Track Performance" scale (see Table 7.2). Arturz described the process by which these habits were developed through the cultivation of a common language, and the means by which they serve to bind the team together and create common goals:

By the second year, we were working on the statistical knowledge, so we can have a language so that we can see the tendency or use a graphic, it's descriptive statistics, not really something analytical. At first, we were afraid

**TABLE 7.3**
**MNT Member Ratings of System Effectiveness**

| EXTENT TO WHICH SYSTEMS ARE EFFECTIVE: | Overall Avg. of All Teams in Sample (N = 166) | APST | BPT | SST | LLT | HRPT |
|---|---|---|---|---|---|---|
| **CONTEXT & NORMS** | | | | | | |
| Feedback & Recognition | 5.3 | 5.2 | 5.9 | 5.2 | 5.5 | 6.4 |
| Training & Resources | 4.8 | 5.3 | 5.5 | 5.0 | 5.6 | 6.1 |
| Team Norms | 5.2 | 5.0 | 5.7 | 4.2 | 5.9 | 6.8 |
| **KNOWLEDGE MANAGEMENT** | | | | | | |
| Contact | 4.3 | 4.9 | 5.2 | 2.9 | 4.4 | 4.6 |
| Global Integration | 4.5 | 3.9 | 4.9 | 5.3 | 4.6 | 4.3 |
| Local Responsiveness | 4.6 | 5.3 | 4.5 | 4.0 | 4.2 | 3.3 |
| Codification: Team | 4.9 | 4.3 | 5.3 | 3.5 | 5.2 | 5.9 |
| Innovativeness | 4.7 | 4.6 | 4.8 | 3.9 | 4.6 | 5.1 |
| Codification: Organizational | 4.9 | 4.4 | 5.3 | 4.5 | 4.4 | 5.9 |

about the statistics and didn't want to do it. We had a meeting with say fifty persons or seventy five persons, and were shown the basics of the statistics and people were afraid of using the statistics. But we learned there that when we are going to teach something in the training, we teach it when you are using it, not just give the knowledge and then you can use it ten month later. What we are doing now is that you teach the statistics at the time that you have the group working, that you have something that you learn, and then you can use it, as any other tool. That was something that we learned a lot of years ago. If for example, take our department mission not to have accidents, because accidents are something that in a manufacturing environment you cannot have, then you can have a graph that tells you how many accidents you have in January and February and March. And all that, you can put in some place where everybody knows about what's happening in the area. So the idea was that the people use the statistics to express what their mission is.

The President of Biomedco had this to say about development of these rules and habits in the team:

What you need is skills to work in a group and skills like know how to deal with conflict, the skill to assert conflict, to not avoid conflict. We have a problem in this plant. People here, they don't like conflict and I see that and sometimes I get frustrated. They don't like conflict. They shy away from conflict. But if you are able to deal with that, you will come out better off. Some people that are too aggressive or too ambitious, sometimes they disregard other people and they turn people off, and if you learn the skill to do this, you will be able to get all this energy out. So it's also a skill, people that work in teams have to know how to verbalize the relationship, you know. I'm trying to learn that, how to ask questions to people in a way that you're soliciting ideas rather than giving instruction.

A Biomedco team developer contributed this insight, indicating that the habits and rituals help to overcome cultural differences and set common expectations:

It's very important, this education of how to participate in a meeting because there are some people for instance, who just listen. They don't say anything and they listen and listen and at the end they want to say something but by the time they say something it is too late. The group already has made up their mind. So, you have to early on, try to build on ideas from other people and get to a point. I find that the Puerto Ricans, what I find is cultural in Biomedco, is that people kind of keep quiet. They get, I don't know if it is intimidated or, I don't know what it is, but they believe that sometimes it is impolite also to come up and say something, that it may be in conflict with his ideas. So that's the skills that we have to develop. In other words, how do I build up on his idea. A year or so ago, I felt that the way that I was asking questions was too directive. Already by asking the question, I was showing what was my position. Then people say, "why do you ask me, you already have the answer." So I have to learn to say, "what have you thought about this?" or "what do you think about this?" The other thing in this culture is that people in this culture like strong people. That's a problem. They see when you are polite and, they see this as a weakness. So I think that here in Puerto Rico we need people to, early on in the meetings, get into the theme and build up on the other people's ideas. We have to force people to talk or to teach people how to ask open ended questions so that everybody should come forward.

The BPT has come quite far in learning to develop the equilibrium in key catalysts like hierarchy, using processes such as rules and rituals to develop strong group level elements. We will return to the issue of hierarchy below as we discuss two additional teams, in a somewhat different organizational context with much less support.

## SALES AND SERVICE TEAM (SST)

Before the merger, everybody was modality-focused and they did their own thing. They didn't help each other as much in the metro team, in my opinion. These guys have, I guess, developed, in my opinion, a camaraderie. They're still working at it, and there're still problems, in my opinion, but it's the best I've been a part of.

—*Christian, Sales Specialist, Sales and Service Team, Medco*

**Context.** The third team we would like to highlight in our sample, the Sales and Service Team (SST), is different from both the APST and BPT in many ways. Perhaps most importantly, the SST is cross-functional, consisting two of members who are in are in sales and six members who are engineers that perform service calls. All are focused on high-end medical equipment, specifically, diagnostic and imaging equipment such as x-ray machines, ultrasound machines, and CAT scan machines. The second unique feature of the SST is the organizational structure in which it is embedded. The sales employees had previously been part of one organization ("Salesco") and the service personnel had been part of a second, separate organization ("Servco"). These two units were recently merged, and along with a research and development organization, created "Medco." Within Medco, there are approximately 45 sales and service teams organized by geographic area.

Medco is one business unit that acts as an independent profit center within a large, highly diversified multinational firm ("Genco"). According to their annual reports, although diverse in terms of product scope, all Genco units are focused on learning, competition, excellence, achievement and striving for new frontiers. They insist on excellence and are intolerant of bureaucracy. They strive to act in a boundaryless fashion, always searching for and applying the best ideas regardless of their source. They prize global intellectual capital and the people that provide it. They purposely build diverse teams to maximize innovation and have a decentralized structure. They are legendary for attitudes like "only 'A' players are desired." Corporate communications describe the "right" leadership teams as those with "the agility and speed to seize the big opportunities we know this changing world will present us."

Like the BPT, all of the SSTs can be considered "work teams" since they have on-going responsibility for producing services. Their membership is stable, full-time, and well-defined. Figure 7.3 depicts the particular SST we focus upon, with eight members representing the "Northern Territories" in Canada. There are six men and two women on the team. Four different national backgrounds and one ethnicity are represented on the team. Members range in age from 31 to 48 years old and most have a technical degree or certificate; the team leader (Steve) has a bachelor's degree. Tenure in the organization ranges from 5 to 25 years, and team tenure ranges from less than 1 year to 4 years. For the most part, the members of the SST occupy the position of "Field Engineer," with the exception of the two members in sales who have the title "Sales Specialists." Steve's title is Area Service Manager. Given all these various demographic characteristics , the SST received a high score on team heterogeneity, but a moderate faultline score (see Fig. 7.3).

The SST had been in existence for approximately four years when we first began our work with them. It is currently a fairly low performing team. As detailed in Table 7.1, internal team customers rated the team fairly low on indicators of outcome effectiveness. The team received moderate scores on process effectiveness. Our model highlights two key elements in this team that are suffering—affect and differentiated goals—and three processes that need improvement—rules, structuration and rituals. The most critical catalysts in this context are leadership and the organizational systems. We describe each of these factors next.

**Individual and Group Elements.** A key issue the SST faces might have been guessed based on the goal structure: the sales personnel have quite different goals than do the service personnel. To some extent, their goals are even mutually exclusive. To put it quite simply, the more diagnostic machines the field engineers are able to repair, the fewer machines the salesmen can sell! From Medco's standpoint, the merger made sense given that a combined sales/service force heightens the customer's experience. The purchasing specialist at a large hospital, for example, can work with one point of contact through out both the purchase process and the ownership period. This instills trust and a sense of reliability in Medco's products. However, from the team members' point of view, the sales/service structure has posed a challenge. For example, when asked to describe the function of the team, Glenn, a Field Engineer in the service end of the business, defined it quite narrowly:

Medco Northern Territories Region: Sales and Service Team

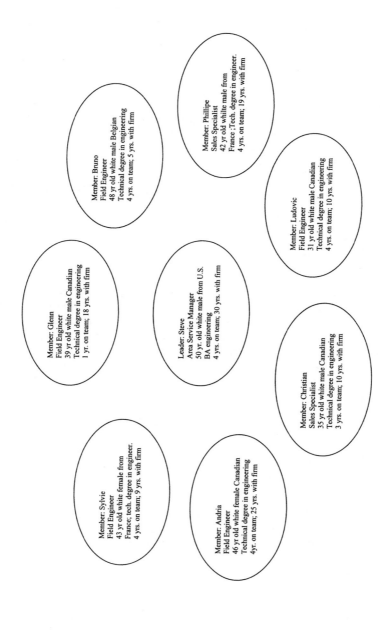

Member: Sylvie
Field Engineer
43 yr old white female from
France; tech. degree in engineer.
4 yrs. on team; 9 yrs. with firm

Member: Glenn
Field Engineer
39 yr old white male Canadian
Technical degree in engineering
1 yr. on team; 18 yrs. with firm

Member: Bruno
Field Engineer
48 yr old white male Belgian
Technical degree in engineering
4 yrs. on team; 5 yrs. with firm

Member: Phillipe
Sales Specialist
42 yr old white male from
France ;Tech. degree in engineer.
4 yrs. on team; 19 yrs. with firm

Member: Andria
Field Engineer
46 yr old white female Canadian
Technical degree in engineering
4yr. on team; 25 yrs. with firm

Leader: Steve
Area Service Manager
50 yr. old white male from U.S.
BA engineering
4 yrs. on team; 30 yrs. with firm

Member: Ludovic
Field Engineer
31 yr old white male Canadian
Technical degree in engineering
4 yrs. on team; 10 yrs. with firm

Member: Christian
Sales Specialist
35 yr old white male Canadian
Technical degree in engineering
3 yrs. on team; 10 yrs. with firm

FIG. 7.3.    Sales and Service Team.

Glenn: The first thing that popped into my head was, "to serve the customer." You know, to take care of, to serve the customer. That is the function of our team, bottom line. 'Cause without our customers we wouldn't be successful.

Interviewer: Right. But ... elaborate a little bit on that ... how does that split between what you do as a service person and the salesperson work?

Glenn: I mean, my function is, as I get service calls, my function is to take care of the equipment. That is the minimum qualification, in my opinion, and we've talked a lot about this, to be a service engineer, is to be able to technically take care of the equipment. Now, the service role is changing, where that's all it used to be, and now it's turning more into a role of not only to technically take care of the equipment but to get more involved with the customer when it comes to the opportunities to potentially order new equipment that are coming about.

Phillipe, one of the SST's two salespeople, also discussed this issue candidly:

So where I fit into all this is from the sales standpoint. I'm the guy that obviously goes out and sells the equipment. These [field engineer] guys have been more involved in helping me sell equipment than I've ever had on any other team. So where in my previous sales experience, I was the guy going out there, doing all the talking, doing all this 'n' that ... these guys [on this SST], when I need something done, a lot of times, I'll call 'em up. I'll say, "If you're in this account, you know, could you say this to so and so, or give this to so and so, or, or help me understand what's goin' on there, so that I can help form my strategy?" So, you know, our involvement as a team really has developed quite a bit in this area. I'm getting more involved in service opportunities. I'm selling service contracts like I've never sold before. I don't turn a wrench or anything, but I'm making sure that for my team, if I hear anything, I let them [the field engineers] know.

Perhaps as a direct result of the differentiated goals on the team, the affect of team members is generally negative. Team members responded in interviews in a manner that indicated stress, negative feelings for the team, and general burnout. Bruno, the Belgian Field Engineer on the team, had been observing other SSTs and made the following comparison:

When I look at other teams, I see that both the sales and service guys take ownership of the accounts. They take, they have passion, a passion for the business. And they, they ... wanna succeed as bad as, you know, as bad as I do. When you ask those FEs, "Why do you think we're so successful now?" They think it's because the sales rep and the service manager have allowed them to kind of open their wings, you know, expand a little bit or, or be more involved. On our team, I didn't feel that. The sales reps, sometimes they think they're on a different level, which really irritates me. They do their own thing, you know, and they don't get the team involved. So in some of the other teams, the FEs are the best I've ever seen. And they take ownership, and they have a passion for the business. They in turn say, "Look, you guys, our service manager allows us to make more decisions and the sales rep gets us more involved in, in the sales cycles and stuff like that."

In addition to the negative affect on the SST, this quote also highlights a second key issue on the team pertaining to leadership, discussed next.

**Catalysts.** As we discussed in the previous section on the BPT, the delicate equilibrium to be maintained in teams between ambiguity and hierarchy poses a real challenge, particularly for MNTs. Whereas the BPT was highly successful at achieving an optimal amount of self-management, particularly given the cultural context, we found the relative lack of self-management and decision-making authority in the SST to be somewhat puzzling. As demonstrated in Table 7.2, the SST had, in fact, the least amount of encouragement for self-management responsibilities, and the least decision making authority on all eight sub-scales. As noted by Kirkman and Gibson (2001), Canadians tend to be low on power distance, which tends to bode well for self-management and participation in decision-making. However, the French and Belgians tend to be somewhat higher on power distance (Trompenaars, 1997). Since members with the latter two national backgrounds comprise 40% of the team, this may pose somewhat of a challenge for determining the appropriate degree of self-management, but in general, our observations would indicate that the team is currently ready, willing, and able to accept more decision-making authority. This was evidenced in an interview with Sylvie, a French Field Engineer, who commented:

We have one ultimate leader, and that's our area service manager, Steve. But we also have other, like I was talking about earlier, CT, MR and X-ray modality leaders. And we have area leaders, each geographic area has a focal point. And it's usually a veteran person that has a lot of experience and is, is looked up to for their opinions and their knowledge. But on the other hand, I think you could teach everyone to have that capacity to be a leader and to run their own business and everything.

When pushed for an example of how this might work, Sylvie had relayed a description of another manager she had worked with in another company:

There were times when he did direct us, that this is something that we need to pay special attention to as a team, but he also would prefer that the team would come up with a solution for that. He didn't dictate or mandate certain behaviors or anything. His first choice was always to let the team resolve it amongst themselves. I think he believed that we as a team would come up with the most palatable answer to a particular issue or whatever. Rather than him dictating. But he did have expertise, and he would dictate something to us if we couldn't come up with an answer.

A potential barrier to increased local responsibility is that the organizational systems at Medco, and more generally at the parent company Genco, focus on alignment, as opposed to adaptability (Gibson & Birkinshaw, 2000). In the academic literature, alignment has come to mean that common behaviors throughout an organization are directed toward the achievement of shared goals. Thus, alignment keeps a business focused through clear objectives and a broadly shared vision. Until recently, scholars had posited that companies with high levels of alignment were "built to last," and that the task of leadership was to get the right fit among such key institutional systems as strategy, metrics and rewards (O'Toole & Pasternack, 2001). But not all institutional alignment is good. In fact, the empirical work conducted by Gibson and Birkinshaw in conjunction with the WEF/BAH research team (discussed in chap. 5) revealed the existence of two quite different types of alignment, which we call "Big A" and "little a." For example the positive "A" variety found at Continental Airlines keeps all employees focused on the importance of on-time arrivals. But at a formerly agile company like Hewlett-Packard, negative "a" alignment was until quite recently anchored in habits of the past. This can lead to bureaucracy, and even become deadly when there is a need for fast decision-making (O'Toole & Pasternack, 2001). In today's high-speed world, companies need to detect changes in the external environment and to act quickly with the full force of their resources. Inflexible "a" alignment simply gets in the way. That's where adaptability comes in.

As evidence of this "a" alignment, the SST received the highest scores on global integration than any other team in this chapter, indicating that there is a great deal of pressure on the team to adopt standardized work practices promoted by Medco, and more generally, by Genco (see Table 7.3). The team also received the lowest scores on innovation, scoring a mere 3.9 on a 7-point scale for which 4.7 was the overall average. It did not appear to be that Medco (or Genco for that matter) ignores the possibility that teams can share, learn and adapt, but rather that workable solutions are not easy to come by. Ludovic, a Canadian Field Engineer, described the situation as follows:

> Interviewer: How do you personally learn about ideas to change the way you work, change the way a team works?
>
> Ludovic: I'd say, it comes down to region meetings. Being driven by the region manager. At our '97 kickoff we had best practice sharing, and there were six reps that got up and presented different aspects.
>
> Interviewer: How did you pick out which ones you were gonna share?

Ludovic: No. The managers decided, you know, there were two regions that came together, and they decided that, they know, I think they have a good feel for who their successful members are in certain areas. So they looked at their own individual players and decided who have done the best job in their opinion and then asked them to present. Um, as we get together, you know, that's how I see a lot of the best practice sharing going on.

Interviewer: Do you feel like when those practices, the best practices are shared, do you get a feeling that people really go, take away from it and implement things

Ludovic: It's not too successful, unfortunately.

Interviewer: And why do you think that is?

Ludovic: Because people are too busy. I mean, we're so doggone busy trying to get done what we gotta get done that we, you know … maybe, it probably would help us. But, you know, we gotta finish this list here, and then try to find time to implement some of those things. They have a lot of great ideas, but to bring 'em back, and to implement those as you're going along, it's hard. I mean, it would be better if there was, "do this one thing." Somehow we need to do better at getting just one thing.

**Processes.** Beyond the relative lack of decision-making authority and the overemphasis on alignment, the SST is also entrenched in some very stable and habitual rituals which tend to be similar to other SSTs within Medco. On the one hand, this eliminates uncertainty and ambiguity, and creates shared history, but on the other, it reduces the sense-making process, and the ability to really move beyond the "tried and true." A key ritual the team does seem to be missing out on, however, is the celebration of accomplishments. This is evidenced by their particularly low score on our survey scale measuring this aspect of self-management—the team received a 4.5 on this scale that has an average of 5.4. In a sales and service environment, in which measuring progress toward goals is a relatively straightforward process, it was particularly disheartening that reaching major milestones as a team were not celebrated, acknowledged, or rewarded. The focus at Medco was on individual performance. Christian, the Canadian sales specialist, had this to say about such a focus:

Christian: I mean, sometimes people are more selfish than others, but they're not looking at the whole picture; they're not looking at the key, you know, if there's success factors or what it takes to be successful long-term. They're looking at today and not the future as well, and what, you know, how things can be affected if you don't get involved in the team.

Interviewer: Would you say that individual achievement or collective achievement is more valued at Medco?

Christian: I would say it's been individual in the past; I know they're trying to change that. But it seems that there is a lot of individual awards. They're starting to try to make this more focused on a team environment, a team win and that kind of stuff. But there's still a lot, you know, we go to our meetings, kick-off meetings and it's individual awards, you know.

Interviewer: And as I understand it, your salary really is ultimately based on your individual goals, correct?

Christian: Correct. I mean, from a sales—especially from a sales perspective—how well I do, and I hate to say "I," because it's really my team has done so well for me, last year, we had the best, I had the best year I ever had last year because of my team. But you're right: my salary reflects how well ultimately, how many orders I get in, how many contracts I sign, and that kind of stuff.

Moving on to the fourth team to be discussed here, we see some similar issues, being resolved somewhat more effectively, in a different context.

## LOGISTICS LEADERSHIP TEAM (LLT)

Because what it is, is really, it's the whole supply chain. I mean we start at marketing with the order or with the customer wherever we get the order from, and we end at manufacturing. We don't get into there but anything else, that has to do with the product in the middle of that, is us. Customer service, product handling, transportation, demand planning functions, and inventory control.
—*Fred, U.S. Director of Logistics, Photoco Southern Americas Region*

**Context.** The Logistic Leadership Team consists of 6 members, each of whom represents logistics (i.e., receiving, warehousing and distribution) operations in a different region of Latin America or South America. The team had been in existence for approximately three years when we first began our work with them. Using the categorization scheme developed by Cohen and Bailey (1997), the team considers itself a management team. Management teams are composed of managers of various subunits within an organization. They coordinate and provide direction to sub-units and are typically responsible for overall performance of a business unit or functional area. Members have authority and decision making power because of their rank in the organization.

Figure 7.4 depicts the LLT, indicating the demographic characteristics of each team member. Six nations and two ethnicities are represented on the team. There is one woman and five men on the team. Members range in age from 28 to 47 years, education ranges from no college (one member), to a technical degree (one member), to bachelor's degrees (2 members), and master's degrees (2 members). Tenure in the organization ranges from 5 to 26 years, and team tenure ranges from 2 years to 3 years. Most team members consider themselves in service or operations. Heterogeneity is high on this team, but potential for faultlines is moderate.

Photoco Southern Americas Region: Leadership Logistics Team

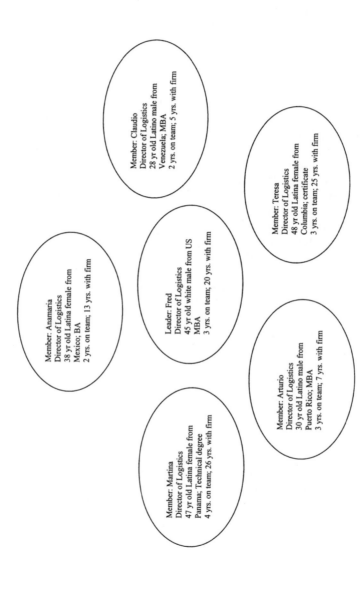

Member: Claudio
Director of Logistics
28 yr old Latino male from
Venezuela; MBA
2 yrs. on team; 5 yrs. with firm

Member: Anamaria
Director of Logistics
38 yr old Latina female from
Mexico; BA
2 yrs. on team; 13 yrs. with firm

Member: Teresa
Director of Logistics
48 yr old Latina female from
Columbia; certificate
3 yrs. on team; 25 yrs. with firm

Leader: Fred
Director of Logistics
45 yr old white male from US
MBA
3 yrs. on team; 20 yrs. with firm

Member: Martina
Director of Logistics
47 yr old Latina female from
Panama; Technical degree
4 yrs. on team; 26 yrs. with firm

Member: Arturio
Director of Logistics
30 yr old Latino male from
Puerto Rico; MBA
3 yrs. on team; 7 yrs. with firm

FIG. 7.4.  Logistics Leadership Team.

216 ᨊᨀ CHAPTER 7

All the members of the LLT are employed by "Photoco," a company that develops, manufactures, sells, distributes, and services imaging equipment and support products such as film and developing paper. According to the Photoco annual report, the organization is striving to develop a world-class, results-oriented culture providing consumers and customers with many options in terms of their core products, bringing differentiated, cost-effective solutions to market quickly and with flawless quality through a diverse team of energetic employees. Their core values are respect for the dignity of the individual, uncompromising integrity, trust, credibility, and continuous improvement. Photoco has been struggling for several years. The company is fragmented as a result of divesting and downsizing. The focus has been on cost reduction and reinforcing the traditional, established excellence of a long-standing product line.

Within this environment, the LLT is moderately effective, both in terms of outcomes and processes. The team is meeting most major objectives and functioning well. Our MNT model would suggest that this is due primarily to positive affect and clear expectations at the individual level and a strong hybrid culture and common goals at the group level. Clear rules, roles and structuration are also important to maintaining the effectiveness of this team. To move the team beyond average performance, our model focuses attention on several key catalysts in this context, including supportive organizational systems, task constraints, and technology. Each of these are addressed in turn next.

**Individual and Group Elements.**   A critical success factor for the LLT is that Fred, the team leader, has worked very hard to set clear expectations for the team. This has eliminated ambiguities and task uncertainty. One of the Vice President of Operations in a region represented on the LLT had this to say about the clarity of expectations on the team:

> I think he [Fred] is one of the success stories because his team does have measurement. The warehouse, for instance, has had many measurements. It's more, you know, perfect delivery and, you know, did they put it away right and do they have a whole bunch of things in place. He has the same thing as I do, in that he has a lot of people reporting into him. He's very good at it. He's very good as a supervisor. Creating, you know, expectations, measuring against those expectations, letting people know, coming here once a month for a week, you know, and meeting and sitting down one on one and I think he's been very very good at this.

When asked to comment on his own leadership style, Fred mentioned that he has tried to develop an open communication climate, which as we reviewed earlier, is conducive to conflict resolution, and critical on an MNT. Fred stated,

My leadership team, I think is extremely effective. And a lot of it's because we got the five people that report to me are really very good. And, I mean, we come out of there with a list of action items and those people get 'em done. And I shouldn't say those people because I have, I usually have half of the items, because they usually delegate upward pretty well. But, you know, nobody's afraid to say anything about anything. And, everybody takes it really well. You know the attitude on the team is really good. We're all almost like friends, there's no hierarchy there. And I take as much grief as anybody else does.

The clarity of expectations set for the team, together with Fred's leadership style have encouraged a set of common goals and a hybrid culture. This was recognized as a key facet of the team's relatively good performance. For example, when asked what kinds of things might derail a team, Arturio, the Puerto Rican Director of Logistics said,

I think, again, the lone wolf approach. Being a maverick or out on your own … is one that would hurt, hurt a team. I think another thing that pulls a team down is, is disgruntlement or frustration, or, you know, we're all busy but saying, "Why do I need to help? Why do I need to go out there and do it? I'm busy," and that kind of stuff is a negative.

Interestingly, as mentioned above, the LLT scored very high on measures of heterogeneity and received a moderate score on our measure of potential faultlines that might divide the team into subgroups. But the team appeared to have overcome at least some of the problems often associated with fractionation by developing a hybrid culture. The commonalities in values, preferences, and styles that exist within this cluster of Latin cultures were a good starting point. However, despite these commonalities, differences in cultures and contexts certainly exist. Each of the team members mentioned factors unique to their own regional environment. The United States has trouble hiring. Columbia has difficulty with technical support. Venezuela has had difficulty motivating line workers. But by setting a clear set of team-based objectives—that included specific metrics for measuring quality of distribution-related tasks—that all members have bought into, Fred helped to bridge these differences.

**Processes.** A key challenge facing the LLT is the tight deadline environment they face in their work as directors of the basic receiving and shipping of Photoco products. Particularly due the sensitive nature of many of the products (light sensitive papers and film), delivery can be tricky. Unfortunately, the team received a fairly low rating from internal team customers on the team outcome dimension of Timeliness (see Table 7.1). Together with customer satisfaction (which was also rated relatively low), these two components of the team's outcome effectiveness must be the focus of improvement efforts. Two key processes—rules and structuration—may help assist the team in this endeavor. Martina, the Director of Logistics in Panama, had this to say about the lack of structure in the LLT:

> Martina: I think we talk, we meet a lot, and that's great, and we do make decisions. But I think we need to set up more structure on when, when we're gonna have the decision made. You know, more timely decisions, in my opinion.
>
> Interviewer: So that kind of direction might help. If Steve could just say, "We need to make this choice" and start putting a little pressure on some kind of deadline, would that help?
>
> Martina: Right. I think we need quite a bit. And you're right; maybe we don't have enough direction. We try to do meetings, and you know, we're supposed to go two hours and we go four hours. That type of thing. It's just ... that happens. Sometimes you get so many different personalities. But again the team still is a great team, but we're still developing and there's some personality conflicts, and you know, you gotta try to work through those.

**Catalysts.**    In this environment, with team members so geographically dispersed, a critical challenge is determining the best technologies for communicating and collaborating. As we discussed in chapter 2 and again in chapter 5, the research in this domain has not yet given clear guidelines about when to use face-to-face meetings, and when to use conference calls or email. The LLT has used a strategic combination of face-to-face meetings and teleconferences to accomplish its work. Arturio, the Director of Logistics in Puerto Rico, had this to say about how the team has dealt with this challenge:

> The six of us meet quarterly, and then we also have conference calls monthly, and we really, the six of us, really run the business of our department. So that's the purpose of that team is to make sure that we know the performance measures are okay, to make sure that the business is running right, make sure the customers are happy, and make sure we give marketing what they want. Then there are what we have, what we call operational teams in each country. And, for example, the operational team here in Puerto Rico is all the team leaders plus me and the planning supervisor. Okay. And we meet on a monthly basis the week after Ana gets the performance measures, and we go over every one of those to make sure that, that, to make sure we're either meeting them, or if we're not meeting them, what the problem is and then what the corrective action would be.

Several team members felt that the conference calls were the least effective means of communicating, and in fact prefer the face-to-face meetings. For example, Claudio, the Director of Logistics in Venezuela, commented:

> We have a conference call monthly, but that's just more information sharing. Cause really, Panama's telling him what they did that month, and the other

five are listening. So then I tell them what we did, and the other five listen to me. Once in a while somebody will raise an issue that, you know, that the other guys will say, "Well, wait a minute. What did you say?" But it's still information sharing. I mean, there not a lot of common actions being taken in that. Okay. So that, if that's the purpose of that team, it works well. Okay. So if you say this team is just to share information. Yeh, it works fine for that. But is it action-oriented? No.

Perhaps the key point here is not that the teleconference is imperfect as a mechanism, but that the team could use the sessions more wisely to go beyond the barebones information meeting. We address this again in subsequent sections of this chapter and in our final chapter.

A final catalyst to change in the LLT has been the frequent membership changes they have experienced. This has resulted in less shared history and shared understanding among the team and a continuous process of re-establishing norms. Teresa, the Director of Logistics for Columbia, had this to say about the environment:

> We've been through so much organization change and churn that, um, it hardly seems like you start to get a cohesive group together and they change the whole structure of the organization again, and now there's new players. Management just for the businesses here has changed three times in the last year. I mean, how can you build a team when that keeps happening, because every leader has a different perspective on how to build the team.

As a leader, Fred struggles with the consequences. He described the implications of membership changes that come with organizational structure changes as follows:

> One thing that has gotten in the way of our teamwork is this downsizing stuff. Cause I think this started a suspicion in the back of everybody's mind that, of yeh, we're going to work together to make this more efficient, and then you're going to fire somebody. So, it's increase productivity and now it's going to mean some guys, you know, are out. It's still in the back of their minds. So, why do you want to work so hard? [laughter, pause]. It's okay the way it is. So, you do have to kind of get over that, and you have to stress the benefits. But, that's bad, that's bad, especially in our area. In the Latin American region of Photoco, because we've gotten a lot of that recently, so they've seen a lot of jobs disappear.

In contrast, most of the team members recognized that turnover is not necessarily a terrible thing in an organization. Uncertainty that comes with merger, acquisition or divestiture can motivate the team to develop a more adaptable skill set, as described by Anamaria, the Director of Logistics for Mexico:

We've got to come together real quick, work as a team, because you never know what tomorrow is gonna be like. Whereas, other organizations that I've seen haven't been through as much change. And they may have great teams, but I think the culture and the environment hasn't grown quite as much as our organization.

One of the means by which the team has dealt with the high turnover is the increased emphasis on documentation. Our survey scale, "Team Codification" with in the Knowledge Management domain captures this effort (see Table 7.3). The LLT scored the highest among the five teams on this scale, which indicates new practices developed by the team are identified and documented. Practices that are highly codified are typically easier to access for new members, and easier to share with other teams. This is a particularly impressive accomplishment, given that the tendency to share ideas openly, in the presence of a hierarchy may run contrary to the high power distance in the many of the Latin American and South American cultures. Fred, the team leader, explained it like this:

> Now it's a little different, because it's a different culture here, obviously, in Latin America than in the U.S., and I've noticed a difference working in Atlanta and in coming here. In Atlanta, the guys are not bashful to tell you anything. Now here, they're not as open, especially, because of the bosses coming from Miami kind of thing. It's harder to build that team kind of thing because they're waiting for you to give them the answer. And that's the hardest thing I've had to overcome probably, and I think I've done it like with the logistics leaders here, at least one of them. And I'll tell you what, I mean, those situations where they've suggested something and it hasn't been right are very few. For example, Claudio, that guy, he's got a million ideas. I'm surprised. I think in a previous life he was an inventor. You know, he always had a plan. And now he's less bashful to come up. I'll be walking around looking, and he'll say, "Hey, you know what? I've thought about this [pause]." And ninety percent of the stuff he suggests we end up doing. Okay. Now there is, there's no question, okay, there's like the island mentality, the "manyana" kind of thing. There's no question, and that's for sure cultural. But I don't think it's the culture of them, I think it's the culture of how they were managed.

The last team we discuss faces many of the same challenges confronting the LLT group. Although the nature and structure of the team is very different, the environment is similar.

## HUMAN RESOURCE PROJECT TEAM

> The group that I'm working with, many of us haven't met one another, never and we're always on the phone yet I find that, it's my perception, or I may be totally wrong, but the group that I have is very dynamic. I mean I can almost feel it on the phone that they're really enthused and they really want to get

this going and they really want to be part of this project. They feel that and maybe the reason is twofold, also saying, "Look we believe the message has been to them that we really believe that you can benefit from this one and this is really important for the company. So the message has been this is really important, you're going to be working on something super-powerful, super-important, changing the organization. So they've come into it, you know, really willing to roll up their sleeves, and let's get at it, but it's not easy.
—*Maria, Human Resource Director, Puerto Rico, Photoco*

**Context.** The Human Resource Project Team (HRPT) consists of 6 members, each of whom represents human resources in a different region of Latin America or South America. Using the categorization scheme developed by Cohen and Bailey (1997), the team considers itself a project team. Project teams are time limited. They produce a short term output, such as a new product or service to be marketed by the company. Project Teams typically work on a nonrepetitive task that requires application of judgment, knowledge and expertise. Often project teams are multifunctional or multidisciplinary, however, members of the HRPT are all in Human Resources. The team had been in existence for approximately 3 years when we first began our work with them. In this sense, it is an unusual project team in that it has a longer life than many project teams. Also interesting, as discussed later, is that this team stands in direct contrast to the LLT in that it has very little face-to-face contact.

The members of the HRPT are also employed by Photoco (i.e., the same organization that employs the LLT) that is involved in developing, manufacturing, selling, distributing, and servicing imaging equipment and products. Again, it is significant to note that the organization has been struggling for several years and involved in numerous waves of divestiture and downsizing. The focus has been on cost reduction and reinforcing the traditional, established excellence of a long-standing product line.

Figure 7.5 depicts the HRPT, indicating the demographic characteristics of each team member. Five nations and one ethnicity are represented on the team. There are four women and one man on the team. Members range in age from 35 to 55 years, education range from a bachelor's degree (4 members) to a master's degree (2 members). Tenure in the organization ranges from 4 years to 18 years, and team tenure ranges from 1 year to 4 years. All team members have the title, "Director of Human Resources" in their region. The team is relatively heterogeneous, but has a low potential faultlines score.

Of all the teams described in this chapter, the HRPT is the most troubled. The team received the lowest ratings of all five teams from internal team customers on both outcome effectiveness and process effectiveness. For this team, several group elements that our MNT model highlights appear to be underlying these low ratings: differentiated goals, low coop-

Photoco Southern Americas Region: Human Resources Project Team

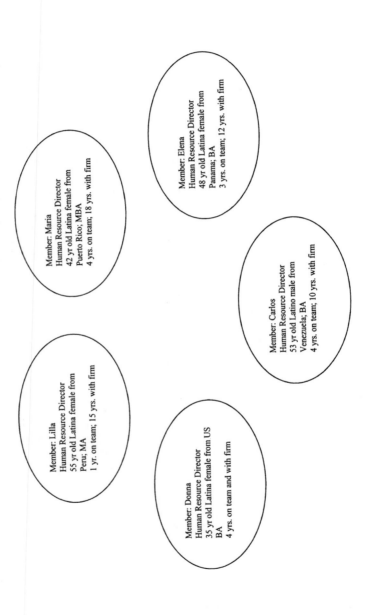

Member: Lilla
Human Resource Director
55 yr old Latina female from
Peru; MA
1 yr. on team; 15 yrs. with firm

Member: Maria
Human Resource Director
42 yr old Latina female from
Puerto Rico; MBA
4 yrs. on team; 18 yrs. with firm

Member: Elena
Human Resource Director
48 yr old Latina female from
Panama; BA
3 yrs. on team; 12 yrs. with firm

Member: Donna
Human Resource Director
35 yr old Latina female from US
BA
4 yrs. on team and with firm

Member: Carlos
Human Resource Director
53 yr old Latino male from
Venezuela; BA
4 yrs. on team; 10 yrs. with firm

FIG. 7.5.   Human Resource Project Team.

eration, and lack of shared meaning. These have impacted interpersonal affect and social awareness, two key individual elements in our model. Examining team processes of social contact and development of a shared history in the HRPT is also somewhat informative. Finally, several catalysts are critical, in particular task constraints, technology, and leadership. Each of these are discussed in greater detail below.

**Group and Individual Elements.**   Our interviews and observations with the HRPT indicate the perhaps the most critical element of this team are the differentiated goals and priorities that members each have in the team. These differences stem from the fact that members each represent different geographic regions that each have a unique set of challenges and environmental constraints or inducements, and they have had few face-to-face opportunities to resolve these differences. Maria, the HR Director from Puerto Rico described this structure as follows:

> So for those five different country clusters, there would be a person such as myself that would also be responsible for their own country office like I am here in Puerto Rico, but then also for a cross-country kind of team. So I really don't report for instance, to the GM here in Puerto Rico, he's more of my peer, versus what used to be in the good old days as some managers would say, my boss. I have an expanded country GM who resides in Miami so I work for him but I report into the HR Director for the Southern Americas region. So we have a matrix situation. Which any matrix situation can be confusing. I personally don't have a problem with it, but I know it's probably not the case all over.

As demonstrated in this quote, the HRPT is aware of the potential conflicts that arise with differentiated goals in a matrix structure. Indeed, the establishment of this project team was intended to address this issue. As the Venezuelan HR Director (Carlos) expressed,

> In this project, we are going across businesses looking at everybody and everybody's different needs. We're just going through an assessment right now of interviewing managers and seeing what their needs are. I think it's been a great exercise itself. It has been very, very helpful for me to have them actually do something, and finally see a product, a deliverable. Now I finally have something, I did something and that is going to fall well into the whole big picture.

A second key group element in the HPRT that is related to the differentiated goals is the relative lack of cooperation across the geographic areas, outside the confounds of the project itself. Maria was particularly upset by the lack of assistance across countries, but also uncertain how much to "push" this cooperation, demonstrating the challenge of maintaining the delicate equilibrium between conflict and consensus, as evidenced in the following interview excerpt:

> I don't see that cooperation much across country teams. I mean I don't see them helping each other ... and maybe there's just not a need to do that. I mean, maybe they are so different, maybe they should be kept Puerto Rico, Panama, Peru, etc. You know, who is to say that everybody has to work the way I'm working. In the past, her set up or strategy has been, I work with group leaders at each site and they work on their own individual situations. There is no need to go across countries. Why now?

The lack of cooperation may be due to cultural preferences. Certain members appeared less willing or able to play the role of knowledge partners, thus, members are unable to reap the benefits of the knowledge sharing that takes place during the project. As expressed by Donna, the HR Director from the United States:

> The people in Panama also have always been left alone and I think they're very happy if you just leave them alone. They're a stickler on that. Again this is my perception about the culture that I've seen in Panama. They're very, "we know what we need to do, and we'll do it."

The low level of cooperation is exacerbated by the high levels of individual sensitivity and strong awareness of the mianzi aspect of face. As described in chapter 4, mianzi captures the aspect of face that reflects a person's interactions with others in her society. Like bark on a tree, face protects the inside of a person and creates an ecological system in which others can live and flourish. As pointed out by Earley and Randel (1997), a key aspect of mianzi is guilt and shame felt by team members who are uncertain whether they are living up to the expectations of others in the team. Some of the members of the HRPT are sensitive to these issues, and adjust their interpersonal relations accordingly, however the ability (or awareness) to do so varies in the team. As expressed by Maria,

> They [the members from Panama] are very sensitive, very proud. I notice that some care has to be taken, on how you address certain issues because you can offend them easily ... I had one person in Panama [Elena] and I knew she had a lot of work and I wanted to help her because we had a program here that I understood she didn't have. I said, "well why don't you send me the information and I'll enter it here in this program and this will help us." Well I could even tell over the phone that she felt, you know as the Japanese would say, she lost face. I said, "Look its not that you can't do it, it's not that you haven't done your job, its just that you have too much. And it's my responsibility to help you and I need to help you on this." I could almost hear the tears coming out of her eyes, because she felt that she had let me down. She came over for two weeks and worked very closely with my other HR rep

here on getting them and I think now she sees the benefit of doing that, but at first it was really "No, no, no I'll do it, I'll do it Saturday. I'll come in, whatever time it takes.

This quote also illustrates the high level of stress, and often negative affect, that accompanies the challenges of working on a team with differentiated goals. Fragmented goals and a loose reporting structure has resulted in a weak hybrid culture. This feeds into a general sense of independence and a lack of integration across members.

*Processes.*　　Teams with differentiated goals often have difficulty working through a constructive conflict resolution process. The HRPT is no exception. Of all the team process scales on the survey, the team received particularly low scores from internal customers on effective conflict resolution, scoring 4.1 on the seven point scale, with the average for this dimension being 5.0 (see Table 7.1). As we described in chapter 6, certain linking processes, in this case social contact and creation of a shared history, predict whether and how conflict produced by differentiated goals will impact individual team members sense of identity, affect, and role in the team. Carlos, the team member from Venezuela, had this to say about the positive impact of social contact:

> We feel we have a very powerful system right now, an HR system which is brand new and we think, we know, we can get a lot out of it. Now for that particular piece I really think we're going to need to come together as a group, you know face-to-face and have some kind of a workshop and work on that. Because there are just some pieces that need that continuity, of you know even if it is in a room eight hours or two or three days, you need to have that interaction, you need to get those juices flowing and not stop after an hour conference call. Just when you are like sort of warming up, you know the clock is ticking. Some point in time you just need that face to face.

Despite comments such as these, the team has had very few opportunities for face to face interaction Carlos speaks of so highly.

*Catalysts.*　　A number of catalysts have proceeded the current state of ineffectiveness in the HRPT. First and foremost is a state of task uncertainty within the team. As we dis cussed in chapter 5, under conditions of high task uncertainty, strategies are not known, and thus must be established through a lengthy process of interaction and examination in the team in which assumptions are checked, educated guesses are made and tested, and additional information is gathered and exchanged. Decreasing task uncertainty, and increasing routineness, can have a very positive impact on MNTs. As reviewed earlier, Pelled, Eisenhardt, and Xin (1997) demonstrated that task routineness diminishes the association between diversity and task conflict.

When tasks are well-defined and straightforward, team members have little need to exchange opinions or challenge each other. Hence, in teams with routine tasks, even if members have diverse backgrounds, there is only minimal room for task conflict based on those backgrounds. In teams with uncertain tasks, there is more room for task conflict, so group members with diverse backgrounds are more likely to exchange opposing opinions and preferences derived from their backgrounds. The tendency for diversity to trigger task conflict may therefore be heightened by task uncertainty and diminished by task routineness. There was a general acknowledgment of this among the HRPT. Maria, for example, argued for developing more clarity around the team's task, She stated,

> It is best if you can identify the product, the actual whatever is being produced by this particular team. That's easier in some functional areas than others. In the HR area or in customer service, well customer service is probably a little easier too, but info systems, finance, HR, those are a little more difficult to identify what is the end product. And so one of the things that I hope to do with this project, the interviews are just the first step, but a second step would be to have teams within companies identify what it is their common denominator or their common product. What features of this product are important? How can we measure the quality of this product, if you will? And it might be something that's not real, you know, sort of intangible. But yet maybe we could come up with some ways of identifying that yes, this is a good product or no, this is not a good product or yes, this is a good outcome or no, this is not a good outcome. And then measuring that, taking a baseline measure of that and then coming back later and finding out if some of the things the company's doing in terms of the HR programs, like this team project, will improve those products.

A critical catalyst that can help to re-establish equilibrium in the team with regard to the task constraints is the team's technology. Most team members agreed that more face-to-face time will help to define the task, establish common goals, and reduce some of the negative outcomes, both team level and individual level, being experienced by the team. As Donna, the team member from the United States, stated:

> If we would have been face-to-face it probably would've been a lot easier to communicate in a way that would be maybe more sensitive to how she [Elena] was feeling and she could have seen your body language and all that. But over the phone all you can go on is the words, the language that your using and sometimes that doesn't do it when you communicate.

Ultimately, this group likely failed because they never had the opportunity to develop any real common sense of teamness, common goals, or even a consistent sense of their "project."

A second critical catalyst the team must address is the equilibrium between role ambiguity and hierarchy. As demonstrated in Table 7.2, the HRPT received the highest ratings for all of the self-management scales. They also reported the highest levels of discretion in decision making. However, given the cultural proclivities of many of the team members, this may be a key factor underlying their struggles. As reviewed in chapter 7, Kirkman and Shapiro's research suggests that the cultural values of those in Latin American countries, particularly the high level of power distance could reduce the initial acceptance of self-management by team members, particularly if self-management is introduced in totality without much training or support. This seemed to be the case within the HRPT. Discussing his manager's style, Carlos remarked:

> She will look at our mission. And from there, she'll be hands-off. She just really does not get involved in the day-to-day activity. She's there if you need her. She says, "Just tell me if we're in trouble—that's all I want to know."

Many of the team members appeared uncomfortable with this hands-off approach. Internal team customers noticed this state of affairs, and in fact, cited it as an underlying cause of the lack of customer satisfaction with the team's output. As one team customer stated

> They are just learning. I would say they are going through a learning phase. Many have been with the company, I would say, probably over fifteen years, so they're used to "I have a supervisor and my supervisor tells me, move this box, do this, do that." Now their boss is in Miami and they have to sort of make those decisions so I think they're struggling from the old system into this team concept system where they share the group leadership and the people will be coming to them for direction or coordination of work load if they have a problem.

As we discuss next, critical for this team is to establish a strategic progression from external direction toward self-management, that includes training for individual members to develop the skills necessary to do so, much as did the BMPT.

## IMPLEMENTATION AND DESIGN OF MNTs

In these five teams, we have witnessed the importance of several design factors that are critical to managing the work structure, social structure, and functional processes. Many of these same design factors—context, group structure, technology, people, and process—are factors highlighted by traditional models of group effectiveness (see Cohen and Bailey, 1997 for a review). For example, leadership is a key feature of group structure. All the teams we have described have struggled with the balance between external direction and self-management that confronts all teams, but this struggle is made all the more salient when members of different national backgrounds join an MNT with differing expectations for leadership. The most effective teams in our sample, such as the BPT, have successfully resolved this balance. However, many teams, such as the SST have yet to achieve this balance, given the particular cultural context in which they are embedded.

Second, creation of hybrid cultures in MNTs, and resulting shared understanding and shared goals, will, in large part, depend on information technologies. At a minimum level, members of virtual teams need to be able to use electronic communication. To achieve high levels of effectiveness, however, it will be necessary to also create norms for basic use and dynamic repositories of shared team knowledge (Cohen and Gibson, 2001). In particular, differences in information technology platforms and tools, and insufficient support for the implementation and use of technologies, can be major barriers to integration. Critically important in a team with a high degree of geographic dispersion, such repositories will contain electronic versions of reports, drawings, meeting notes, prototypes, along with rules and procedures for use. Stein and Zwass (1997) refer to such repositories as organizational memory information systems. Again, all the MNTs in our sample have struggled with information technologies, but the more effective, such as the APST have arrived at an optimal use of the varying technologies available to them, based on the nature of their task and their varying needs throughout the team's life cycle. In contrast, the HRPT has not been able to fully develop functional technology usage.

Finally, we would argue that people and processes fall hand-in-hand to determine effective conflict resolution in MNTs, and that the more successful MNTs in our sample have explicitly addressed these key design factors through selection, training, and ongoing maintenance of norms and routines. Many have accomplished this through socialization and basic meeting management. The APST did this through by recruiting group members with different and/or unique combinations of attributes to reduce the probability of subgroup formation and the kinds of intragroup conflicts they can cause. Likewise, training to improve self-management skills, documentation, and tracking are key processes that have become habitual in the BPT, and ultimately help to explain its success. In contrast, we saw a lack of these factors in the HRPT.

Armed with these basic design factors, MNTs can go a long way to improving effectiveness and maintaining functionality, essentially overcoming barriers to successful performance across cultural boundaries.

## SUMMARY

In this chapter, we have described five teams we have investigated in conjunction with a multiyear project examining the implementation of teams in multinational organizations. In each team, several individual and group elements, processes, and catalysts are critical to the current level of team functioning, helping to explain both high performance and performance barriers. As such, the features of our MNT model can also be utilized to direct interventions, and serve as key points of leverage in increasing the effectiveness of MNTs. In addition, the model helps to direct future research by highlighting the most impactful arenas for additional investigation. We elaborate on these two functions of the MNT model in our last chapter, and draw a few final conclusions and observations.

# 8  Conclusions and a Research Agenda

The purpose of our monograph has been to both extend and consolidate the evolving literature on multinational teams. In the past 2 decades, the topic of multinational teams, their composition and functioning, has received increasing attention from organizational scholars. Of course, the very idea of a multinational team is the product of a very practical business offshoot of globalization. That is, if it were not for the globalization of business, few organizational scholars would be particularly concerned with multinational teams. Even a topic such as international and cross-cultural negotiation would likely not be a central issue in our thinking. But this is simply not the world that we now face. Businesses are global, people are continually interacting with one another across national boundaries, and the nature of organizational behavior must now be conceptualized in terms of culture-specific versus culture-general processes and actions. That is, the emic and etic aspects of behavior must be taken into careful consideration as any theory of human action and interaction is formulated. An emic (or insider's) perspective adopts an interpretative frame, examining behavior from within the system (Pike, 1966). Typically, only one culture is investigated in-depth and the assumption is that constructs are unique to each culture, rather than general across cultures. In contrast, an etic (or outsider's) perspective examines behavior from a position outside the system, comparing the same phenomenon across many cultures for the purpose of comparison (Pike, 1966). Understood from an etic perspective, constructs should be general to all cultures, albeit may be experienced in a unique manner in each.

## REVIEW OF DOMAINS ADDRESSED

The topic of teams in organizations has been the focus of many, many papers, chapters, and books. Team and group dynamics is an entire sub-area within the fields of social psychology and sociology and literally thousands of articles have been written on the topic with work dating back to the 1800s. From an organizational context, much of the early work done in industrial psychology concerned itself with the nature of groups and teams for understanding workplace productivity. One classic example is the Coch and French (1948) study of the Harwood Pajama factory looking at the potential advantage of participative decision-making in employee effectiveness. They found that group participation resulted in a higher level of goal commitment and performance than in two other conditions of no-participation and participation by a representative. This study complemented other work at the time including work by Elton Mayo and his colleagues (the "Hawthorne Studies"), and Lewin, Lippett, and White (1939) on leadership style and participation.

These various studies gave rise to a large wave of research on teams in organizations and it has culminated with a plethora of books on the topic such as the utility of worker involvement and self-managed teams (Cohen & Ledford, 1994; Mankin, Cohen, & Bikson, 1996; Mohrman, Cohen & Mohrman, 1995) from the University of Southern California school, the role of technology (e.g., Ancona & Caldwell, 1992; Ancona & Chong, 1996; Goodman & Associates, 1986) from the Carnegie school and MIT, and specific research by organizational scholars including Gersick (1988), George (1990), and Hackman (1976, 1990), among others. To complement this work has been additional research by people such as Graham (1985), Putnam and Poole (1987), and Leung (1997) on group negotiation and Erez and Locke and their colleagues on participative goal-setting (e.g., Earley & Erez, 1991; Latham, Erez & Locke, 1988; Locke & Latham, 1990).

The area having received least attention that has only recently taken a front position in the literature is the subject of teams dynamics in an international context, or what we refer to broadly as a multinational team. It is for this reason that we turned our attention to the development and presentation of a comprehensive framework for understanding teams in an international and cross-cultural context.

Some scholars have suggested that a fundamental theory of psychology or organizational behavior is exactly that—fundamental and therefore equally applicable to all people. That is, a principle underlying a psychological framework, such as Skinner's (1938) stimulus-response operant conditioning, is culture free and universal. Such a search for psychological universals has been a very difficult one (e.g., see Lonner's chapter in Triandis & Berry's 1980 *Handbook of Cross-Cultural Psychology*) providing few convincing universal laws of action. As we are writing this concluding chapter, one of the most significant scientific discoveries has been announced—the complete mapping of the human genome. Biologists, medical researchers, chemists, etc. now have a complete description of the fundamental building blocks of human life. The promise of cures for various illnesses including cancer, Parkinson's disease, and diabetes to name a few, now seem realistic and achievable in our lifetime. More fundamental, we now have a seemingly accurate description of human life—granted from a specific viewpoint. How close are scholars in the psychological and behavioral sciences from claiming such a feat?

While our modest attempt at describing the functioning and interactions underlying multinational teams is in no way comparable to mapping the human genome or describing string theory in physics or mapping the universe by the astronomer, we have attempted to provide an initial step toward understanding the most basic of human interactions across cultural and national boundaries. A fundamental facet of humanity is social interaction and exploration. These two principles will inevitably give rise to the opportunities for people to form into groups and teams across cultural boundaries. A student of history quickly observes that people have been crossing such boundaries and forming such alliances since the first social interactions began. Of course, many such actions in the past were for purposes of conquest and domination. Some might argue that multinational and transnational companies are engaging in the very same practices! But our basic point is that people are bound by principles of interaction and exploration. It is for this reason, among others, that we developed our thinking on this topic.

Based on a rather mundane but important practical motivation, we wrote this book as an aid for researchers and practitioners who are concerned with multinational teams. The first author had an amusing (but somewhat disconcerting) incident with an MBA student who questioned the need to emphasize international practices in learning HRM. The student was a former employee of a major U.S. automobile manufacturer! Few business and industries lie insulated from international competition and such landmark American companies as "Chrysler," "Best Foods," and "Ben and Jerry's Ice Cream" have been acquired by "foreigners" (e.g., by Germany's Daimler-Mercedes-Benz and by the Dutch–British multinational company, Unilever). Therefore, the topic of multinational teams lies at the heart of effective globalization for a company.

These international mergers give rise to multinational teams mandated, among other things to coordinate business activity, explore new markets, coordinate international strategy, and create new products. With the creation of multinational teams is the concern of how to operate and run them effectively; controlling team direction and action without stifling the potential synergies and creativity they may experience.

## CONTRIBUTIONS OF OUR FRAMEWORK

As we stated, our purpose has been to present a comprehensive framework for understanding multinational teams. We examined various features and dynamics underlying these teams. In our framework, we addressed multinational teams using multiple levels of analysis as well as various types of dynamic linkages. Our microlevel of analysis emphasized the individual-level elements of team members including such characteristics as trust and expectations, respect and moral character, affective sensitivity, confidence and efficacy, and social awareness. This was companioned with group elements such as competition, fractionation, hybrid culture, shared understanding, common goals, and group confidence.

These various elements of team member and team were linked to one another through several dynamics. First, we described the rules and roles that people use as they interact with one another. People are role-making and rule determining because these processes enable them to understand their personal functioning in a social structure. That is, we seek roles that help us maintain or improve our social status and we look to rules and norms within a team to help us understand our position and duties relative to other team members. These linking processes are of critical importance for a multinational team since many of the anchors that we use to define ourselves in the social milieu are absent. In addition, we rely on social contracts as a means of predicting the enforcement of agreed upon roles. Our social contracts are a means through which we enforce enacted roles. Likewise, we draw upon a shared history within a team as a way of judging the fairness and appropriateness of others' actions. It is this function as an evaluation tool that gives rise to people developing a shared history in the first place. Without such a common history, team members are unable to judge consistently others' actions within the team.

We discussed as well several linking mechanisms that connect the work and social structure catalysts that we described in our framework. We discussed three general linking processes including: roles, rituals, and structuration, and social enactment. Roles reflect a persons sense of identity. By rituals, we referred to those institutionally-derived patterns of a team that are associated with meaningful events (e.g., celebrating team success for a project completed). Structuration is Giddens's concept of people creating a future social structure in accordance with their present expectations. Finally, we used the idea of social enactment, or the engaging of particular actions and behavior as a way of reasserting one's position in a hierarchy. In a sense, social enactment reflects the idea of posturing and behaving as a signaling mechanism to maintain one's social stature. These three linking processes connect the most macro-level catalysts of our model.

Two general categories of macro-level catalysts in the framework can be contrasted: *social structure catalysts*, such as third parties, subgroups, cooperation versus competition, and hierarchy/leadership; and *work structure catalysts,* such as timing, task constraints, technology, supportive organization, resource changes, and goal focus. The social structure catalysts refer to team-level aspects of how people interact with one another. As an example, the importance of subgroups in the emerging social structure is that they often give rise to divisiveness within the team and a "we versus them" mind-set. The work structure catalysts describe structural characteristics of where, when, and how team members are likely to interact as a team. For example, the use of technology as a means of facilitating team interaction across vast geographic distances is becoming increasingly frequent. We discussed many of the advantages and drawbacks of such work structure catalysts.

Taken together, our framework has integrated individual, team, and workplace characteristics looking at how various elements of these entities are linked through various social mechanisms. We have not provided direct links to even more macro levels of analysis such as company governance issues, industry practices, political constraints so our model is clearly intended as a mid-range theory of multinational team functioning. Likewise, we have not restricted our framework to a single theory such as social identity theory or structuration theory.

## THE IMPORTANCE OF EQUILIBRIUM

The common theme that does underlies our model refers back to a point we made early in our exposition, namely, that these various elements and processes operate according to an optimality principle of integration and differentiation. That is, there is some regulatory set-point at any given point in time for the extent to which elements and processes push toward integration versus pull toward differentiation. This is true at multiple levels of analysis. Just as individuals seek optimal levels of integration and differentiation (Brewer, 1993), we argue that teams do as well. Ultimately, as we think about the nature of team functioning we must return to the idea of an equilibrium point.

Throughout the book we have argued that there are regulatory points around which team processes hover. This is not to suggest that such points are static or singular. We have not argued that teams seek to achieve an optimal level of, say, distinctive ingroup identity (separation from other groups but inclusion in the general social structure of the company) and remain there. The equilibrium regulation that we have discussed is much more analogous to the dynamic regulation point described in nonlinear dynamics, or so-called Chaos Theory (Gleick, 1987). That is, each group (and group member) moves in a quasi-oscillatory fashion between the pulls of integration and differentiation. As a team member, this is reflected by the tension described by Brewer in her Optimal Distinctiveness Theory (1993) we presented earlier. Each team member simultaneously seeks to be a unified member of her team while wishing to remain as a distinct and independent entity. Further, this tension creates a constant movement to-and-fro of inclusion/exclusion with an oscillatory point dependent on external factors such as the cultural context of the society. For example, in Thailand there is a generally high power distance with relatively low to moderate collectivism (Earley, 1999; Komin, 1991). This manifests itself in individual team member values as a tension of loyalty and duty to the team while resenting such an imposition as a restriction of personal liberty. Thai social structure emphasizes deference to more powerful others ("krengjai") and personal obligation ("bunkhun") reflecting features of what westerners often think of as collectivism. Krengjai may lead an individual to *avoid* asking a friend or superior for help so as to avoid creating an excessive bunkhun (Klausner, 1993). Thus, Thai culture emphasizes independence and deference rather than social collectivism (Earley, 1999).

At a team level, a similar tension is observed as multinational teams seek to regulate integration and differentiation from their external environment. Integration is an important stepping stone of legitimacy for a multinational team. It is important for any team but especially important for a multinational team that often must establish its importance and credentials to its larger, organizational home. As the institutional theorists describe (e.g., DiMaggio & Powell, 1983; Scott & Meyer, 1994) practices such as mimetic isomorphism (copying the practices of others) provide a perceived legitimacy of one entity in the presence of others. Thus, a multinational team within a company may seek out the practices of other such teams within the company and copy their actions to legitimate their own existence.

At the same time, however, is a desire to retain a separate identity that distinguishes ones own team from others within the company. There is a balance point beyond which a team loses its collective sense of identity separate from other teams within the organization. A manager from a sporting goods and sportswear manufacturer working in Asia commented of his team experience (personal conversation with the first author),

One of the striking experiences that I had as [company X] put together these marketing teams for Asia and Europe is that to be successful, and make a big splash, we had to show them how we were different. During our early meetings, we decided that we needed a team name and something to keep us different than the other regional marketing teams. Our team name that we came up with was the Mongoose team because we were fast and able to tackle anything. We even had t-shirts printed up with a Mongoose on it because I thought it would keep us feeling like we were a real team. The funny thing is that after some other teams heard about us, they came up with their own names.

This illustrates the importance of a team maintaining its independence from other teams as it operates within a company. Unique identities provide a team with an opportunity to keep unique accomplishments identified with them as well as provide autonomy. Our framework, then, has emphasized a number of individual and group-level elements that are regulated according to a general principle of dynamic equilibria and subject to change by various social and work-structure catalysts. These catalysts give rise to change through a number of linking processes. In the face of these catalysts, the challenge for the MNT is to re-establish the equilibrium.

## A NEW RESEARCH AGENDA FOR THE STUDY OF MULTINATIONAL TEAMS

Our emphasis in this book has not only been to describe and discuss the key elements and processes underlying multinational teams, but also to review existing research and suggest some possible new venues for investigation and theory development. In this section, we turn our attention to a sampling of research issues that we consider central at this point in the development of the literature. For sake of convenience, we organize this section into three subsections: content and conceptual issues, methodo-logical issues, and practice and implementation issues.

**Content and Conceptual Issues.** Probably the most important conceptual issue facing the researcher of multinational teams is the identification of fundamental principles that drive these teams. That is, what are the reasons and motives for why these teams operate as they do and how can we use this knowledge to understand them better?

**Identity.** One of the most common conceptual frameworks drawn from to understand multinational teams has been that of an Identity framework, most often Social Identity Theory and Self Categorization Theory (Tajfel, 1982; Turner, 1987). As we discussed earlier in the book, these complementary theories look at the way individuals within teams attach themselves to groups and how this impacts group functioning. Individuals are thought to be motivated by a desire for inclusion into social groups as a means of enhancing personal ego. That is, we join groups because they reinforce our sense of personal importance. By attaching ourselves to certain groups, and devaluing other groups, we distinguish ourselves as important and worthy. It is a primal desire of all people to define and assert their significance in the social milieu (Earley, 1997; Erez & Earley, 1993; Goffman, 1959; Hu, 1944; Ting-Toomey & Cocroft, 1994; Turner, 1987).

This suggests that in a multinational team, individuals are motivated by a desire to distinguish themselves from strangers in other groups by integrating themselves into their particular group. They are attracted to teams having members who can provide social reinforcement and reaffirmation of self worth. Such an argument can be applied to various types of groups and it is not unique to the multinational team. For example, we see this same argument applied extensively to the diversity and demography literatures (e.g., Lawrence, 1997; Tsui et al., 1992). Even though the diversity and demography literatures diverge concerning predictions of team outcomes such as turnover and performance, they both posit that team members are motivated by a desire for self enhancement.

**Status and Power.** A related theoretical explanation for team development is that of status hierarchy and power (e.g., Earley & Mosakowski, 2000; Ravlin, Thomas, & Ilsev, 2000). One explanation for team dynamics is that people seek to establish their position in a social hierarchy as a way of understanding their role on a team, and that this sorting process is particularly difficult on a multinational team. The reason such a sorting process is problematic on a multinational team is because many of the social cues for establishing dominance are inconsistent, lacking, or contradictory. This is not the case for a domestic team since members come from a common culture for which there is a much greater degree of overlap concerning status cues. For example, a team composed of all Chinese managers may not agree concerning all of the details of status, but there is a general consensus shared concerning respect for age and position (job title). One does not need to "learn" this hierarchy. However, if we mix a Chinese manager with an U.S. manager for whom age is not a relevant status marker, it becomes more complicated for the two managers to understand relative status. Complicate this further by introducing more team members having multidimensional status markers and we can see the unique challenge of understanding status in a multinational team (Earley & Mosakowski, 2000).

**Conflict.** A related vein of work has come from individuals who examine multinational teams from a perspective of conflict and group functioning (e.g., Ravlin et al., 2000; Weldon & Jehn, 1995). According to Ravlin et al. (2000), when organizational groups are composed of members of multiple cultures, a primary concern is that conflict between members of different cultural backgrounds will impede group effectiveness. In order to understand this dynamic, Ravlin and colleagues developed a framework looking at the influences of belief systems regarding values and status, and the roles that recognition of, agreement with, and acceptance of these beliefs by members in subgroups. Further, they focus on how these processes generate latent and manifest conflict within the group. Drawing from a variety of theories, Ravlin and colleagues focus on the nature of power held by various team members as well as potential conflict attributable to value incongruence among members. Their point is that multinational teams are likely to experience unclear status hierarchies as well as incongruent member values that will result in potential conflict and sub-group formation. How a team might be created and implemented is a de-sign question that they address using a conflict and power perspective.

**Collective Cognition.**    A related approach comes from those scholars who seek to understand multinational teams from a shared mind-set per-spective, or a collective cognition view (e.g., Gibson, 2000b; Klimoski & Mo-hammed, 1994). According to this view, an important element for understanding team functioning are the shared mental representations that team members have about the world around them. For example, when the team acts and feedback is available about performance, this information is likely to generate a feedback loop. Feedback is first perceived, then filtered and stored. Group members share subjective impressions of what has oc-curred or what may occur and these impressions are utilized to form future cognitions (Gibson, 2000b). This is a critical issue because these collective interpretations are eventually stored in the team's memory and can form the basis for future performance throughout the life of the team. When the information is positive, this may encourage accumulation of more knowl-edge, and repetition of the cycle of collective cognition. When the feedback is negative, it will likely encourage re-examination.

Building in the notion of shared understanding and collective cognition, Earley and Mosakowski (2000) discussed the importance of a hybrid cul-ture. A strong culture exists if these rules, expectations, and roles are shared (Rohner, 1987; Schweder & LeVine, 1984). They argued that a hy-brid culture provides a common basis for mutual understanding within the multinational team, and more importantly, that the act of creating a hybrid culture is itself an important bonding element. By creating a hybrid culture, team members are more likely to empathize with one another, develop common goals and purpose, and have improved communication.

Although there is promise with the idea of a hybrid culture to explain why some groups fail and others thrive, it is static in the sense that achieving a hy-brid culture is seen as the important outcome of group interaction. Once achieved, it is unclear how a group might subsequently change and evolve. Is the hybrid culture a sufficiently integrating experience for team members that as they are confronted with new challenges and catalysts they will "work through them"? In as much as a hybrid culture captures a number of elements such as common goals, shared understanding, and communica-tion, it sheds substantial light on multinational teams as they evolve over time. However, it seems that while this is an important feature of a success-ful multinational team, it is only a partial picture of such success.

**Evolution and Change.**    All of these perspectives tend to emphasize the nature of team members' values and status as a means of understanding team dynamics. Unfortunately, an element lacking from these per-spectives is the impetus for change and evolution of a team. That is, these conceptual perspectives might establish initial formation and develop-ment of a multinational team, but they are inadequate for addressing the subsequent dynamics underlying the changes that occur throughout a team's lifespan. Even Brewer's optimality model falls somewhat short since there is no reason for a group to change once an optimal point of in-tegration/differentiation has been experienced. In our framework, we pro-vide two general classes of forces that give rise to continual evolution (and revolution) in a multinational team, namely, the social and work structure catalysts. These endogenous and exogenous influences explain why teams do not grind to a halt after establishing a team status hierarchy, feel-ings of member self worth, or sense of inclusion. We are not suggesting that previous approaches are inert and stagnant, rather that the longitudi-nal or dynamic component of these theories and models is somewhat lacking. A multinational team (perhaps more so than most other types of teams given its unique setting) is constantly changing because its environ-ment is inherently unstable and dynamic. Multinational teams cannot be isolated from the general business environment in the way that other teams might be (e.g., Apple Computer's classic isolation of the Macintosh design team).

What we describe a unique feature of the multinational team, now be-comes a critical research need—the dynamic and changing aspect of this type of team. Researchers need to focus on examining the catalysts for change for multinational teams, rather than relying on unidimensional ex-planations of team member interaction such as interpersonal attraction, self worth, or conflict. Again, we are not negating the importance of these principles for understanding a multinational team, but these represent a very incomplete understanding of how they evolve.

For example, as we have discussed a perspective recently introduced to the literature that has much potential is the idea of faultlines, hypothetical dividing lines that may split a group into subgroups based on one or more attributes (Lau & Murnighan, 1998). In our use of this concept to analyze our case examples presented in chapter 7, we found the faultline notion to be both helpful and limiting in many ways. The core idea of a faultline is quite useful we think in as much as it provides an opportunity for looking at demographic characteristics in a multidimensional fashion. Not only can we include multiple characteristics in a common group assessment, these characteristics can vary in relative value to group members (some differ-ences are more important than others). The problem we faced, however, is that these relative weightings of characteristics differ across team mem-bers of a multinational team—often, they differ very significantly. Although individual differences would suggest that people differ in their relative weights attached to various characteristics within any culture, this problem is magnified as we cross cultural and national boundaries as is inevitable with multinational teams.

Take, for example, our case of the APST team. In terms of nationality, the potential for conflict based on subgroups seems high since there are eight nations represented across 12 team members. However, the difficulty with predicting subgroups based on potential faultlines is that we have to make assumptions as to what are the salient characteristics in the computation of the faultlines. What if the various members do not perceive the same traits as relevant for their "faultlines"? In the APST, for example, based on our quotes, it appears that gender is a significant issue for several of the members. Thus, gender appears quite salient in the formation of subgroups. However, nationality is not mentioned by the team members. Does this mean that they do not view one another in terms of national differences? Or is it that they have moved beyond seeing one another in terms of national differences (given the length of time that they have been together as a team perhaps they have moved beyond national differences)? Or is it that national differences are sufficiently fundamental that they view them as background and a given aspect of their differences? A faultline approach is fraught with difficulties for multinational teams for these reasons and we return to this in the next subsection on methodological issues.

Of the various perspectives that we discussed in our book, one framework having received scant attention in the literature for understanding multinational teams (for an exception see Maznevski, 1994 and Butler, 2000) is that of structuration theory. To reiterate, structuration is a concept from Giddens (1984) who proposed that people within any given social structure not only react to their surroundings, but they also create those surroundings in the future through their present actions. It is this idea that he referred to as "colonization of the future" and it suggests that peoples' concept of "the way things are" and their goals will give rise to actions that ensure such future states are achieved. More importantly, people constantly recreate the social structures that house them as time moves forward. The importance of this type of perspective is that it provides a dynamic perspective on what might otherwise be viewed as largely static. Even the few studies assessing longitudinal effects for diverse teams (e.g., Watson et al.'s 1993) often argue that static results occur if sufficient time is provided for in a research design. In the case of Watson et al., the authors argued that diverse teams will overcome initial performance limitations relative to homogeneous teams provided that they are given sufficient time to develop. Thus, few researchers have addressed the complexities of the longitudinal aspects of team dynamics in any comprehensive fashion.

In our framework, a longitudinal component cannot be ignored since the social and work catalysts are constantly introduced, removed, evolving, and incorporating. For example, technology is a prime example of an influence that is ever changing and so it will continually require a multinational team to adapt and evolve. Likewise, group membership often changes and each new entrant gives rise to many new challenges to a group such as change in social hierarchy, leadership structure, and interaction patterns. Membership changes are a dynamic process described by Earley and Mosakowski as requiring rediscovery of status markers. For example, a team having members with varying status markers (e.g., an Israeli who has religion, ethnicity, and age as cues, a Thai who has age, education, and gender, an American who has race, gender, and wealth) gives rise to a continual reconfiguration of status hierarchy. Their argument is that as team members become accustomed with one another, they will no longer view themselves in terms of differing nationalities. Instead, they now view one another according their own status hierarchy, and this potentially leads to additional divisions and subgroup formation. As Adler (1991) suggested, an expatriate female manager sent to Japan is first seen as foreign, or "gaijin" rather than female per se. It is only after familiarity and inclusion in the ingroup that additional characteristics might become evoked. Ironically, this suggests that initial acceptance might give rise to subsequent rejection of status!

*Multidimensionality.* Another important research question that needs to be addressed is how to consolidate the various individual research perspectives that have been drawn upon by researchers. As we described, scholars have examined multinational teams using many different theories and perspectives. Our framework attempts to provide a general umbrella for these various perspectives rather than drawing from any single organizing principle. This is both a strength and weakness of our approach. On the one hand, we provide for a richness of explanations through our various elements and catalysts. This multidimensionality enables a researcher to draw from a number of influences to understand multinational teams. On the other hand, the plethora of influences and elements creates confusion and complexity. The parsimony offered using a single explanatory system (e.g., Social Identity Theory or Status Hierarchy Theory) is abandoned as what we view to be overly simplistic and limited. It is too easy to find multinational teams in real life that contradict the terms dictated by any single and simple explanation.

We encourage researchers to move beyond the use of a single explanation for understanding multinational teams at this time. These teams are too complex to be reduced to single explanations. At the same time, we do not advocate the opportunistic evoking of different theoretical explanations for each and every aspect of a team's dynamics. Rather, we argue that a framework such as ours will provide an organizing context for various effects and influences observed in multinational teams.

***Methodological Issues and New Directions.*** An important facet to future research of multinational teams is the use of longitudinal designs as a means of understanding how various catalysts operate. Such designs are important, not simply to watch how one effect might play itself out, but rather, longitudinal designs are essential to capture the phenomena of "catalysis" in multinational teams. Without such designs, one cannot accurately assess the role of various catalysts, nor the relative importance of various linking processes that we described.

***Time Frame.*** Of course, with the adoption of a longitudinal design come a number of relevant questions. First, what is the appropriate timeframe to study the various effects? Do we need to observe a team for a week, a month, a year? The frequency and duration of observations have important implications for the findings obtained in longitudinal research. For example, sampling excerpts of conversations in 30 second intervals over the course of a 3-hour team meeting will present a very different picture of conflict resolution than would sampling the same team's meetings in a more general fashion over the course of 3 months. Given the variability of notions of time across cultures (e.g., Gibson et al., 2000; Hall, 1983; Hofstede & Bond, 1988; Levine & Bartlett, 1984; Levine, West, & Reis, 1980; Mosakowski & Earley, 2000), it seems that determining the proper timeframe for a longitudinal design will be difficult and largely based on empirical experience.

A second question from a longitudinal perspective is when to expect stable oscillations to occur between points of integration and differentiation. If these stable equilibria are achievable, when might we expect to observe them? Perhaps these oscillations coincide with critical stages of progression, such as the now out of fashion "forming," "storming," "norming" view of group development? Or are there critical time points of punctuated equilibrium for a multinational team such as those described by Gersick (1988) in task-performing groups? Our knowledge of the impact of task and context on teams would suggest that the introduction or development of the key catalysts are critical junctures at which to examine multinational teams.

***Field Versus Laboratory.*** Perhaps somewhat more controversial is a recommendation that we complement field research with additional laboratory work on multinational teams. There has been an emphasis placed on fieldwork by a number of scholars who suggest that multinational teams must be organizational teams. This is not really legitimate in our view. Just as teams can arise for many purposes (McGrath, 1984) and take on many different styles and lifespans, multinational teams may be better understood if we look increasingly at laboratory-based teams to capture some of the dynamics that we have described in this book. As with any method, there are inherent limitations of such an approach, but a laboratory approach will be fruitful for some aspects such as introducing membership changes in status, altering technology, or changing team resources. Further, some of the longitudinal effects that we described might be examined in a laboratory setting since many of the early developmental effects observed in field teams have been described in laboratory teams.

*Level of Analysis.* A more fundamental methodological issue for study multinational teams is common to understanding any type of team, namely, how can constructs be represented at various levels of analysis. This is a problem confronting any researcher who seeks to cross levels of analysis in research but it is of tantamount importance to the researcher of multinational teams because there are so many levels and layers that must be addressed. As we introduced in our opening chapter, this is a fundamental challenge in understanding the complexity of multinational teams.

To begin, the concept of culture must be represented in this type of research at three distinct levels—individual, team, and society. Of course, the societal level is the most traditional view of culture and is well represented in work by many researchers (e.g., Hofstede, 1991; Kluckhohn & Strodtbeck, 1961; Schwartz, 1993; Triandis, 1994). This level of analysis views a cultural dimension such as a value as a characteristic of an intact social system (Rohner, 1984). Culture at this level is often measured with survey items aggregated to the country level (Hofstede, 1980b) or ascribed to a given society based on observations of that society's institutions and artifacts (Kluckhohn & Strodtbeck, 1961).

In addition to the societal level, culture represented at an individual level of analysis is not without precedent in the recent literature. Cross-cultural organizational behavior and psychology research sometimes employs an individual differences approach to culture (e.g., Earley, 1989; Triandis, 1990). For example, Triandis, Bontempo, Vilareal, Masaaki, and Lucca (1988) distinguish between the cultural and individual level of values held concerning individualism-collectivism. At a societal level, the terms of individualism and collectivism apply. At an individual level, Triandis et al. advocate use of the terms idiocentrism and allocentrism for the psychological value orientation. An increasing number of researchers have used culture as an individual differences characteristic in their research, and this has enabled them to keep consistent constructs measured at an individual level and cultural level leading to improved prediction (Earley & Mosakowski, 1995; Leung & Bond, 1989).

*Culture at the Team Level.* What has been less frequently studied, and only really now emerging in the literature, is the dilemma facing the teams researcher. That is, how does one represent culture at a team level? This is not unique to culture since a team, or group, level of various constructs can be problematic. Take, for example, the concept of efficacy. Gibson et al. (2000) examined three separate operationalizations of group (collective) efficacy including an aggregation of individual estimates of their personal capability, aggregation of individual estimates of their group's capability, and a discussion method of group members deciding on a single judgment (through group discussion) concerning their group's capability. Using this technique to measure group-efficacy, a group is presented with a rating scale to use in forming a single response to a question about its sense of efficacy with regard to a given task objective. This single response is obtained through open discussion and interaction as group members review previous experience, situational constraints, and factors which may be expected to facilitate the group's performance. Such an approach eliminates the calculation of statistical indicators of inter-member agreement and allows for more open interaction within the group similar to that which might occur as groups go about their everyday work tasks.

Indeed in their comparisons of operationalizations, Gibson et al. found a small advantage for the discussion method. However, Bandura (1997, September, personal conversation) has suggested that collective efficacy should not be assessed using a group discussion method because it is likely to be contaminated by a social desirability influence and, therefore, distorted. Indirect support for his supposition was provided in Earley (1999) who showed that in hierarchical (high power distance) cultures, the group leader had an inordinate influence over their team's collective efficacy judgment. Still, previous research suggests that a promising avenue for measurement of group-level phenomena is through a group discussion

Thus, how can we combine individual judgments, or distill a society's global perspective, to assess a team's disposition? In the Earley (1999) study as well as Eby and Dobbins (1997), Gibson (1999, 2000a), Kirkman, Gibson, & Shapiro (2001), and Thomas (1999), culture was represented at a team level as an aggregation of team members' perceptions. That is, culture is assessed as an individual differences concept (each person's personal values) and then aggregated mathematically as an average "culture" score for their team. Safeguards such as WABA tests are employed to assure that variation in values among experimental groups exceeds that of within-group effects to support the aggregation procedure. In some cases (e.g., Cox, Lobel, & McCleod, 1991), cultural background is inferred based upon team member demographic qualities and imposed consistently across team members (e.g., Black and Hispanic team members are inferred as culturally distinct from Anglo team members on a dimension such as individualism and collectivism).

However, these still remain inadequate strategies in our view. Is the arithmetic average of five team members' personal values equivalent to their team's culture on some dimension(s)? Gibson et al. argued that a consensus method is superior to other aggregation approaches for collective efficacy because it satisfies several of the criteria important for a group-level construct outlined by Bar-Tal (1990) including: (1) the construct must reflect the group as a whole, rather than the individual members as separate units, (2) group members should agree with regard to the construct, (3) the construct must discriminate among groups, and (4) the origin of the construct must reflect the processes of interaction that occur within the group.

The discussion method of obtaining group efficacy scores begins to address the fourth requirement for group constructs—that the origin of the construct reflects the processes of interaction within the group. That this requirement is being fulfilled is most evident when one examines the key influences on the formation of group performance beliefs (Gibson, 2000c). Although individual members of a group come and go, there remains within the group a socially constructed and collectively shared history as evidenced by group norms, routines, and patterns of interaction. Each individual's private assessment may not accurately reflect the collective history that characterizes the group in comparison with other groups. In contrast, a discussion approach better reflects the pattern of interactions and connections between members, and heeds the advice of Morgeson & Hoffmann (1999), who argue:

> The investigation of construct at the collective level should begin with an understanding of the interaction of members [of the group]. Because these interactions allow collective constructs to emerge and be maintained, focusing on the interactions that define and reinforce the collective phenomenon can provide a better understanding of how collective phenomenon arise and continue, particularly in the face of contextual or membership changes. Such understanding is facilitated by explicitly identifying systems of ongoing and events, particularly those events that lend structure to collective phenomenon. (p. 257)

Thus, it may be that the "distortion" Earley (1999) described in his study is not actually a distortion; group interaction resulting in disproportionate influence of one team member over another may well reflect the true nature of a team construct such as collective efficacy or team culture. Thus, researchers need to begin assessing various team-level constructs relevant to multinational teams using a variety of methods and not impose any single method without truly considering its merits.

**Cultural Relativity of Perceptions.** A related problem to the one we have just discussed is the nature of faultlines and relative ratings of status characteristics. We described some of these difficulties in our conceptual directions section of this chapter. Basically, we argue that any distinctions derived from an analysis of status-related characteristics in a society (e.g., faultlines per Lau & Murnighan, 1998; status markers per

Earley, 1999; relational demography per Tsui et al., 1992) is limited by the relative importance of these markers as perceived by each of the team members. Thus, a proper analysis of status demarcation requires a thorough knowledge of team members' perceptions and evaluations of these characteristics. It is insufficient to assume that characteristics such as gender, race, and education are significant and meaningful markers for particular team members, even if they come from a culture in which these markers are significant. Again, the issue becomes one of assessing constructs at an individual and team level of analysis rather than imposing cultural-level characteristics uniformly across all people from that culture.

As we mentioned in chapter 7, the analysis derived from Lau and Murnighan's (1998) faultlines notion is useful in as much as it points out that combinations of status characteristics are important. This is the fundamental point made by Hughes (1971) in his discussion of primary and secondary status-determining traits. However, from an empirical position, this makes assessing faultlines within a team much more complicated and difficult. Take just a few of our case studies as examples of the challenge that we face. In our team called "HRPT," we are confronted with several classification dilemmas. This is a troubling team because national heterogeneity is high while cultural heterogeneity is not if one looks at the idea of anglo versus latino/hispanic cultures. In fact, it is possible to argue that given the countries involved, there are actually just two groups represented—North America/home office and Central/South America. Subgroups might easily be formed on the strong faultline of anglo vs. latin american groups.

This is an important illustration that simply relying on country coding is problematic and that country-based delineations reflect culture quite imperfectly. What is really crucial are the *perceptions* of cultural faultlines within the team. However, determining what are the relative traits central to determining a team's faultlines remains difficult and problematic. Thus, for the researcher the problem of using status markers as a predictor for potential division within a multinational team remains.

**Technologies.** A final topic to which we will return in the final section of this chapter that is relevant for methodological examination, is what role does technology play in the assessment and study of multinational teams? Although the impact of technology on group work has been studied extensively (e.g., DeSanctis & Poole, 1994; Goodman & Associates, 1986; Hackman, 1990; Mankin, Cohen, & Bikson, 1996), this question becomes of central importance in understanding even the mundane functioning of multinational teams. Technology has become one of the linking mechanisms whereby companies can maintain such teams. From a methodological viewpoint, the problem becomes one of capturing the interactions that may occur from distant conversations. If such interactions were solely made using a single means, such as e-mail, then it might be possible to monitor interactions using some type of groupware or GDSS technique. Even a printout of relevant e-mails that could be content analyzed would be possible. However, technology is rarely used in such a unidimensional fashion. Instead, team members from multinational groups interact using a variety of electronic means including e-mail, video and teleconferencing, two-way telephone, electronic whiteboards, and faxes. The difficulty for the researcher is somehow capturing the various types of communications and assessing their impact on the dynamics of a multinational team.

The first step is to determine what are the various methods that are drawn upon by these teams to maintain contact and get their work done. This is a largely empirical question that might be assessed through interviewing multinational teams. The second step would be to individually assess each of these methods in isolation to understand their separate contribution to team dynamics. Finally, we recommend examining how the various combinations of technology are used and impact these teams. It is likely that field observations would be needed for such an endeavor, possibly including the simultaneous observation of various team members. Ultimately, it may not be possible for a single researcher to properly assess the nature and impact of technology on a multinational team since the sheer complexity and time constraints would make it a complex task. We advocate multinational research teams to accomplish this worthwhile endeavor.

## PRACTICE / IMPLEMENTATION ISSUES

There are a wide array of problems that confront a company wishing to implement a multinational team because MNTs are subject to many difficulties. In this section, we focus on four fundamental issues of team implementation: the role of direct versus technology-mediated interaction, team governance and self-management, team composition, and lifespan.

*Technology-mediated Interaction.* One example of a difficulty confronting a multinational team is the lack of opportunity for the team to meet face-to-face. This is an important point because many people assert that technology (e-mail, videoconference, etc.) can substitute for face-to-face (see Canney-Davison & Ward, 1999 for a review of this debate). Our findings suggest this "substitution effect" is not well supported, as evidenced in the quote from the "Photoco" HRPT:

> The group that I'm working with, many of us haven't met one another, never and we're always on the phone yet I find that, it's my perception, or I may be totally wrong, but the group that I have is very dynamic. I mean I can almost feel it on the phone that they're really enthused and they really want to get

this going and they really want to be part of this project. (Maria, Human Resource Director, Puerto Rico, Photoco)

We can contrast this with a subsequent quote by Maria who comments,

I don't see it that cooperation much across country teams. I mean I don't see them helping each other ... and maybe there's just not a need to do that. I mean, maybe they are so different, maybe they should be kept Puerto Rico, Panama, Peru, etc. You know, who is to say that everybody has to work the way I'm working. In the past, her set up or strategy has been, I work with group leaders at each site and they work on their own individual situations. There is no need to go across countries. Why now?

And with Carlos (from Venezuela) who argues,

Now for that particular piece I really think were going to need to come together as a group, you know face to face and have some kind of a workshop and work on that. Because there are just some pieces that need that continuity, of you know even if it is in a room eight hours or two or three days, you need to have that interaction, you need to get those juices flowing and not stop after an hour conference call. Just when you are like sort of warming up, you know the clock is ticking. Some point in time you just need that face to face.

Likewise, the U.S. director observed a difficulty she had in inadvertently causing a Panamanian colleague to lose face over a matter of some personnel practices. It was only after careful facework (Goffman, 1959) that the Panamanian colleague was able to regain lost ground.

The most important, and difficult, circumstance confronting the implementation of a multinational team is that of managing the distances without losing the "humanity" and "personality" of the team itself. There remains something quite primal and fundamental about humans when they encounter one another directly rather than through the mediated realm of e-mail, video-conferencing, and other electronic means. At least with technology as it is currently available, we remain skeptical that it will provide an adequate substitute for direct encounters of team members.

Is there an exception to this assertion? Can technology overcome the need for humans to directly engage one another? Certainly, in some brave new world there are many possibilities but this is the topic for some other forum. However, we might suggest that technology can substitute for face-to-face encounters after certain critical events occur. That is, the key question is what is it about the direct contact that is useful? How long does this contact need to occur for this desired effect to take place, and why is it that direct contact leads to such mixed results as we described in chapter 7 (e.g., team APST versus team HRPT)?

***Strategies for Technological Mediation.*** One of the key points that we made in the presentation of our general model is that during the initial phases of team interaction, there is an important need for a team to establish its own sense of purpose, direction, and rules for interaction. This is what various people have called the "hybrid" or "third" culture (Casmir, 1992; Earley & Mosakowski, 2000). The critical point is that a multinational team, as with any team, needs to have a common basis for interaction and shared purpose. Lacking this, the team fragments and a "subgroup mentality" takes precedent. An effective team has a unified sense of purpose and members know how to communicate with one another. To achieve these goals requires intensive, direct interaction before the various bonds of trust and mutual understanding might develop. Of course, this point is central to someone coming from a high context culture (Earley & Erez, 1997; Glenn & Glenn, 1981; Hall, 1976).

High and low-context cultures influence the style of communication in normal interaction as well as conflict resolution. Individuals in low-context cultures are better able to separate conflicts from the person involved in the conflict than individuals in high context cultures. In high context cultures to disagree openly or confront someone in public is a severe blow and an extreme insult, causing both sides to *lose face*, especially in the case of superior-subordinate communication. People in high-context cultures cannot separate between the person and the conflict issue, and they invest a lot of effort in the search for a solution and the process of solving the conflict as they try to empathize and avoid direct confrontation. In high context cultures, face is very important and it is tied closely with "honor," "shame," and "obligation" (Earley, 1997). Therefore, members of high-context cultures have more other-face concerns than in low-context cultures, and they try to avoid direct confrontation.

Our point is that in implementing a multinational team, particular care must be taken for teams having high context members. Many of the subtle communication cues that are needed by someone from a high context culture may be lacking. For example, in Japanese business culture, characteristics of the person making a statement—his position, status, timing, and so on—are critical to understanding the true intent of the statement (Graham & Sano, 1984). Often what is left unsaid is more central to the position of the speaker than what is actually said (Hall, 1959). Without direct contact, people from a high context cultural background may miss the cues needed for proper interpretation of interactions. Even for low context cultures there appears to be something fundamental about direct contact. The western saying, "You can't trust a person if they won't look you directly in the eye" reflects the fundamental importance of direct interaction for group development.

If we assume that direct contact is critical to multinational team success, then an obvious question becomes, how long is direct contact needed and when? This is not a simple question because so little research has been done on these teams, and even less of it has focused on such temporal aspects of team development. From practical experience, the first author has seen field teams come together effectively with as little as 20 hours of direct contact time. Likewise, teams having had 50 hours of direct contact time or more have been observed to self destruct. Much of the key to predicting the success of a team comes from the quality and direction of the initial interaction and whether or not a hybrid culture is established.

By carefully scheduling their face to face interaction, MNTs need to strive for design that enables specialists characterized by functional, cultural, and/or organizational differences, to combine their expertise and develop innovative solutions to problems. As we suggested earlier, this requires a balancing of a integration and differentiation. The team must agree on a vision, shared agenda, and common priorities, but at the same time, the team must learn to cultivate and take advantage of differences which increase creativity and innovation. Timing and pacing become critical. The team must decide when to keep issues open and when to narrow them down and focus energies on achieving those shared objectives.

Openly discussing the areas of expertise and specialties, and the values held by each partners' organization and national culture is the first step in balancing convergence and divergence. What is it that each partner represents and contributes? What are the norms, ways of thinking, and world views institutionalized in a given partner's context? During initial face to face meetings, the answers to these questions are probably best sought by breaking out into partner groups and discussing areas of expertise and values within each subgroup first. Then, the subgroups should come together and share their attributes. Again, finding the overlaps, but also identifying the unique areas of expertise and the unique cultural values held.

Next, we suggest the MNT create a project map in which critical decision and action points are depicted. At which points is it important to emphasize the unique values and areas of expertise? At which points is collaboration essential? A project timeline for convergence and divergence should then be created taking into consideration the areas of expertise represented by each partner. Face-to-face meetings and telephone conferences should be planned to coincide with the points at which collaboration is essential, again taking into consideration the particular areas of expertise (and values) represented across partners.

**Governance.**    A second implementation issue concerns the governance of multinational teams. That is, how much direction should the team receive from outside the team? There have been a number of studies during the past several decades addressing the importance of self-managed work teams (e.g., Cohen & Ledford, 1994; Kirkman & Shapiro, 1997; Kirkman & Rosen, 1997; Manz & Sims, 1993; Trist, Susman, & Brown, 1977). By an autonomous of self-managed work team, we are referring to a team whose members have responsibility for such things as managing their own actions, planning and scheduling work, decision control over work-related decisions, and job assignments. Although this team form has received recent attention in the literature (e.g., Kirkman & Shapiro, 1997), it is a traditional concept stemming from the notion of worker democracy and autonomy reflected in the 1950s and 1960s (cf. Cherns, 1976; Erez & Earley, 1993; Thorsrud & Emery, 1970). In Europe, an approach related to what we now call self-managed work teams, known as the Socio-Technical System, or Autonomous Work Groups, was developed on the team level in countries such as England, Sweden, and Norway. The sociotechnical approach attempts to optimize the integration of the social and technical aspects of the work system. Furthermore, the sociotechnical approach takes into consideration the interplay between the organization and its environment, and in particular, the cultural values that specify the norms, rules, and regulations of behavior in organizations.

Sociotechnical interventions almost always involve the design of jobs on the group level, and they implement the five principles of individual job enrichment on the group level—team autonomy, team responsibility, feedback on performance, and task meaningfulness as enhanced by skill variety and by task identity and significance. However, one of the disadvantages of the sociotechnical system as viewed by U.S. experts is that it "does not adequately deal with differences among organization members in how they respond to work that is designed for the sociotechnical perspective" (Hackman & Oldham, 1980). This critique may be a partial answer for some of the observations that we made with our case analyses from chapter 7. That is, the individualistic values held in the United States, that result in greater concern for individual differences than for groups, may be a divisive factor in teams.

In our case studies provided in chapter 7, the team having the most difficulties had the most self-management and autonomy. The HRPT had extremely high scores with regard to self-management and decision-making autonomy and, yet, its performance was among the lowest of our teams. We are not suggesting that self-managed teams and autonomy are inherently problematic for multinational teams. However, it is quite clear that self-management and autonomy is not a simple cure-all for any team, let alone a multinational team. What appears the most critical point is the relationship of team management style to the cultural values of team members and the hybrid culture that they develop. In the case of HRPT, it seems clear that a unified culture has not been developed. Thus, self management is not terribly promising since it provides team members with an opportunity to pursue their independent interests and not share in common purpose. As Kirkman and Shapiro (1997, 2000a) argue, an important mediating characteristic of self-managed work teams is that group members are open and interested in sharing responsibilities. This is the point that Erez and Earley (1993) argued in their contingency approach to integrating work practices with cultural and personal context. It is an important question, however, as to how much external control should a multinational team have imposed on it by the parent organization.

**Strategies for Governance.** We would argue that several leadership functions are most critical in MNTs: leadership must communicate direction, motivate people to accomplish a vision, and capitalize on cross-organizational and multicultural synergies. These activities can be carried out by an external leader, by a leader internal to the team, or shared among team members. The choice of which strategy to utilize when should be based on the length of time a team has been existence and the relative competencies of team members. But basically, the challenges are the same regardless of the strategy. First, the leader must have a thorough understanding of the deliverables of the team, and the expectations of the key stakeholders. Second, the leader must understand the agendas and priorities of each partner in the team. Third, the leader needs to understand what motivates and "turns on" both the stakeholders (e.g., customers) and the members. Sometimes deliverables, expectations, agendas, and motivations are one in the same. More often, however, the leader must weave these components together to inspire the team to achieve. This involves establishing a clear direction that incorporates all of the components. Finally, equally important, MNT leaders must also monitor progress and recognize and celebrate successes. Monitoring progress means keeping track of actions taken toward the accomplishment of each agenda item, and fulfillment of each deliverable or expectation. It is critical to recognize major successes (such as a positive evaluation by a key stakeholder). It is also important to celebrate minor successes that may only be viewed as successes by certain partners. A status report on all actions taken toward objectives, all expectations fulfilled, and all deliverables achieved is a good way to kick off each face-to-face meeting and teleconference.

**Team Composition.** Team membership and composition is another central design issue for a multinational team. A great deal of our book has been devoted to the nature of team membership and its implications for team dynamics. Of course, we have spoken as if team members' abilities to perform their assigned duties are inconsequential and this is not our intent—we presume that the members chosen for a multinational team will have met some minimal requisite level of competence with regard to their actual work assignment. Thus, we have focused on the proper team composition assuming work competence.

Fractionated teams have poor performance, internal conflict, and are likely to fall apart. Likewise, team members must be receptive to the notion of the independence inherent in a multinational team. So what are the important characteristics of team members? At this point, we can only speculate on what we have seen in actual teams and what this might imply about the "ideal" candidate for a multinational team.

In terms of personal traits and skills, there is no question that empathy and relational understanding are central to the multinational team member. An ability to understand and empathize with others is critical for the development of a hybrid culture. If a person is able to get within the mind-set of fellow team members, it is more likely that she will be able to communicate with them effectively and avoid unnecessary conflict. Furthermore, drawing from the recent literature on personality theory, or what has been called the "Big Five," we find other clues to important team member characteristics. Big Five refers to a five-factor model of personality traits including extroversion, neuroticism, agreeableness, openness, and conscientiousness (McCrae & Costa, 1987). This model posits that five basic traits underlie personality structure in terms of fundamental content.

The five factors underlying personality reflect the basis of personal and social evaluations of a target individual. Extroversion reflects characteristics such as being sociable, fun-loving, affectionate, friendly, and talkative. It corresponds to more traditional concepts such as talkativeness, liveliness, etc. The key factors accounting for the extroversion factor appear to be sociability, cheerfulness, activity level, assertiveness, and sensation seeking. Neuroticism reflects a dimension that is widely accepted in personality and clinical psychology. It is reflected by characteristics such as worrying, insecure, self-consciousness, and temperament. People high on neuroticism may adopt irrational beliefs like self-blame, possess disturbed thoughts, and experience emotional distress (McCrae & Costa, 1987). The third factor, agreeableness, reflects a broad dimension capturing agreeableness versus antagonism. People who are low on agreeableness (high on antagonism) seem to set themselves against others, they are mistrustful and skeptical, uncooperative, stubborn, and rude. Their sense of attachment to others is weak, and in extreme cases, individuals resemble social outcasts. The fourth personality trait is conscientiousness and is contrasted with undirectedness. Conscientiousness is reflected by adjectives including hardworking, ambitious, scrupulous, energetic, persevering, and having a strong will to achieve. A person high on conscientiousness is purposeful and guided by goals and plans whereas a person high on undirectedness is lazy, unguided, and disorganized. Finally, the fifth personality trait was originally referred to as culture (Norman, 1963) reflecting such traits as intelligence, sophistication, and intellectual curiosity. More recently, McCrae and Costa (1985, 1987) provide evidence and further analyses supporting a modification of this trait to be more accurately called openness. By openness to experience, it is meant that an individual is original, imaginative, has broad interests, and is daring and interested in new experiences. Openness is associated with intelligence but it should not be confused as being the same thing. Although people high in openness are often intelligent, there is not necessarily a high correlation between the two constructs, and they load on separate factors in analytic models (McCrae & Costa, 1987).

The key point in this discussion is an employee's personal judgments, and those of external referents, are related to personality. For example, a person who is high on openness and agreeableness is likely to be someone able to seek out information from fellow team members about their proclivities and inclinations. This information gathering is essential for establishing a hybrid culture.

Of course, a central question is the directionality of these traits as well as their universality. In a high context culture (Hall, 1959; Witkin & Berry, 1975), high extroversion may be associated with ignoring social norms and rules, a trait considered to be undesirable. Likewise, agreeableness might be viewed as a lack of commitment and energy for a highly masculine (Hofstede, 1980b) culture with its emphasis on a fast-paced and aggressive approach to life. Our point is that although the five personality traits appear to occur in a wide variety of cultures, this does not mean that using them to capture the potential a person has for success as a multinational team member will guarantee success. The relative contribution of each factor to the social perception process is likely to vary as a function of culture (Smith & Bond, 1994). For instance, a culture stressing individualism is likely to place a high value on an openness dimension since "doing your own thing" (Triandis, 1989) is predicated on an assumption of openness to experience. In an authoritarian and hierarchical culture (e.g., high-power distance), conscientiousness and dedication to one's role in society is likely to be a highly valued characteristic. As team members encounter one another having differing perceived personality characteristics (of differing value in their own culture), troubles may occur due to potential misunderstanding.

A second consideration is that there are likely to be a number of culture-specific personality traits in any given culture not encompassed by a five-factor model (Earley, 1997). Bond (1996, personal conversation) has commented that Hong Kong Chinese typically generate an eight-factor model that subsumes a five-factor approach. For example, a number of additional personality traits (modesty, social conformity, and group dedication) arise in Hong Kong Chinese culture which are not contained in a five-factor model. A final, and related, problem concerns the way one might combine personal and social judgments of fellow members' goals using personality constructs. In some cultures people are more aware of their actions and, therefore, hide their true intent from others. Thus, the interpersonal awareness of a high context culture team member might provide him with the skills to hide personal goals. This is likely to hinder the development of a common culture and understanding within the team.

**Strategies for Team Composition.** What, then, is the "ideal" composition of a multinational team? The important consideration is not who is on the team per se, but how to overcome potential difficulties associated with particular combinations. For example, a team having people with one or two homogeneous backgrounds is problematic because it is likely to witness subgroup formation and fragmentation within the team. This tendency toward fragmentation might be overcome if team members are focused on mutual goals and purpose. Likewise, their personal openness and interest in others may enable them to come together as a unified team.

In most teams the communication climate can be described as either supportive or defensive, which in turn results in a pattern of conflict that is either functional or dysfunctional (Lumsden & Lumsden, 1993). In a supportive climate, ideas are shared freely, conflict is based on the task, conflict resolution is open and perceived as fair, and problem solutions are well understood and mutually accepted. In a defensive climate, ideas are suppressed, conflict becomes related to personality issues, conflict resolution is "behind-the-scenes" and unsatisfying to many, and problem solutions are not understood nor well accepted by all. Communication climate relate directly to the type of conflict resolution that teams engage in. Effective MNTs are willing to openly confront the issues when dysfunctional group and interpersonal dynamics hinder progress. This requires building a supportive communication climate. A supportive climate is open, trusting, inclusive, challenging and rewarding. A defensive climate is closed, blaming, alienating, discouraging, and punishing. A climate develops when team members respond to an initial risk or disclosure on the part of one member (or partner). When someone in the team discloses information or takes a risk, how does the team respond? A supportive response involves, spontaneity, empathy, a problem-orientation, flexibility and engenders a sense of equality among members. This in turn, results in trust and openness in the team, which in turn encourages future risk and disclosure, thus increasing openness and trust, and creating a cycle of support. On the other hand, a defensive response involves evaluation, control, strategic maneuvering, superiority, and certainty. This in turn, results in loss of trust and withdrawal, which results in self-protection, and closed mindedness, thus increasing distrust and producing divisions within the team, creating a cycle of division.

Within the context of a supportive climate, functional and constructive conflict resolution can occur. Functional conflict resolution involves critical evaluation of ideas. It is open and predictable. Members provide an accurate representation of their own needs and concerns, but focus on shared agenda and objectives. Time is devoted to finding solutions to problems and utilizing logical processes in which ideas are given consideration based on merit. Functional conflict can be contrasted with dysfunctional conflict. Dysfunctional conflict seldom produces resolution.

You can recognize dysfunctional conflict because evaluation is focused on the behavior and personality of other members, rather than on ideas. Bad stereotypes of others are developed. Personal goals are pursued rather than shared goals, and personal needs are often disguised rather than openly shared. Discussions are secretive and unpredictable. Time is devoted to non-rational and irrational arguments.

One way to address communication climate in MNTs is for members to conduct a "fishbowl" exercise. During a segment of a team meeting, two members of the team are asked to serve as observers (or outside observers are asked to conduct the observation). The observers sit outside the action, observing the team interaction inside the team (the fish in the fish bowl). The observers record supportive and defensive reactions to disclosures, without attaching names to the reactions, simply recording the statements that were made. After about an hour, the team should stop the interaction and do a "process check." Observers can report back to the team the number of supportive and defensive reactions (without mentioning names). The team might then discuss how defensive reactions could have been supportive. This same exercise can be conducted to address conflict resolution directly. Observers can record instances in which characteristics of functional conflict were demonstrated and instances in which dysfunctional conflict was demonstrated (again, keeping the instances anonymous). After an hour of interaction, the team should discuss ways in which the conflict could have been dealt with in a more constructive manner. Using this technique, the MNT can come to a better understanding of the various member approaches and how they combine to create a culture and climate inside the team.

Finally, we wish to point out that the various ages of MNTs and the circumstances under which they operate makes it very difficult to predict what will be the critical characteristics on which to base team processes. For example, in the case of our team SST, service versus sales is a key dimension mentioned by team members concerning their differences. In other teams (e.g., HRPT) it might be nationality or regionality or gender. As we said earlier, it is difficult to predict what characteristics will be salient overtime. The lifespan and length the teams have been together is clearly an issue worth addressing in contrast to other more short-term teams that we see discussed in the literature (e.g. Earley & Mosakowski, 2000).

## SUMMARY

As we discussed at the outset, our purpose in developing this book was to address an apparent gap in the literature on teams. Despite the popularity of multinational teams from a pragmatic viewpoint (companies are using these teams increasingly), little work has been developed to provide a comprehensive model for them. We have seen a number of important first steps in work by such authors as Earley and Mosakowski (2000), Elron (1997), Gibson (2000a, 2000b, 2000c), Gibson & Vermeulen (2000), Kirkman & Shapiro (1997), Maznevski & Chudoba (2000), and Ravlin et al. (2000), just to name a few. Our purpose in writing this book is to provide a more general framework to guide subsequent research on this critical topic.

Our model focused on various features of the team's members, their interactions as a team, and the organizational context in which they operate. We used the concept of integration and differentiation as a general force guiding the specific processes that link various levels of analysis in our model. From this, we derived a number of implications and suggestions for future research. What we close with is a restatement of the nature of the problem we address in this book. Without question, multinational teams are not merely a management fad to be abandoned in the future. The globalization of business necessitates a cross-border approach to work with an increasing reliance on multinational teams. How and why these unique teams function cannot be addressed by the plethora of standard prescriptions for domestic teams despite the relatively recent nature of their publication (e.g., Duarte & Synder, 1999; Sundstrom & Associates, 1999; Thompson, 2000). It is only through a rethinking of the concept of teams that we may understand the unique forces operating in a global business environment.

# APPENDIX A

1.] Could you tell us a little about what you do and the teams you work with?

2.] Who is on the teams? How are these members selected? How are responsibilities divided?

3.] What is the function of the teams [what outputs do they provide]?

4.] Who is the team's "customer" [internal or external]?

5.] Who receives the teams' work [who is directly downstream in the process]?

6.] How is performance monitored and rewarded?

7.] What kind of feedback do teams receive about performance?

8.] How do you know when you have done a good job?

9.] Do you believe the teams are effective? Why or why not?

10.] Do the teams have leaders? What are the responsibilities of the leader?

11.] Who does the team report to? Does it interact with other teams?

12.] Would the teams benefit from more direction? Who should provide it? In what format?

13.] What are the key factors that contribute to and/or inhibit the success of the teams?

14.] How are practices shared in this organization?

15.] To what extent does headquarters dictate practices?

16.] Is individual achievement or collective achievement more important in this organization?

17.] Is individual achievement or collective achievement more important in this country?

18.] What facets of the culture here impact teams, either positively or negatively?

19.] What metaphors [or mental images] do people use for teams in this country?

20.] Do you have anything else you would like to add?

# APPENDIX B

## TEAM EFFECTIVENESS

1 = very inaccurate; 2 = mostly inaccurate; 3 = slightly inaccurate;
4 = uncertain; 5 = slightly accurate; 6 = mostly accurate;
7 = very accurate

### GOALS

1. This team fulfills its mission.
2. This team accomplishes its objectives.
3. This team meets the requirements set for it.
4. This team achieves its goals.
5. This team serves the purpose it is intended to serve.

### CUSTOMERS

1. This team's customers are satisfied.
2. This team's customers are happy with the team's performance.
3. This team is responsive to its customers.
4. This team fulfills the needs of its customers.
5. This team responds to external demands.

### TIMELINES

1. This team meets its deadlines.
2. This team wastes time.
3. The team provides deliverables (e.g., products, or services) on time.
4. This team is slow.

5. This team adheres to its schedule.
6. This team finishes its work in a reasonable amount of time.

## QUALITY
1. This team has a low error rate.
2. This team does high-quality work.
3. This team consistently provides high-quality output.
4. This team is consistently error free.
5. This team needs to improve the quality of its work.

## PRODUCTIVITY
1. This team uses too many resources.
2. This team is productive.
3. This team is wasteful.
4. Inputs used by this team are appropriate for the outputs achieved.
5. This team is efficient.

## TEAM PROCESSES

## CONFLICT
1. There are personality problems on this team.
2. There is cooperative thinking in this team.
3. This team resolves conflict well.
4. Members of this team are open to new ideas.
5. There is hostility among members.

## ATTITUDES
1. This team has fun.
2. Members of this team have a good attitude.
3. There is a high level of energy on this team.
4. Members of this team are committed to the team.
5. There is a relaxed atmosphere in this team.

## COMMUNICATION
1. There is poor information flow in this team.
2. Members of this team keep in touch effectively.
3. There is open communication in this team.
4. Everyone has a chance to express their opinion.
5. Members feel free to make negative comments.
6. We maintain a high level of idea exchange.
7. One or two members tend to dominate the discussion.

## COHESION

1. Members of this team help one another.
2. Members of this team stick together.
3. Members of this team encourage one another.
4. We show a high level of support for teamwork.
5. Individual members are highly integrated into our team.
6. We have a high level of cohesion in our team.
7. Team members share a common commitment to our team.

## SELF-MANAGEMENT

Please answer each of the following questions about the person who serves as an external leader for your team. This is the person in a leadership position who is responsible for supervising your team. It is the one person who works most closely with your team to provide direction. This person is generally not considered a member of your team. The name of this person appears on your cover letter. Note: Your responses are completely confidential. Your supervisor will not have access to individual ratings. Use the following scale:

1 = very inaccurate; 2 = mostly inaccurate; 3 = slightly inaccurate;
4 = uncertain; 5 = slightly accurate; 6 = mostly accurate;
7 = very accurate

1. Our leader encourages us to go over an activity before we attempt it.
2. Our leader encourages us to set goals for our group performance.
3. Our leader encourages us to be critical of ourselves when we do poorly.
4. Our leader encourages us to feel good about ourselves if we do a good job.
5. Our leader encourages us to expect high performance from our group.
6. Our leader encourages us to be aware of our level of performance.

## DECISION MAKING

How much input does your team have in the following decisions?
    1 = no input; 2 = very little input; 3 = a little input; 4 = uncertain;
    5 = some input; 6 = a lot of input; 7 = complete input
(you make the decision)

1. How you develop your skills and abilities.
2. Planning and scheduling of your work.
3. Planning and determining goals.
4. Who will be on the team.
5. Decisions concerning leadership inside the team.
6. Performance evaluation for the team.
7. Task assignments within the team.
8. Performance evaluations for team members (peer reviews).

## KNOWLEDGE MANAGEMENT

Please answer the following questions about your team. Use the following scale.
    1 = very inaccurate; 2 = mostly inaccurate; 3 = slightly inaccurate;
    4 = uncertain; 5 = slightly accurate; 6 = mostly accurate;
    7 = very accurate

1. This organization has a formal system to capture good ideas made by teams.
2. This organization attempts to centrally collect best practices.
3. This organization has a formal system to share good ideas with other teams.
4. This organization emphasizes that teams should record know-how and information.
5. If a new way of doing work is introduced, it often comes from within the team.
6. This team comes up with many new ideas about how work should be done.
7. This team avoids changing our methods of work.
8. This team is frequently the source of ideas that are copied by other teams.
9. This team carefully documents how we do our work.
10. This team has a formal system to capture our good ideas.
11. This team attempts to record our best practices.

12. Our processes are well-documented.
13. This team faces unique challenges that other teams of the same type do not.
14. Our customers' needs vary widely.
15. Most teams like this one face similar demands.
16. New processes typically need modification before they will work for this team.
17. This organization pressures our team to use standard procedures.
18. This team often must follow work practices developed outside the team.
19. This team feels strongly connected to the larger organization.
20. There are other teams in this organization serving the same function as this team.
21. This team depends on other teams to get our work done.
22. Members of this team have frequent contact with members of other similar teams.
23. This team often must interact with other teams to complete our tasks.
24. Members of this team regularly attend technical meetings, training courses, and other events with members of other similar teams.

## TEAM NORMS

Do the following statements describe your team? Circle the number that indicates how accurate the statement is with regard to your team. Use the following scale:

1 = very inaccurate; 2 = mostly inaccurate; 3 = slightly inaccurate;
4 = uncertain; 5 = slightly accurate; 6 = mostly accurate;
7 = very accurate

1. It is clear in our team what is acceptable behavior and what is not acceptable.
2. Our team has clear standards for the behavior of team members.
3. This team has a high level of activity.
4. This team meets frequently enough to be effective.
5. This team has clear priorities.
6. We fail to organize our time well.
7. We are comfortable with the roles we play in the team.
8. The workload is distributed unfairly in this team.
9. In this team, we plan our work effectively.

## ORGANIZATIONAL CONTEXT

Please use the scale below to answer questions about the organization in which your team works.

1 = very inaccurate; 2 = mostly inaccurate; 3 = slightly inaccurate;
4 = uncertain; 5 = slightly accurate; 6 = mostly accurate;
7 = very accurate

1. My team is recognized by management when we perform well.
2. The physical place where we do our work is adequate for what we have to do.
3. Our team has all the materials, supplies, or equipment needed to perform our task.
4. The training I have received is adequate for me to perform my job very well.
5. I am recognized by management when I perform well on my team.
6. This team receives feedback about our team-level performance.
7. I receive feedback about my personal performances on the team.
8. The training I have received is adequate for me to be an effective member of my team.

## DEMOGRAPHICS

AGE _____ SEX: M  or  F [circle one]
In what country were you born? COUNTRY _____
In which country have you lived the longest?
COUNTRY _____ YEARS LIVED THERE _____
Of all the countries you have lived in, which country do you identify with the most? COUNTRY _____

ETHNICITY:
[circle one}

1 = African American/Black
2 = American Indian/Alaskan
3 = Asian
4 = Pacific Islander
5 = Hispanic/Latino
6 = White/Non-Hispanic

Highest educational level achieved:
[circle one]

1 = High school
2 = Associate's degree
3 = Technical degree/certificate
4 = Bachelor's degree
5 = Master's degree
6 = Doctorate

| Highest degree received from: | Functional area: [circle one] |
|---|---|
| 1 = Small private<br>   (note: small = less than<br>   1000 students)<br>2 = Large private<br>3 = small public<br>   (note: small = less than<br>   1000 students)<br>4 = large public | 1 = Accounting<br>2 = Information Systems<br>5 = Sales<br>4 = Production/operations<br>5 = Sales<br>6 = Marketing<br>7 = Service<br>8 = Human resources |

Number of years employed in organization: _____
Number of years in management _____
How long has this team been in existence?
_____ years/months/weeks [circle one]
How long have you been on this team?
_____ years/months/weeks [circle one]
How many people are on your team? _____

# References

Abelson, R. P. (1976). Script processing, attitude formation and decision making. In J. S. Carroll & J. W. Payne (Eds.), *Cognition and social behavior* (pp. 33–46). Hillsdale, NJ: Lawrence Erlbaum Associates.

Abrams, D., Wetherell, M., Cochrance, S., Hogg, M. A., & Turner, J. C. (1990). Knowing what to think by knowing who you are: Self-categorization and the nature of norm formation, conformity, and global polarization. *British Journal of Social Psychology, 29*, 97–119.

Adler, N. J., & Ghadar, F. (1990). International strategy from the perspective of people and culture: The North American context. In A. M. Rugman (Ed.), *Research in global strategic management: International Business Research for the Twenty-First Century; Canada's new research agenda* (Vol. 1, pp. 179–205).

Adler, N. J. (1991). *International dimensions of organizational behavior* (2nd ed.). Boston, MA: PWS-Kent.

Adler, N. J., Brahm, R., & Graham, J. L. (1992). Strategy implementation: A comparison of face-to-face negotiations in the People's Republic of China and the United States. *Strategic Management Journal, 13*, 449–466.

Alvesson, M. (1993). *Cultural perspectives on organizations*. Cambridge: Cambridge University Press.

Amason, A. (1996). Distinguishing the effects of functional and dysfunctional conflict on strategic decision making: Resolving a paradox for top management teams. *Academy of Management Journal, 39*, 123–148.

Amburgey, T. L., Kelly, D., & Barnett, W. P. (1993). Resetting the clock: The dynamics of organizational-change and failure. *Administrative Science Quarterly, 38*(1), 51–73.

Ancona, D., & Chong, C. (1996). Entrainment: Pace, cycle, and rhythm in organizational behavior. In B. M. Staw & L. L. Cummings (Eds.), *Research in organizational behavior* (Vol. 18, pp. 251–284). Greenwich, CT: JAI Press.

Ancona, D. G., & Caldwell, D. F. (1992). Demography and design: Predictors of new product team performance. *Organization Science, 3*(3), 321–341.

Anderson, P., & Tushman, M. L. (1990). Technological discontinuities and dominant designs: A cyclical model of technological change. *Administrative Science Quarterly, 35*(4), 604–633.

Apgar, M. (1998). The alternative workplace: Changing where and how people work. *Harvard Business Review,* May–June: 121–139.

Argote, L., & McGrath, J. E. (1993). Group processes in organizations: Continuity and change. In C. L. Cooper & I. T. Robertson (Eds.), *International review of industrial and organizational psychology* (pp. 333–389). Chichester, England: John Wiley.

Argyle, M., Henderson, M., Bond, M. H., Iizuka, Y., & Contarello, A. (1996). Cross-cultural variations in relationship rules. *International Journal of Psychology, 21,* 287–315.

Argyris, C., & Schon, D. (1978). *Organizational learning: A theory of action perspective.* Reading, MA: Addison-Wesley.

Armstrong, D. J., & Cole, P. (1995). Managing distance and differences in geographically distributed work groups. In S. E. Jackson & M. N. Ruderman (Eds.), *Diversity in work teams: research paradigms for a changing workplace* (pp. 187–215). Washington, DC: American Psychological Association.

Arthur, W. B. (1988). Self-reinforcing mechanisms in economics. In P. W. Anderson, K. J. Arrow, & D. Pines (Eds.), *The economy as an evolving complex system* (pp. 9–31). Redwood City, CA: Addison-Wesley.

Arthur, W. B. (1989). Competing technologies, increasing returns, and lock-in by historical events. *Economic Journal, 99,* 116–131.

Asch, S. (1956). Studies of independence and conformity: A minority of one against a unanimous majority. *Psychological Monographs, 70,* (9) (Whole No. 416).

Ashton, T. (1991). George T. Shaheen. *Chief Executive, 66,* 16.

Axel, H. (1996). Company experiences with global teams. *HR Executive Review, 4*(2), 3–18.

Axelrod, R. (1976). *Structure of decisions.* Princeton: Princeton University Press.

Bales, R. F. (1953). The equilibrium problem in small groups. In T. Parsons, R. F. Bales, & E. A. Shils (Eds.), *Working papers in the theory of action.* Glencoe, IL: Free Press.

Bandura, A. (1986). *Social foundations of thoughts and action: A social cognitive theory.* Englewood Cliffs, NJ: Prentice-Hall.

Bandura, A. (1997). *Self efficacy.* Englewood Cliffs, NJ: Prentice-Hall.

Bantel, K. A., & Jackson, S. E. (1989). Top management and innovations in banking: Does the composition of the top team make a difference? *Strategic Management Journal, 10,* 107–124.

Bar-Tal, D. (1990). *Group beliefs.* New York: Springer-Verlag.

Barley, S. R. (1986). Technology as an occasion for structuring: Evidence from observations of CT scanners and the social order of radiology departments. *Administrative Science Quarterly, 31,* 78–108.

Barley, S. R. (1990). The alignment of technology and structure through roles and networks. *Administrative Science Quarterly, 33,* 24–60.

Barley, S. R,. & Tolbert, P. S. (1997). Institutionalization and structuration: Studying the links between action and institution. *Organization Studies, 18*(1), 93–117.

Barnett, W. P. (1997). The dynamics of competitive intensity. *Administrative Science Quarterly, 42*(1), 128–160.

Baron, J. N., & Cook, K. S. (1992). Process and outcome: Perspectives on the distribution of rewards in organizations. *Administrative Science Quarterly, 37,* 191–197.

Bartlett, C. A., & Ghoshal, S. (1987). Managing Across Borders: New Strategic Requirements. *Sloan Management Review,* 7–17.

Bartlett, C. A., & Ghoshal, S. (1990). Matrix management: Not a structure, a frame of mind. *Harvard Business Review,* July/August, 138–145.

Bartlett, C. A., & Ghoshal, S. (1991). Global strategic management: Impact on the new frontiers of strategy research. *Strategic Management Journal, 12,* 5–16.

Bazerman, M. H., Loewenstein, G. F., & White, S. B. (1992). Reversals of preference in allocation decisions: Judging an alternative versus choosing among alternatives. *Administrative Science Quarterly, 37,* 220–240.

Beaumont, P. B. (1992). The U.S. human resource literature: A review. In G. Salaman et al. (Eds.), *Human resource strategies.* London: Sage.

Beck, B. E. F., & Moore, L. F. (1985). Linking the host culture to organizational variables. In P. J. Frost, et al. (Eds.), *Organizational culture* (pp. 335–354). Beverly Hills, CA: Sage.

Beer, M., & Walton, E. (1990). Developing the competitive organization: Interventions and strategies. *American Psychologist, 5,* 154–161.

Beinhocker, E. D. (1999). Robust adaptive strategies. *Sloan Management Review, 40*(3), 95.

Benedict, R. (1946). *The chrysanthemum and the sword.* Boston: Houghton Mifflin.

Bennett, M. J. (1986). A developmental approach to training for intercultural sensitivity. *International Journal of Intercultural Relations, 10,* 179–196.

Berger, J., Conner, T. L., & Fisek, M. H. (1974). *Expectation states theory: A theoretical research program.* Cambridge, MA: Winthrop Publishers, Inc.

Berger, J., Fisek, M. H., Norma, R. Z., &. Zelditch, M. Jr. (1977). *Status characteristics and social interaction.* New York: Elsevier.

Berger, J., &. Zelditch, M. (Eds.). (1985). *Status, rewards, and influence.* San Francisco: Jossey-Bass.

Berlyne, D. E. (1967). Arousal and reinforcement. In D. Levine (Ed.), *Nebraska symposium on motivation* (pp. 1–110). Lincoln, NE: University of Nebraska Press.

Berman, J. J., Murphy-Berman, V., Singh, P., & Kumar, P. 1984, September. *Cross-cultural similarities and differences in perceptions of fairness.* Paper presented at the International Congress of Psychology, Acapulco, Mexico.

Berry, J. W. (1971). Ecological and cultural factors in spatial perceptual development. *Canadian Journal of Behavioral Science, 3,* 324–336.

Berry, J. W. (1980). Social and cultural change. In H. C. Triandis & R.W. Brislin (Eds.), *Handbook of cross-cultural psychology* (pp. 211–280). Boston: Allyn & Bacon.

Berry, J. W. (1997). Individual and group relations in plural societies. In C. S. Granrose & K. Oskamp (Eds.), *Cross-cultural workgroups* (pp. 17–35). Thousand Oaks, CA: Sage Publications.

Bettenhausen, K. L. (1991). Five years of groups research: What we have learned and what needs to be addressed. *Journal of Management, 17*(2), 345–381.

Bettenhausen, K. L., & Murnighan, J. K. (1985). The emergence of norms in competitive decision-making groups. *Administrative Science Quarterly, 30,* 350–372.

Bies, R. J. (1987). The predicament of injustice: The management of moral outrage. In L. L. Cummings & B. M. Staw (Eds.), *Research in organizational behavior* (vol. 9, pp. 289–319). Greenwich, CT: JAI Press.

Blau, P. M. (1977). *Inequality and heterogeneity.* New York: Free Press.

Blau, P. M. (1989). *Exchange and power in social life.* Newark, NJ: Transaction Publishers.

Bluedorn, A. C., & Denhardt, R. B. (1988). Time and organizations. *Journal of Management, 14,* 299–320.

Blumer, H. (1969). *Symbolic interactionism; Perspective and method.* Englewood Cliffs, NJ: Prentice-Hall.

Bochner, S., & Ohsako, T. (1977). Ethnic role salience in racially homogeneous and heterogeneous societies. *Journal of Cross-Cultural Psychology, 8,* 477–492.

Bochner, S., & Perks, R. W. (1971). National role evocation as a function of cross-national interaction. *Journal of Cross-Cultural Psychology, 2,* 157–164.

Boland, R. J., & Tenkasi, R. V. (1995). Perspective taking and perspective making in communities of knowing. *Organization Science, 6*(4), 350–372.

Bond, M. H., Leung, K. L., & Wan, C. K. (1982). How does cultural collectivism operate? The impact of task and maintenance contributions on reward distributions. *Journal of Cross-Cultural Psychology, 13*(2), 186–200.

Bond, M. H., & Lee, P. W. H. (1981). Face-saving in Chinese culture: A discussion and experimental study of Hong Kong students. In A. Y. C. King & R. P. L. Lee (Eds.), *Social life and development in Hong Kong* (pp. 288–305). Hong Kong: Chinese University Press.

Bond, M. H., Wan, K., Leung, K., & Giacalone, R. A. (1985). How are responses to verbal insult related to cultural collectivism and power distance? *Journal of Cross-Cultural Psychology, 16,* 111–127.

Bontempo, R., Lobel, S. A., & Triandis, H. C. (1989). *Compliance and value internalization among Brazilian and U.S. students.* Manuscript submitted for publication.

Borgatta, E. F., & Stimson, J. (1963). Sex differences in interaction characteristics. *Journal of Social Psychology, 60,* 89–100.

Boudreau, M., Loch, K. D., Robey, D., & Straud, D. (1998). Going global: Using information technology to advance the competitiveness of the virtual transnational organization. *The Academy of Management Executive, 12*(4), 120–130.

Boyacigiller, N., & Adler, N. J. (1991). The parochial dinosaur: Organizational science in a global context. *Academy of Management Review, 16,* 262–290.

Bradley, J. (1989). *TACT, Version 1, User's Guide.* Toronto, Canada: University of Toronto Computing Services.

Brett, J. M., Tinsley, C. H., Janssens, M., Barsness, Z. I., & Lytle, A. L. (1997). New approaches to the study of culture I/O psychology. In P. C. Earley & M. Erez (Eds.), *New perspectives on international industrial and organizational psychology* (pp. 75–129). San Francisco: Jossey-Bass.

Brewer, M. B. (1993). Social identity, distinctiveness, and in-group homogeneity. *Social Cognition, 11*(1), 150–164.

Brewer, M. B., & Kramer, R. M. (1985). The psychology of intergroup attitudes and behavior. *Annual Review of Psychology, 36,* 219–243.

Brewster, C. (1995). Towards a "European" model of human resource management. *Journal of International Business Studies,* First Quarter.

Brockner, J., Grover, S., O'Malley, M., & Reed, T. (1993). Threat of future layoffs, self-esteem, and survivors' reactions: Evidence from the laboratory and the field. *Strategic Management Journal, 14,* 153–166.

Brown, J. S., & Duguid, P. (1991). Organizational learning and communities of practice: Toward a unified view of working, learning, and innovation. *Organization Science, 2,* 40–57.

Brown, S. L., & Eisenhardt, K. M. (1998). *Competing on the edge: Strategy as structured chaos.* Boston, MA: Harvard Business School Press.

Burke, P. J., & Reitzes, D. C. (1991). An identity theory approach to commitment. *Social Psychology Quarterly, 54*(3), 239–251.

Butler, C. (2000). Unpublished doctoral dissertation, London Business School.

Butler, C., & Earley, P. C. (2001). National diversity and social structural concerns of work groups. In C. Cooper, S. Cartwright, & P. C. Earley (Eds.), *Handbook of organization culture* (pp. 53–84). London: Blackwell Publishers.

Byrne, D. (1971). *The attraction paradigm.* New York: Academic Press.

Campbell, D. T. (1958). Common fate, similarity, and other indices of the status of aggregates of persons as social entities. *Behavioral Science, 3,* 14–25.

Campbell, J. P. (1990). Modeling the performance prediction problem in industrial and organizational psychology. *Handbook of Industrial & Organizational Psychology* (2nd ed.) (pp. 687–732). Palo Alto: Consulting Psychologists Press.

Campion, M. A., & Lord, R. G. (1982). A control systems conceptualization of the goal-setting and changing process. *Organizational Behavior and Human Decision Processes, 30*(2): 265–287.

Campion, M. A., Medsker, G. J., & Higgs, A. C. (1993). Relations between work group characteristics and effectiveness: Implications for designing effective work groups. *Personnel Psychology, 46,* 823–850.

Canney-Davison, S., & Ward, K. (1999). *Leading international teams.* London: McGraw-Hill.

Cannon-Bowers, J. A., & Salas, E. (1990). Cognitive psychology and team training: Shared mental models in complex systems. Paper presented at the annual meeting of the Society for Industrial and Organizational Psychology, Miami, Florida.

Cannon-Bowers, J. A., Salas, E., & Converse, S. A. (1993). Shared mental models in expert team decision-making. In N. J. Castellan (Ed.), *Individual and group decision making* (pp. 221–246). Hillsdale, NJ: Lawrence Erlbaum Associates.

Carroll, G. R. (1984). Dynamics of publisher succession in newspaper organizations. *Administrative Science Quarterly, 29,* 303–329.

Carroll, G. R., & Swaminathan, A. (1991). Density dependent organizational evolution in the American brewing industry from 1633 to 1988. *Acta Sociologica, 34,* 155–175.

Carroll, G. R., & Harrison, J. R. (1998). Organizational demography and culture: Insights from a formal model and simulation. *Administrative Science Quarterly, 43,* 637–667.

Cascio, W. F. (1989). *Managing human resources: Productivity, quality of work life, profits.* New York: McGraw Hill.

Casmir, R. (1992). Third-culture building: A paradigm shift for international and intercultural communication. *Communication Yearbook, 16,* 407–428.

Chen, C. (1995). New trends in reward allocation preferences: A Sino–U.S. comparison. *Academy of Management Journal 38,* 408–428.

Chen, P. Y., & Spector, P. E. (1992). Relationships of work stressors with aggression, withdrawal, theft, and substance abuse: An exploratory study. *Journal of Occupational and Organizational Psychology, 65,* 177–184.

Cherns, A. B. (1976). Behavioral science engagements-taxonomy and dynamics. *Human Relations, 29*(10), 905–950.

Choi, I., & Nisbett, R. E. (1998). Situational salience and cultural differences in the correspondence bias and actor–observer bias. *Personality and Social Psychology Bulletin, 24,* 949–960.

Choi, I., Nisbett, R. E., & Norenzayan, A. (1999). Causal attribution across cultures: Variation and universality. *Psychological Bulletin, 125,* 47–63.

Choi, I., Nisbett, R. E., & Smith, E. E. (1997). Culture, categorization, and inductive reasoning. *Cognition, 65,* 15–32.

Chuang, Y. C. (1998). The cognitive structures of role norms in Taiwan. *Asian Journal of Social Psychology, 1,* 239–251.

Clark, T. A. R., & Mallory, G. R. (1996). The cultural relativity of human resource management: Is there a universal model? In T. A. R. Clark (Ed.), *European human resource management*. Oxford: Blackwell.

Clark, T. A. R., & Pugh, D. (1997). *Convergence and divergence in European HRM: An exploratory polycentric study*. Paper presented at the European Academy of Management Conference, Dublin, June, 1997.

Clarke, P. (1971). *Lancashire and the new liberalism*. Cambridge: Cambridge University Press.

Coch, L., & French, J. R. P. (1948). Overcoming resistance to change. *Human Relations, 1*, 512–532.

Cohen, S., & Gibson, C. B. (2001). *Creating Conditions for Virtual Team Effectiveness*. Working paper, University of Southern California.

Cohen, B. P., &. Zhou, X. (1991). Status processes in enduring work groups. *American Sociological Review, 56*, 179–188.

Cohen, S. G., & Ledford, G. E., Jr. (1994). The effectiveness of self-managing work teams: A quasi-experiment. *Human Relations, 47*, 643–676.

Cohen, S. G., & Bailey, D. E. (1997). Trends in team effectiveness research: From the shop floor to the executive suite. *Journal of Management, 23*, 239–290.

Collins, R. (1988). Theoretical continuities in Goffman's work. In P. Drew & A. Wootton (Eds.), *Erving Goffman: Exploring the interaction order* (pp. 41–63). Boston: Northeastern Press.

Compton, J. L. (1980). Indigenous folk media in rural development in South and Southeast Asia. In D. W. Brokensha, D. M. Warren, & O. Werner (Eds.), *Indigenous knowledge systems and development* (pp. 307–320). Lanham, MD: University Press of America.

Comstock, D. E., & Scott, W. R. (1977). Technology and the structure of subunits: Distinguishing individual and workgroup effects. *Administrative Science Quarterly, 22*, 177–202.

Coombs, R., & Hull, R. (1998). 'Knowledge management practices' and path-dependency in innovation. *Research Policy, 27*(3), 237–253.

Corner, P. D., & Kinicki, A. (1997). *Team process as a mediator between top management team demography and financial performance: An initial empirical investigation*. Working paper, University of Waikato, New Zealand.

Corner, P. D., Kinicki, A. J., & Keats, B. W. (1994). Integrating organizational and individual information processing perspectives on choice. *Organization Science, 5*(3), 294–308.

Cox, T. H. (1993). *Cultural diversity in organizations*. San Francisco, CA: Berett-Koehler.

Cox, T. H., Lobel, S. A., & McLeod, P. L. (1991.) Effects of ethnic group cultural differences on cooperative and competitive behavior on a group task. *Academy of Management Journal, 34*(4), 827–847.

Crandall, N. F., & Wallace, M. J. (1998). *Work and rewards in the virtual workplace*. New York: AMACOM.

Cray, D., & Mallory, G. R. (1998). *Making sense of managing culture.* London: Thomson Business Press.

Cummings, L. L. (1984). Compensation, culture, and motivation: A systems perspective. *Organizational Dynamics, 12*(3), 33–44.

Curall, S. C., & Judge, T. A. (1995). Measuring trust between organizational boundary role persons. *Organizational Behavior and Human Decision Processes, 64*(2), 151–170.

Cushman, P. (1990). Why the self is empty: Toward a historically situated psychology. *American Psychologist, 45,* 599–611.

Daft, R. L., Lengel, R. H., & Trevino, L. K. (1987). Message equivocality, media selection and manager performance: Implications for information systems. *MIS Quarterly, 11*(3), 355–368.

Davis, J. H., Schoorman, F. D., Mayer, R. C., & Tan, H. H. (2000). The trusted general manager and business unit performance: Empirical evidence of a competitive advantage. *Strategic Management Journal, 21,* 563–576.

Davison, S. C. (1994). Creating a high performance international team. *Journal of Management Development, 13,* 81–90.

Dawe, A. (1978). Theories of social action. In T. Bottomore & R. Nisbet (Eds.). *A History of Sociological Analysis* (pp. 418–456). London: Heinemann.

Deaux, K. (1996). Social identification. In E. T. Higgins & A. W. Kruglanski (Eds.), *Social Psychology.*

DeMatteo, J. D. (1997). *Rewarding the team: An investigation of the direct and indirect effects of team-based reward practices on team cooperation and performance.* Unpublished doctoral dissertation. University of Tennessee, Knoxville.

DeSanctis, G., & Jackson, B. M. (1994). Coordination of information technology: Team-based structures and computer-based communication systems. *Journal of Management Information Systems, 10,* 85–110.

DeSanctis, G., & Poole, M. S. (1994). Capturing the complexity in advanced technology use: Adaptive structuration theory. *Organization Science, 5*(2), 121–147.

Deutsch, M. (1961). The face of bargaining. *Operations Research, 9,* 886–897.

Deutsch, M. (1973). *The resolution of conflict.* New Haven, CT: Yale University Press.

Deutsch, M. (1980). Fifty years of conflict. In L. Festinger (Ed.), *Four decades of social psychology* (pp. 46–77). New York: Oxford University Press.

Devanna, M. A., Fombrun, C. J., & Tichy, N. N. (1984). A framework for strategic human resource management. In C. J. Fombrun, N. N. Tichy, & M. A. Devanna (Eds.), *Strategic human resource management.* New York: Wiley.

Dierickx, I., & Cool, K. (1989). Asset stock accumulation and sustainability of competitive advantage. *Management Science, 35,* 1504–1511.

DiMaggio, D. J., & Powell, W. W. (1983). The iron cage revisited: Institutional isomorphism and collective rationality in organizational fields. *American Sociological Review, 48,* 147–160.

Donnenwerth, G. V., & Foa, U. G. (1974). Effects of resource class on retaliation to injustice in interpersonal exchange. *Journal of Personality and Social Psychology, 29,* 785–793.

Dorfman, P. W., & Howell, J. P. (1997). Managerial leadership in the U.S. and Mexico: Distant neighbors or close cousins? In C. S. Granrose & K. Oskamp (Eds.), *Cross-cultural workgroups* (pp. 234–264). Thousand Oaks, CA: Sage Publications.

Doucet, J., & Jehn, K. (1997). Analyzing hard words in a sensitive setting: American expatriates in communist China. *Journal of Organizational Behavior, 18,* 559–582.

Dougherty, D. (1992). Interpretive barriers to successful product innovation in large firms. *Organization Science, 3,* 179–202.

Dowe, T. (1997). The netizen. *Wired, 5,* 53–56, 184–185.

Duarte, D. L., & Synder, N. T. (1999). *Mastering virtual teams: Strategies, tools and techniques that succeed.* San Francisco, CA: Jossey-Bass Publishers.

Duhaime, I. M., & Schwenk, C. R. (1985). Conjectures on cognitive simplification in acquisition and divestment decision making. *Academy of Management Review, 10,* 287–295.

Dulebohn, J. H., & Martocchio, J. J. (1998). Employee perceptions of the fairness of work group incentive pay plans. *Journal of Management, 24,* 469–488.

Duncan, R., & Weiss, A. (1979). Organizational learning: Implications for organization design. In L. L. Cummings & B. M. Staw (Eds.), *Research in organizational behavior* (vol. 1, pp. 75–124). Greenwich, CT: JAI.

Earley, P. C. (1985). The influence of information, choice and task complexity upon goal acceptance, performance and personal goals. *Journal of Applied Psychology, 70,* 481–491.

Earley, P. C. (1987). Intercultural training for managers: A comparison of documentary and interpersonal methods. *Academy of Management Journal, 30,* 685–698.

Earley, P. C. (1989). Social loafing and collectivism: A comparison of the United States with the People's Republic of China. *Administrative Science Quarterly, 34,* 565–581.

Earley, P. C. (1991). East meets West meets Mideast: Further explorations of collectivistic and individualistic work groups. *Academy of Management Proceedings,* (vol. 1, pp. 205–209).

Earley, P. C. (1993). East meets West meets Mideast: Further explorations of collectivistic and individualistic work groups. *Academy of Management Journal, 36,* 319–348.

Earley, P. C. (1994). The individual and collective self: An assessment of self-efficacy and training across cultures. *Administrative Science Quarterly, 39,* 89–117.

Earley, P. C. (1997). *Face, harmony, and social structure: An analysis of organizational behavior across cultures.* New York: Oxford University Press.

Earley, P. C. (1999). Playing follow the leader: Status-determining traits in relation to collective efficacy across cultures. *Organizational Behavior and Human Decision Processes, 80,* 1–21.

Earley, P. C., & Erez, M. (1991). Time dependency effects of goals and norms: An examination of alternative methods to influence performance. *Journal of Applied Psychology, 76,* 717–724.

Earley, P. C., & Erez, M. (1997). *The Transplanted Executive*. N.Y.: Oxford University Press.

Earley, P. C., & Gibson, C. B. (1998). Taking stock in our progress: 100 years of solidarity and community. *Journal of Management, 24,* 265–304.

Earley, P. C., Gibson, C. B., & Chen, C. (1999). How did I do versus how did we do? Intercultural contrasts of performance feedback search and self-efficacy in China, Czechoslovakia, and the United States. *Journal of Cross-Cultural Psychology, 30,* 596–621.

Earley, P. C., & Kanfer, R. (1985). The influence of component participation and role models on goal acceptance, goal satisfaction and performance. *Organizational Behavior and Human Decision Processes, 36,* 378–390.

Earley, P. C., & Laubach, M. (in press). Cross-cultural perspectives on work groups: Linking culture with context. In M. Gannon & K. Newman (Eds.), *Handbook of culture*. London: Blackwell Publishers.

Earley, P. C., & Lind, E. A. (1987). Procedural justice and participation in task selection: Control-mediated effects of voice in procedural and task decisions. *Journal of Personality and Social Psychology, 52,* 1148–1160.

Earley, P. C., & Mosakowski, E. M. (2000). Creating hybrid team cultures: An empirical test of transnational team functioning. *Academy of Management Journal, 43,* 26–49.

Earley, P. C., & Mosakowski, E. (1995). A framework for understanding experimental research in an international and intercultural context. In B. J. Punnett & O. Shenkar (Eds.), *Handbook of International Management Research* (pp. 83–114). London: Blackwell Publishers.

Earley, P. C., & Randel, A. E. (1997). Self and other: Face and sork group dynamics. In C. S. Granrose & S. Oskamp (Eds.), *Cross-cultural work groups* (pp. 113–134). Claremont, CA: The Claremont Symposium on Applied Social Psychology.

Earley, P. C., & Singh, H. (1995). International and intercultural research: What's next? *Academy of Management Journal, 38,* 1–14.

Eberhard, W. (1967). *Guilt and sin in traditional China*. Berkeley: University of California Press.

Eby, L., & Dobbins, G. H. (1997). Collectivistic orientation in teams: An individual and group level analysis. *Journal of Organizational Behavior, 18*(3), 275–295.

Ekman, R., & Davidson, J. (1994). *The nature of emotion*. New York: Oxford University Press.

Elron, E. (1997). Top management teams within multinational corporations: Effects of cultural heterogeneity. *Leadership Quarterly, 8,* 393–412.

Elron, E., Shamir, B., & Ben-Ari, E. (1998). *Why don't they fight each other? Cultural diversity and operational unity in multinational forces*. Working paper, Hebrew University, Jerusalem.

Elsass, P. M., & Graves, L. M. (1997). Demographic Diversity in Decision-Making Groups: The Experiences of Women and People of Color. *Academy of Management Review, 22*(4), 946–973.

Ely, R. J. (1995). The power in demography: Women's social constructions of gender identity at work. *Academy of Management Journal, 38,* 589–634.

Emerson, R. M. (1962). Power-dependence relations. *American Sociological Review, 27,* 31–41.

England, G. W. (1983). Japanese and American management: Theory Z and beyond. *Journal of International Business Studies, 14,* 131–141.

Ensher, E. A., & Murphy, S. E. (1997). Effects of race, gender, perceived similarity, and contact on mentor relationships. *Journal of Vocational Behavior, 50*(3), 460–481.

Epstein, J. (1977). *Along the gringo trail*. Berkeley, CA: And/Or Press.

Erez, M. (1986). The congruence of goal-setting strategies with socio-cultural values and its effects on performance. *Journal of Management, 12,* 83–90.

Erez, M. (1994). Interpersonal communication systems in organizations, and their relationships to cultural values, productivity and innovation: The case of Japanese corporations. *Applied Psychology: An International Review.*

Erez, M., & Arad, R. (1986). Participative goal-setting: Social, motivational and cognitive factors. *Journal of Applied Psychology, 71,* 591–597.

Erez, M., & Earley, P. C. (1987). Comparative analysis of goal-setting strategies across cultures. *Journal of Applied Psychology, 72,* 658–665.

Erez, M., & Earley, P. C. (1993). *Culture, self-identity, and work*. New York: Oxford Press.

Erez, M., Earley, P. C., & Hulin, C. (1985). The impact of participation upon goal acceptance and performance: A two-step model. *Academy of Management Journal, 28,* 50–66.

Erez, M., & Kanfer, F. H. (1983). The role of goal acceptance in goal-setting and task performance. *Academy of Management Review, 8,* 454–463.

Farh, J. L., Earley, P. C., & Lin, S. C. (1997). Impetus for action: A cultural analysis of justice and extra-role behavior in Chinese society. *Administrative Science Quarterly, 42,* 421–444.

Feldman, D. C. (1984). The development and enforcement of group norms. *Academy of Management Review, 9,* 47–53.

Ferris, G. R., & Wagner, J. A. (1985). Quality circles in the United States: A conceptual reevaluation. *Journal of Applied Behavior Science, 21,* 155–167.

Fiedler, F. E. (1966). The effect of leadership and cultural heterogeneity on group performance: A test of the contingency model. *Journal of Experimental Social Psychology, 2,* 237–264.

Fischhoff, B., & Goitein, B. (1984). The informal use of formal models. *Academy of Management Review, 9*(3), 505–512.

Fiske, A. P. (1991). *Structures of social life: The four elementary forms of human relations: communal sharing, authority ranking, equality matching, market pricing*. New York: The Free Press

Fiske, D. W., & Maddi, S. R. (1961). *Functions of varied experience*. Homewood, IL: Dorsey.

Fiske, S. T., & Neuberg, S. L. (1990). A continuum of impression formation, from category-based to individuating process: Influence of information and motivation of attention and interpretation. *Advances in Experimental Social Psychology, 23*, 1–74.

Fiske, S. T., & Taylor, S. E. (1984). *Social cognition*. Reading, MA: Addison-Wesley.

Fleck, L. (1979). *Genesis and development of a scientific fact*. Chicago: University of Chicago.

Foa, E. B., & Foa, U. G. (1976). Resource theory of social exchange. In J. W. Thibaut, T. T. Spence, & R. C. Carson (Eds.), *Contemporary topics in social psychology*. Morristown: General Learning.

Foa, U. G., & Foa, E. B. (1974). *Societal structures of the mind*. Springfield, IL: Charles C. Thomas.

Foa, U. G., Glaubman, H., Garner, M., Tornblom, K. Y., & Salcedo, L. N. (1987). Interrelation of social resources: Evidence of pancultural invariance. *Journal of Cross-Cultural Psychology, 18*, 221–233.

Foa, U. G., Converse, J. Jr., Tornblom, K. Y., & Foa, E. B. (1993). *Resource theory: Explorations and applications*. San Diego: Academic Press

Forgas, J. P., & Bond, M. H. (1985). Cultural influences on the perception of interaction episodes. *Personality and Social Psychology Bulletin, 11*, 75–88.

Foschi, M. (1996). Double standards in the evaluation of men and women. *Social Psychology Quarterly, 59*(3), 237–254.

French, J. R. P., & Raven, B. (1959). The bases of social power. In D. Cartwright (Ed.), *Studies in social power* (pp. 150–167). Ann Arbor: Institute for Social Research, University of Michigan.

Galbraith, J. (1973). *Designing complex organizations*. Menlo Park, CA: Addison-Wesley.

Galbraith, J. (1974). Organization design: An information processing view. *Interfaces, 4*, 28–36.

Gallagher, D., Diener, E., & Larsen, R. J. (1989). *Individual differences in affect intensity: A moderator of the relation between emotion and behavior*. Unpublished manuscript, Department of Psychology, University of Illinois, Urbana-Champaign.

Gardner, H. (1993). *Multiple intelligences : The theory in practice*. New York : Basic Books.

Garfinkel, H. (1967). *Studies in ethnomethodology*. Englewood Cliffs, NJ: Prentice-Hall.

Gasser, L. (1986). The integration of computing and routine work. *ACM Transactions on Office Information Systems, 4*(3), 205–225.

Gecas, V. (1982). The self concept. *Annual Review of Psychology, 8,* 1–33.

Geertz, C. (1973). *The interpretation of cultures.* New York: Basic Books.

George, J. M. (1990). Personality, affect, and behavior in groups. *Journal of Applied Psychology, 75*(2), 107–116.

Gersick, C. J. G. (1988). Time and transition in work teams: Toward a new model of group development. *Academy of Management Journal, 31,* 9–41.

Gersick, C. J. G. (1989). Marking time: Predictable transitions in task groups. *Academy of Management Journal, 32,* 274–309.

Gersick, C. J. G., & Hackman, J. R. (1990). Habitual routines in task-performing groups. *Organizational Behavior and Human Decision Processes, 47,* 65–97.

Ghoshal, S., & Bartlett, C. B. (1990). The multinational corporation as an interorganizational network. *Academy of Management Review, 15,* 603–625.

Ghoshal, S., Korine, H., & Szulanski, G. (1994). Interunit communication in multinational corporations. *Management Science, 40,* 96–110.

Gibson, C. B. (1994). The impact of national culture on organization structure: Evidence from cross-cultural interviews. In S. B. Prasad (Ed.), *Advances in international comparative management* (vol. 9, pp. 3–37). Greenwich, CT: JAI Press.

Gibson, C. B. (1995). *The determinants and consequences of group-efficacy in work organizations in U.S., Hong Kong, and Indonesia.* Unpublished doctoral dissertation, University of California, Irvine.

Gibson, C. B. (1996). Do you hear what I hear? A framework for reconciling intercultural communication difficulties arising from cognitive styles and cultural values. In M. Erez & P. C. Earley (Eds.), *New perspectives on international industrial organizational psychology.* San Francisco, CA: Jossey-Bass.

Gibson, C. B. (1997). Do you hear what I hear? A framework for reconciling intercultural communication difficulties arising from cognitive styles and cultural values. In M. Erez & P. C. Earley (Eds.), *New perspectives on international industrial/organizational psychology* (pp. 335–362). San Francisco, CA: Jossey-Bass.

Gibson, C. B. (1999). Do they do what they believe they can? Group-efficacy beliefs and group performance across tasks and cultures. *Academy of Management Journal, 42*(2), 138–152.

Gibson, C. B. (2000a). *The efficacy advantage: Factors influencing the formation of group-efficacy across cultures.* Working paper, University of Southern California.

Gibson, C. B. (2000b). *From accumulation to transformation: Phases and cycles of collective cognition in work groups.* Working paper, University of Southern California.

Gibson, C. B. (2000c). *We think we can, we think we can: An integrative review of theory and research regarding group performance beliefs.* Working paper, University of Southern California.

Gibson, C. B., & Birkinshaw, J. (2000). *Creating the capacity for organizational renewal: Alignment and adaptability in the multinational context.* Working paper, University of Southern California.

Gibson, C. B., & Kirkman, B. L. (2000). Our Past, present, and future in teams: The role of human resource professionals in managing team performance. In A. I. Kraut & A. K. Korman (Eds.), *Changing concepts and practices for human resource management: Contributions from industrial-organizational psychology.* San Francisco: Jossey-Bass.

Gibson, C. B., Randel, A. E., & Earley, P. C. (2000). Understanding group-efficacy: An empirical test of multiple assessment methods. *Group and Organization Management, 25*(1), 67–97.

Gibson, C. B., & Saxton, T. (2001). *Consultants in the cupboard: how third-party involvement affects team strategic decision outcomes.* Working paper, University of Southern California.

Gibson, C. B., & Vermeulen, F. (2000). *Teams engaging in learning behavior: An empirical investigation of stimuli and impediments.* Working paper, University of Southern California.

Gibson, C. B., & Zellmer-Bruhn, M. (2000). *Intercultural analysis of the meaning of teamwork: Evidence from six multinational corporations.* Working paper, University of Southern California.

Gibson, C. B., Zellmer-Bruhn, M., & Schwab, D. P. (2000). *Developing a measure of team effectiveness for multinational organizations.* Working paper, University of Southern California.

Giddens, A. (1971) repr. 1972. *Capitalism and modern social theory: An analysis of the writings of Marx, Durkheim and Max Weber.* London: [s.n.].

Giddens, A. (1984). *The constitution of society.* Cambridge: Polity.

Giddens, A. (1991). *Modernity and self-identity.* Cambridge: Polity Press.

Giles, H., Coupland, N., & Coupland, J. (1991). Accommodation theory: Communication, contexts, and consequences. In H. Giles, N. Coupland, & J. Coupland (Eds.), *Contexts of accommodation: Developments in applied sociolinguistics* (pp. 1–68). Cambridge, England: Cambridge University Press.

Ginsberg, A. (1990). Connecting diversification to performance: A sociocognitive perspective. *Academy of Management Review, 15*(3), 514–535.

Ginsberg, A., & Abrahamson, E. (1991). Champions of change and strategic shifts: The role of internal and external change advocates. *Journal of Management Studies, 28*(2), 173–190.

Gioia, D. A., & Manz, C. C. (1985). Linking cognition and behavior: A script processing interpretation of vicarious learning. *Academy of Management Review, 10*(3), 527–539.

Gioia, D. A., & Poole, P. P. (1984). Scripts in organizational behavior. *Academy of Management Review, 9*(3), 449–459.

Gist, M. E., & Mitchell, T. R. (1992). Self-efficacy: A theoretical analysis of its determinants and malleability. *Academy of Management Review, 17*(2), 183–211.

Gleick, J. (1987). *Chaos: Making a new science.* New York: Viking.

Gleick, J. (1999). *Faster: The acceleration of just about everything.* New York: Pantheon Books.

Glenn, E. S., & Glenn, C. G. (1981). *Man and mankind: Conflicts and communications between cultures* . Norwood, NJ: Ablex Publishing Co.

Glenn, E., Witmeyer, D., & Stevenson, K. (1977). Cultural styles of persuasion. *International Journal of Intercultural Relations, 1,* 52–56.

Goffee, R., & Jones, G. (1996). What holds the modern company together? *Harvard Business Review,* November–December.

Goffee, R., & Jones, G. (1998). *The character of a corporation: How your company's culture can make or break your business.* New York: Harper Business.

Goffman, E. (1959). *The presentation of self in everyday life.* Garden City: Doubleday.

Goleman, D. (1995). *Emotional intelligence.* New York: Bantam Books.

Golembiewski, H., & McConkie, M. (1975). The centrality of interpersonal trust in group processes. In C. L. Cooper (Ed.), *Theories of group processes* (pp. 131–186). New York: Wiley.

Gomez-Casseres, B. (1994). Group versus group: How alliances networks compete. *Harvard Business Review, 72*(4), 62–78.

Goodman, P. S., & Associates. (1986). *Designing effective work groups.* San Francisco: Jossey-Bass.

Goodman, P. S., Ravlin, E. C., & Schminke, M. (1990). Understanding groups in organizations. In L. L. Cummings & B. M. Staw (Eds.), *Leadership, Participation, and Group Behavior* (pp. 323–385). Greenwich, CT: JAI Press.

Goto, S. G. (1997.) Majority and minority perspectives on cross-cultural interactions. In C. S. Granrose & K. Oskamp (Eds.), *Cross-cultural workgroups.* Thousand Oaks, CA: Sage Publications.

Graham, J. L. (1981). The role perception of time in consumer research. *Journal of Consumer Research, 7,* 335–342.

Graham, J. L. (1985). The influence of culture on the process of business negotiations: An exploratory study. *Journal of International Business Studies, 14,* 79–94.

Graham, J. L., & Sano, Y. (1984). *Smart bargaining: Doing business with the Japanese.* Cambridge: Ballinger Publishing Company.

Granovetter, M. (1985). Economic action and social structure: The problem of embeddedness. *American Journal of Sociology, 91,* 481–510.

Granrose, C. S., & Oskamp, K. (1997). Cross-cultural socialization of Asian employees in U.S. organizations. In C. S. Granrose, & K. Oskamp (Eds.), *Cross-cultural workgroups* (pp. 181–211). Thousand Oaks, CA: Sage Publications.

Granrose, C. S., & Oskamp, K. (1997). *Cross-cultural workgroups.* Thousand Oaks, CA: Sage Publications.

Gratton, L., Hailey, V. H., Stiles, P., & Truss, C. (1999). *Strategic human resource management: Corporate rhetoric and human reality.* Oxford: Oxford University Press.

Greenberg, J., & Folger, R. (1983). Procedural justice, participation, and the fair process effect in groups and organizations. In P. Paulus (Ed.), *Basic group processes* (pp. 235–256). New York: Springer-Verlag.

Greiner, L. E., & Metzger, R. O. (1983). *Consulting to Management*. Englewood Cliffs, NJ: Prentice-Hall.

Grimshaw, D. J., & Kwok, F. T. S. (1998). The business benefits of the virtual organization. In M. Igbaria and M. Tan (Eds.), *The virtual workplace*. Hershey, PA: Idea Group Publishing.

Gruenfeld, D., Thomas-Hunt, M. C., & Kim, P. H. (1998). Cognitive flexibility, communication strategy, and integrative complexity in groups: Public versus private reactions to majority and minority status. *Journal of Experimental Social Psychology, 34*, 202–226.

Gruenfeld, L. W., & MacEachron, A. E. (1975). A cross-national study of cognitive style among managers and technicians. *International Journal of Psychology, 10*, 27–55.

Gudykunst, W. B., & Kim, Y. (1984). *Communicating with strangers*. New York: Random House.

Gudykunst, W. B., Ting-Toomey, S., & Chua, E. (1988). *Culture and interpersonal communication*. Beverly Hills, CA: Sage.

Gulati, R. (1995). Does familiarity breed trust? The implications of repeated ties for contractual choices in alliances. *Academy of Management Journal, 38*, 85–112.

Guzzo, R. A., & Shea, G. P. (1994). Group Performance and Intergroup Relations in Organizations. In M. D. Dunnette & L. M Hough (Eds.), *Handbook of industrial and organizational psychology* (2nd ed.). Palo Alto: Consulting Psychologists Press.

Guzzo, R. A., & Waters, J. A. (1982). The expression of the affect and the performance of decision-making groups. *Journal of Applied Psychology, 67*, 67–74.

Guzzo, R. A., Yost, P. R., Campbell, R. J., & Shea, G. P. (1993). Potency in groups: Articulating a construct. *British Journal of Social Psychology, 32*, 87–106.

Habermas, J. (1979). *Knowledge and human interest*. Boston: Beacon Press.

Hackman, J. R. (1976). Groups in organizations. In Marvin D. Dunnette (Ed.), *Handbook of industrial and organizational psychology* (pp. 1455–1525). Chicago, I.: Rand McNally Press.

Hackman, J. R. (1990). Introduction. In J. R. Hackman (Ed.), *Groups that work (and those that don't)* (pp. 1–22). San Francisco: Jossey-Bass.

Hackman, J. R., & Oldham, G. R. (1980). *Work redesign*. Reading, MA: Addison-Wesley.

Hahn, F. H. (1984). *Equilibrium and macroeconomics*. Oxford: Basil Blackwell.

Hall, E. T. (1959). *The silent language*. New York: Anchor Press.

Hall, E. T. (1976). *Beyond culture*. Garden City, New York: Doubleday.

Hall, E. T. (1983). *The dance of life: The other dimension of time*. Garden City, NY: Anchor Press.

Hambrick, D. C., Cho, T. S., and Chen, M. (1996). The influence of top management team heterogeneity on firms' competitive moves. *Administrative Science Quarterly, 41*, 659–684.

Hambrick, D. C., Davison, S. C., Snell, S. A., & Snow, C. C. (1998). When groups consist of multiple nationalities: Towards a new understanding of the implications. *Organization Studies, 19,* 181–205.

Hambrick, D. C., & Mason, P. A. (1984). Upper echelons: The organization as a reflection of its top managers. *Academy of Management Review, 9,* 193–206.

Hampden-Turner, C., & Trompenaars, F. (1994). *The seven cultures of capitalism.*

Handy, C. (1995). Trust and the virtual organization. *Harvard Business Review, 73*(3), 40–50.

Hannan, M., & Freeman, J. (1977). The population ecology of organizations. *American Journal of Sociology, 82,* 929–940.

Harkins, S. G., & Petty, R. E. (1983). Social context effects in persuasion. In P. B. Paulus (Ed.), *Basic group processes* (pp. 147–178). New York: Springer-Verlag.

Harris, S. G., & Sutton, R. I. (1986). Functions of parting ceremonies in dying organizations. *Academy of Management Journal, 29*(1), 5–31.

Harstone, M., & Augoustinos, M. (1995). The minimal group paradigm: Categorization into two versus three groups. *European Journal of Social Psychology, 25,* 179–193.

Haslam, N., & Fiske, A. P. (1992). Implicit relationship prototypes: Investigating five theories of the cognitive organization of social relationships. *Journal of Experimental Social Psychology, 28,* 441–474.

Hawes, F., & Kealey, D. J. (1981). An empirical study of Canadian technical assistance. *International Journal of Intercultural Relations, 5,* 239–258.

Hawthorne, M. (1994). The computer in literary analysis: Using TACT with students. *Computers and the Humanities, 28*(1), 19.

Hebb, D. O. (1955). Drives and the CNS (conceptual nervous system). *Psychological Review, 62,* 243–254.

Heifetz, R. A., & Laurie, D. L. (1997). The works of leadership. *Harvard Business Review, 75,* 124–134.

Heilman, M. E., & Hornstein, H. A. (1992). *Managing human forces in organizations.* Homewood, IL: Irwin.

Heiss, J. S. (1962). Degree of intimacy and male-female interaction. *Sociometry, 25,* 197–208.

Hill, J. W., & Kolb, D. K. (1998). *Chemistry for changing times* (8th ed). Upper Saddle River, NJ: Prentice-Hall.

Hinings, C. R., Brown, J. L., & Greenwood, R. (1991). Change in an autonomous professional organization. *Journal of Management Studies, 28*(4), 375–393.

Hitson, H. M. (1959). *Family patterns and paranoidal personality structure in Boston and Burma.* Cambridge, MA: Radcliff College.

Hofstede, G. (1980a). *Culture's consequences: International differences in work related values.* Newbury Park, CA: Sage.

Hofstede, G. (1980b). Motivation, leadership and organization: Do American theories apply abroad? *Organizational Dynamics,* Summer, 42–63.

Hofstede, G. (1991). *Culture and organizations: Software of the mind*. London: McGraw-Hill.

Hofstede, G. (1993). Cultural constraints in management theories. *Academy of Management Executive, 7*(1), 81–94.

Hofstede, G., & Bond, M. H. (1988). The Confucius connection: From cultural roots to economic growth. *Organizational Dynamics,* Spring, 4–21.

Hofstede, G., Neuijen, B., Ohayv, D. D., & Sanders, G. (1990). Measuring organizational cultures: A qualitative and quantitative study across twenty cases. *Administrative Science Quarterly, 35,* 286–316.

Hollander, E. P. (1964). *Leaders, groups, and influence*. New York: Oxford University Press.

Holmes, H., Tantongtavy, S., & Tomizawa, R. (1995). *Working with the Thais*. Bangkok, Thailand: White Lotus Publishers.

Homans, G. C. (1958). Social behavior as exchange. *American Journal of Sociology, 63,* 597–606.

Homans, G. C. (1961). *Social behavior: Its elementary forms*. New York: Harcourt Brace & World.

House, R. J. (1998). Globe project. *Personal Communication*. November.

House, R. J., Spangler, W. D., & Woycke, J. (1991). Personality and charisma in the U.S. presidency: A psychological theory of leader effectiveness. *Administrative Science Quarterly, 36,* 364–396.

House, R. J., & Rousseau, D. (1995). *On the bifurcation of OB or if it ain't meso it ain't OB*. Working paper, The Wharton School, University of Pennsylvania

Howes, M. (1980). The uses of indigenous technical knowledge in development. In D. W. Brokensha,

Hu, H. C. (1944). The Chinese concepts of 'face.' *American Anthropologist, 46,* 45–64.

Huber, G. P., & Daft, R. L. (1987). The information environments of organizations. In F. M. Jablin, L. L. Putnam, K. H. Roberts, & L. W. Porter (Eds.), *Handbook of organizational communication*. Beverly Hills, CA: Sage.

Huber, G., & Glick, W. H. (1993). Sources and forms of organizational change. In G. P. Huber & W. H. Glick (Eds.), *Organizational change and redesign: Ideas and insights for improving performance* (pp. 3–18). New York: Oxford Press.

Hui, C. H., & Triandis, H. C. (1985). Measurement in cross-cultural psychology. *Journal of Cross-Cultural Psychology, 16,* 131–152. *Introduction to Hitachi and modern Japan*. (1986). Tokyo: Hitachi Ltd.

Hughes, E. C. (1971). *The sociological eye: Selected papers*. Chicago: Aldine-Atherton, Inc.

Huselid, M. A., Jackson, S. E., & Schuler, R. S. (1997). Technical and strategic human resource management effectiveness as determinants of firm performance. *Academy of Management Journal, 40*(1), 171–188.

Huston, T. L., Geis, G., & Wright, R. (1976). The angry samaritans. *Psychology Today,* June: 61–85.

Hutchins, E. (1991). The social organization of distributed cognition. In L. B. Resnick, J. M. Levine, & S. D. Teasley (Eds.), *Perspectives on socially shared cognition* (pp. 283–307). Washington, DC: American Psychological Association.

Ibarra, H. (1992). Homophily and differential returns: Sex differences in network structure and access in an advertising firm. *Administrative Science Quarterly, 37*, 422–477.

Innis, H. A. (1991). *The bias of communication*. Toronto: University of Toronto Press.

Ishii, H. (1990, Winter). Cross-cultural communication and computer supported co-operative work. *Whole Earth Review*, Winter (vol. 69, pp. 48–52).

Jackson, S. E. (1992a). Team composition in organizational settings: Issues in managing an increasingly diverse work force. In S. Worchel, W. Wood, & J. A. Simpson (Eds.), *Group process and productivity* (pp. 138–176). Newbury Park, CA: Sage.

Jackson, S. E. (1992b). Consequences of group composition for the interpersonal dynamics of strategic issue processing. In P. Shrivastava, A. Huff, & J. Dutton (Eds.), *Advances in strategic management* (vol. 89, pp. 345–382). Greenwich, CT: JAI Press.

Jackson, S. E., May, K. E., & Whitney, K. (1995). Understanding the dynamics of diversity in decision-making teams. In R. A. Guzzo, E. Salas, & Associates (Eds.), *Team effectiveness and decision making in organizations* (pp. 204–261). San Francisco, CA: Jossey-Bass Publishers.

Jackson, S. E., Salas, E., & Associates. (1992). *Diversity in the workplace: Human resources initiatives*. New York: Guilford Press.

Jackson, S. E., & Schuler, R. S. (1995). Understanding human resource management in the context of organizations and their environments. In M. R. Rosenzweig & L. W. Porter (Eds.), *Annual Review of Psychology* (vol. 46, pp. 237–264). Palo Alto: Annual Reviews.

Jackson, S. E., Stone, V. K., & Alvarez, E. B. (1992). Socialization amidst diversity: The impact of demographics on work team oldtimers and newcomers. *Research in Organizational Behavior, 15*, 45–109.

Janis, I. L. (1982). *Groupthink: Psychological studies of policy decisions and fiascoes*. Boston: Houghton-Mifflin.

Jehn, K. A. (1995). A multi-method examination of the benefits and detriments of intragroup conflict. *Administrative Science Quarterly, 40*, 256–282.

Jehn, K. A., Chadwick, C., & Thatcher, S. M. B. (1997). To agree or not to agree: The effects of value congruence, individual demographic dissimilarity, and conflict on workgroup outcomes. *The International Journal of Conflict Management, 8*, 287–305.

Jehn, K. A., Northcraft, G. B., & Neale, M. A. (1999). Why differences make a difference: A field study of diversity, conflict, and performance in workgroups. *Administrative Science Quarterly, 44*(4), 741–763.

Jemison, D. B., & Sitkin, S. B. (1986). Corporate acquisitions: A process perspective. *Academy of Management Review, 11*, 145–163.

Johnson, B., & Rice, R. E. (1987). *Managing organizational innovation*. New York: Columbia University Press.

Johnson, S. T. (1993). Work teams: What's ahead in work design and rewards management. *Compensation & Benefits Review, 25,* 35–41.

Jones, J. M. (1988). Cultural differences in temporal perspectives. In J. E. McGrath (Ed.), *The social psychology of time: New perspectives* (pp. 21–38). Beverly Hills, CA: Sage.

Joshi, A., & Caligiuri, P. M. (2000). *Geographically distributed teams: A social network perspective on effectiveness and cohesion*. Working paper, Rutgers University.

Joynt, P., & Warner, M. (1996). *Managing across cultures: Issues and perspectives*. London: Thomson Business Press.

Jun, J. S., & Muto, H. (1995). The hidden dimensions of Japanese administration: Culture and its impact. *Public Administration Review, 55*(2), 125–135.

Kagan, S., Knight, G., & Martinez-Romero, S. (1982). Culture and the development of conflict resolution style. *Journal of Cross-Cultural Psychology, 13,* 43–59.

Kanin-Lovers, J., & Cameron, M. (1993). Team-based reward systems. *Journal of Compensation & Benefits, 8,* 56–60.

Kanter, R. M., & Eccles, R. G. (1992). Making network research relevant to practice. In N. Nohria & R. G. Eccles (Eds.), *Networks and organizations: Structure, form and action* (pp. 521–527). Boston: Harvard Business School Press.

Karambayya, R., & Brett, J. M. (1989). Managers handling disputes: Third-party roles and perceptions of fairness. *Academy of Management Journal, 32*(4), 687–704.

Katz, D., & Kahn, R. L. (1978). *The social psychology of organizations* (2nd ed.). New York: Wiley.

Katz, R. (1982). The effects of group longevity on project communication and performance. *Administrative Science Quarterly, 27,* 81–104.

Katzenbach, J. R., & Smith, D. K. (1993). *The wisdom of teams-creating the high-performance organization*. Boston, MA: Harvard Business School Press.

Kauffman, S. (1995). *At home in the universe*. New York: Oxford University Press.

Keck, S. L. (1997). *Culture and turbulent contexts in transnational top management team performance*. Paper presented at the 1997 Academy of Management Meeting, Boston, MA.

Kelley, H. H., & Thibaut, J. W. (1978). *Interpersonal relations: A theory of interdependence*. New York: Wiley.

Kenkel, W. F. (1957). Differentiation in family decision-making. *Sociology and Social Research, 42,* 18–25.

Kerr, N. (1983). Motivation losses in small groups: A social dilemma analysis. *Journal of Personality and Social Psychology, 45,* 819–828.

Kets de Vries, M. F. R., & Miller, D. (1986). Personality, culture, and organization. *Academy of Management Review, 11,* 266–279.

Kiesler, S., Siegel, J., & McGuire, T. (1984). Social psychological aspects of computer-mediated communication. *American Psychologist, 39,* 1123–1134.

Kihlstrom, J. F., & Cantor, N. (1984). Mental representations of the self. In L. Berkowitz (Ed.), *Advances in experimental social psychology* (vol. 17, pp. 2–48). New York: Academic Press.

Kihlstrom, J. F., Cantor, N., Albright, J. S., Chew, B. R., Klein, S. B., & Niedenthal, P. M. (1988). Information processing and the study of the self. *Advances in Experimental Social Psychology* (vol. 21, pp. 145–178). San Diego, CA: Academic Press.

Kim, P. H. (1997). When what you know can hurt you: A study of experiential effects on group discussion and performance. *Organizational Behavior and Human Process, 69*(2), 165–177.

Kirchmeyer, C., & Cohen, A. (1992). Multicultural groups: Their performance and reactions with constructive conflict. *Group & Organization Management, 17*(2), 153–170.

Kirkman, B. L., Gibson, C. B., & Shapiro, D. (In press). *"Exporting" teams: Enhancing the implementation and effectiveness of work teams in global affiliates.* Organizational Dynamics.

Kirkman, B. L., & Rosen, B. (1997). A model of work team empowerment. In R. W. Woodman & W. A. Pasmore (Eds.), *Research in organizational change and development* (vol. 10, pp. 131–167). Greenwich, CT: JAI Press.

Kirkman, B. L., & Shapiro, D. L. (1997). The impact of cultural values on employee resistance to teams: Toward a model of globalized self-managing work team effectiveness. *Academy of Management Review, 22*(3), 730–745.

Kirkman, B. L., & Shapiro, D. L. (2000a). The impact of cultural values on job satisfaction and organizational commitment in self-managing work teams: The mediating role of employee resistance. In press, *Academy of Management Journal.*

Kirkman, B. L., & Shapiro, D. L. (2000b). *The impact of employee cultural values on productivity, cooperation, and empowerment in self-managing work teams.* Working paper, University of North Carolina, Greensboro.

Kirzner, I. M. (1973). *Competition and entrepreneurship.* Chicago, IL: University of Chicago Press.

Klausner, W. J. (1993). *Reflections on Thai culture.* Bangkok, Thailand: The Siam Society.

Klein, K., Dansereau, F., & Hall, R. (1994). Level issues in theory development, data collection, and analysis. *Academy of Management Review, 19,* 195–229.

Klimoski, R., & Mohammed, S. (1994). Team mental model: Construct or metaphor? *Journal of Management, 20,* 403–437.

Kluckhohn, C. (1954). *Culture and behavior.* New York: Free Press.

Kluckhohn, F., & Strodtbeck, F. (1961). *Variations in Value Orientation.* Westport: Greenwood Press.

Komin, S. (1991). *Psychology of the Thai people.* Bangkok, Thailand: National Institute of Development Administration (NIDA).

Kozan, M. K. (1989). Cultural influences on styles of handling interpersonal conflicts: Comparisons among Jordanian, Turkish, and U. S. managers. *Human Relations, 42,* 787–799.

Kramer, R. M., & Tyler, T. R. (Eds.) (1996). *Trust in organizations: Frontiers of theory and research.* Thousand Oaks, CA: Sage Publications.

Kymlicka, W. *Multicultural citizenship.* New York: Oxford University Press.

Lambert, W. (1977). The effects of bilingualism on the individual: Cognitive and sociocultural consequences. In P. A. Hurnbey (Eds.), *Bilingualism: Psychological, social, and educational implications* (pp. 15–27). New York: Academic Press.

Langfield-Smith, K. (1992). Exploring the need for a shared cognitive map. *Journal of Management Studies, 29*(3), 349–368.

Larkey, L. K. (1996). Toward a theory of communicative interactions in culturally diverse workgroups. *Academy of Management Review, 21*(2). 463–491.

Larson, A. W. (1978). Apperceptual style and intercultural communication. In F. L. Casmir (Ed.), *Intercultural and international communication.* Washington DC: University Press of America.

Larson, J. R., & Christensen, C. (1993). Groups as problem-solving units: Toward a new meaning of social cognition. *British Journal of Social Psychology, 32,* 5–30.

Latanè, G., Williams, K. D., & Harkins, S. (1979). Many hands make light the work: The causes and consequences of social loafing. *Journal of Personality and Social Psychology, 32,* 822–832.

Latham, G. P., Erez, M., & Locke, E. A. (1988). Resolving scientific disputes by the joint design of crucial experiments by the antagonists: Application to the Erez-Latham dispute regarding participation in goal setting. *Journal of Applied Psychology (Monograph), 73,* 753–772.

Lau, D. C., & Murnighan, J. K. (1998). Demographic diversity and faultlines: The compositional dynamics of organizational groups. *Academy of Management Review, 23,* 325–340.

Lawler, E. E., III. (1986). *High involvement management.* San Francisco: Jossey-Bass.

Lawrence, B. S. (1997). Perspective: The blackbox of organizational demography. *Organization Science, 8.*

Lawrence, P. (1991). The personnel function; An Anglo-German comparison. In C. Brewster and S. Tyson (Eds.), *International comparisons in human resource management.* London: Pitman.

Lazarus, R. S. (1991). *Emotion and adaptation.* New York: Oxford University Press.

Lazarus, R. S., & Lazarus, B. N. (1994). *Passion and reason: Making sense of our emotions.* New York: Oxford University Press

Lea, M., & Spears, R. (1995). Love at first byte? Building personal relationships over computer networks. In J. T. Wood & S. Duck (Eds.), *Under-studied relationships: Off the beaten track* (pp. 197–240). London: Sage.

Leonard-Barton, D. (1995). *Wellsprings of knowledge: Building and sustaining the sources of innovation*. Boston, MA: Harvard Business School Press.

Leung, K. (1997). Negotiation and reward allocations across cultures. In P. C. Earley & M. Erez (Eds.), *New perspectives on international industrial/organizational psychology* (pp. 640–675). San Diego, CA: Jossey-Bass.

Leung, K., & Bond, M. (1984). The impact of cultural collectivism on reward allocation. *Journal of Personality and Social Psychology, 47,* 793–804.

Leung, K., & Bond, M. (1989). On the empirical identification of dimensions for cross-cultural comparison. *Journal of Cross-Cultural Psychology, 20,* 133–151.

Leung, K., & Park, H. (1986). Effects of interactional goal on choice of allocation rule: A cross-national study. *Organizational Behavior and Human Decision Processes, 37,* 111–120.

Leviatan, U., & Rosner, M. (1980). *Work and organization in kibbutz industry*. Norwood, PA: Norwood Publications.

Levine, R. V. (1997). *A geography of time*. New York: Basic Books.

Levine, R. V., & Bartlett, K. (1984). Pace of life, punctuality and coronary heart disease in six countries. *Journal of Cross-Cultural Psychology, 15,* 233–255.

Levine, R. V., West, L. J., & Reis, H. T. (1980). Perceptions of time and punctuality in the United States and Brazil. *Journal of Personality and Social Psychology, 38*(4), 541–550.

Levy, R. (1973). *The Tahitians*. Chicago, IL: University of Chicago Press.

Lewin, K., Lippett, R., & White, R. K. (1939). Patterns of aggressive behavior in experimentally created "social climates." *Journal of Social Psychology, 10,* 271–299.

Lickel, B., Hamilton, D. S., Wieczorkowska, G., Lewis, A., Sherman, S. J., & Uhles, A. N. (1998). *Varieties of groups and the perception of group entitativity*. Unpublished paper.

Lim, S. G., & Murnighan, J. K. (1994). Phases, deadlines, and the bargaining process. *Organizational Behavior and Human Decision Processes, 58,* 153–171.

Lin, X., & Germain, R. (1998). Sustaining satisfactory joint venture relationships: The role of conflict resolution strategy. *Journal of International Business Studies, 29,* 179–196.

Lincoln, J. R. (1990). Japanese organizations and organization theory. In B. M. Staw & L. L. Cummings (Eds.), *Research in organizational behavior vol. 12* (pp. 255–294). Greenwich, CT: JAI Press.

Lincoln, J. R., Hanada, R., & Olson, J. (1981). Cultural orientation and individual reactions to organizations: A study of employees of Japanese armed forces. *Administrative Science Quarterly, 26,* 93–115.

Lind, E. A., & Earley, P. C. (1992). Procedural justice and culture. *International Journal of Psychology, 27,* 227–242.

Lind, E. A., & Tyler, T. R. (1988). *The social psychology of procedural justice*. New York: Plenum.

Lindsley, D. H., Brass, D. J., & Thomas, J. B. (1995). Efficacy-performance spirals: A multilevel perspective. *Academy of Management Review, 20,* 645–678.

Lipnack, J., & Stamps, J. (1997). *Virtual teams: Reaching across space, time, and organizations with technology*. New York: John Wiley.

Liska, A. E. (1992). *Social threat and social control*. Albany, NY: SUNY Press.

Littler, C., & Salaman, G. (1984). *Class at work. The design, allocation and control of jobs*. London. Batsford.

Loasby, B. J. (1991). *Equilibrium and evolution*. New York: Manchester University Press.

Locke, E. A., & Latham, P. G. (1990). *A theory of goal setting and task performance*. Englewood Cliffs, NJ: Prentice-Hall.

Locke, E. A., & Schweiger, D. M. (1979). Participation in decision-making: One more look. In B. M. Staw & L. L. Cummings (Eds.), *Research in organization behavior* (pp. 265–339). Greenwich, CT.: JAI Press.

Lord, R. G., & Foti, R. J. (1985). Schema theories, information processing, and organizational behavior. In H. P. Sims & D. A. Gioia (Eds.), *The thinking organization* (pp. 21–48). San Francisco: Jossey Bass.

Lord, R. G., & Kernan, M. C. (1987). Scripts as determinants of purposeful behavior in organizations. *Academy of Management Review, 12*, 265–277.

1990. M & A demographics of the decade: The top 100 deals of the decade. *Mergers & Acquisitions, 25*, 107–112.

Lumsden, G., & Lumsden, D. (1993). *Communicating in Groups and Teams. Sharing Leadership*. Belmont, CA: Wadsworth.

Lynd, H. (1958). *On shame and the search for identity*. New York: Harcourt Brace.

Lytle, A., Brett, J. M., Barness, Z. I., Tinsley, C. H., & Janssens, M. (1995). A paradigm for confirmatory cross-cultural research in organizational behavior. In B. M. Staw and L. L. Cummings (Eds.), *Research in Organizational Behavior, 17*, 167–214.

Majchrzak, A., Rice, R. E., Malhotra, A., King, N., & Ba, S. (2000). *Technology adaptation: The case of a computer-supported virtual team*. Working paper, University of Southern California.

Majchrzak, A., Rice, R. E., Malhotra, A., King, N., & Ba, S. (2000). Technology adaptation: The case of a computer-supported inter-organizational virtual team. *MIS Quarterly, 24*(4), 569–600.

Mankin, D., Cohen, S. G., & Bikson, T. K. (1996). *Teams and technology: Fulfilling the promise of the new organization*. Boston, MA: Harvard Business School Press.

Mann, L. (1980). Cross cultural studies of small groups. In H. C. Triandis & R. W. Brislin (Eds.), *Handbook of Cross-Cultural Psychology* (Vol. 15). Boston: Allyn & Bacon.

Manz, C. C., & Sims, H. P., Jr. (1993). *Business without bosses: How self-managing teams are building high performance companies*. New York: Wiley.

March, J. G. (1953). Husband–wife interaction over political issues. *Public Opinion Quarterly, 17*, 461–470.

March, J. G. (1991). Exploration and exploitation in organizational learning. *Organization Science. 2*(1), 71–86.

Markides, C. C. (1999). A dynamic view of strategy. *Sloan Management Review, 40*(3), 55–60.

Markus, H. R., & Kitayama, S. (1991). Culture and the self: Implications for cognition, emotion, and motivation. *Psychological Review, 98,* 224–253.

Markus, H., & Wurf, E. (1987). The dynamic self-concept: A social psychological perspective. *Annual Review of Psychology, 38,* 299–337.

Markus, M. L. (1994). Electronic mail as the medium of managerial choice. *Organizational Science, 5,* 502–527.

Marsella, A. J. (1994). The measurement of emotional reactions to work: Conceptual, methodological, and research issues. *Work and Stress, 8,* 153–176.

Martin, J. (1992). *Cultures in organizations: Three perspectives.* New York: Oxford University Press.

Martin, J. N., & Hammer, M. R. (1989). Behavioral categories of intercultural communication competence: Everyday communicators' perceptions. *International Journal of Intercultural Relations, 13,* 303–332.

Marwell, G., & Hage, J. (1970). The organization of role-relationships: A systematic description. *American Sociological Review, 35,* 884–900.

Matsui, T., Kakuyama, T., & Onglatco, M. L. (1987). Effects of goals and feedback on performance in groups. *Journal of Applied Psychology, 72,* 407–415.

Maznevski, M. L. (1994). Understanding our differences: Performance in decision-making groups with diverse members. *Human Relations, 47*(5), 531–552.

Maznevski, M. L., & Chudoba, K. M. (2000). Virtual transnational teams: An adaptive structuration approach to understanding their performance. *Organization Science.*

Maznevski, M. L., & Peterson, M. F. (1997). Societal values, social interpretations, and multinational teams. In C. S. Granrose & K. Oskamp (Eds.), *Cross-cultural workgroups* (pp. 61–89). Thousand Oaks, CA: Sage Publications.

McAuley, P. C., Bond, M. H., & Kashima, E. (2001). *Towards Defining Situations Objectively: Culture-level Analysis of Role Dyads in Hong Kong and Australia.* Unpublished paper.

McClelland, D. C. (1961). *The achieving society.* Princeton, NJ: Van Nostrand.

McCrae, R., & Costa, P. (1987). Validation of the five-factor model of personality across instruments and observers. *Journal of Personality and Social Psychology, 52*(1), 1–90.

McGrath, J. E. (1984). *Groups: Interaction and performance.* Englewood Cliffs, NJ: Prentice-Hall.

McGrath, J. E. (1988). *The social psychology of time.* Newbury Park: Sage.

McGrath, J. E., Berdahl, J. L., & Arrow, H. (1995). Traits, expectations, culture, and clout: The dynamics of diversity in work groups. In S. Jackson & M. Ruderman (Eds.), *Diversity in workteams: Research paradigms for a changing workplace* (pp. 17–45). Washington, DC: American Psychological Association.

McGrath, J. E., & Kelly, J. R. (1986). *Time and human interaction: Toward a social psychology of time.* New York: Guilford Press.

McGrath, J. E., & Rotchford, N. L. (1983). Time and behavior in organizations. In L. L. Cummings & B. M. Staw (Eds.), *Research in Organizational Behavior* (pp. 57–101). Greenwich, CT.: JAI Press.

McKelvey, B. (1982). *Organizational systematics: Taxonomy, evolution, classification*. Berkeley, CA: University of California Press.

McKenna, K. Y. A., & Bargh, J. A. (1998). Interpersonal relations and group processes: coming out in the age of the internet: Identity demarginalization through virtual group participation. *Journal of Personality and Social Psychology, 75*(3), 681–698.

McLeod, P. L., & Lobel, S. A. (1992). The effects of ethnic diversity on idea generation in small groups. *Academy of Management Best Papers Proceedings* (pp. 227–231).

Mead, G. H. (1934). *Mind, self and society*. Chicago, IL: University of Chicago Press.

Mead, M. (1967). *Cooperation and competition among primitive people*. Boston: Beacon.

Meglino, B. M., & Ravlin, E. C. (1998). Individual values in organizations: Concepts, controversies, and research. *Journal of Management, 24*, 351–389.

Mellinger, G. D. (1956). Interpersonal trust as a factor in communication. *Journal of Abnormal and Social Psychology, 52*, 304–309.

Messick, D. M., & Mackie, D. M. (1989). Intergroup relations. *Annual Review Psychology, 40*, 45–81.

Miles, R. E., & Snow, C. C. (1978). *Organization strategy, structure, and process*. New York: McGraw-Hill.

Milgrom, P., & Roberts, J. (1993). *Complementarities and fit: Strategy, structure, and organizational change*. Unpublished manuscript, Stanford University.

Milliken, F. J., & Martins, L. L. (1996). Searching for common threads: Understanding the multiple effects of diversity in organizational groups. *Academy of Management Review, 21*, 402–433.

Mitchell, W. (1989). Whether and when? Probability and timing of incumbents' entry into emerging industrial subfields. *Administrative Science Quarterly, 34*(2), 208–230.

Mitchell, W. (1991). Dual clocks: Entry order influences on incumbent and newcomer market share and survival when specialized assets retain their value. *Strategic Management Journal, 12*(2), 85–100.

Miyahara, A. (1984, June). *A need for a study to examine the accuracy of American observers' perceptions of Japanese managers' communication styles*. Paper presented at the Eastern Communication Association Convention, Philadelphia.

Moghaddam, F. M. (1997). Change and continuity in organizations: Assessing intergroup relations. In C. S. Granrose & K. Oskamp (Eds.), *Cross-cultural workgroups* (pp. 36–60). Thousand Oaks, CA: Sage.

Mohr, L. (1971). Organizational technology and organization structure. *Administrative Science Quarterly, 16*, 444–459.

Mohrman, S., Cohen, S., & Mohrman, A. (1995). *Designing team-based organizations*. San Francisco: Jossey-Bass.

Mohrman, S. A., Gibson, C. B., & Mohrman, A. (2001) Doing research that's useful to practice: A model and empirical investigation. *Academy of Management Journal*.

Monier, E. L. (1999, August). *On team mental models: The role of cognitive convergence in problem solving and team cohesiveness*. Paper presented at the Academy of Management Meeting, Chicago, IL.

Morgan, P., & Baker, K. (1985). Building a professional image: Improving listening behavior. *Supervisory Management*, November, 34–38.

Morgeson, F. P., & Hofmann, D. A. (1999). The structure and function of collective constructs: Implications for multilevel research and theory development. *Academy of Management Review, 24*(2), 249–265.

Morris, M. W., Nisbett, R. E., & Peng, K. (1995). Causality across domains and cultures. In D. Sperber, D. Premack, & A. J. Premack (Eds.), *Causal cognition* (pp. 577–614). New York: Oxford University Press.

Morrison, A. M., & Von Glinow, M. A. (1990). Women and minorities in management. *American Psychologist, 45,* 200–208.

Mosakowski, E. (1998). Entrepreneurial resource, organizational choices, and competitive outcomes. *Organization Science, 9,* 625–643.

Mosakowski, E., & Earley, P. C. (2000). A selective review of time assumptions in strategy research. *Academy of Management Review, 25,* 796–812.

Mulder, M. (1977). *The daily power game*. Leiden: Martinus Nijhoff Social Sciences Division.

Murphy-Berman, V., Berman, J., Singh, P., Pachuri, A., & Kumar, P. (1984). Factors affecting allocation to needy and meritorious recipients: A cross-cultural comparison. *Journal of Personality and Social Psychology, 46,* 1267–1272.

Myerson, D., & Martin, J. (1987). Cultural change: An integration of three different views. *Journal of Management Studies, 24,* 623–647.

Nemeth, C. J. (1985). Dissent, group process, and creativity. *Advances in Group Processes, 2,* 57–75.

Nemeth, C. J. (1986). Differential contributions of majority and minority influence. *Psychological Review, 91,* 23–32.

Nemiro, J. E. (1998). *Creativity in virtual teams*. Unpublished doctoral dissertation, Claremont Graduate School, Claremont, CA.

Neuberg, S. L. (1989). The goal of forming accurate impressions during social interactions: Attenuating the impact of negative expectancies. *Journal of Personality and Social Psychology, 56,* 374–386.

Neuberg, S. L., & Fiske, S. T. (1987). Motivational influences on impression formation: Outcome dependency, accuracy-driven attention, and individuating processes. *Journal of Personality and Social Psychology, 53,* 431–444.

Nishida, H. (1985). Japanese intercultural communication competence and cross-cultural adjustment. *International Journal of Intercultural Relations, 9*(3), 247–269.

Norman, W. T. (1963). Toward an adequate taxonomy of personality attributes: Replicated factor structure. *Journal of Abnormal and Social Psychology, 66,* 574–583.

Nuttin, J. (1985). *Future time perspective and motivation.* Hillsdale, NJ: Lawrence Erlbaum Associates.

Nuttin, J., & Lens, W. (1985). *Future time perspective and motivation.* Louvain, Belgium: Leuven University Press.

O'Dwyer, G., Giser, A., & Lovett, E. (1997). Groupware and reengineering: The human side of change. In D. Coleman (Ed.), *Groupware: Collaborative strategies for corporate LANs and intranets.* Upper Saddle River, NJ: Prentice-Hall.

O'Hara-Devereaux, M., & Johansen, R. (1994). *Globalwork: Bridging distance, culture and time.* San Francisco: Jossey-Bass.

O'Reilly, C. A., III, Caldwell, D. F., & Barnett, W. P. (1989). Work group demography, social integration, and turnover. *Administrative Science Quarterly, 34,* 21–37.

Ohbuchi, K., & Takahashi, Y. (1994). Cultural styles of conflict management in Japanese and Americans: Passivity, covertness, and effectiveness of strategies. *Journal of Applied Social Psychology, 24,* 1345–1366.

Olson, M. (1965). *The logic of collective action.* Cambridge, MA: Harvard University Press

Orasanu, J., Fischer, U., & Davison, J. (1997). Cross-cultural barriers to effective communication in aviation. In C. S. Granrose & K. Oskamp (Eds.), *Cross-cultural workgroups* (pp. 134–162). Thousand Oaks, CA: Sage.

Organ, D. W. (1990). The motivational basis of organizational citizenship behavior. In B. M. Staw & L. L. Cummings (Eds.), *Research in organizational behavior, 12,* 43–72. Greenwich, CT: JAI Press.

Orlikowski, W. J. (1992). The duality of technology: Rethinking the concept of technology in organizations. *Organization Science, 3*(3), 398–427.

Orlikowski, W. J., Yates, J., Okamura, K., & Fujimoto, M. (1995). Shaping electronic communication: The metastructure of technology in the context of use. *Organization Science, 6*(4), 423–443.

Orru, M., Biggart, N. W., & Hamilton, G. G. (1991). Organizational isomorphism in East Asia. In W. W. Powell and D. J. DiMaggio (Eds.), *The new institutionalism in organizational analysis* (pp. 361–389). Chicago: University of Chicago Press.

Ostroff, C. (1993). Comparing correlations based on individual-level and aggregated data. *Journal of Applied Psychology, 78,* 569–582.

O'Toole, J., & Pasternack, B. (2001). *When leadership is an organizational trait.* Working paper, University of Southern California.

Ouchi, W. G. (1980). Markets, bureaucracies and clans. *Administrative Science Quarterly, 25,* 129–141.

Ouchi, W. G., & Jaeger, A. M. (1978). Type Z organization: Stability in the midst of mobility. *Academy of Management Review, 5,* 305–314.

Parker, L. (1994). Working together: Perceived self- and collective-efficacy at the workplace. *Journal of Applied Social Psychology, 24,* 43–59.

Parks, C. D., & Cowlin, R. (1995). Group discussion as affected by number of alternatives and by a time limit. *Organizational Behavior and Human Decision Processes, 62,* 276–275.

Parsons, T., & Shils, E. A. (1951). *Toward a general theory of action.* Cambridge: Harvard University Press.

Pelled, L. H. (1996). Demographic diversity, conflict and work group outcomes: An intervening process theory. *Organization Science, 7*(6), 615–631.

Pelled, L. H., Eisenhardt, K. M., & Xin, K. R. (1999). Exploring the black box: An analysis of work group diversity, conflict and performance. *Administrative Science Quarterly, 44,* 1–28.

Pelled, L. H., Ledford, G. E., & Mohrman, S. A. (1998). Individual demographic dissimilarity and organizational inclusion: A field investigation. *Academy of Management Proceedings* (vol. 1, pp. 241–245).

Perrow, C. (1972). *Complex organizations: A critical essay.* Glenview, IL: Scott, Foresman.

Pervin, L. A. (1976). A free-response description approach to the analysis of person-situation interaction. *Journal of Personality and Social Psychology, 34,* 465–474.

Peteraf, M., & Shanley, M. (1997). Getting to know you: A theory of strategic group identity. *Strategic Management Journal, 18* (Special Issue Supplement, Summer), 165–186.

Pettigrew, A. (1985). *The awakening giant: Continuity and change in ICI.* London: Basil Blackwell.

Pfeffer, J. (1983). Organizational demography. In B. M. Staw & L. L. Cummings (Eds.), *Research in organizational behavior* (vol. 4, pp. 299–357). Greenwich, CT: JAI Press.

Piers, G., & Singer, M. B. (1971). *Shame and guilt: A psychoanalytic and cultural study.* New York: W. W. Norton.

Pike, K. L. (1966). *Language in relation to a unified theory of the structure of human behavior.* The Hague: Mouton.

Pitt-Rivers, J. (1954). *The people of the sierra.* New York: Criterion Books.

Pondy, L. R., Frost, P. J., Morgan, G., & Dandridge, T. C. (1982). *Organizational symbolism.* Greenwich, CT: JAI Press.

Poole M. S., & Jackson, M. H. (1993). Communication theory and group support systems. In L. M. Jessup & J. S. Valacich (Eds.), *Group support systems: New perspectives* (pp. 121–147). Old Tappan, NJ: Macmillan.

Popping, R. (1997). Computer programs for the analysis of text transcripts. In C. W. Roberts (Ed.), *Text analysis for the social sciences* (pp. 209–221). Mahwah, NJ: Lawrence Erlbaum Associates.

Powell, W. W., & DiMaggio, P. J. (1991). *The new institutionalism in organizational analysis.* Chicago, IL: University of Chicago Press.

Prandy, K. (1998). Class and continuity in social reproduction: An empirical investigation. *The Sociological Review, 46*(2), 340–364.

Prahalad, C. K., & Bettis, R. A. (1986). The dominant logic: A new linkage between diversity and performance. *Strategic Management Journal, 7*, 485–501.

Prussia, G. E., & Kinicki, A. J. (1996). A motivational investigation of group effectiveness using social-cognitive theory. *Journal of Applied Psychology, 81*, 187–198.

Putnam, L. L., & Poole, M. S. (1987). Conflict and negotiation. In F. M. Jablin, L. L. Putnam, K. H. Roberts, & L. W. Porter (Eds.), *Handbook of organizational communication: An interdisciplinary perspective* (pp. 549–599). Newbury Park, CA: Sage.

Rallu, J. L. (1998). Les categories statistiques utilisees dans les DOM-TOM depuis le debut de la Presence Francaise. *Population, 3*, 589–608.

Ranson, S., Hinings, R., & Greenwood, R. (1980). The structuring of organizational structures. *Administrative Science Quarterly, 28*, 314–337.

Rappoport, A. (1959). Critiques of game theory. *Behavior Science, 4*, 49–66.

Ravlin, E. C., Thomas, D. C., & Ilsev, A. (2000). Beliefs about values, status, and legitimacy in multicultural groups: Influences on intra-group conflict. In P. C. Earley & H. Singh (Eds.), *Innovations in international and cross-cultural management* (pp. 58–83). Thousand Oaks, CA: Sage Publications.

Rawls, J. (1971). *A theory of justice.* Cambridge: Harvard University Press.

Reger, R. K., & Huff, A. S. (1993). Strategic groups: A cognitive perspective. *Strategic Management Journal, 14*(2), 103–123.

Rice, R. E. (1994). Network analysis and computer mediated communication systems. In S. Wasserman & J. Galaskiewicz (Eds.), *Advances in social and behavioral science from social network analysis* (pp. 167–203). Newbury Park, CA: Sage.

Ridgeway, C., & Walker, H. A. (1995). Status structures. In K. Cook, G. A. Fine, J. S. House (Eds.), *Sociological perspectives on social psychology.* Needham Heights, MA: Allyn & Bacon.

Riley, P. (1983). A structurationist account of political culture. *Administrative Science Quarterly, 28*, 414–437.

Robinson, R. B. (1982). The importance of "outsiders" in small firm strategic planning. *Academy of Management Journal, 25*(1), 80–93.

Rohner, R. P. (1987). Culture theory. *Journal of Cross-Cultural Psychology, 18*, 8–51.

Rohner, R. P. (1984). Toward a conception of culture for cross-cultural psychology. *Journal of Cross-Cultural Psychology, 15*(2), 111–138.

Rokeach, M. (1973). *The nature of human values.* New York: Free Press.

Romanelli, E., & Tushman, M. L. (1986). Inertia, environment, and strategic choice: A quasi-experimental design for comparative-longitudinal research. *Management Science, 32*(5), 608–621.

Romanelli, E., & Tushman, M. L. (1994). Organizational transformation as punctuated equilibrium: An empirical test. *Academy of Management Journal, 37*(5), 1141–1166.

Rosaldo, R. (1989). *Culture and truth*. Boston: Beacon Press.

Rosch, M., & Segler, K. G. (1987). Communication with the Japanese. *Management International Review, 27*(4), 56–67.

Rossi, A. M., & Todd-Mancillas, W. R. (1985). A comparison of managerial communication strategies between Brazilian and American women. *Communication Research Reports, 2*, 128–134.

Rosenzweig, P. M., & Nohria, N. (1994). Influences on human resource management practices in multinational corporations. *Journal of International Business Studies, 25*, 229–251.

Rotter, J. B. (1971). Generalized expectancies for interpersonal trust. *American Psychologist, 26*(5), 443–452.

Rousseau, D. M. (1985). Issues of level in organizational research: Multi-level and cross-level perspectives. *Research in Organizational Behavior, 7*, 1–37.

Rousseau, D. M., Sitkin, S. B., Burt, R., & Camerer, C. (1998). Not so different after all: A cross-discipline view of trust. *Academy of Management Review, 23*(3), 393–404.

Rubenowitz, S. (1974). Experiences in industrial democracy and changes in work organizations in Sweden. *Psckologiska Institutionen, vol. 2:* Goteborgs Universitet.

Saavedra, R., Earley, P. C., & Van Dyne, L. (1993). Complex interdependence in task-performing groups. *Journal of Applied Psychology, 71*, 61–72.

Sahay, S., & Walsham, G. (1997). Social structure and managerial agency. *Organization Studies, 18*(3), 415–444.

Salovey, P., & Mayer, J. D. (1990). Emotional Intelligence. *Imagination, Cognition, and Personality, 9*(3), 185–211.

Sampson, E. E. (1989). The challenge of social change for psychology: Globalization and psychology's theory of the person. *American Psychologist, 44*, 914–921.

Sandel, M. J. (1982). Liberalism and the limits of justice. Cambridge, England: Cambridge University Press.

Sastry, M. A. (1997). Problems and paradoxes in a model of punctuated organizational change. *Administrative Science Quarterly, 42*(2), 237–275.

Sathe, V. (1985). *Culture and related corporate realities*. Homewood IL: Richard D. Irwin, Inc.

Saxton, T. (1995). The impact of third parties on strategic decision-making: Roles, timing, and organizational outcomes. *Journal of Organizational Change Management, 8*(3), 47–62.

Scarbrough, H. (1998). Pathological dependency? Core competencies from an organizational perspective. *British Journal of Management, 9*(3), 219–232.

Schank, R. C., & Abelson, R. P. (1977). *Scripts, plans, goals, and understanding: An inquiry into human knowledge structures*. Hillsdale, NJ: Lawrence Erlbaum Associates.

Schein, E. H. (1985). *Organizational culture and leadership*. San Francisco: Jossey-Bass.

Schneider, B. (1975). Organizational climate: An essay. *Personnel Psychology, 28*, 447–479.

Schneider, S. C. (1989). Strategy formulation: The impact of national culture. *Organization Studies, 10*(2), 149–168.

Schneider, S. C. (1993). Conflicting ideologies: Structural and motivational consequences. *Human Relations, 46*(1), 45–64.

Schneider, S. C., & Angelmar, R. (1993). Cognition in organizational analysis: Who's minding the store. *Organizational Studies, 14*(3), 347–374.

Schneider, S. C., & Barsoux, J. L. (1997). *Managing across cultures*. Hemel Hempstead: Prentice-Hall.

Schneider, S. C., & De Meyer, A. (1991). Interpreting and responding to strategic issues: The impact of national culture. *Strategic Management Journal, 12*, 307–320.

Schuler, R. S., Dowling, P. J., & De Cieri, H. (1993). An integrative framework of strategic international human resource management. *Journal of Management, 19*, 419–459.

Schurr, P. H., & Ozanne, J. K. (1985). Influences on exchange processes: Buyers' preconceptions of a seller's trustworthiness and bargaining toughness. *Journal of Consumer Research, 11*(4), 939–954.

Schuster, J. R., & Zingheim, P. K. (1993). "New pay" strategies that work. *Journal of Compensation & Benefits, 8*, 5–9.

Schwartz, S. H. (1992). The universal content and structures of values: Theoretical advances and empirical tests in 20 countries. In M. P. Zanna (Ed.), *Advances in Experimental Social Psychology* (vol. 25, pp. 1–65). New York: Academic Press.

Schwartz, S. H. (1993). Cultural dimensions of values: Toward an understanding of national differences. Unpublished paper.

Schwartz, S. H., & Bilsky, W. (1987). Toward a universal psychological structure of human values. *Journal of Personality and Social Psychology, 53*, 550–562.

Schweder, R. A., & LeVine, R. A. (1984). *Culture theory: Essays on mind, self and emotion*. New York: Cambridge University Press.

Scott, W. R., & Meyer, J. W. (1994). *Institutional environments and organizations: Structural complexity and individualism*. Thousand Oaks, CA: Sage.

Shackelford, S., Wood, W., & Worchel, S. (1996). Behavioral styles and the influence of women in mixed-sex groups. *Social Psychology Quarterly, 59*(3), 284–293.

Shamir, B. (1990). Calculations, values, and identities: The sources of collectivistic work motivation. *Human Relations, 43*, 313–332.

Sherif, M. (1966). *In common predicament: Social psychology of intergroup conflict and cooperation*. Boston: Houghton Mifflin.

Sherman, S. J., Judd, C. M., & Park, B. (1989). Social cognition. *Annual Review of Psychology, 40*, 281–326.

Shrivastava, P. (1983). A typology of organizational learning systems. *Journal of Management Studies, 20*, 9–21.

Sidanius, J., Pratto, F., & Rabinowitz, J. L. (1994). Gender, ethnic status, and ideological asymmetry. *Journal of Cross-Cultural Psychology, 25,* 194–216.

Skinner, B. F. (1953). *Science and human behavior.* New York: Macmillan.

Smircich, L., & Calas, M. B. (1986). Organizational culture: A critical assessment. *Annual Review of Sociology, 2,* 228–263.

Smith, K. A., Olian, J. D., Sims, H. P., O'Bannon, D. P., & Scully, J. A. (1994). Top management team demography and process: The role of social integration and communication. *Administrative Science Quarterly, 39,* 412–438.

Smith, P. B., & Bond, M. H. (1994). *Social psychology across cultures.* Boston: Allyn & Bacon.

Smith, P. B., & Bond, M. H. (1998). *Social psychology across cultures* (2nd ed.). London: Prentice Hall International.

Smith, P. B., Dugan, S., & Trompenaars, F. (1996). National culture and the values of organizational employees: A dimensional analysis across 43 nations. *Journal of Cross-Cultural Psychology, 27*(2), 231–264.

Sniezek, J. A., & Henry, R. A. (1990). Revision, weighting, and commitment in consensus group judgment. *Organizational Behavior and Human Decision Processes, 45,* 66–84.

Snow, C. C., Snell, S. A., Canney-Davison, S., & Hambrick, D. C. (1996). Use transnational teams to globalize your company. *Organizational Dynamics, 32* (Spring), 20–32.

Solomon, C. M. (1995). Global teams: The ultimate collaboration. *Personnel Journal, 74*(9), 49–58.

Spadone, R. A. (1992). Internal-external locus of control and temporal orientation among Southeast Asians and White Americans. *American Journal of Occupational Therapy, 46*(8), 713–719.

Sproull, L., & Kiesler, S. (1991). *Connections: New ways of working in the networked organization.* Cambridge, MA: MIT Press.

Stablein, R., & Nord, W. (1989). Practical and emancipatory interests in organizational symbolism: A review and evaluation. *Journal of Management, 11,* 13–28.

Stasser, G. (1991). Facilitating the use of unshared information in decision making groups. Paper presented at the 63rd meeting of the Midwest Psychological Association, Chicago, IL.

Staw, B. M., Sandelands, L. E., & Dutton, J. E. (1981). Threat-rigidity effects in organizational behavior: A multi-level analysis. *Administrative Science Quarterly, 26,* 501–524.

Staw, B. M., & Sutton, R. (1992). Macro organizational psychology. In J. K. Murnighan (Ed.), *Social psychology in organizations: Advances in theory and research* (pp. 350–384). Englewood Cliffs, NJ: Prentice-Hall.

Steers, R. M., Shin Y. K., & Ungsom, G. (1989). *The chaebol: jae boi: Korea's new industrial might.* New York: Harper & Row.

Stein, E. W., & Zwass, V. (1995). Actualizing organizational memory with information systems. *Information Systems Research, 6*(2), 85–117.

Steiner, I. D. (1972). *Group process and productivity*. New York: Academic Press.

Sternberg R. (1985). Implicit theories of intelligence, creativity, and wisdom. *Journal of Personality and Social Psychology, 49*(3), 607–627.

Stets, J. E. (1997). Status and identity in marital interaction. *Social Psychology Quarterly, 60*(3), 185–217.

Storms, P. L., & Spector, P. E. (1987). Relationships of organizational frustration with reported behavioral reactions: The moderating effect of locus of control. *Journal of Occupational Psychology, 60*, 227–234.

Stovel, K., Savage, M., & Bearman, P. (1996). Ascription into Achievement: Models of Career Systems at Lloyds Bank, 1980–1970. *American Journal of Sociology, 91*, 358–399.

Stryker, S. (1980). *Symbolic interactionism: A social structural version*. Menlo Park: Benjamin/Cummings.

Stryker, S. (1987). Identity theory: Developments and extensions. In K. Yardley & T. Honess (Eds.), *Self and identity: Psychosocial perspectives* (pp. 89–103). London: Wiley.

Sujan, H., Sujan, M., & Bettman, J. R. (1988). Knowledge structure differences between more effective and less effective salespeople. *Journal of Marketing Research, 25*, 81–86.

Sundstrom, E., & Associates. (1999). *Supporting work team effectiveness*. San Francisco: Jossey-Bass.

Suryanarayanan, S. (1989). Trends and outlook for U.S. consulting. *Journal of Management Consulting, 5*(4), 3–9.

Tajfel, H. (1982). Social psychology of intergroup relations. *Annual Review of Psychology, 33*, 1–39.

Tajfel, H. H., & Turner, J. C. (1979). An integrative theory of intergroup conflict. In W. G. Austin & S. Worchel (Eds.), *The social psychology of intergroup relations* (pp. 33–47). Monterey, CA.: Brooks/Cole.

Tajfel, H., & Turner, J. C. (1986). The social identity theory of intergroup behaviour. In S. Worchel & W. G. Austin (Eds.), *Psychology of intergroup relations* (pp. 7–24). Chicago: Nelson-Hall.

Tannenbaum, A. S. (1980). Organizational psychology. In H. C. Triandis & R. W. Brislin (Eds.), *Handbook of Cross-Cultural Psychology* (vol 5, pp. 281–334). Boston: Allyn & Bacon.

Taylor, S., Beechler, S., & Napier, N. (1996). Toward an integrative model of strategic international human resource management. *Academy of Management Review, 21*, 959–985.

Tenkasi, R., Mohrman, S. A., & Mohrman, A. M., Jr. (1998). Accelerated learning during transition. In S. A. Mohrman, J. R. Galbraith, E. E. Lawler, III, & Associates (Eds.), *Tomorrow's organization: Crafting winning capabilities in a dynamic world* (pp. 330–361). San Francisco: Jossey-Bass.

Thatcher, S. M. B., Jehn, K. A., & Chadwick, C. (1998). *What makes a difference? The impact of individual demographic differences, group diversity, and conflict on individual performance*. Working paper. The Wharton School, University of Pennsylvania.

Thibaut, J. W., & Kelley, H. H. (1959). *The social psychology of groups*. New York: Wiley.

Thibaut, J. W., & Walker, L. (1975). *Procedural justice: A psychological analysis*. Hillsdale, NJ: Lawrence Erlbaum Associates.

Thoits, P. A., & Virshup, L. K. (1997). Me's and we's: Forms and functions of social identities. In R. D. Ashmore & L. Jussim (Eds.), *Self and identity: Fundamental issues* (pp. 106–133). Oxford: Oxford University Press.

Thomas, D. C. (1999). Cultural diversity and work group effectiveness: An experimental study. *Journal of Cross-Cultural Psychology, 30*(2), 242–263.

Thomas, D. C., Ravlin, E. C., & Wallace, A. (1996). Effect of cultural diversity in work groups. *Research in the Sociology of Organizations, 14,* 1–33.

Thomas, J., & McDaniel, R. (1990). Interpreting strategic issues: Effects of strategy and the information-processing structure of top management teams. *Academy of Management Journal, 33,* 286.

Thompson, J. D. (1967). *Organizations in action*. New York: McGraw-Hill.

Thompson, L. (2000). *Making the team*. Englewood Cliffs, NJ: Prentice-Hall.

Thorsrud, E., & Emery, F. E. (1970). Industrial democracy in Norway. *Industrial Relations, 9,* 187–196.

Tichy, N. M. (1982). Managing change strategically: The technical, political, and cultural keys. *Organizational Dynamics, 11*(2), 59–80.

Ting-Toomey, S. (1985). Toward a theory of conflict and culture. In W. Gudykunst, L. Stewart, & S. Ting-Toomey (Eds.), *Communication, culture and organizational processes* (pp. 71–86). Beverly-Hills, CA: Sage.

Ting-Toomey, S. (1994). *The challenge of facework*. Albany, NY: SUNY Press.

Ting-Toomey, S., & Cocroft, B. (1994). Face and facework: Theoretical and research issues. In S. Ting-Toomey (Ed.), *The challenge of facework: Cross-cultural and interpersonal issues*. SUNY series in human communication processes. Albany, NY: State University of New York Press.

Ting-Toomey, S., Gao, G., Trubinsky, P., Yang, Z., Kim, H. S., Lin, S.-L., & Nishida, T. (1991). Culture, face maintenance and styles of handling interpersonal conflict: A study in five cultures. *The International Journal of Conflict Management: 2*(Oct #4), 275–296.

Tjosvold, D. (1973). *The use of threat by low-power persons in bargaining*. Unpublished doctoral dissertation, University of Minnesota.

Tjosvold, D. (1974). Threat as a low-power person's strategy in bargaining: Social face and tangible outcomes. *International Journal of Group Tensions, 4,* 494–510.

Tjosvold, D. (1983). Social face in conflict: A critique. *International Journal of Group Tensions, 13,* 49–64.

Tjosvold, D., & Huston, T. L. (1978). Social face and resistance to compromise in bargaining. *Journal of Social Psychology, 104,* 57–68.

Tornblom, K. Y., Jonsson, D., & Foa, U. G. (1985). Nationality resource class, and preferences among three allocation rules: Sweden vs. USA. *International Journal of Intercultural Relations, 9,* 51–77.

Tosi, H.(1992). *The environment/organization/person contingency model: A meso approach to the study of organizations*. Greenwich, CT: JAI Press.

Townsend, A. M., DeMarie, S. M., & Hendrickson, A. R. (1998). Virtual teams: Technology and the workplace of the future. *Academy of Management Executive, 12*(3), 17–29.

Triandis, H. C. (1977). *Interpersonal behavior*. Monterey, CA: Brooks/Cole.

Triandis, H. C. (1989). The self and social behavior differing cultural contexts. *Psychological Review, 96*, 506–520.

Triandis, H. C. (1990). Cross-cultural studies of individualism and collectivism. In J. Berman (Ed.), *Nebraska symposium on motivation*. Lincoln: University of Nebraska Press.

Triandis, H. C. (1995). *Individualism and collectivism*. Boulder, CO: Westview.

Triandis, H. C., & Albert, R. D. (1987). Cross-cultural perspectives. In F. M. Jablin, L. L. Putman, K. H. Roberts, & L. W. Porter (Eds.), *Handbook of organizational communication: An interdisciplinary perspective*. Beverly-Hills, CA: Sage Publications.

Triandis, H. C., & Berry, J. (1980). *Introduction. Handbook of cross-cultural psychology* (Vol. 1). New York: Allyn & Bacon.

Triandis, H. C., Bontempo, R., Betancourt, H., Bond, M., Leung, K., Brenes, A., Georgas, J., Hui, H. C., Narim, G., Singha, J. B. P., Verma, J., Spangenberg, J., Tonzard, & H., & de Montmollin, G. (1986). The measurement of etic aspects of individualism and collectivism across cultures. *Australian Journal of Psychology, 38*, 257–267.

Triandis, H. C., Bontempo, R., Vilareal, M. J., Masaaki, A., & Lucca, N. (1988). Individualism and collectivism: Cross-cultural perspectives on self-ingroup relationships. *Journal of Personality and Social Psychology, 54*, 328–338.

Triandis, H. C., Vassiliou, V., & Nassiakou, M. (1968). Three cross-cultural studies of subjective culture. *Journal of Personality and Social Psychology: Monograph Supplement, 8, Part 2*, 1–42.

Trist, E. L., & Bamforth, K. W. (1951). Some social psychological consequences of the longwall method of goal-getting. *Human Relations, 4*, 3–38.

Trist, E. L., Susman, G. I., & Brown, G. R. (1977). An experiment in autonomous working in an American underground coal mine. *Human Relations, 30*, 201–236.

Trompenaars, F. (1997). *Riding the waves of culture*. London: Nicholas Brealey Publishing.

Tsui, A. S., Egan, T. D., & O'Reilly, C. A., III. (1992). Being different: Relational demography and organizational commitment. *Administrative Science Quarterly, 37*, 549–579.

Tuckman, B. W., & Jensen, M. C. (1977). Stages of small group development revisited. *Group and Organizational Studies, 2*, 419–429.

Tung, R. L. (1997). International and intranational diversity. In C. S. Granrose, & K. Oskamp (Eds.), *Cross-cultural workgroups*. Thousand Oaks, CA: Sage.

Turner, J. C. (1985). Social categorization and the self-concept: A social-cognitive theory of group behavior. In E. J. Lawler (Ed.), *Advances in group processes: Theory and research* (vol 2, pp. 77–122). Greenwich, CT: JAI Press.

Turner, J. C. (1987). *Rediscovering the social group*. Oxford: Basil Blackwell.

Tushman, M. L., & Anderson, P. (1986). Technological discontinuities and organizational environments. *Administrative Science Quarterly, 31*(3), 439–465.

Tushman, M. L., & O'Reilly, C. A. (1996). Ambidextrous organizations: Managing evolutionary and revolutionary change. *California Management Review, 38*(4), 8–30.

Tushman, M. L., & Rosenkopf, L. (1992). Organizational determinants of technological change: Toward a sociology of technological evolution. *Research in Organizational Behavior, 14,* 311–347.

Tversky, A., & Kahneman, D. (1986). Rational choice and the framing of decisions. *Journal of Business, 59,* 5251–5278.

Tyre, M. J., & Orlikowski, W. J. (1994). Windows of opportunity—Temporal patterns of technological adaptation in organizations. *Organization Science, 5*(1), 98–118.

Van Dyne, L., Graham, J. W., & Dienesch, R. M. (1994). Organizational citizenship behavior: Construct redefinition, measurement, and validation. *Academy of Management Journal, 37,* 765–802.

Van Maanen, J., & Barley, S. R. (1984). Occupational communities: Culture and control in organizations. In B. M. Staw & L. L. Cummings (Eds.), *Research in organizational behavior* (vol. 6, pp. 287–365). Greenwich, CT: JAI Press.

Van Maanen, J., & Schein, E. H. (1977). Toward a theory of organizational socialization. In B. M. Staw (Ed.), *Research in Organizational Behavior, 1,* 209–264.

Varian, H. R. (1993). *Intermediate Microeconomics* (3rd ed.). New York: W. W. Norton.

Vinokur, A., & Burnstein, E. (1978). Novel argumentation and attitude change: The case of polarization following group discussion. *European Journal of Social Psychology, 8,* 335–348.

Von Mises, L. (1949). *Human action: A treatise on economics*. New Haven: Yale University Press.

Vroom, V. (1964). *Motivation and work*. Englewood Cliffs, NJ: Prentice-Hall.

Walgenbach, P. (1993). *Mittleres management: Aufgaben, funktionen, arbeitsverhalten*. Wiesbaden: Gabler.

Walker, H. A., Illardi, B. C., McMahon, A. M., & Fennel, M. L. (1996). Gender, interaction, and leadership. *Social Psychology Quarterly, 59*(3), 255–272.

Wall, J. A., Jr., & Callister, R. R. (1995). Conflict and its management. *Journal of Management, 21,* 515–558.

Wallbot, H. G., & Scherer, K. R. (1986). How universal and specific is emotional experience? Evidence from 25 countries on five continents. *Social Science Information, 25,* 763–795.

Waller, M. J. (1999). The timing of adaptive group responses to nonroutine events. *Academy of Management Journal, 42,* 127–137.

Waller, M. J., Zellmer-Bruhn, M., & Giambatista, R. C. (1999). *The effects of shifting deadlines on pacing in groups*. University of Illinois, working paper.

Waller, M. J., Zellmer-Bruhn, M., & Giambatista, R. C. (1999). The effects of individual time urgency on group polychronicity. *Journal of Managerial Psychology* (April, pp. 244–256).

Waller, M. J., Gibson, C. B., & Carpenter, M. (2001). Time's arrow: The impact of differences in time perspective on knowledge management speed in multicultural teams. Working paper, University of Illinois.

Walsh, J. P. (1995). Managerial and organizational cognition: Notes from a trip down memory lane. *Organization Science, 6*(3), 280–321.

Walsh, J., Henderson, C., & Deighton, J. (1988). Negotiated belief structures and decision performance: An empirical investigation. *Organizational Behavior and Human Decision Processes, 42*, 194–216.

Walsh, J. P., Wang, E., & Xin, K. R. (1999). Same bed, different dreams: Working relationships in Sino-American joint ventures. *Journal of World Business, 34*, 69–112.

Walther, J. B. (1997). Group and interpersonal effects in international computer-mediated collaboration. *Human Communication Research, 23*(3), 342–369.

Walther, J. B., Anderson, J. F., & Park, D. W. (1994). Interpersonal effects in computer-mediated interaction: A meta-analysis of social and anti-social communication. *Communication Research, 21*, 460–487.

Warkentin, M. E., Sayeed, L., & Hightower, R. (1997). Virtual teams versus face-to-face teams: An exploratory study of a web-based conference system. *Decision Sciences, 28*(4), 975–987.

Watson, W. E., Kumar, K., & Michaelson, L. K. (1993). Cultural diversity's impact on interaction process and performance: Comparing homogeneous and diverse task groups. *Academy of Management Journal, 36*, 590–602.

Weber, M. (1947). *The theory of social and economic organizations*. (T. Parsons, trans.). New York: Free Press.

Webster, M. Jr., & Foschi, M. (1988). *Status Generalization: New Theory and Research*. (Eds.). Stanford, CA: Stanford University Press.

Wegner, D. M. (1987). Transactive memory: A contemporary analysis of the group mind. In B. Mullen & G. R. Goethals (Eds.), *Theories of group behavior* (pp. 185–208). New York: Springer-Verlag.

Weick, K. E. (1969). *The social psychology of organizing*. Reading, MA: Addison-Wesley.

Weick, K. E. (1979). *The social psychology of organizing*, (2nd ed.). Reading, MA: Addison-Wesley.

Weick, K. E. (1990). Cognitive processes in organizations. In L. L. Cummings & B. M. Staw (Eds.), *Information and cognition in organizations* (pp. 185–210). Greenwich, CT: JAI Press.

Weick, K. E. (1993). Organizational redesign as improvisation. In G. P. Huber & W. H. Glick (Eds.), *Organizational change and redesign: Ideas and insights for improving performance* (pp. 346–382). New York: Oxford Press.

Weick, K. E., & Bougon, M. (1986). Organizations as cognitive maps. In H. P. Sims & D. Gioia (Eds.), *Thinking organizations* (pp. 102–135).

Weick, K. E., & Roberts, K. H. (1993). Collective mind in organizations: Heedful interrelating on flight decks. *Administrative Science Quarterly, 38,* 357–381.

Weick, K. E., & Westley, F. (1996). Organizational learning: Affixing an oxymoron. In S. R. Clegg, C. Hardy, & W. R. Nord (Eds.), *Handbook of organization studies* (pp. 440–459). London: Sage.

Weisinger, J. Y., & Salipante, P. F. (1995). Toward a method of exposing hidden assumptions in multicultural conflict. *International Journal of Conflict Management, 6,* 147–170.

Weldon, E., & Gargano, G. M. (1988). Cognitive loafing: The effects of accountability and shared responsibility on cognitive effort. *Personality & Social Psychology Bulletin, 14,* 159–171.

Weldon, E., & Jehn, K. A. 1995. Examining cross-cultural differences in conflict management behavior: A strategy for future research. *International Journal of Conflict Management, 6,* 387–403.

Wellens, A. R. (1993). Group situation awareness and distributed decision making: From military to civilian applications. In N. J. Castellan (Ed.), *Individual and group decision-making* (pp. 267–291). Hillsdale, NJ: Lawrence Erlbaum Associates.

Wellins, R. S., Byham, W. C., & Dixon, G. R. (1994). *Inside teams: How 20 world-class organizations are winning through teamwork*. San Francisco, CA: Jossey-Bass.

West, C. (1984). When the doctor is a "lady": Power, status and gender in physician–patient encounters. *Symbolic Interaction, 7*(1), 87–106.

Westwood, R. I., Tang, S. F. Y., & Kirkbride, P. S. (1992). Chinese conflict behavior: Cultural antecedents and behavioral consequences. *Organization Development Journal, 10,* 13–19.

Williams, K. Y., & O'Reilly, C. A., Jr. (1998). Demography and diversity in organizations: A review of 40 years of research. *Research in Organizational Behavior, 20,* 77–140.

Willmott, H. (1987). Studying managerial work: A critique and a proposal. *Journal of Management Studies, 24,* 249–270.

Wilson, J. Q. (1993). *The moral sense*. New York: Free Press.

Wish, M., Deutsch, M., & Kaplan, S. J. (1976). Perceived dimensions of interpersonal relations. *Journal of Personality and Social Psychology, 33,* 409–420.

Witkin, H. A., & Berry, J. W. (1975). Psychological differentiation in cross-cultural perspective. *Journal of Cross-Cultural Psychology, 6,* 4–87.

Witkin, H. A., & Goodenough, D. R. (1976). Field dependence and interpersonal behavior. *ETS Research Bulletin*, RB-76-12.

World Economic Forum/Booz-Allen & Hamilton. (2000). *Creating the capacity for organizational renewal*. Report presented at the World Economic Forum, Davos, Switzerland, January, 2000.

Wood, R. E. (1986). Task complexity: Definition of a construct. *Organizational Behavior and Human Decision Processes, 37,* 60–82.

Wooldridge, A. (1997). The advice business. *The Economist, 342,* S3–5.

Wyer, R. S., Jr., & Srull, T. K. (1980). The processing of social stimulus information: A conceptual integration. In R. Hastie, T. M. Ostrom, E. B. Ebbesen, R. S. Wyer, Jr., D. L. Hamilton, & D. E. Carlston (Eds.), *Person memory: The cognitive basis of social perception.* Hillsdale, NJ: Lawrence Erlbaum Associates.

Wyer, R. S., & Srull, T. K. (1989). *Memory and cognition in its social context.* Hillsdale, NJ: Lawrence Erlbaum Associates.

Yan, H. (1995). *The concept of 'face' in Chinese proverbs and phrases.* Proverbium. Berkeley, CA: California Folklore Society.

Yang, K. S. (1970). Authoritarianism and evaluation of appropriateness of role behavior. *Journal of Social Psychology, 80,* 171–181.

Yu, X. (1995). Conflict in a multicultural organization: An ethnographic attempt to discover work-related cultural assumptions between Chinese and American co-workers. *International Journal of Conflict Management, 6,* 211–232.

Zaheer, S., Albert, S., & Zaheer, A. (1999). Time scales and organizational theory. *Academy of Management Review, 24,* 725–741.

Zander, A. W., & Medow, H. (1963). Individual and group aspiration. *Human Relations, 16,* 89–105.

Zellmer-Bruhn, M., & Gibson, C. B. (2001). *Team Level Strategic Context: Effects on Innovation & Performance.* Working paper, University of Minnesota.

Zellmer-Bruhn, M., Gibson, C. B., & Aldag, R. (2000). Times flies like an arrow: Tracing antecedents and consequences of temporal elements of organizational culture. In C. L. Cooper, S. Cartwright, & P. C. Earley (Eds.), *Handbook of organizational culture* (pp. 21–52). Sussex, England: Wiley.

Zenger, T. R., & Lawrence, B. S. (1989). Organizational demography: The differential effects of age and tenure distribution on technical communications. *Academy of Management Journal, 32,* 353–376.

Zucker, L. (1987). Institutional theories of organization. *Annual Review of Sociology, 13,* 443–464.

Zuckerman, M. (1979). *Sensation seeking.* Hillsdale, NJ: Lawrence Erlbaum Associates.

Zuckerman, M. (1984). Sensation seeking: A comparative approach to a human trait. *Behavioral and Brain Sciences, 7,* 413–471.

# Author Index

# Subject Index